Gestalt

7

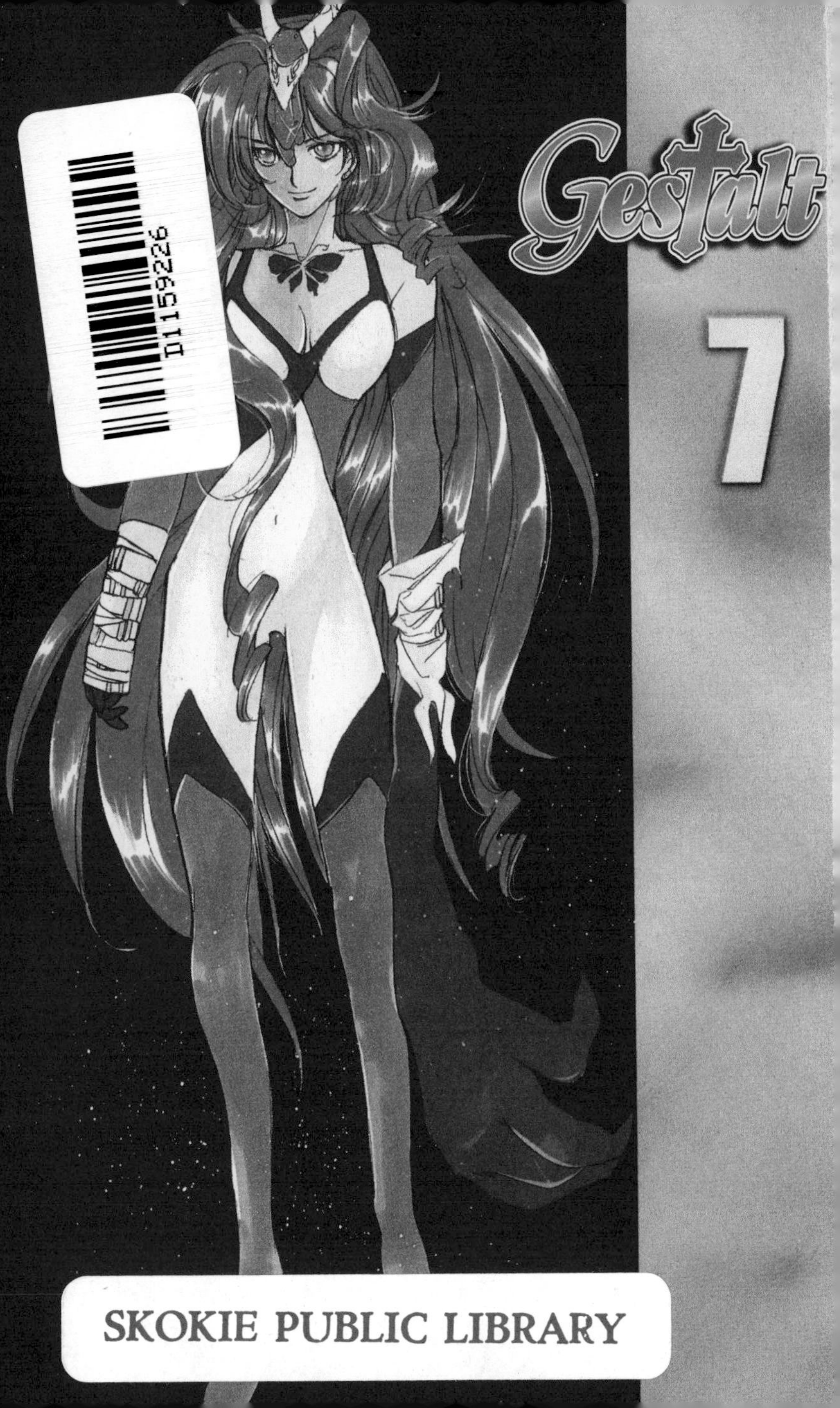

CONTENTS

7

Legend of the Great Beast

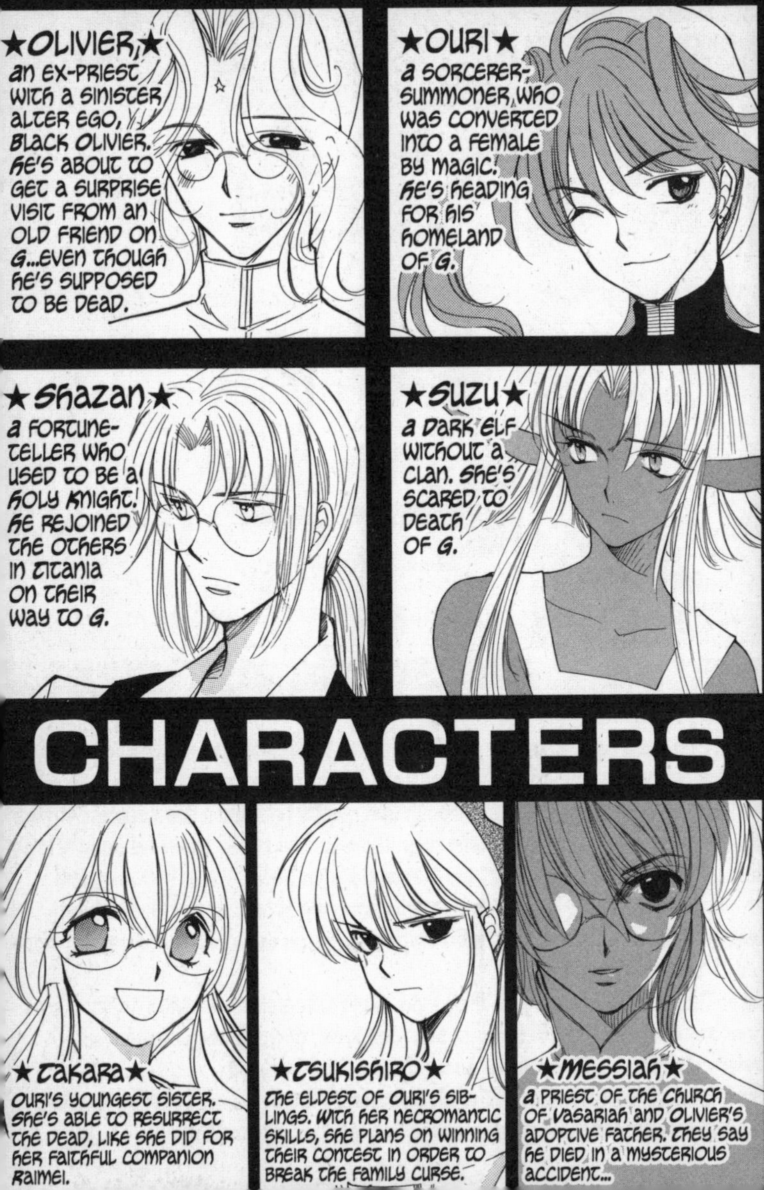
★OLIVIER★
AN EX-PRIEST WITH A SINISTER ALTER EGO, BLACK OLIVIER. HE'S ABOUT TO GET A SURPRISE VISIT FROM AN OLD FRIEND ON G...EVEN THOUGH HE'S SUPPOSED TO BE DEAD.
★OURI★
A SORCERER-SUMMONER WHO WAS CONVERTED INTO A FEMALE BY MAGIC. HE'S HEADING FOR HIS HOMELAND OF G.
★SHAZAN★
A FORTUNE-TELLER WHO USED TO BE A HOLY KNIGHT. HE REJOINED THE OTHERS IN TITANIA ON THEIR WAY TO G.
★SUZU★
A DARK ELF WITHOUT A CLAN. SHE'S SCARED TO DEATH OF G.
CHARACTERS
★TAKARA★
OURI'S YOUNGEST SISTER. SHE'S ABLE TO RESURRECT THE DEAD, LIKE SHE DID FOR HER FAITHFUL COMPANION RAIMEI.
★TSUKISHIRO★
THE ELDEST OF OURI'S SIB-LINGS. WITH HER NECROMANTIC SKILLS, SHE PLANS ON WINNING THEIR CONTEST IN ORDER TO BREAK THE FAMILY CURSE.
★MESSIAH★
A PRIEST OF THE CHURCH OF VASARIAH AND OLIVIER'S ADOPTIVE FATHER. THEY SAY HE DIED IN A MYSTERIOUS ACCIDENT...

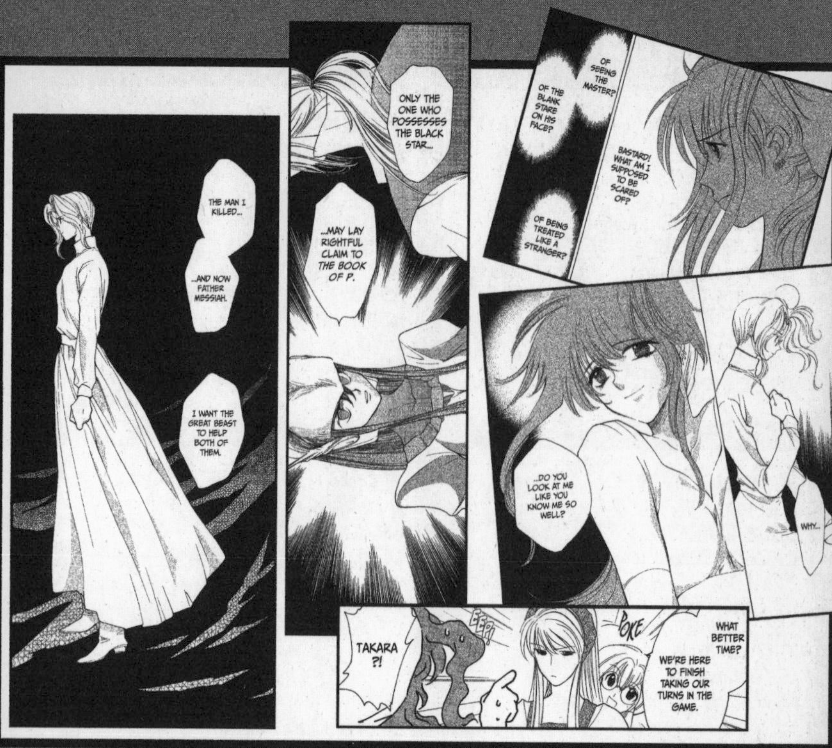
BASTARD! WHAT AM I SUPPOSED TO BE SCARED OF?
OF SEEING THE MASTER?
OF THE BLANK STARE ON HIS FACE?
OF BEING TREATED LIKE A STRANGER?
WHY...
...DO YOU LOOK AT ME LIKE YOU KNOW ME SO WELL?
WHAT BETTER TIME?
WE'RE HERE TO FINISH TAKING OUR TURNS IN THE GAME.
POKE
EEP!
TAKARA ?!
ONLY THE ONE WHO POSSESSES THE BLACK STAR...
...MAY LAY RIGHTFUL CLAIM TO THE BOOK OF P.
THE MAN I KILLED...
...AND NOW FATHER MESSIAH.
I WANT THE GREAT BEAST TO HELP BOTH OF THEM.

Olivier, Ouri, Suzu and Shazan are on their way to the forbidden island of G.
In exchange for the return of his severed arms, Olivier is transported back to Barbaros and loses all his memories of Ouri. Though Ouri quickly falls into a deep depression over this, he pulls himself together in time to go there himself and continue his journey with Olivier. That's when the captain of the Diamond Knight Guard, Ender, shows up and accuses Olivier of killing Father Messiah, triggering the appearance of Black Olivier!
Meanwhile, back in Titania, Shazan finally gets his hands on *The Book of P* and catches up with Ouri and the gang.
Just as Ouri and Ender engage in their fight, Ouri's sisters show up, and Tsukishiro uses her necromancy to call forth demons. She soon loses control of the creatures, but Olivier calls upon his divine power to send them away for good.
Olivier knows the Great Beast of Gestalt represents his only chance to revive Messiah, so the team sets out for the legendary island, leaving the mainland behind...

THE STORY SO FAR

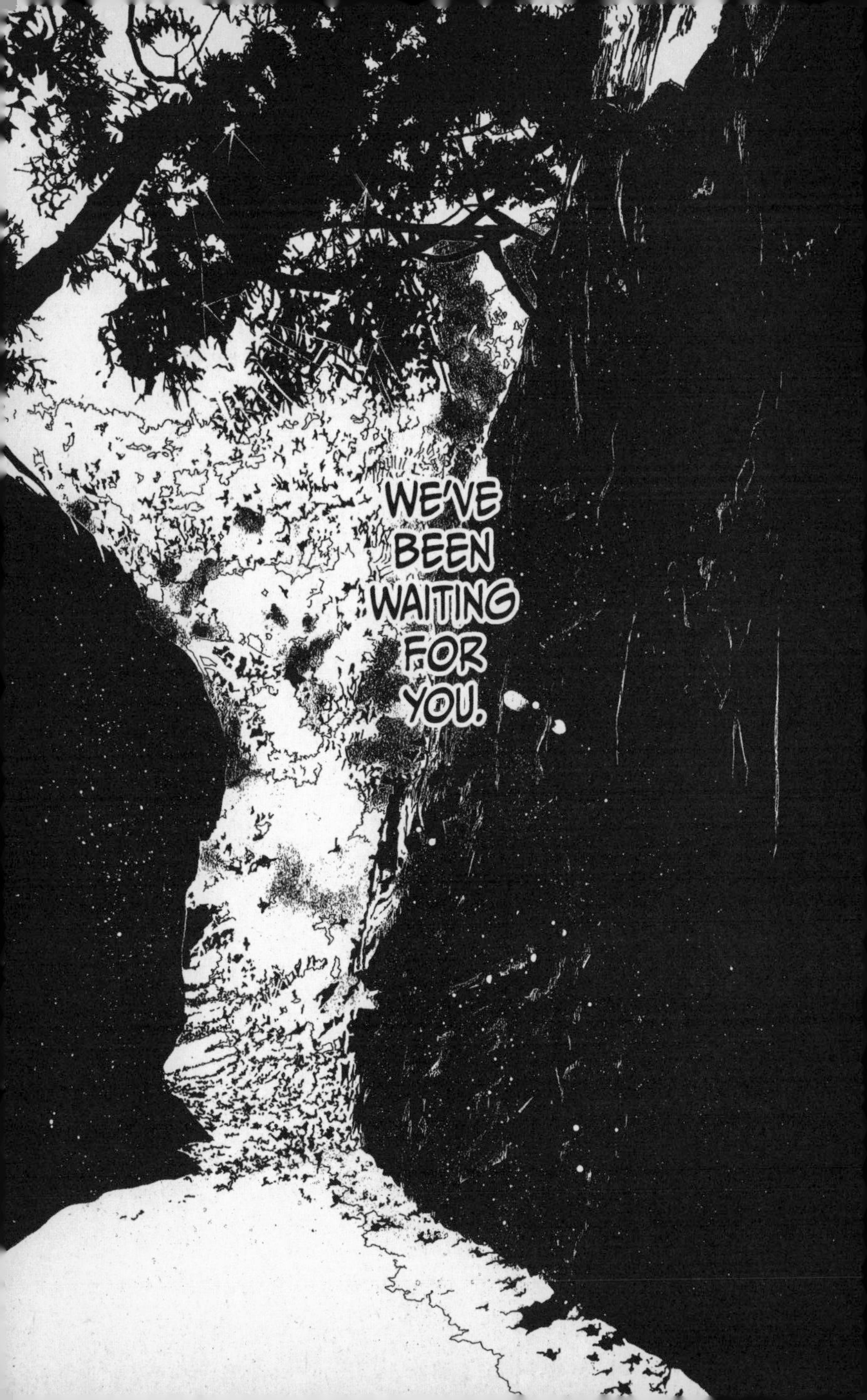
WE'VE BEEN WAITING FOR YOU.

The Gestalt Arc
Chapter 35
Beginning

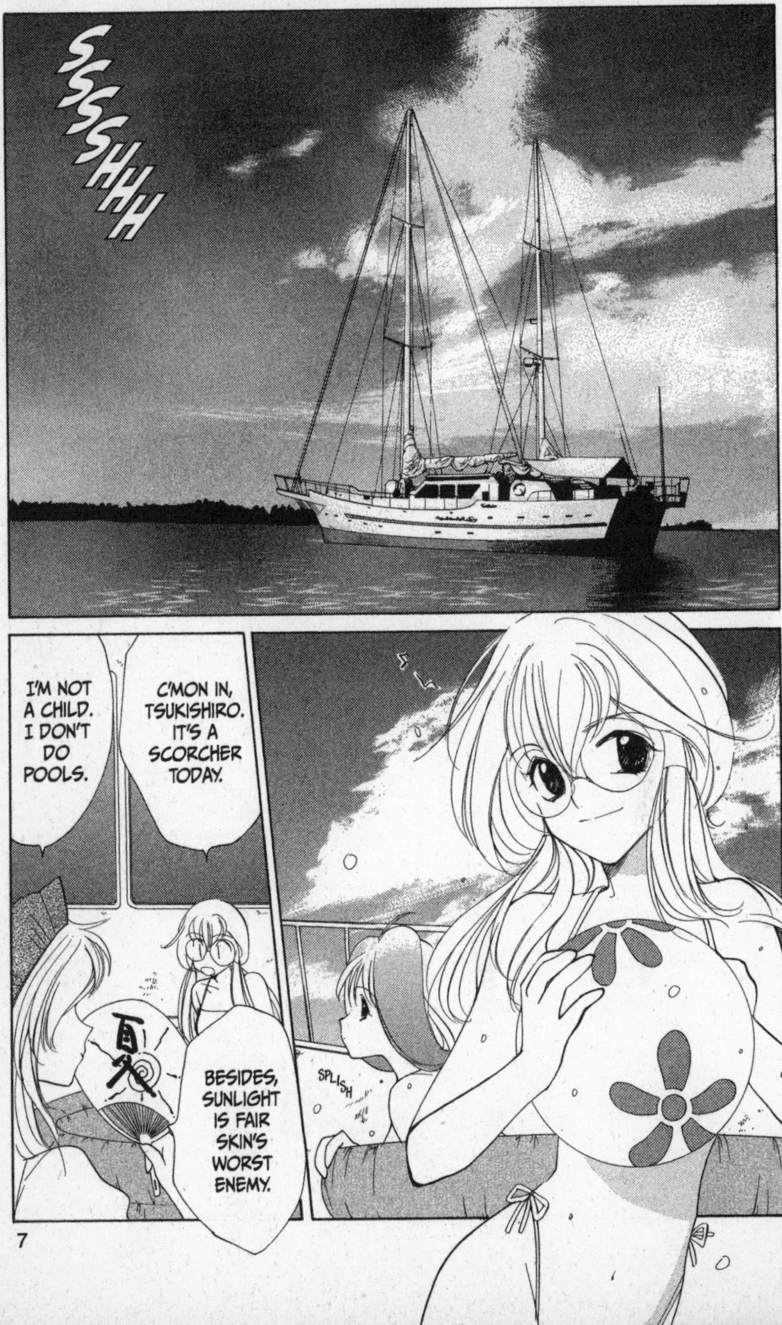
SSSSHHH
SPLISH
C'MON IN, TSUKISHIRO. IT'S A SCORCHER TODAY.
I'M NOT A CHILD. I DON'T DO POOLS.
BESIDES, SUNLIGHT IS FAIR SKIN'S WORST ENEMY.

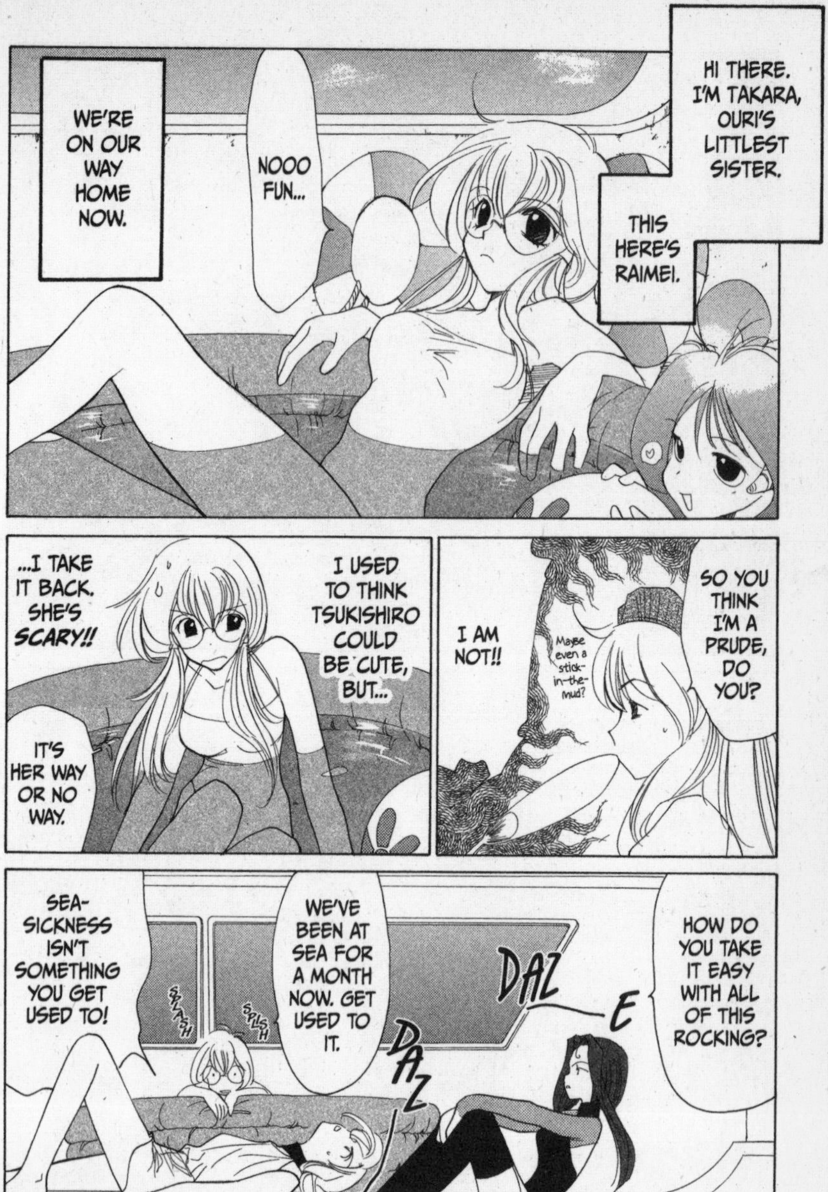
HI THERE. I'M TAKARA, OURI'S LITTLEST SISTER.
THIS HERE'S RAIMEI.
NOOO FUN...
WE'RE ON OUR WAY HOME NOW.
SO YOU THINK I'M A PRUDE, DO YOU?
Maybe even a stick-in-the-mud?
I AM NOT!!
I USED TO THINK TSUKISHIRO COULD BE CUTE, BUT...
...I TAKE IT BACK. SHE'S *SCARY!!*
IT'S HER WAY OR NO WAY.
HOW DO YOU TAKE IT EASY WITH ALL OF THIS ROCKING?
DAZE
DAZE
WE'VE BEEN AT SEA FOR A MONTH NOW. GET USED TO IT.
SPLISH
SPLASH
SEA-SICKNESS ISN'T SOMETHING YOU GET USED TO!

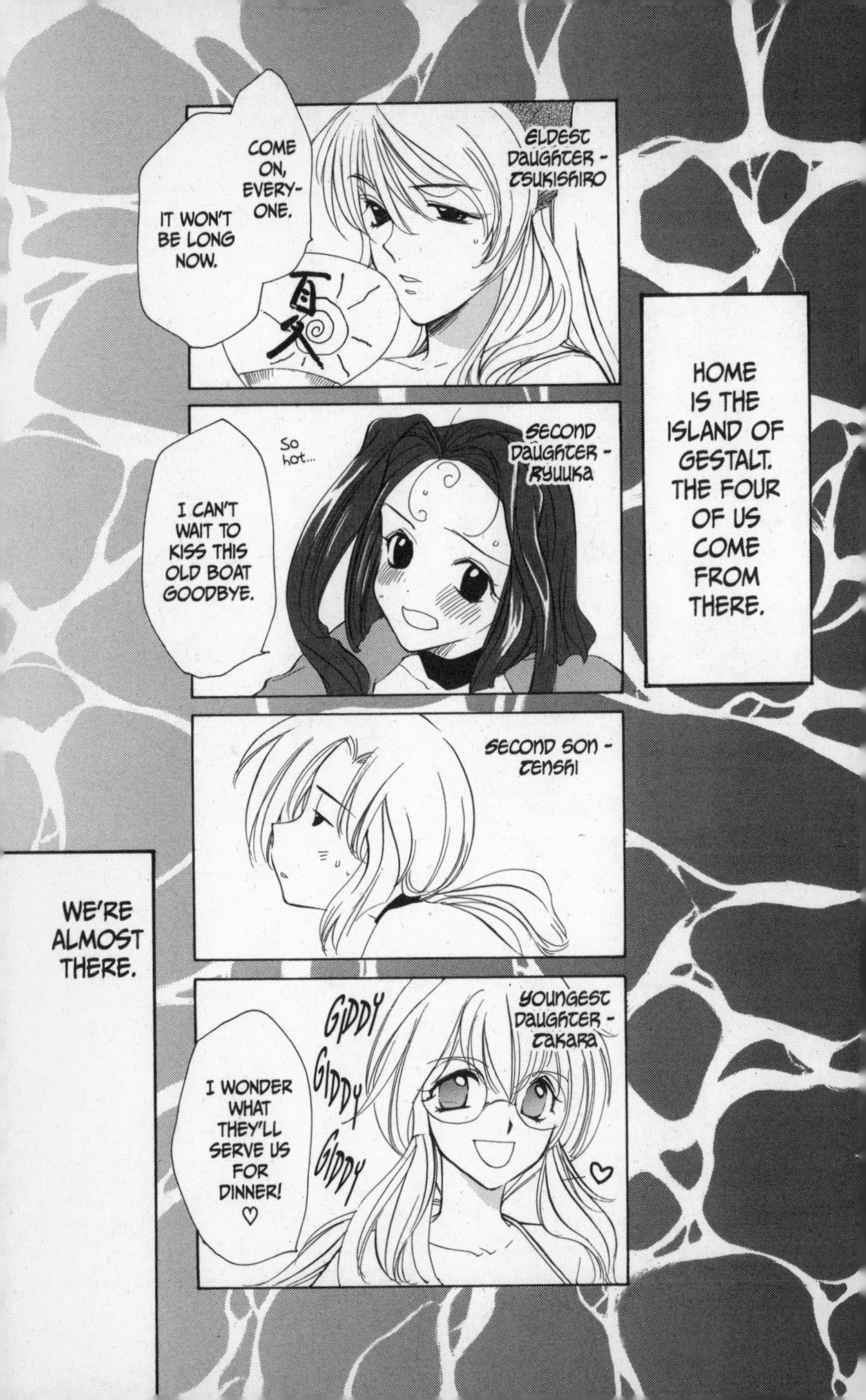
ELDEST DAUGHTER - TSUKISHIRO
COME ON, EVERYONE.
IT WON'T BE LONG NOW.
HOME IS THE ISLAND OF GESTALT. THE FOUR OF US COME FROM THERE.
SECOND DAUGHTER - RYUUKA
So hot...
I CAN'T WAIT TO KISS THIS OLD BOAT GOODBYE.
SECOND SON - TENSHI
WE'RE ALMOST THERE.
YOUNGEST DAUGHTER - TAKARA
GIDDY GIDDY GIDDY
I WONDER WHAT THEY'LL SERVE US FOR DINNER! ♡

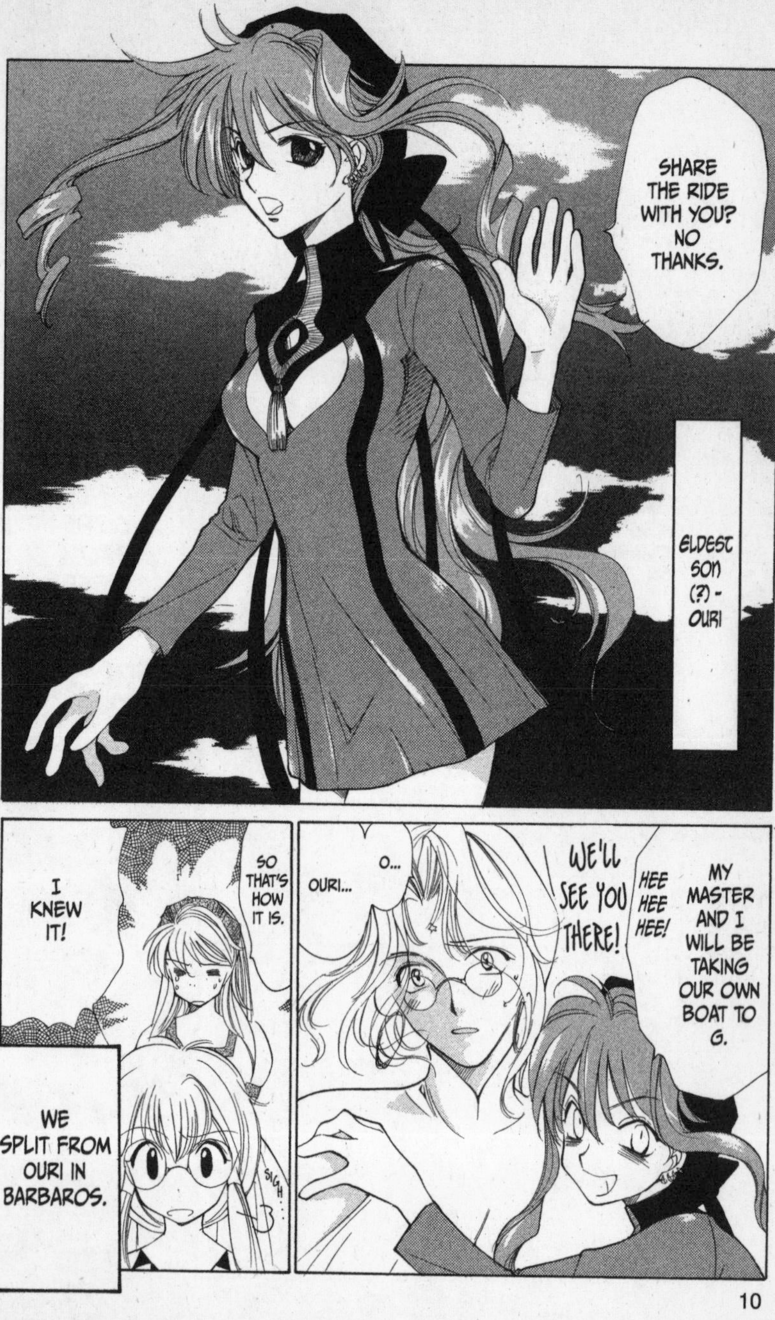
SHARE THE RIDE WITH YOU? NO THANKS.
ELDEST SON (?) - OURI
MY MASTER AND I WILL BE TAKING OUR OWN BOAT TO G.
HEE HEE HEE!
WE'LL SEE YOU THERE!
O... OURI...
SO THAT'S HOW IT IS.
I KNEW IT!
SIGH...
WE SPLIT FROM OURI IN BARBAROS.

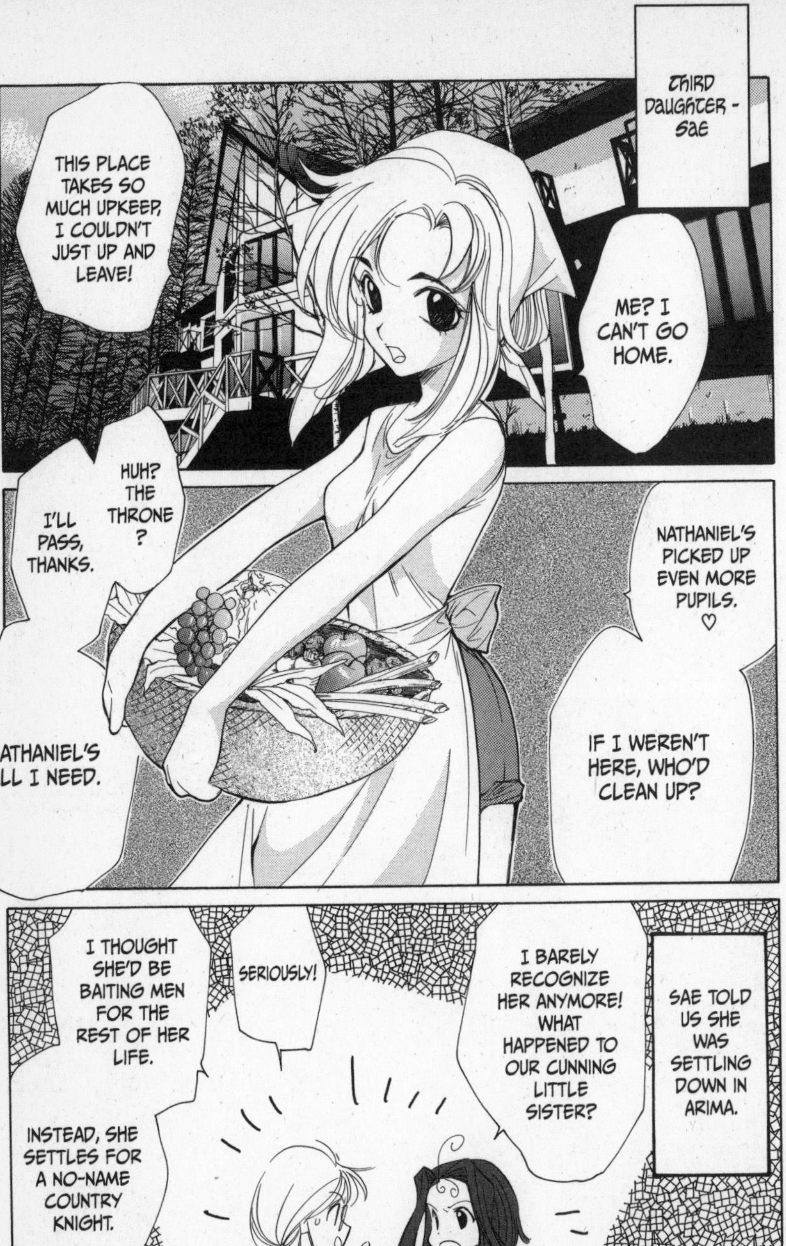
THIRD DAUGHTER - SAE
ME? I CAN'T GO HOME.
THIS PLACE TAKES SO MUCH UPKEEP, I COULDN'T JUST UP AND LEAVE!
NATHANIEL'S PICKED UP EVEN MORE PUPILS. ♡
IF I WEREN'T HERE, WHO'D CLEAN UP?
HUH? THE THRONE?
I'LL PASS, THANKS.
NATHANIEL'S ALL I NEED.
SAE TOLD US SHE WAS SETTLING DOWN IN ARIMA.
I BARELY RECOGNIZE HER ANYMORE! WHAT HAPPENED TO OUR CUNNING LITTLE SISTER?
SERIOUSLY!
I THOUGHT SHE'D BE BAITING MEN FOR THE REST OF HER LIFE.
INSTEAD, SHE SETTLES FOR A NO-NAME COUNTRY KNIGHT.

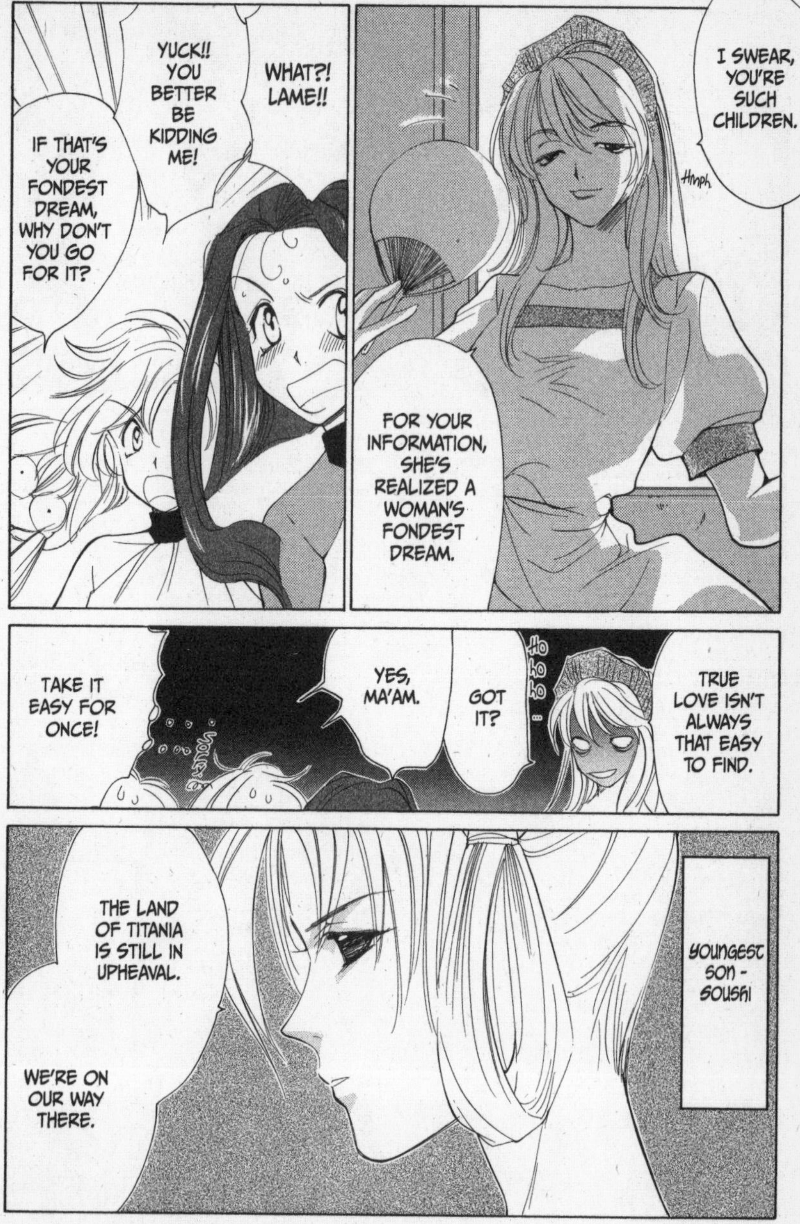
I SWEAR, YOU'RE SUCH CHILDREN.
Hmph.
FOR YOUR INFORMATION, SHE'S REALIZED A WOMAN'S FONDEST DREAM.
WHAT?! LAME!!
YUCK!! YOU BETTER BE KIDDING ME!
IF THAT'S YOUR FONDEST DREAM, WHY DON'T YOU GO FOR IT?
TRUE LOVE ISN'T ALWAYS THAT EASY TO FIND.
Ho ho ho...
GOT IT?
YES, MA'AM.
TAKE IT EASY FOR ONCE!
YOUNGEST SON - SOUSHI
THE LAND OF TITANIA IS STILL IN UPHEAVAL.
WE'RE ON OUR WAY THERE.

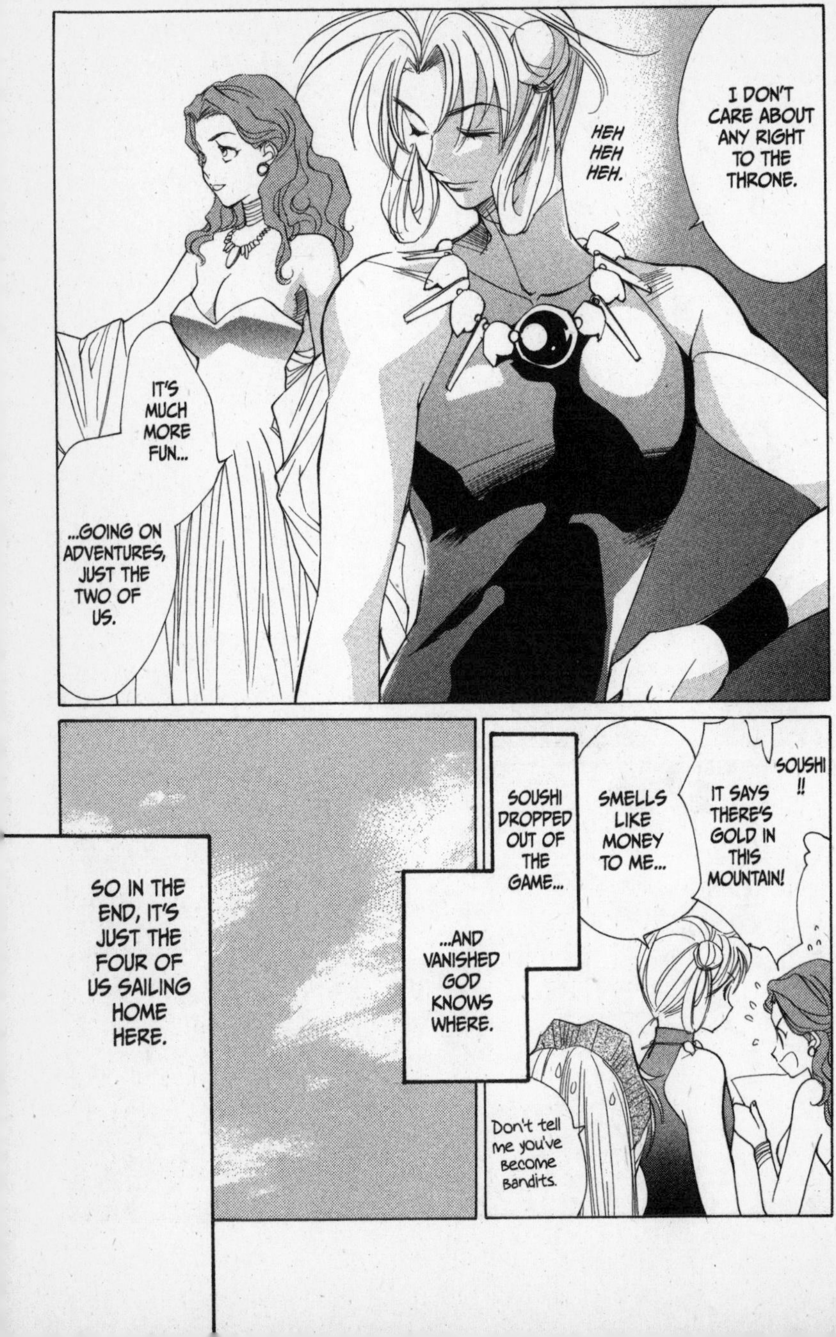
I DON'T CARE ABOUT ANY RIGHT TO THE THRONE.
HEH HEH HEH.
IT'S MUCH MORE FUN...
...GOING ON ADVENTURES, JUST THE TWO OF US.
SOUSHI!!
IT SAYS THERE'S GOLD IN THIS MOUNTAIN!
SMELLS LIKE MONEY TO ME...
SOUSHI DROPPED OUT OF THE GAME...
...AND VANISHED GOD KNOWS WHERE.
Don't tell me you've become bandits.
SO IN THE END, IT'S JUST THE FOUR OF US SAILING HOME HERE.

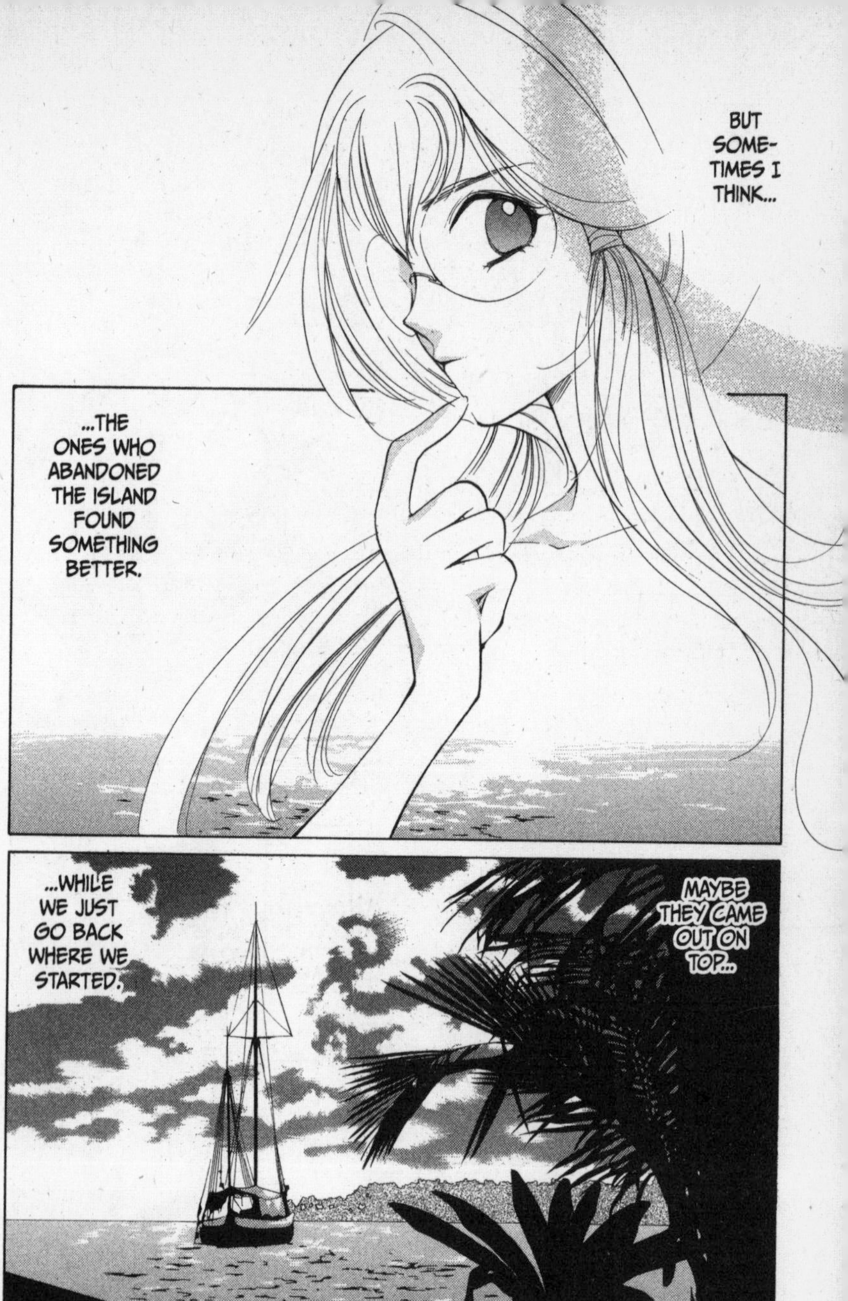
BUT SOMETIMES I THINK...
...THE ONES WHO ABANDONED THE ISLAND FOUND SOMETHING BETTER.
MAYBE THEY CAME OUT ON TOP...
...WHILE WE JUST GO BACK WHERE WE STARTED.

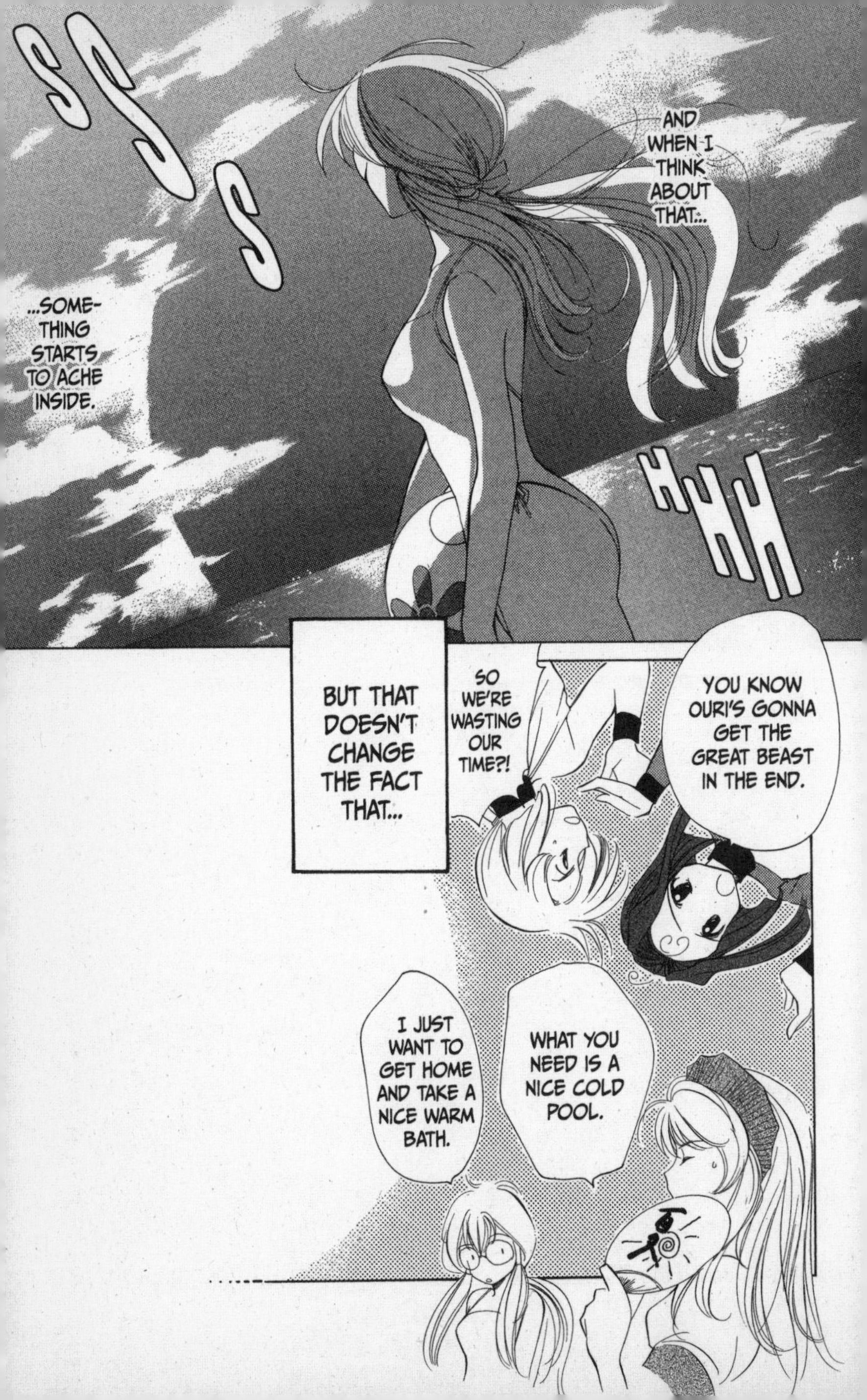
AND WHEN I THINK ABOUT THAT...
...SOMETHING STARTS TO ACHE INSIDE.
YOU KNOW OURI'S GONNA GET THE GREAT BEAST IN THE END.
SO WE'RE WASTING OUR TIME?!
BUT THAT DOESN'T CHANGE THE FACT THAT...
WHAT YOU NEED IS A NICE COLD POOL.
I JUST WANT TO GET HOME AND TAKE A NICE WARM BATH.

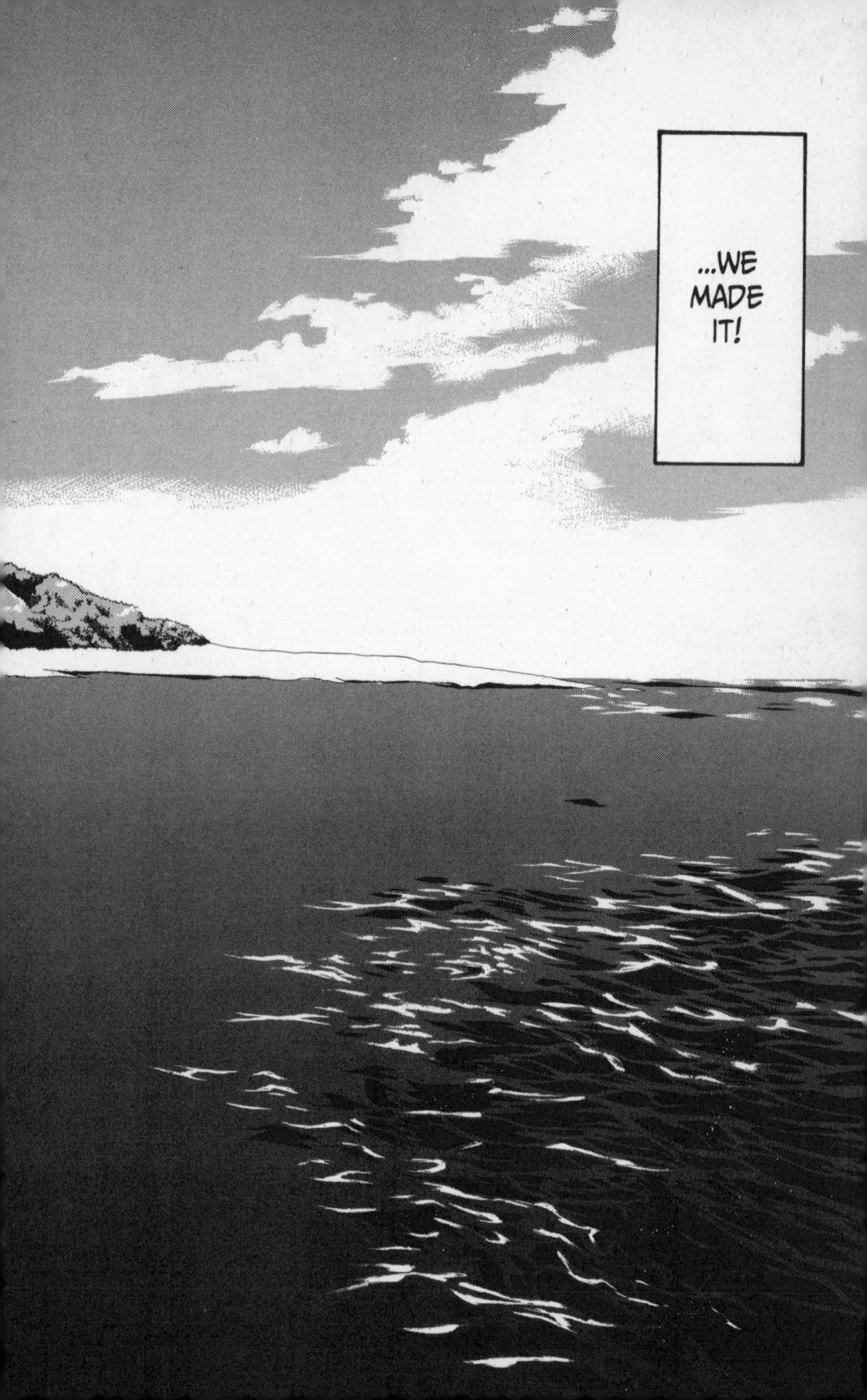
...WE MADE IT!

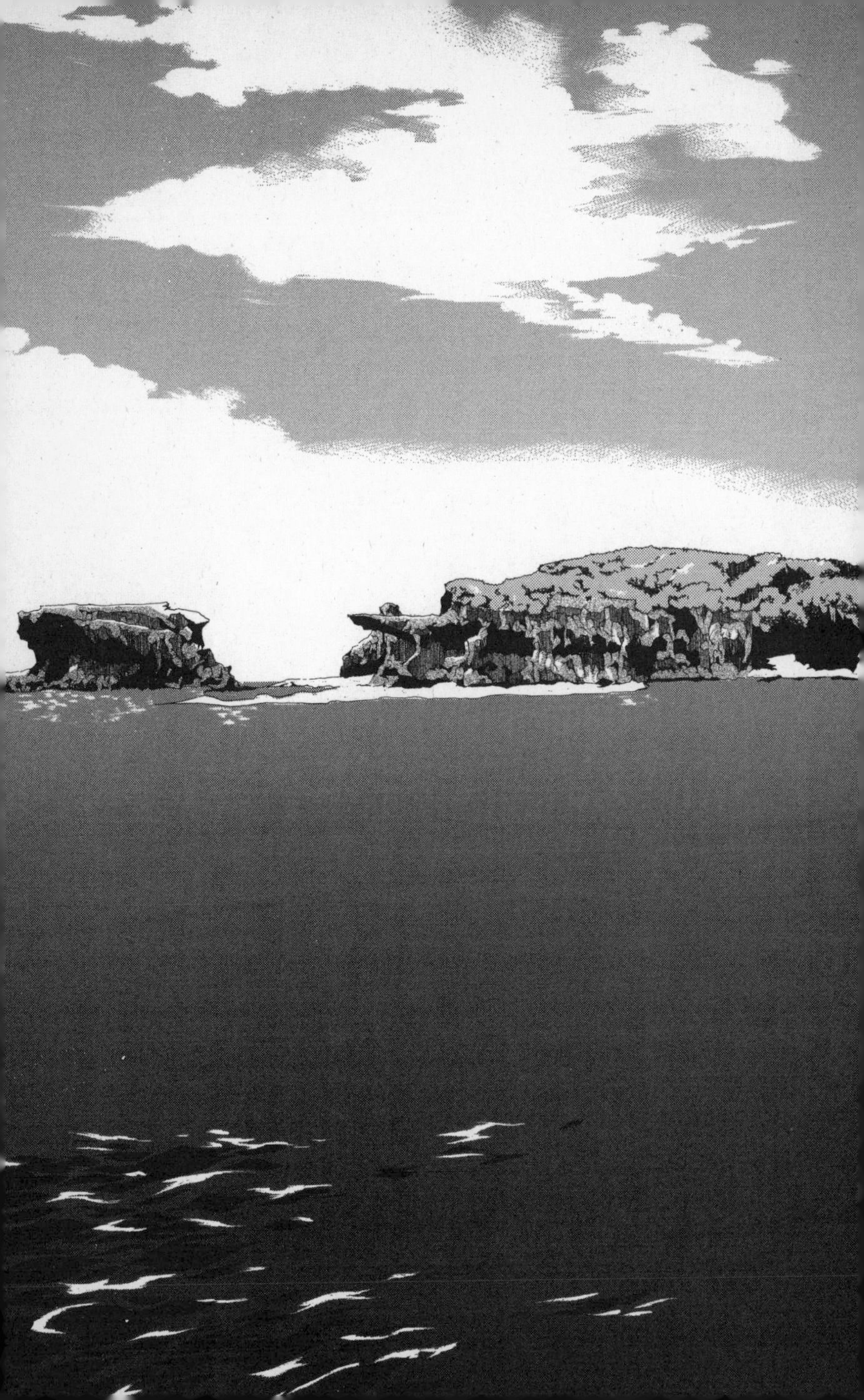

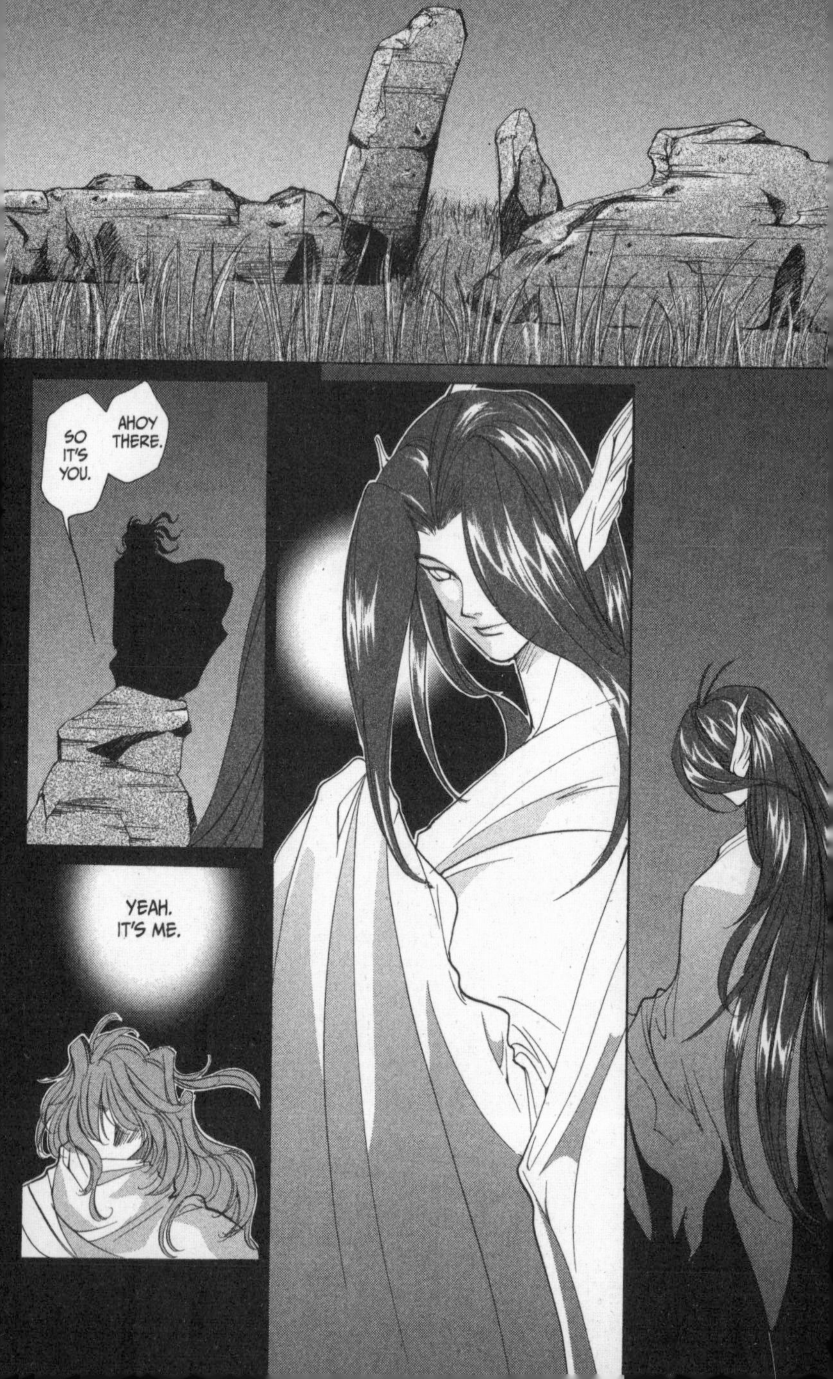
AHOY THERE.
SO IT'S YOU.
YEAH. IT'S ME.

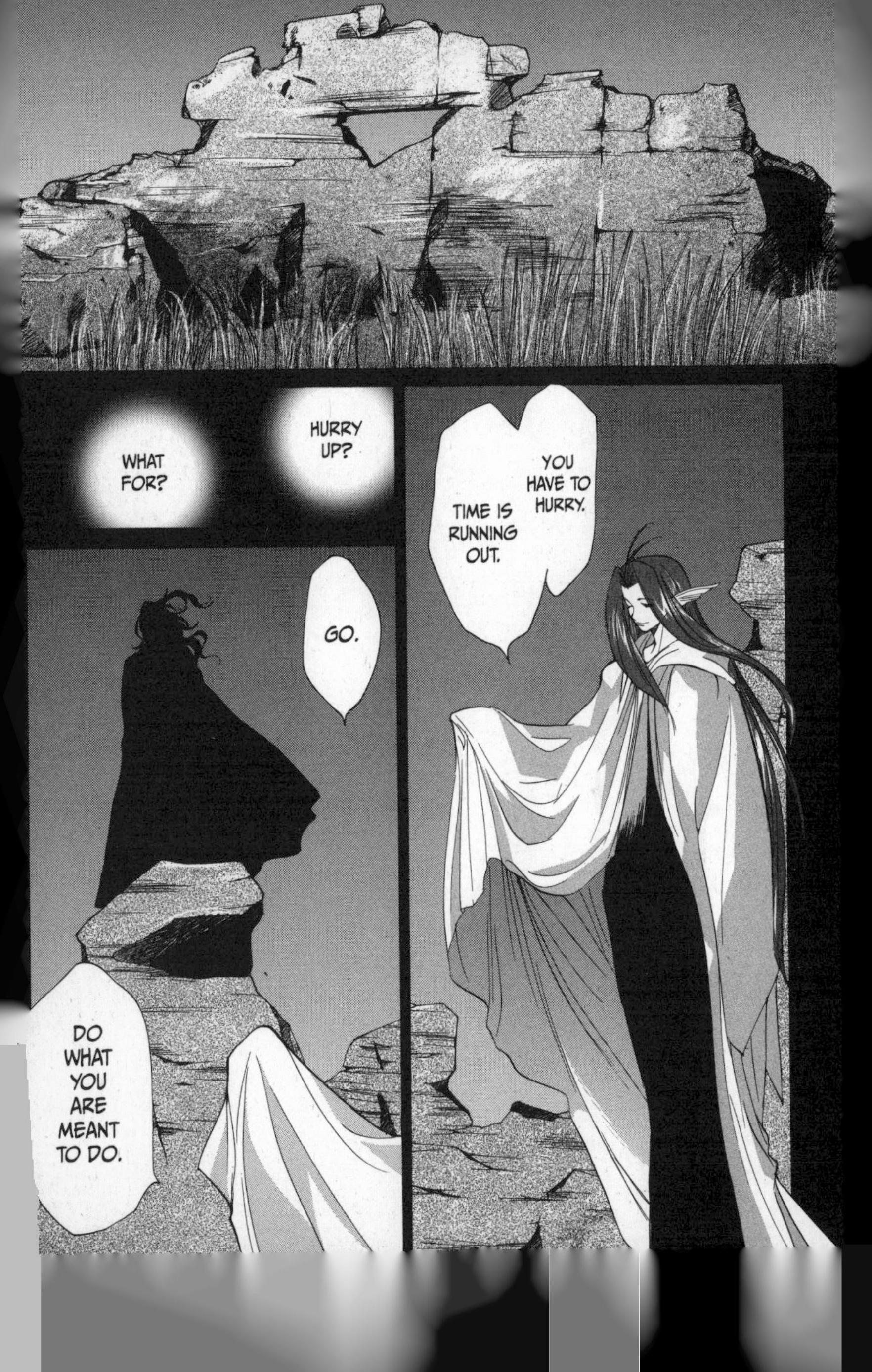
YOU HAVE TO HURRY.
TIME IS RUNNING OUT.
HURRY UP?
WHAT FOR?
GO.
DO WHAT YOU ARE MEANT TO DO.

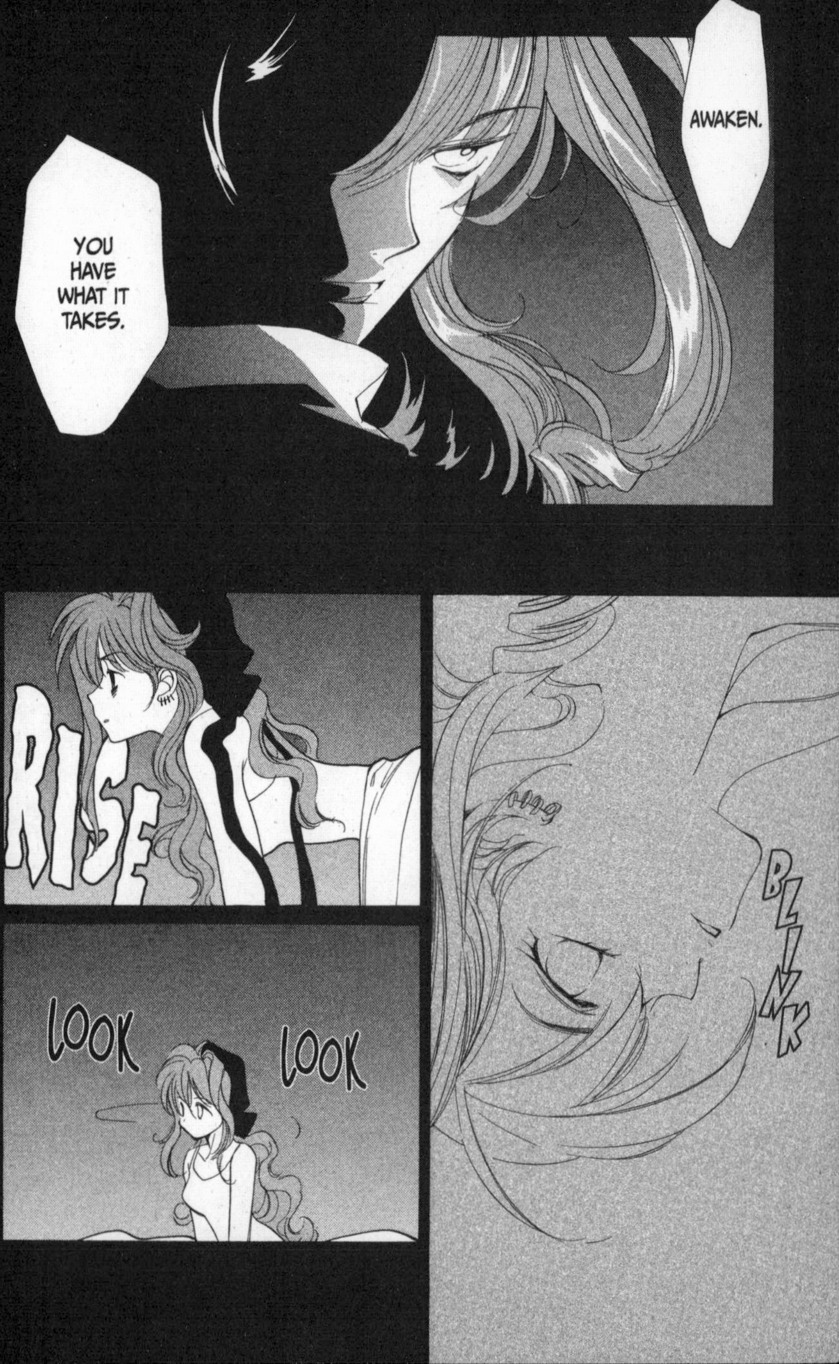
AWAKEN.
YOU HAVE WHAT IT TAKES.
BLINK
RISE
LOOK
LOOK

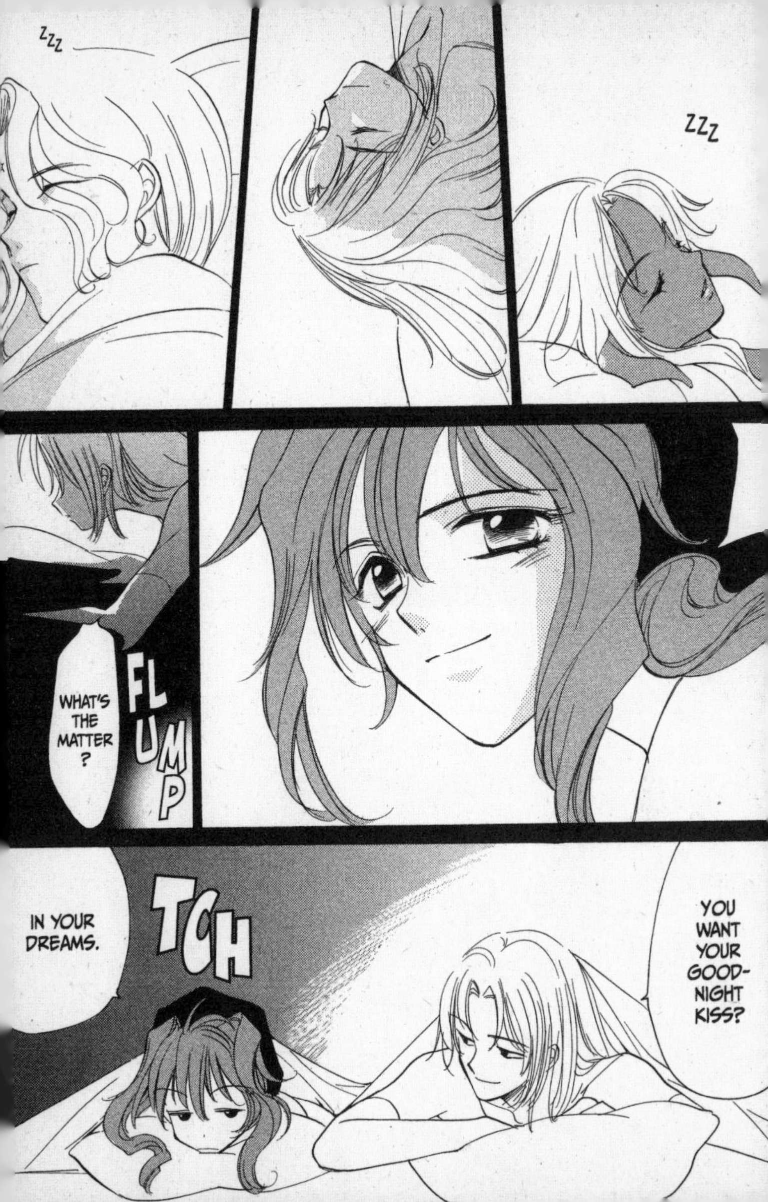
ZZZ
ZZZ
WHAT'S THE MATTER?
FLUMP
YOU WANT YOUR GOOD-NIGHT KISS?
TCH
IN YOUR DREAMS.

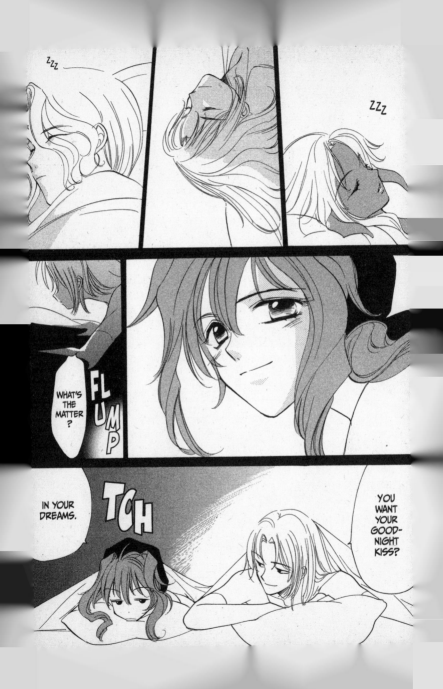

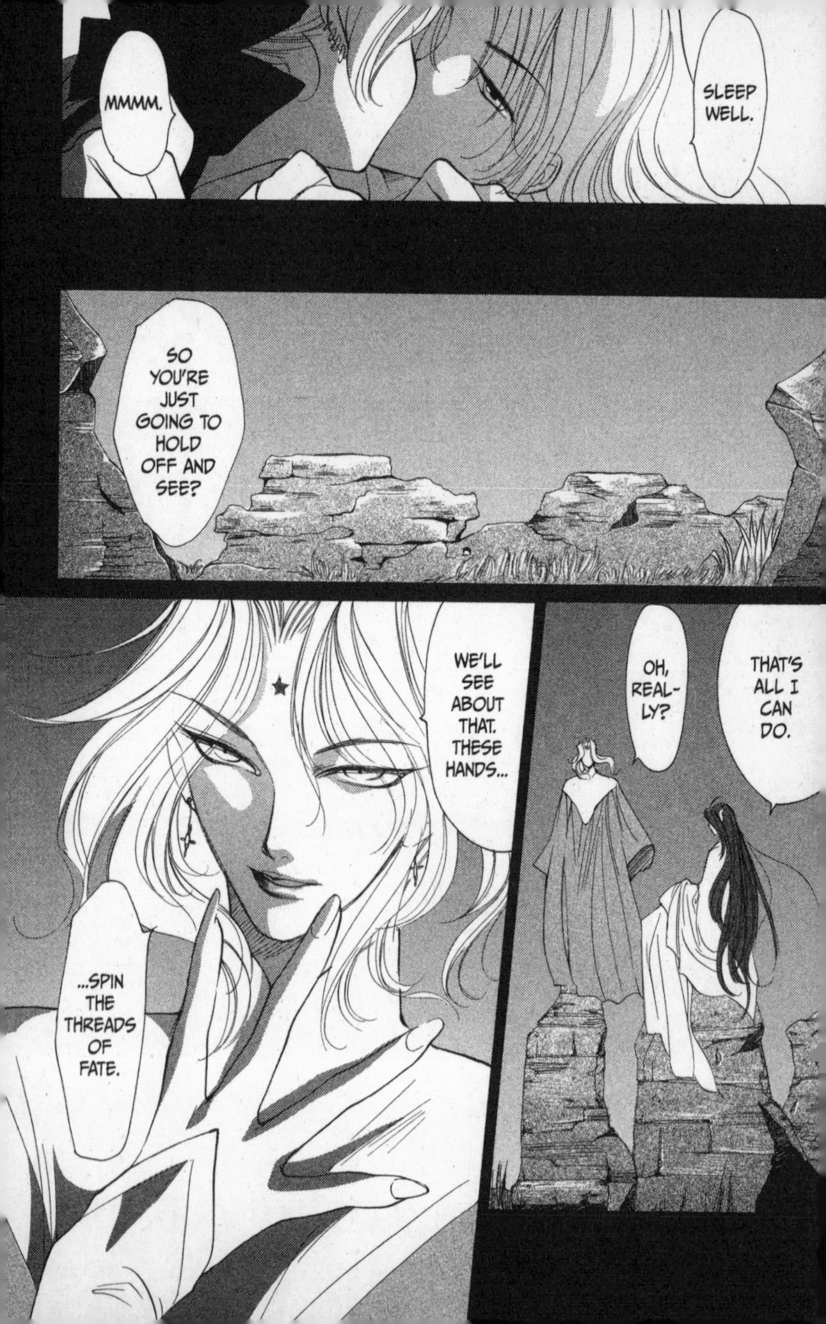
SLEEP WELL.
MMMM.
SO YOU'RE JUST GOING TO HOLD OFF AND SEE?
THAT'S ALL I CAN DO.
OH, REAL-LY?
WE'LL SEE ABOUT THAT. THESE HANDS...
...SPIN THE THREADS OF FATE.

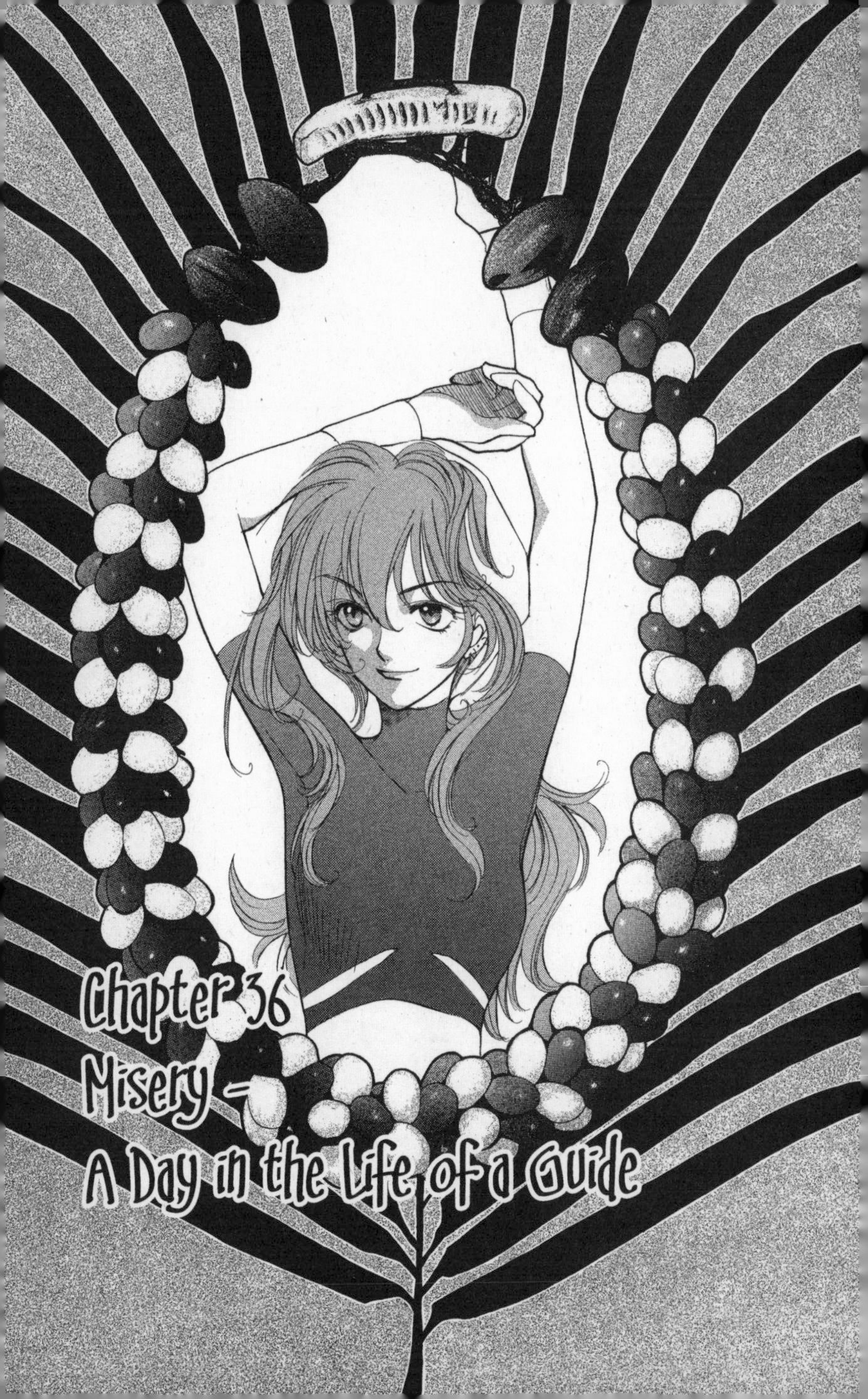
Chapter 36
Misery -
A Day in the Life of a Guide

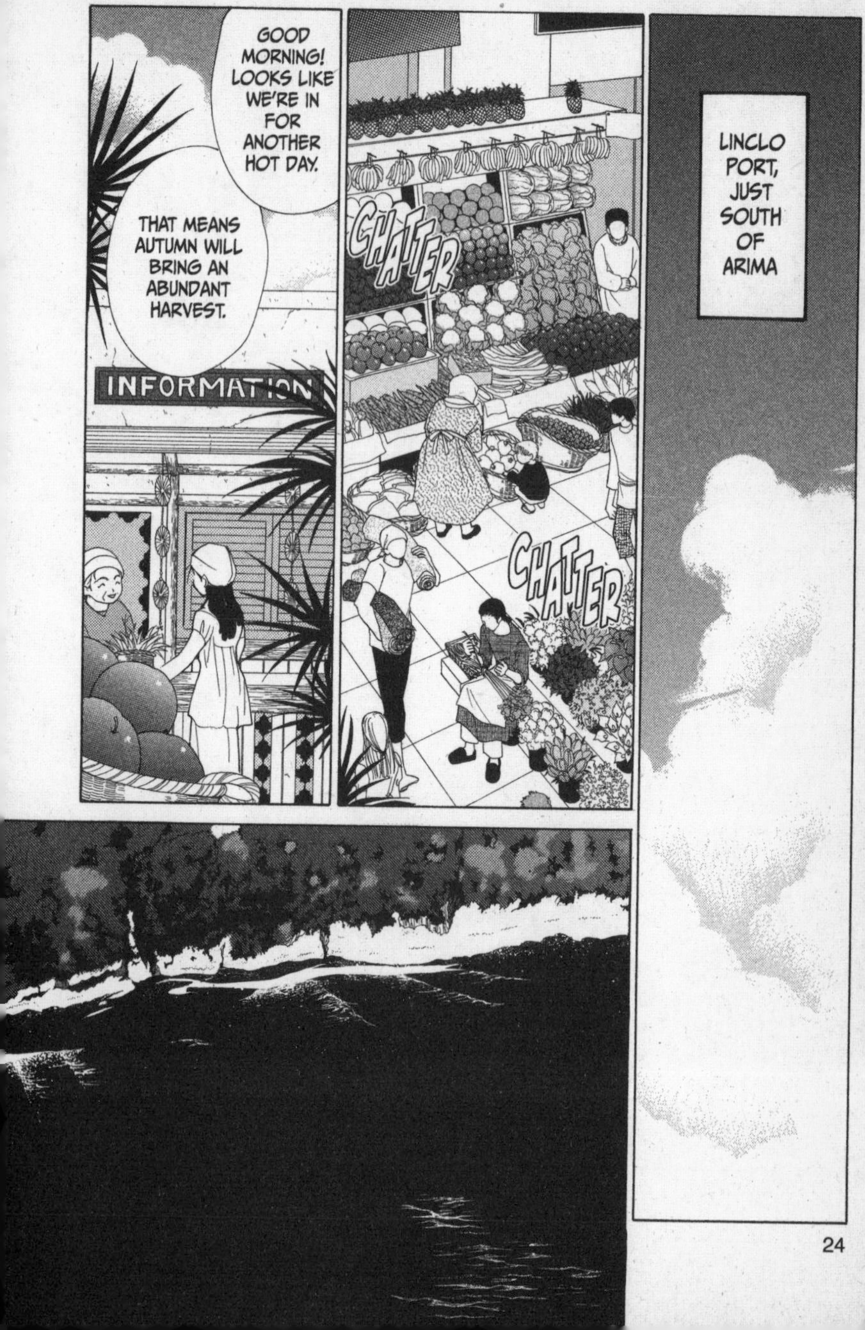
LINCLO PORT, JUST SOUTH OF ARIMA
CHATTER
CHATTER
GOOD MORNING! LOOKS LIKE WE'RE IN FOR ANOTHER HOT DAY.
THAT MEANS AUTUMN WILL BRING AN ABUNDANT HARVEST.
INFORMATION

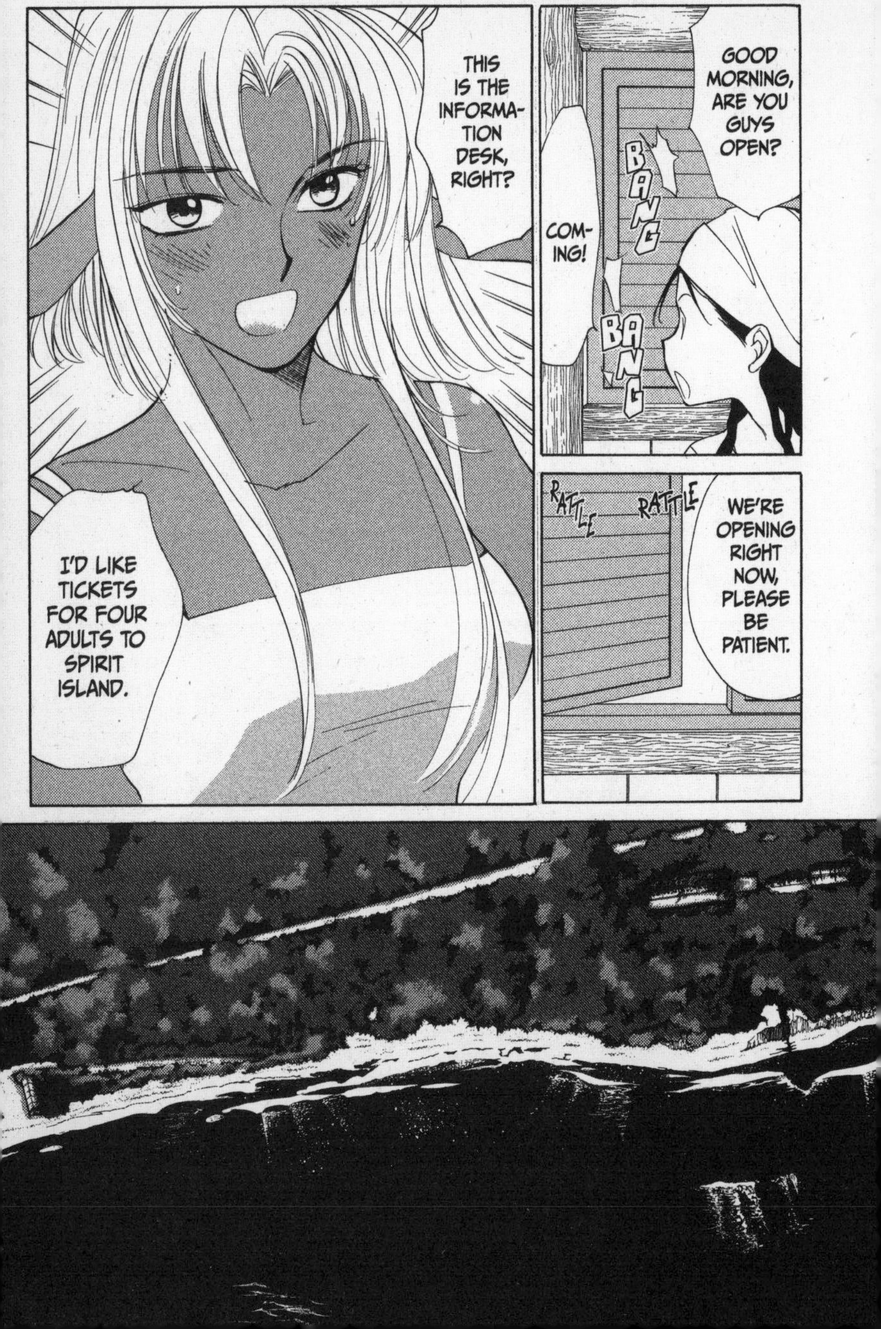
GOOD MORNING, ARE YOU GUYS OPEN?
BANG
BANG
COMING!
RATTLE
RATTLE
WE'RE OPENING RIGHT NOW, PLEASE BE PATIENT.
THIS IS THE INFORMATION-DESK, RIGHT?
I'D LIKE TICKETS FOR FOUR ADULTS TO SPIRIT ISLAND.

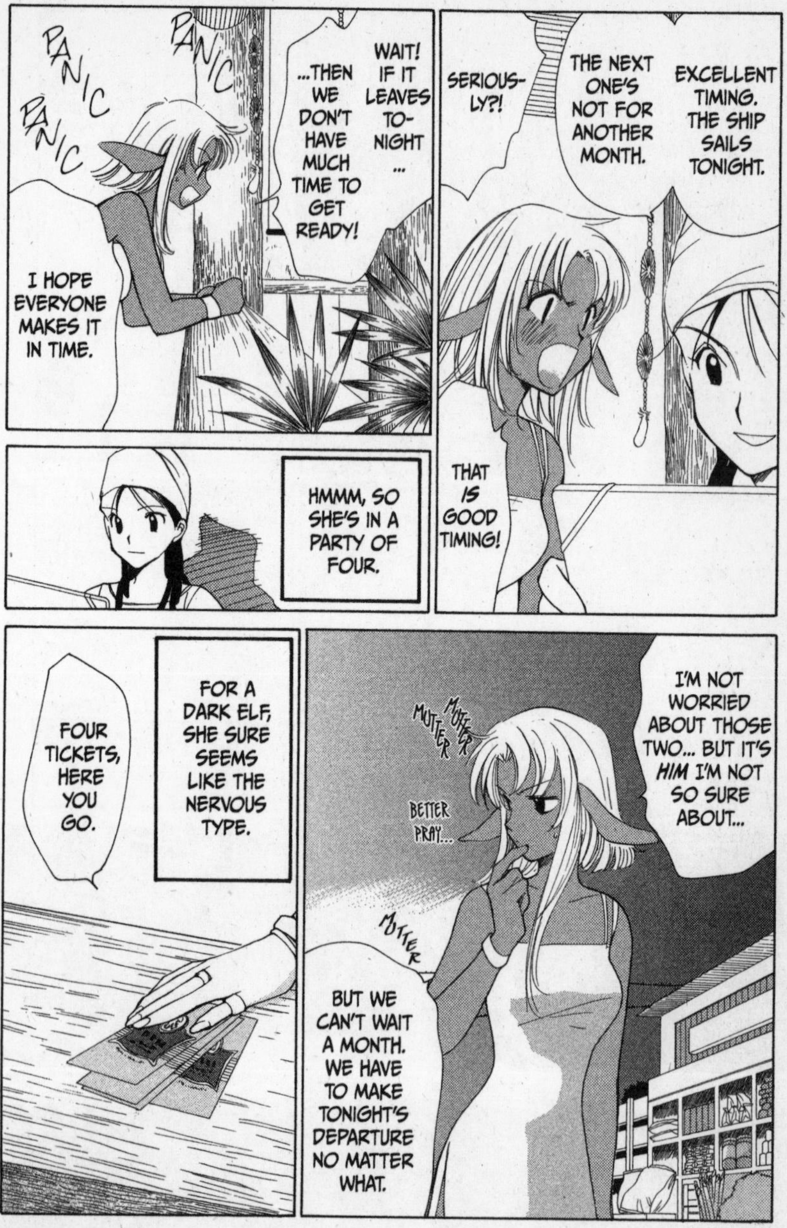
EXCELLENT TIMING. THE SHIP SAILS TONIGHT.
THE NEXT ONE'S NOT FOR ANOTHER MONTH.
SERIOUSLY?!
THAT *IS* GOOD TIMING!
PANIC
PANIC
PANIC
WAIT! IF IT LEAVES TONIGHT...
...THEN WE DON'T HAVE MUCH TIME TO GET READY!
I HOPE EVERYONE MAKES IT IN TIME.
HMMM, SO SHE'S IN A PARTY OF FOUR.
I'M NOT WORRIED ABOUT THOSE TWO... BUT IT'S *HIM* I'M NOT SO SURE ABOUT...
MUTTER
MUTTER
BETTER PRAY...
MUTTER
BUT WE CAN'T WAIT A MONTH. WE HAVE TO MAKE TONIGHT'S DEPARTURE NO MATTER WHAT.
FOR A DARK ELF, SHE SURE SEEMS LIKE THE NERVOUS TYPE.
FOUR TICKETS, HERE YOU GO.

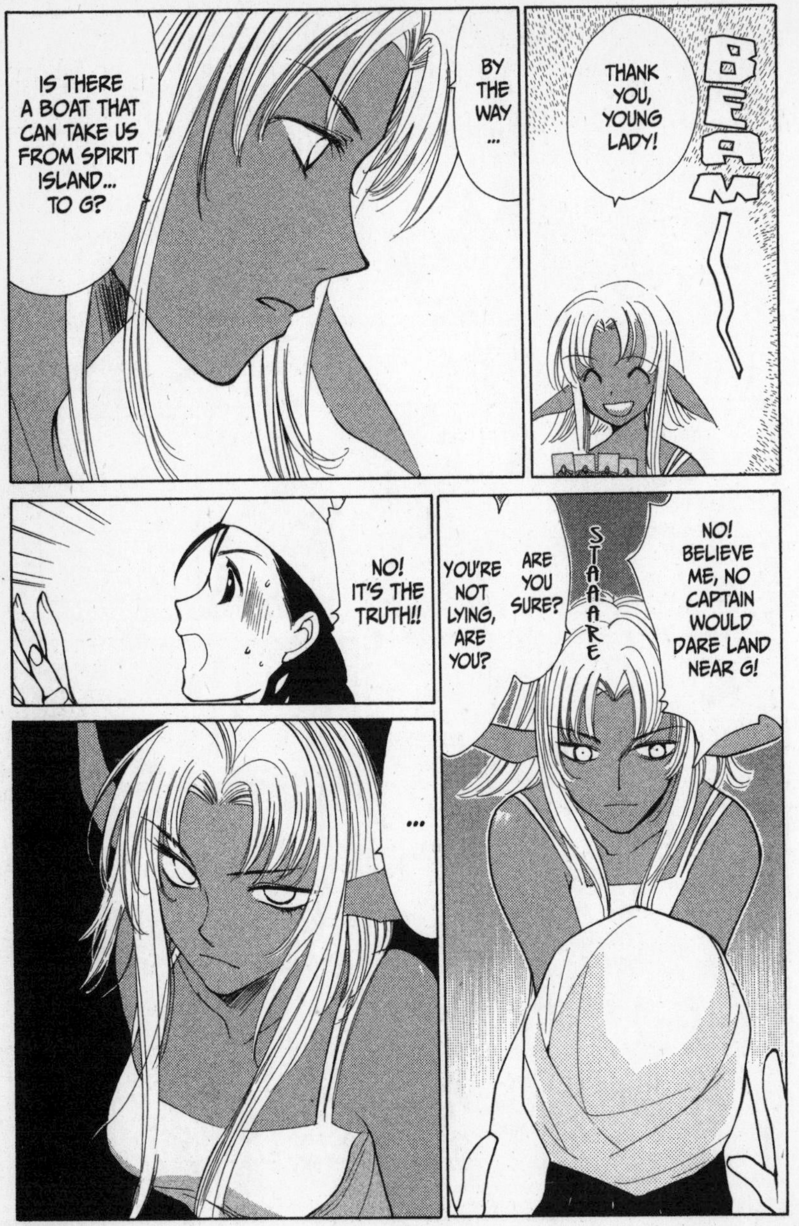
BEAM
THANK YOU, YOUNG LADY!
BY THE WAY...
IS THERE A BOAT THAT CAN TAKE US FROM SPIRIT ISLAND... TO G?
NO! BELIEVE ME, NO CAPTAIN WOULD DARE LAND NEAR G!
STAAARE
ARE YOU SURE?
YOU'RE NOT LYING, ARE YOU?
NO! IT'S THE TRUTH!!
...

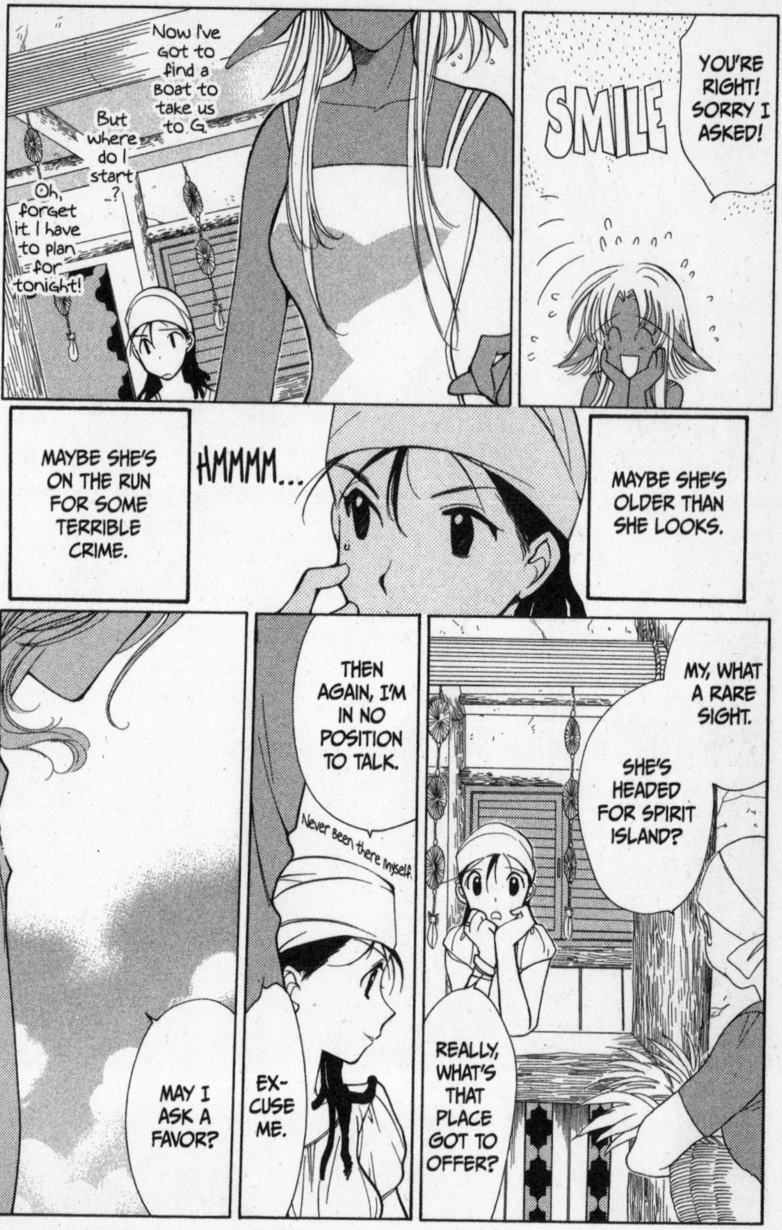
SMILE
YOU'RE RIGHT! SORRY I ASKED!
Now I've got to find a boat to take us to G.
But where do I start ...?
Oh, forget it. I have to plan for tonight!
MAYBE SHE'S OLDER THAN SHE LOOKS.
HMMMM...
MAYBE SHE'S ON THE RUN FOR SOME TERRIBLE CRIME.
MY, WHAT A RARE SIGHT.
SHE'S HEADED FOR SPIRIT ISLAND?
REALLY, WHAT'S THAT PLACE GOT TO OFFER?
THEN AGAIN, I'M IN NO POSITION TO TALK.
Never Been there myself.
EX-CUSE ME.
MAY I ASK A FAVOR?

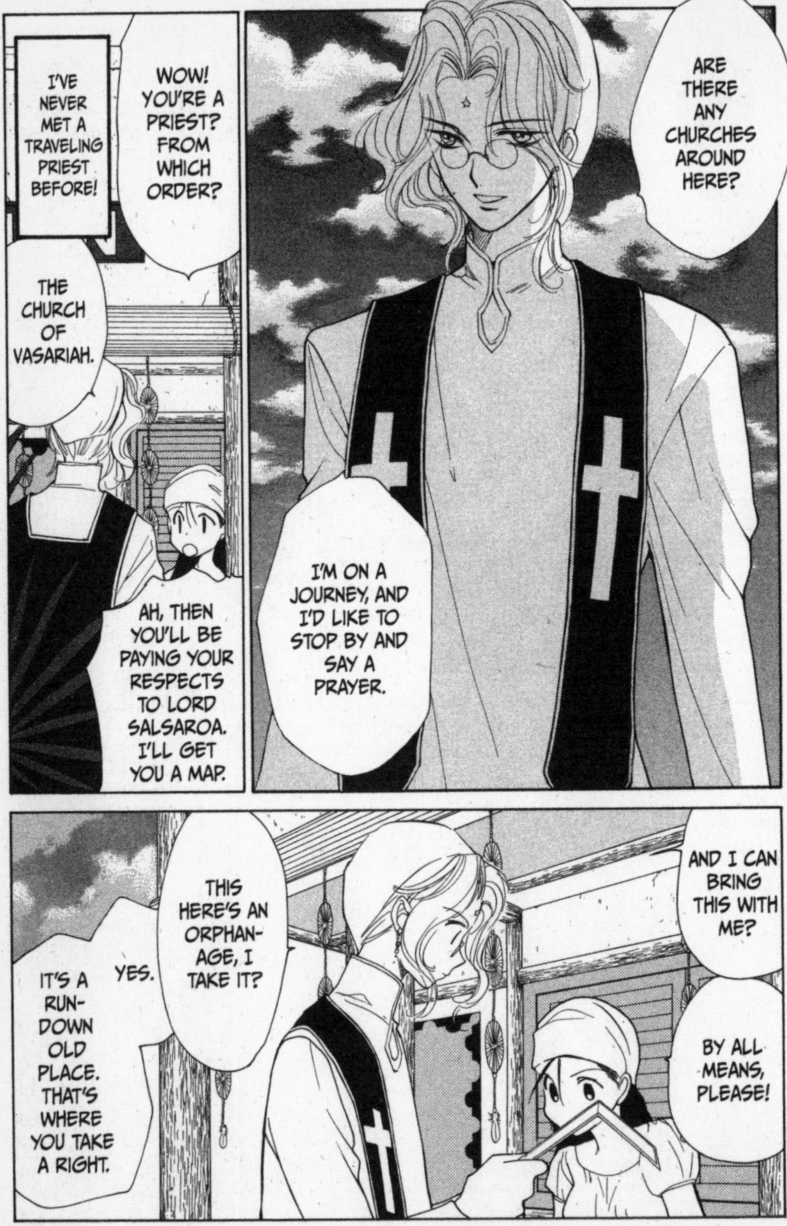
ARE THERE ANY CHURCHES AROUND HERE?
I'M ON A JOURNEY, AND I'D LIKE TO STOP BY AND SAY A PRAYER.
WOW! YOU'RE A PRIEST? FROM WHICH ORDER?
I'VE NEVER MET A TRAVELING PRIEST BEFORE!
THE CHURCH OF VASARIAH.
AH, THEN YOU'LL BE PAYING YOUR RESPECTS TO LORD SALSAROA. I'LL GET YOU A MAP.
AND I CAN BRING THIS WITH ME?
BY ALL MEANS, PLEASE!
THIS HERE'S AN ORPHANAGE, I TAKE IT?
YES.
IT'S A RUN-DOWN OLD PLACE. THAT'S WHERE YOU TAKE A RIGHT.

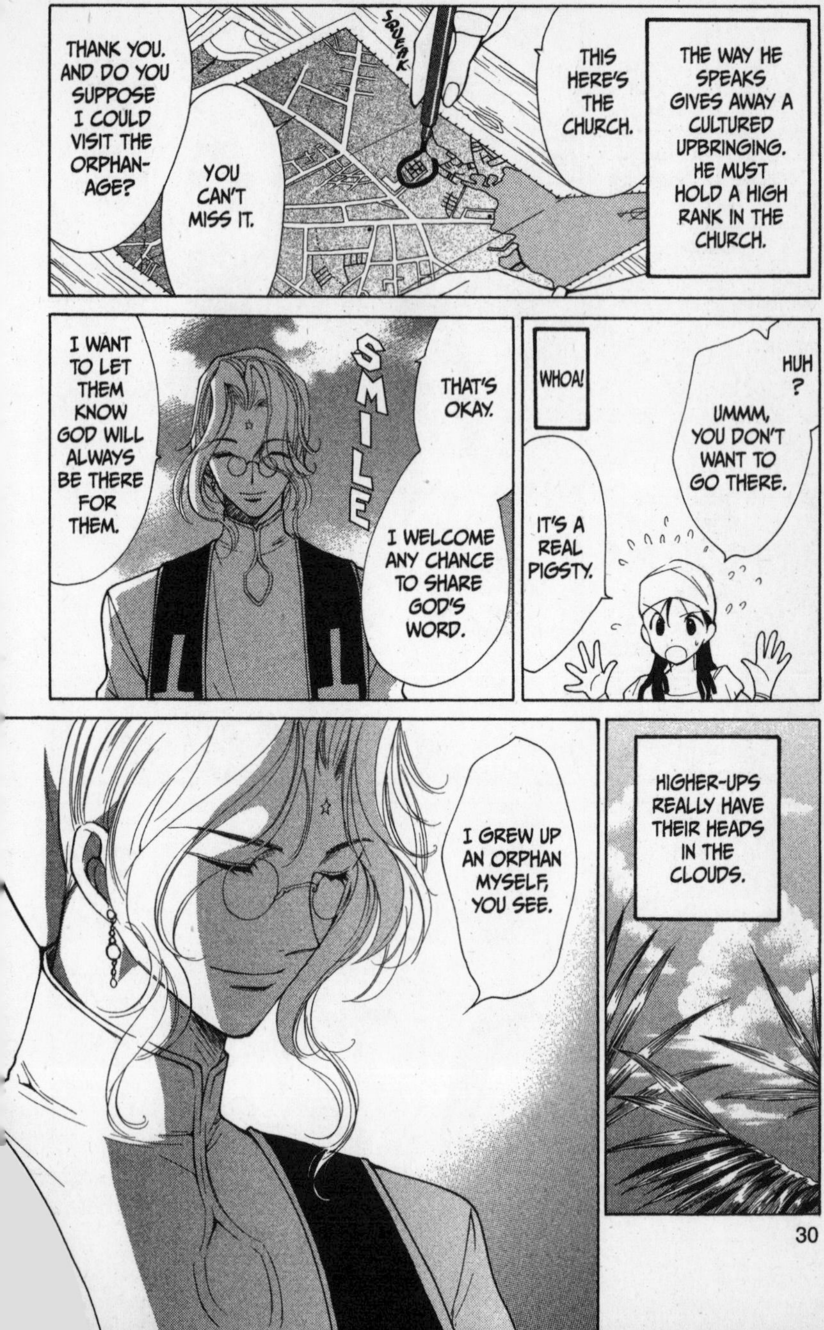
THE WAY HE SPEAKS GIVES AWAY A CULTURED UPBRINGING. HE MUST HOLD A HIGH RANK IN THE CHURCH.
THIS HERE'S THE CHURCH.
SQUEAK
YOU CAN'T MISS IT.
THANK YOU. AND DO YOU SUPPOSE I COULD VISIT THE ORPHAN-AGE?
HUH?
UMMM, YOU DON'T WANT TO GO THERE.
WHOA!
IT'S A REAL PIGSTY.
THAT'S OKAY.
SMILE
I WELCOME ANY CHANCE TO SHARE GOD'S WORD.
I WANT TO LET THEM KNOW GOD WILL ALWAYS BE THERE FOR THEM.
HIGHER-UPS REALLY HAVE THEIR HEADS IN THE CLOUDS.
I GREW UP AN ORPHAN MYSELF, YOU SEE.

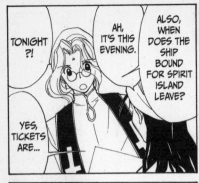

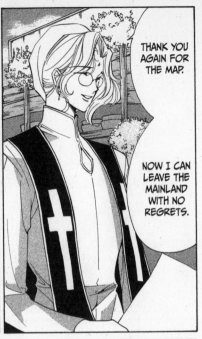

THANK YOU AGAIN FOR THE MAP.
NOW I CAN LEAVE THE MAINLAND WITH NO REGRETS.
ALSO, WHEN DOES THE SHIP BOUND FOR SPIRIT ISLAND LEAVE?
AH, IT'S THIS EVENING.
TONIGHT ?!
YES, TICKETS ARE...
I DON'T NEED A TICKET.
MY FRIEND SHOULD HAVE ALREADY BOUGHT ONE FOR ME.
HUH?
THEN THAT DARK ELF... IS TRAVELING WITH A PRIEST?!
HE'S PROBABLY BEEN THROUGH A LOT MORE THAN IT SEEMS.
YOU DID ME A GREAT FAVOR.
IN RETURN...

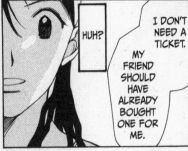

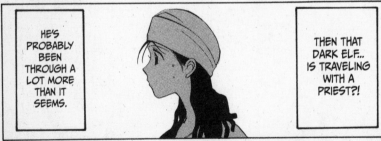

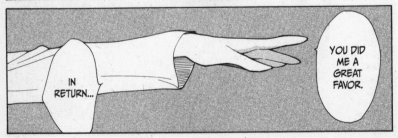

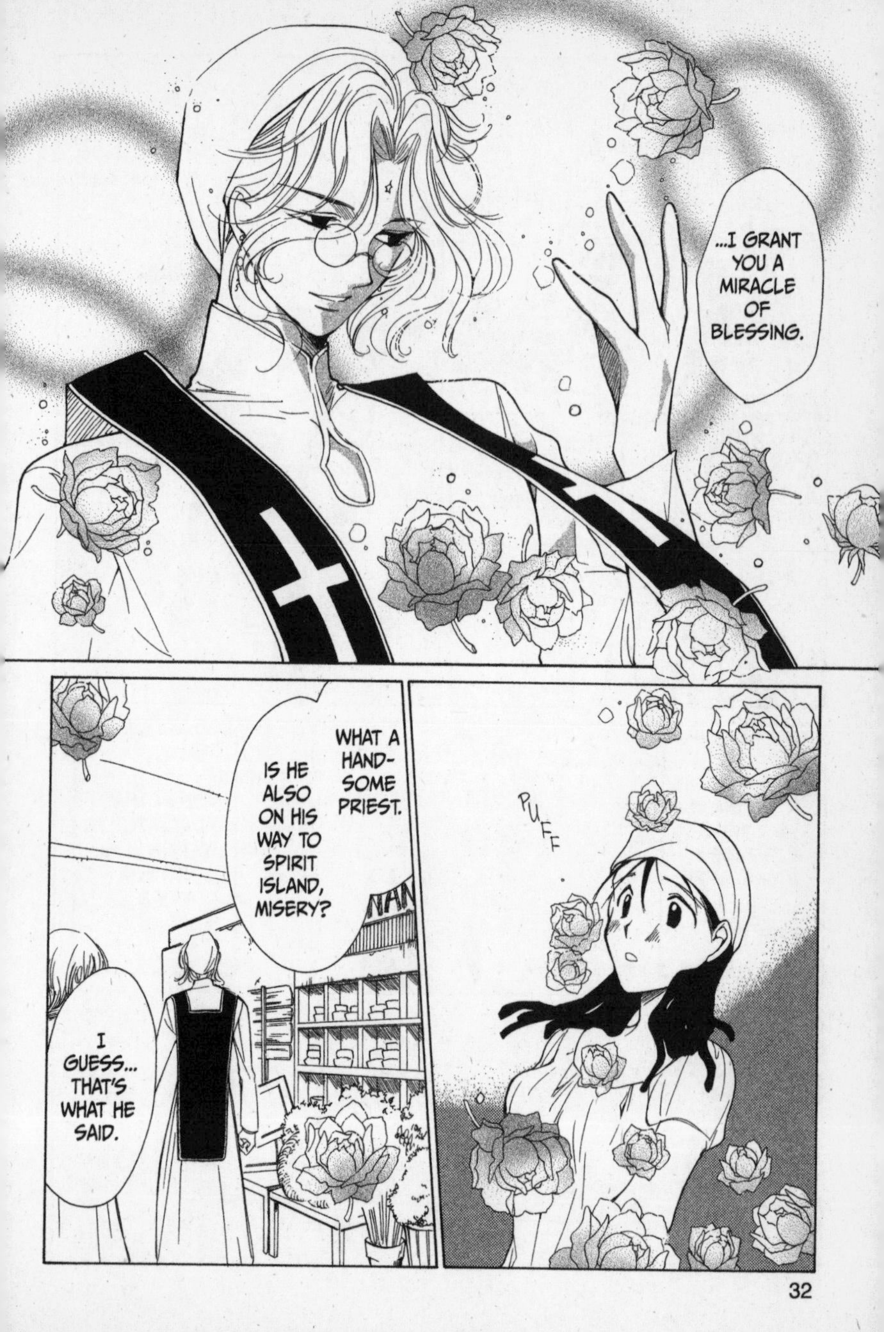
...I GRANT YOU A MIRACLE OF BLESSING.
PUFF
WHAT A HAND-SOME PRIEST.
IS HE ALSO ON HIS WAY TO SPIRIT ISLAND, MISERY?
I GUESS... THAT'S WHAT HE SAID.

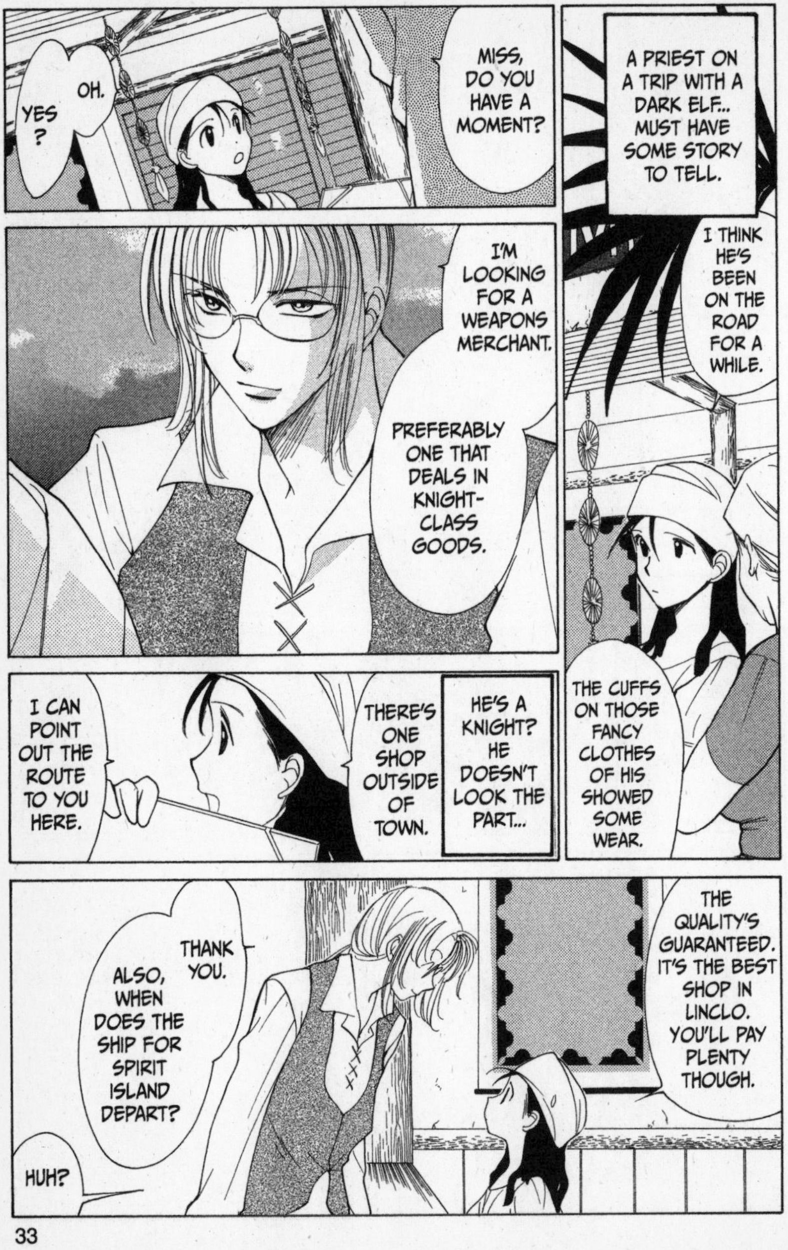
A PRIEST ON A TRIP WITH A DARK ELF... MUST HAVE SOME STORY TO TELL.
I THINK HE'S BEEN ON THE ROAD FOR A WHILE.
THE CUFFS ON THOSE FANCY CLOTHES OF HIS SHOWED SOME WEAR.
MISS, DO YOU HAVE A MOMENT?
OH.
YES?
I'M LOOKING FOR A WEAPONS MERCHANT.
PREFERABLY ONE THAT DEALS IN KNIGHT-CLASS GOODS.
HE'S A KNIGHT? HE DOESN'T LOOK THE PART...
THERE'S ONE SHOP OUTSIDE OF TOWN.
I CAN POINT OUT THE ROUTE TO YOU HERE.
THE QUALITY'S GUARANTEED. IT'S THE BEST SHOP IN LINCLO. YOU'LL PAY PLENTY THOUGH.
THANK YOU.
ALSO, WHEN DOES THE SHIP FOR SPIRIT ISLAND DEPART?
HUH?

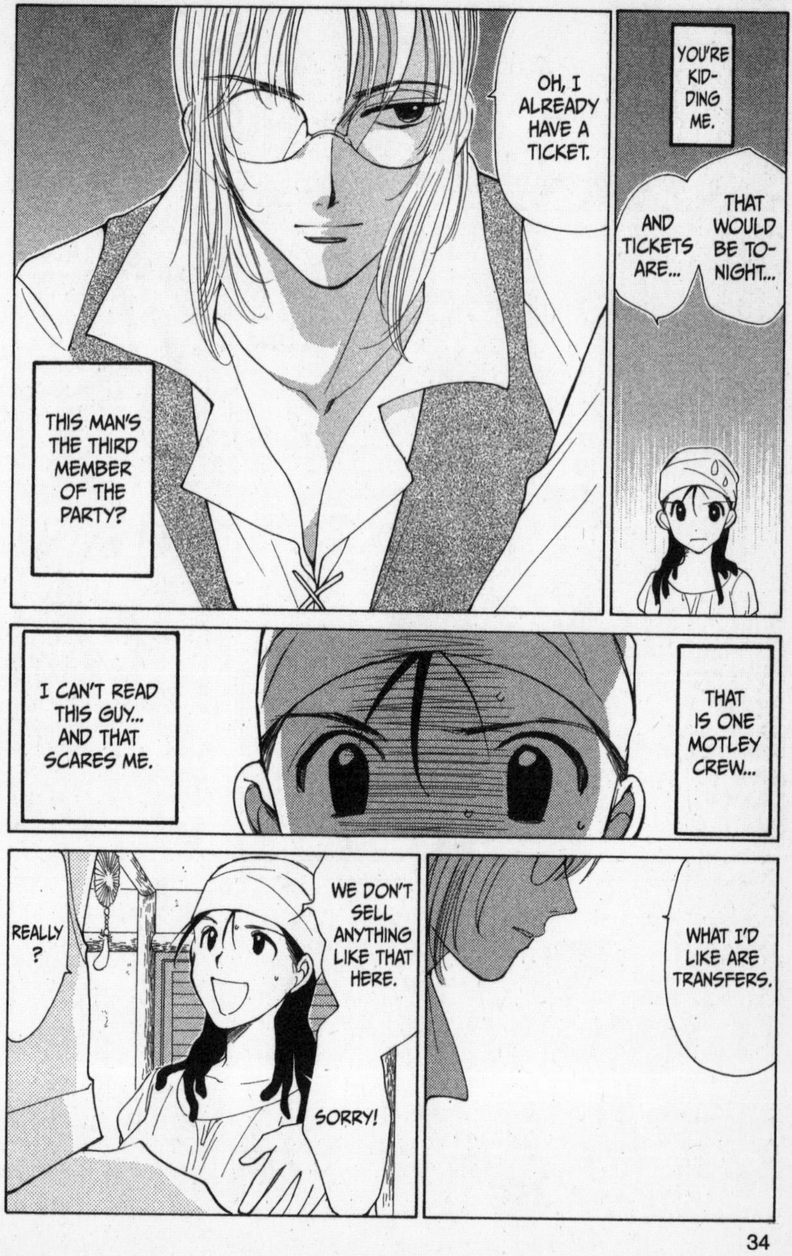
YOU'RE KID-DING ME.
THAT WOULD BE TO-NIGHT...
AND TICKETS ARE...
OH, I ALREADY HAVE A TICKET.
THIS MAN'S THE THIRD MEMBER OF THE PARTY?
THAT IS ONE MOTLEY CREW...
I CAN'T READ THIS GUY... AND THAT SCARES ME.
WHAT I'D LIKE ARE TRANSFERS.
WE DON'T SELL ANYTHING LIKE THAT HERE.
REALLY?
SORRY!

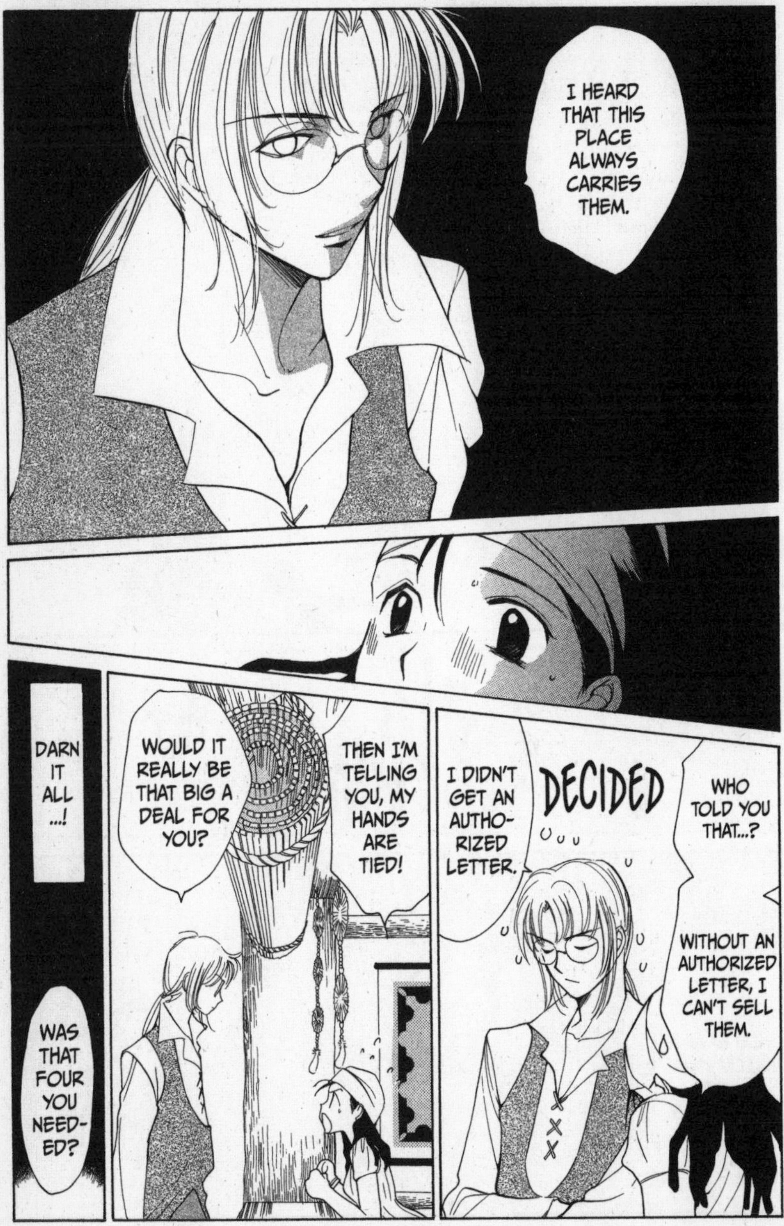
I HEARD THAT THIS PLACE ALWAYS CARRIES THEM.
WHO TOLD YOU THAT...?
DECIDED
I DIDN'T GET AN AUTHO-RIZED LETTER.
WITHOUT AN AUTHORIZED LETTER, I CAN'T SELL THEM.
THEN I'M TELLING YOU, MY HANDS ARE TIED!
WOULD IT REALLY BE THAT BIG A DEAL FOR YOU?
DARN IT ALL ...!
WAS THAT FOUR YOU NEED-ED?

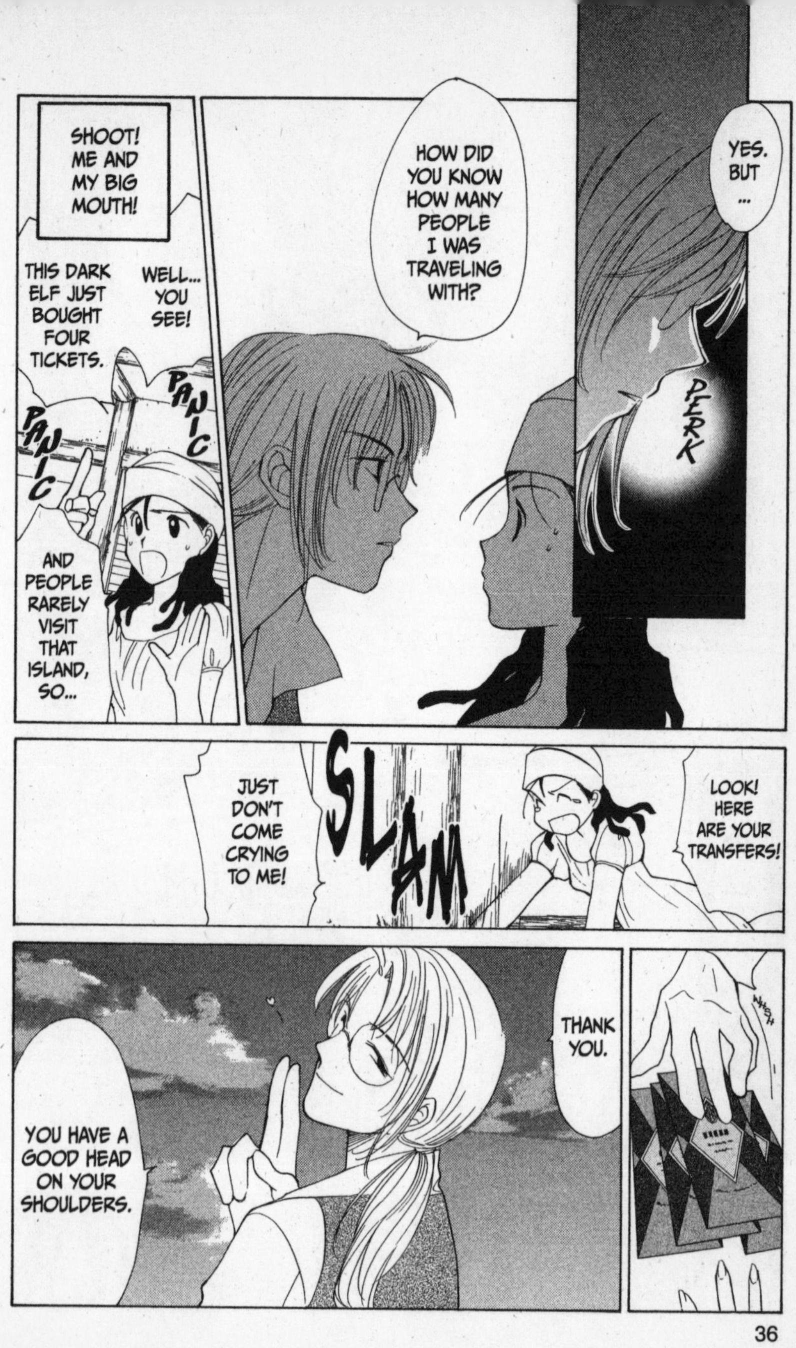
YES. BUT ...
PERK
HOW DID YOU KNOW HOW MANY PEOPLE I WAS TRAVELING WITH?
SHOOT! ME AND MY BIG MOUTH!
WELL... YOU SEE!
THIS DARK ELF JUST BOUGHT FOUR TICKETS.
PANIC
PANIC
AND PEOPLE RARELY VISIT THAT ISLAND, SO...
LOOK! HERE ARE YOUR TRANSFERS!
SLAM
JUST DON'T COME CRYING TO ME!
THANK YOU.
YOU HAVE A GOOD HEAD ON YOUR SHOULDERS.

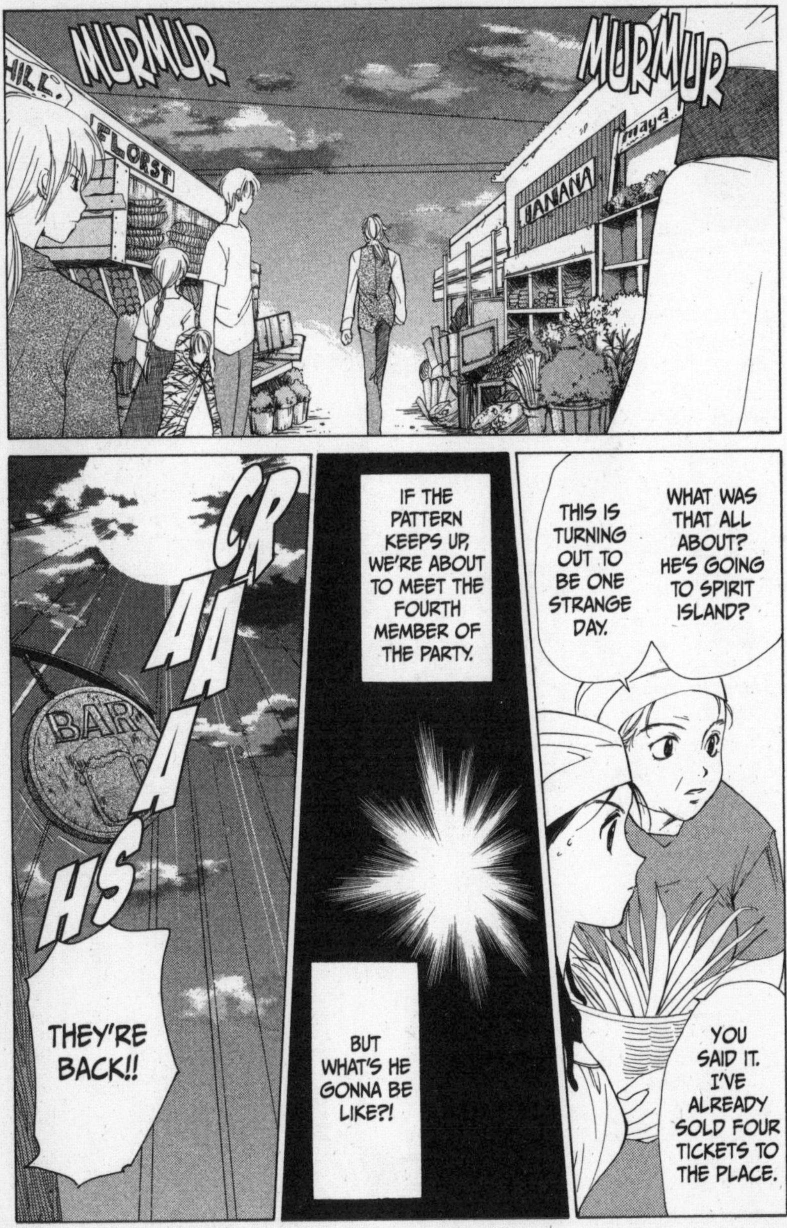
MURMUR
MURMUR
maya
HANANA
HILL.
FLORST
WHAT WAS THAT ALL ABOUT? HE'S GOING TO SPIRIT ISLAND?
THIS IS TURNING OUT TO BE ONE STRANGE DAY.
YOU SAID IT. I'VE ALREADY SOLD FOUR TICKETS TO THE PLACE.
IF THE PATTERN KEEPS UP, WE'RE ABOUT TO MEET THE FOURTH MEMBER OF THE PARTY.
BUT WHAT'S HE GONNA BE LIKE?!
CRAAAASH
BAR
THEY'RE BACK!!

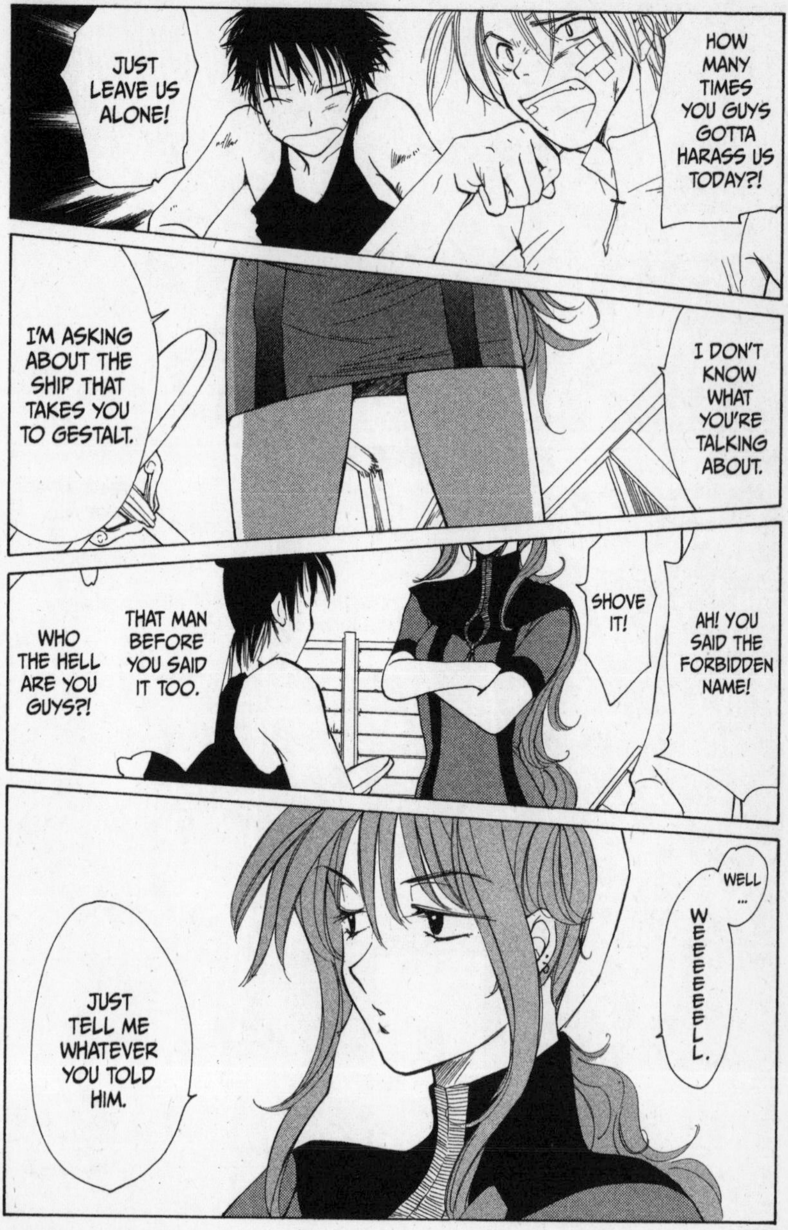
HOW MANY TIMES YOU GUYS GOTTA HARASS US TODAY?!
JUST LEAVE US ALONE!
I DON'T KNOW WHAT YOU'RE TALKING ABOUT.
I'M ASKING ABOUT THE SHIP THAT TAKES YOU TO GESTALT.
AH! YOU SAID THE FORBIDDEN NAME!
SHOVE IT!
THAT MAN BEFORE YOU SAID IT TOO.
WHO THE HELL ARE YOU GUYS?!
WELL ...
WEEEEEELL.
JUST TELL ME WHATEVER YOU TOLD HIM.

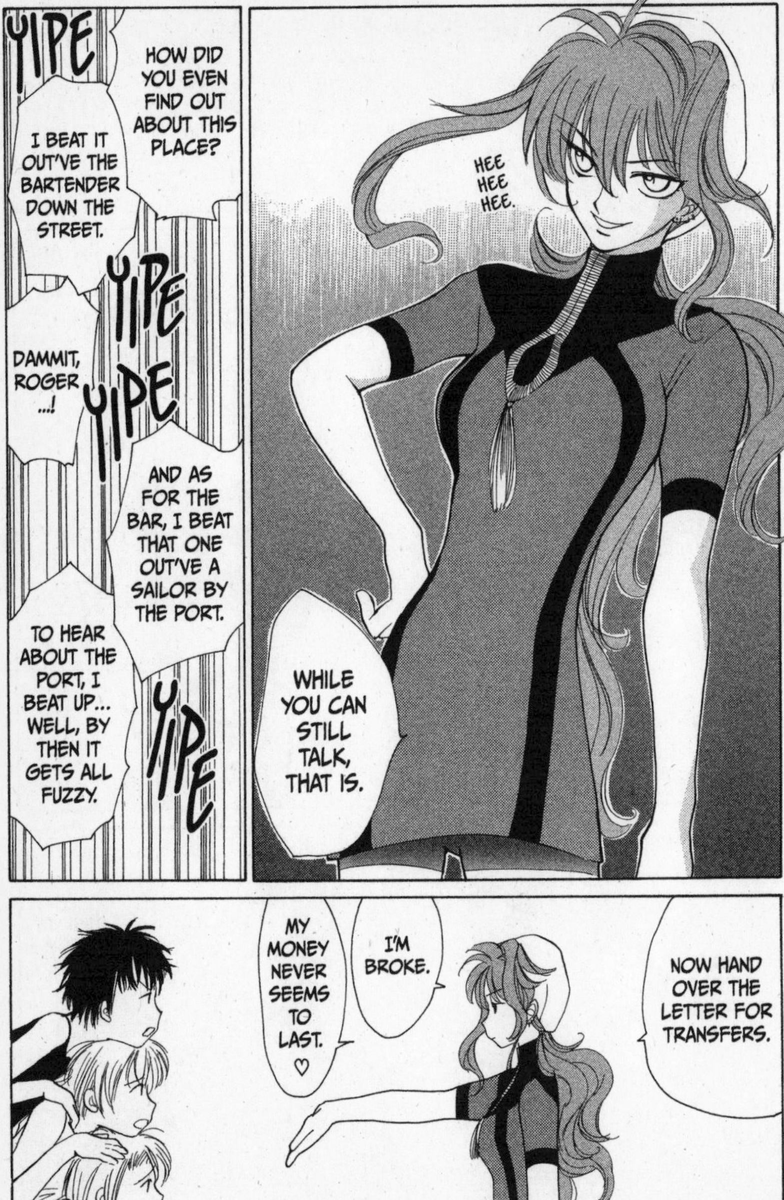
HEE HEE HEE.
WHILE YOU CAN STILL TALK, THAT IS.
YIPE
HOW DID YOU EVEN FIND OUT ABOUT THIS PLACE?
I BEAT IT OUT'VE THE BARTENDER DOWN THE STREET.
YIPE
YIPE
DAMMIT, ROGER ...!
AND AS FOR THE BAR, I BEAT THAT ONE OUT'VE A SAILOR BY THE PORT.
YIPE
TO HEAR ABOUT THE PORT, I BEAT UP... WELL, BY THEN IT GETS ALL FUZZY.
NOW HAND OVER THE LETTER FOR TRANSFERS.
I'M BROKE.
MY MONEY NEVER SEEMS TO LAST. ♡

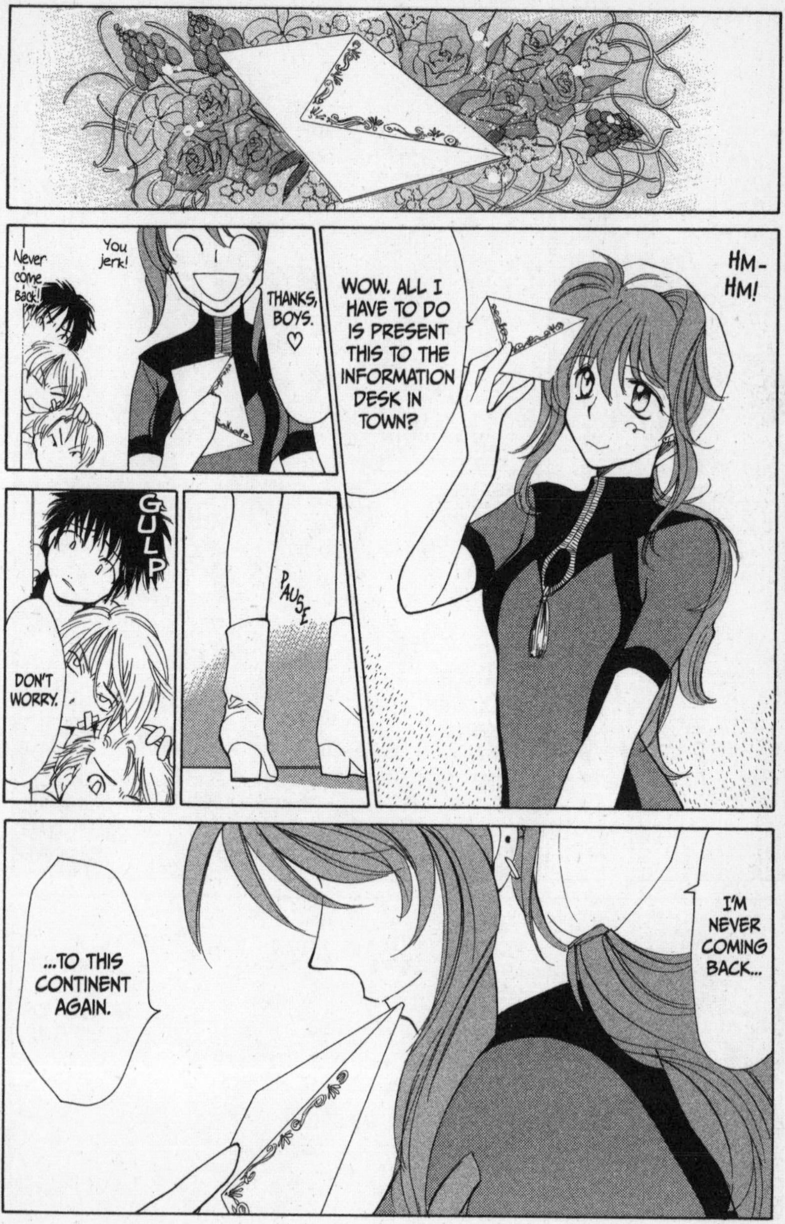
HM-HM!
WOW. ALL I HAVE TO DO IS PRESENT THIS TO THE INFORMATION DESK IN TOWN?
THANKS, BOYS. ♡
You jerk!
Never come back!
PAUSE
GULP
DON'T WORRY.
I'M NEVER COMING BACK...
...TO THIS CONTINENT AGAIN.

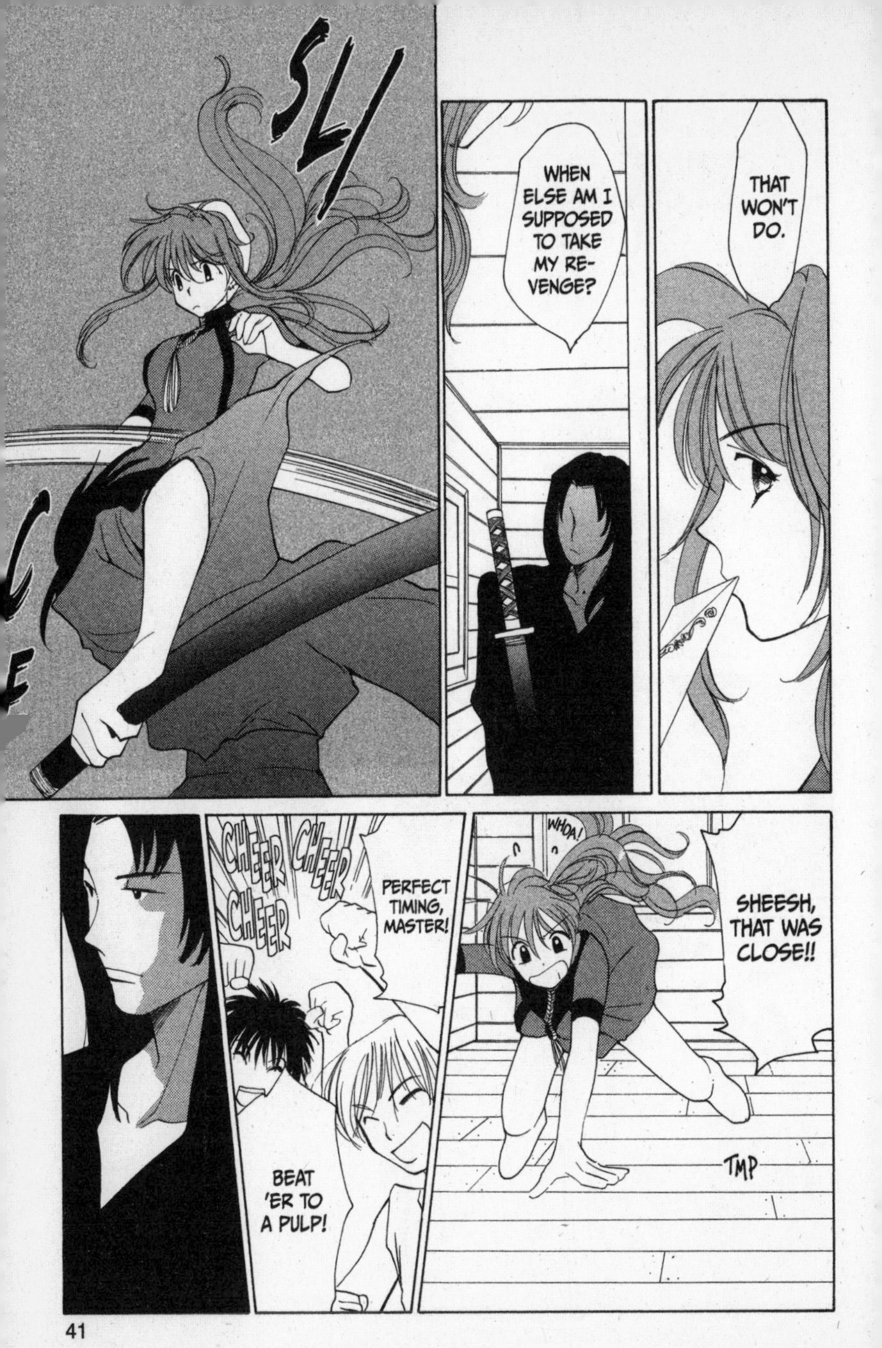
THAT WON'T DO.
WHEN ELSE AM I SUPPOSED TO TAKE MY RE-VENGE?
SLI
CE
WHOA!
SHEESH, THAT WAS CLOSE!!
TMP
PERFECT TIMING, MASTER!
CHEER CHEER
CHEER
BEAT 'ER TO A PULP!

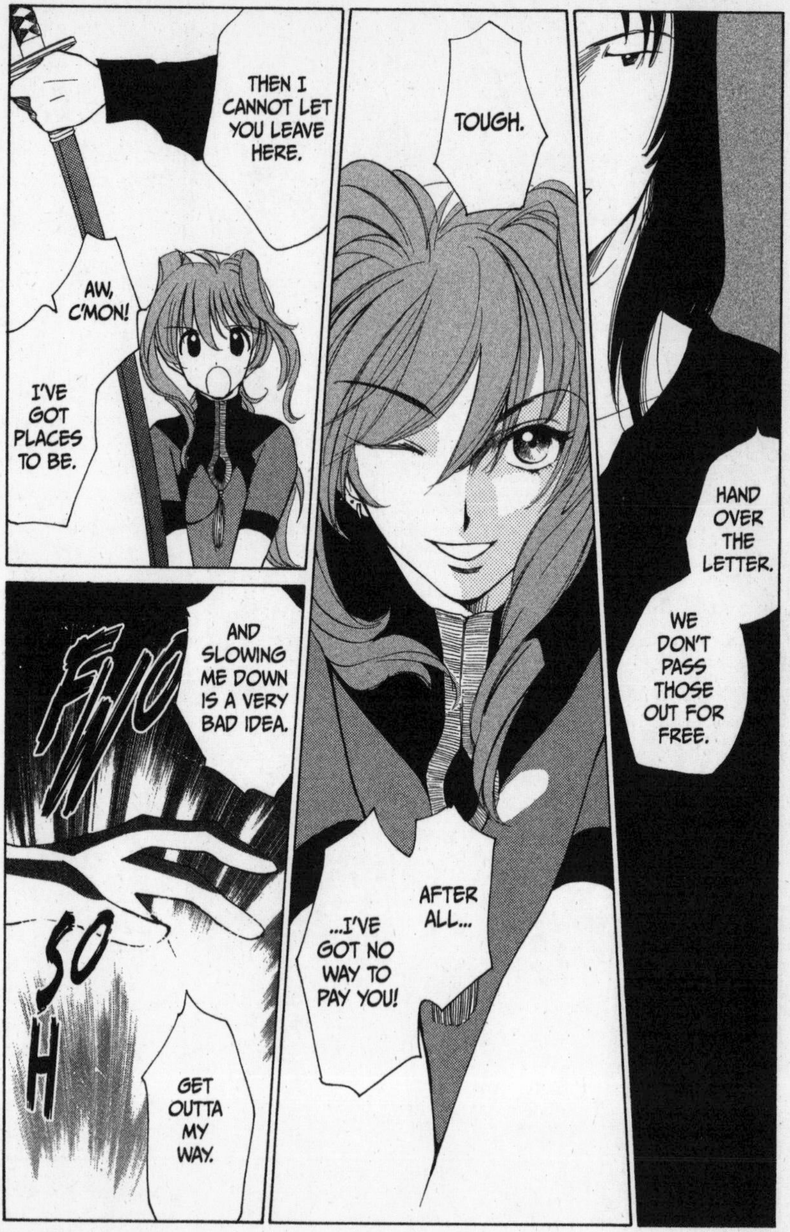
HAND OVER THE LETTER.
WE DON'T PASS THOSE OUT FOR FREE.
TOUGH.
AFTER ALL...
...I'VE GOT NO WAY TO PAY YOU!
THEN I CANNOT LET YOU LEAVE HERE.
AW, C'MON!
I'VE GOT PLACES TO BE.
AND SLOWING ME DOWN IS A VERY BAD IDEA.
GET OUTTA MY WAY.

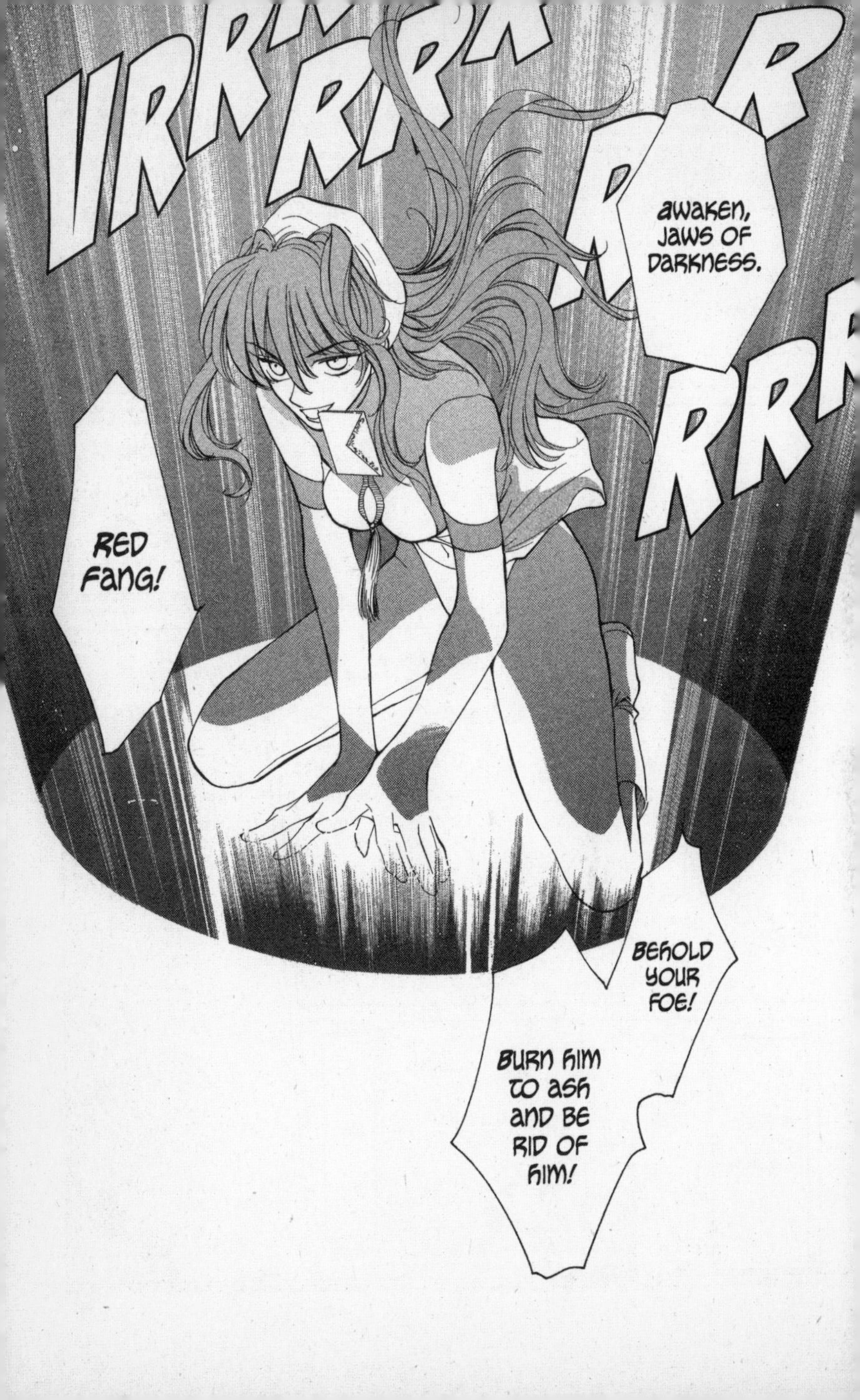

VRRRRRRRRR
Awaken, jaws of darkness.
Red Fang!
Behold your foe!
Burn him to ash and be rid of him!

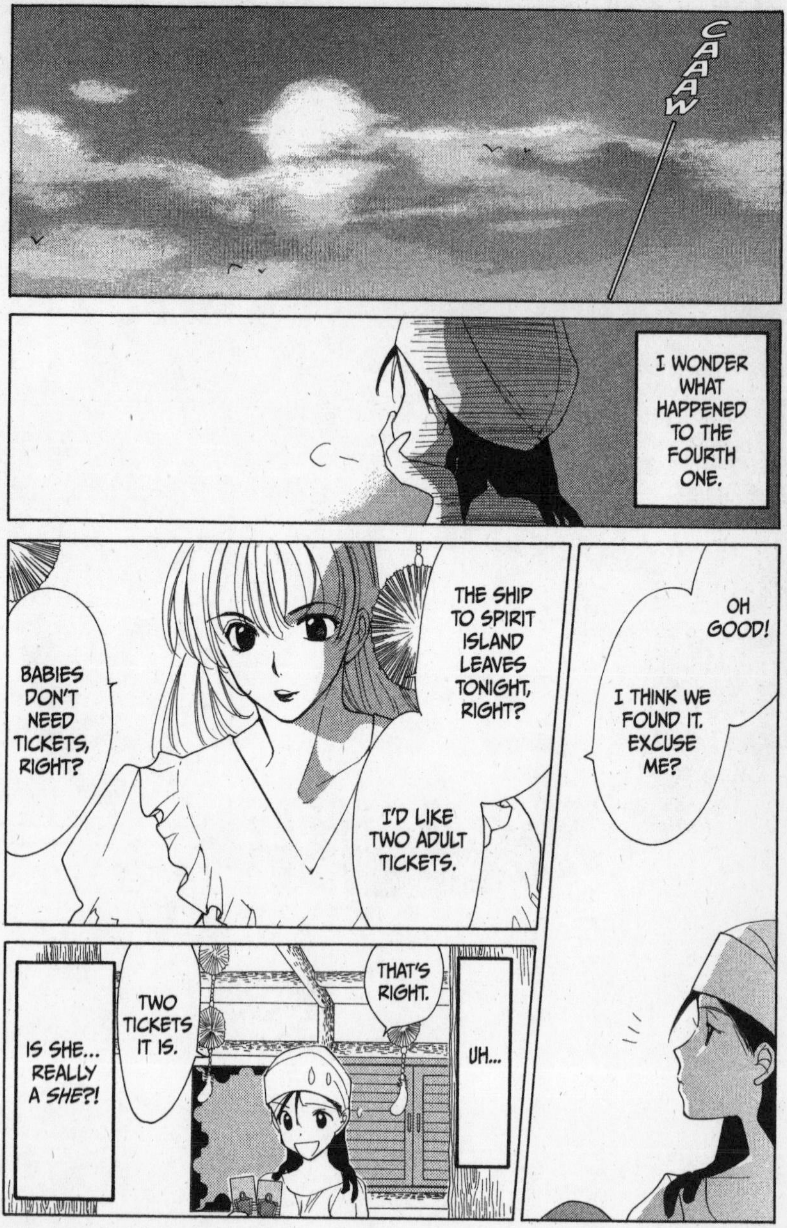
CAAAW
I WONDER WHAT HAPPENED TO THE FOURTH ONE.
OH GOOD!
I THINK WE FOUND IT. EXCUSE ME?
THE SHIP TO SPIRIT ISLAND LEAVES TONIGHT, RIGHT?
I'D LIKE TWO ADULT TICKETS.
BABIES DON'T NEED TICKETS, RIGHT?
UH...
THAT'S RIGHT.
TWO TICKETS IT IS.
IS SHE... REALLY A *SHE*?!

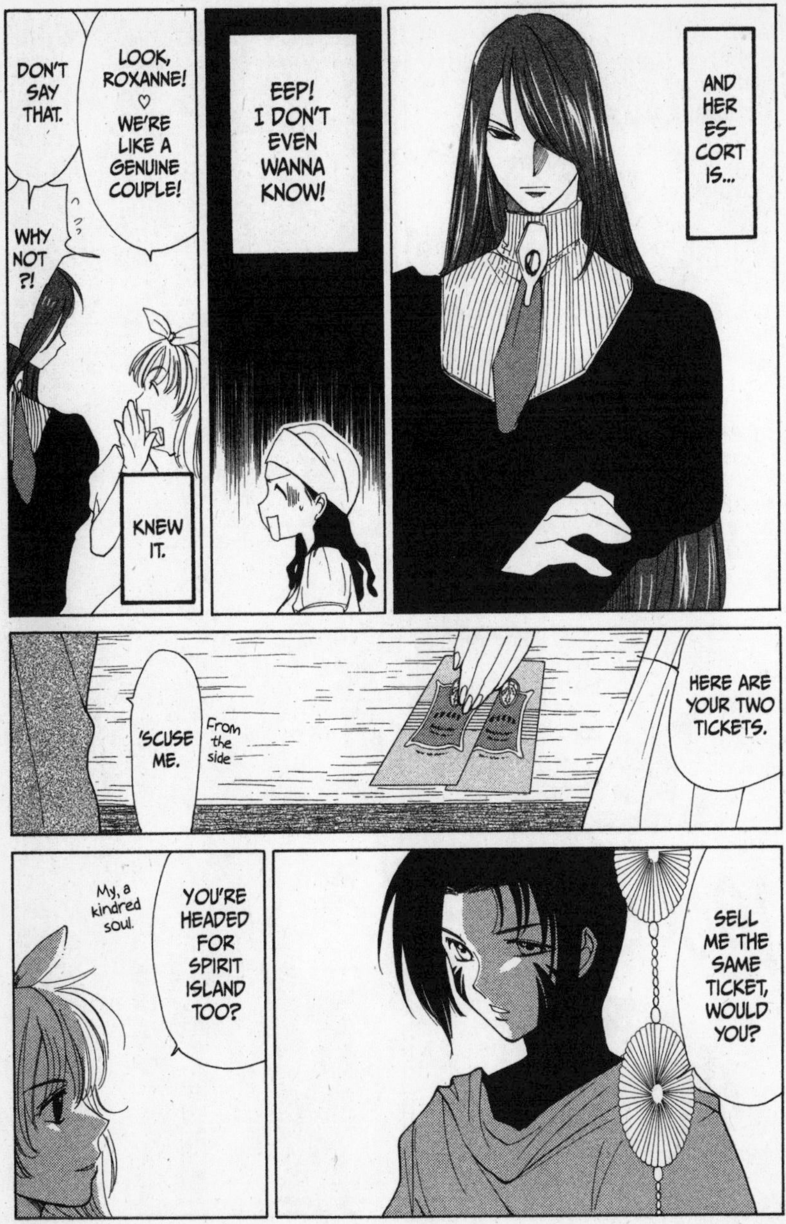
AND HER ES-CORT IS...
EEP! I DON'T EVEN WANNA KNOW!
LOOK, ROXANNE! ♡ WE'RE LIKE A GENUINE COUPLE!
DON'T SAY THAT.
WHY NOT ?!
KNEW IT.
HERE ARE YOUR TWO TICKETS.
'SCUSE ME.
From the side
SELL ME THE SAME TICKET, WOULD YOU?
YOU'RE HEADED FOR SPIRIT ISLAND TOO?
My, a kindred soul.

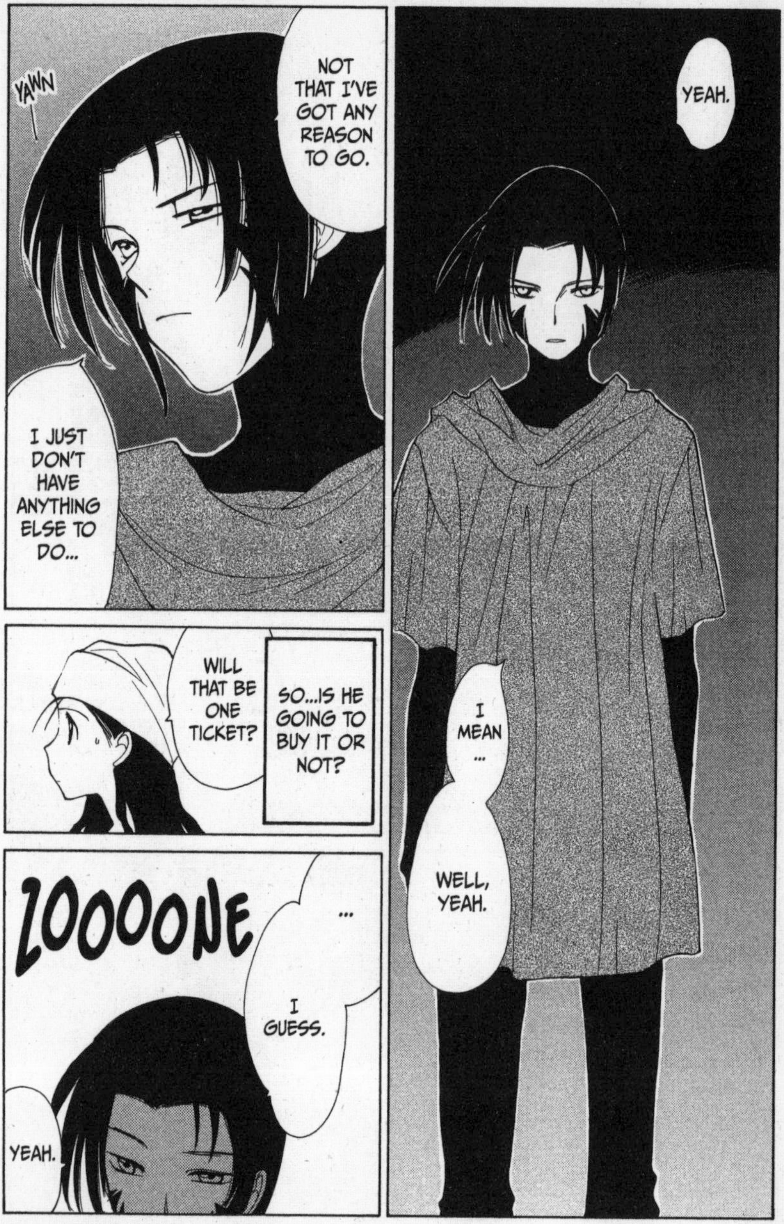
YEAH.
I MEAN...
WELL, YEAH.
NOT THAT I'VE GOT ANY REASON TO GO.
YAWN
I JUST DON'T HAVE ANYTHING ELSE TO DO...
SO...IS HE GOING TO BUY IT OR NOT?
WILL THAT BE ONE TICKET?
... I GUESS.
ZOOOONE
YEAH.

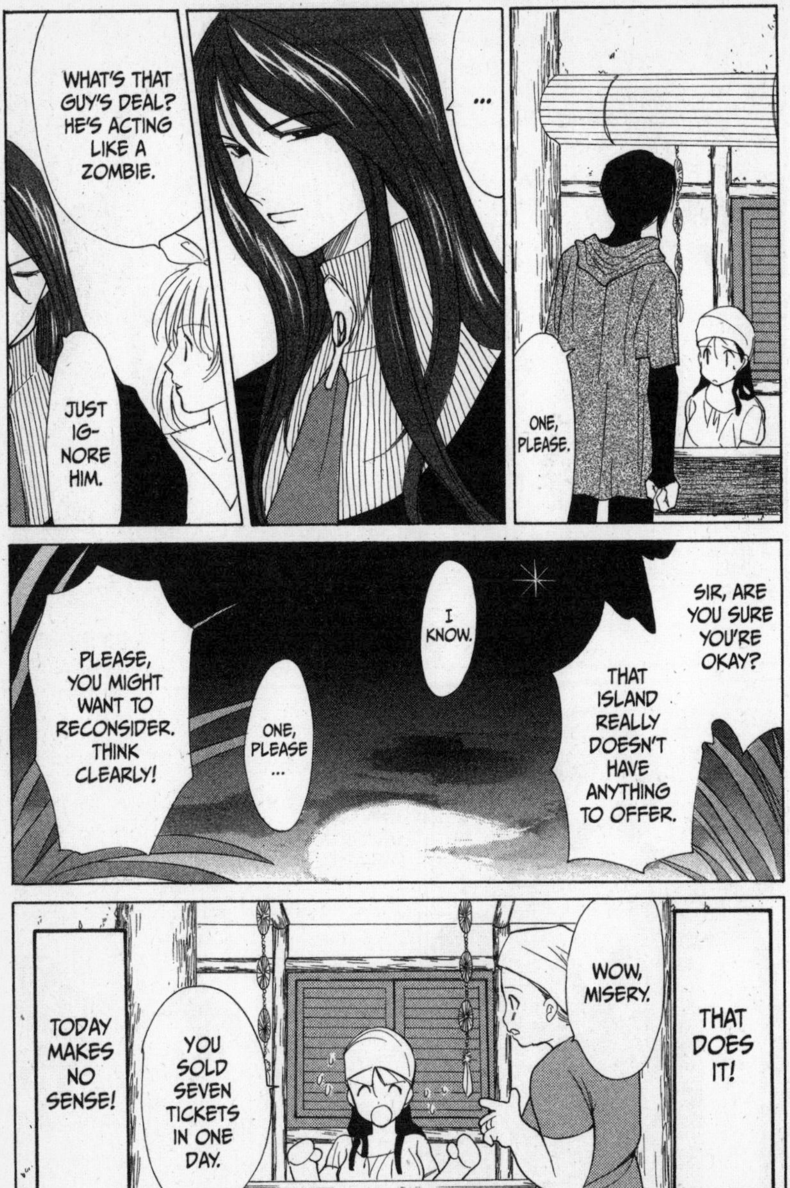
ONE, PLEASE.
...
WHAT'S THAT GUY'S DEAL? HE'S ACTING LIKE A ZOMBIE.
JUST IG-NORE HIM.
SIR, ARE YOU SURE YOU'RE OKAY?
THAT ISLAND REALLY DOESN'T HAVE ANYTHING TO OFFER.
I KNOW.
ONE, PLEASE ...
PLEASE, YOU MIGHT WANT TO RECONSIDER. THINK CLEARLY!
THAT DOES IT!
WOW, MISERY.
YOU SOLD SEVEN TICKETS IN ONE DAY.
TODAY MAKES NO SENSE!

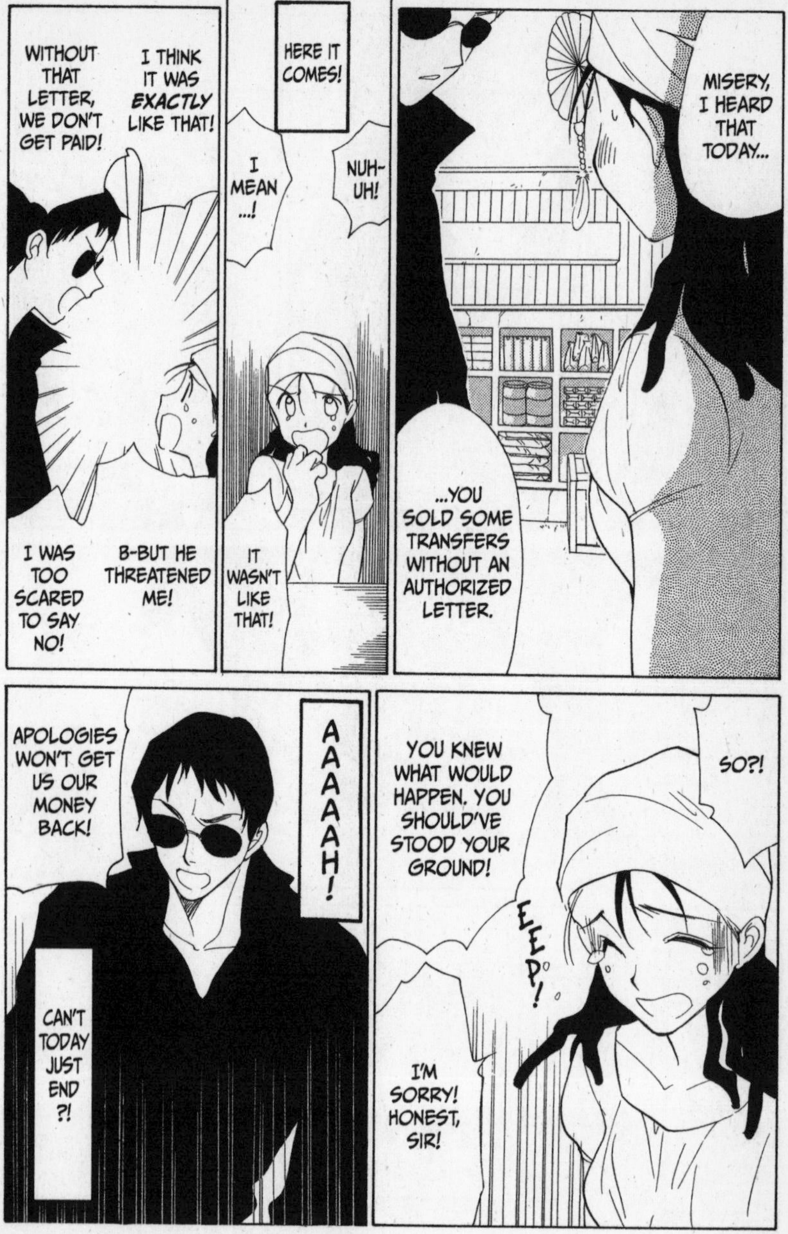
MISERY, I HEARD THAT TODAY...
...YOU SOLD SOME TRANSFERS WITHOUT AN AUTHORIZED LETTER.
HERE IT COMES!
NUH-UH!
I MEAN...!
IT WASN'T LIKE THAT!
I THINK IT WAS *EXACTLY* LIKE THAT!
WITHOUT THAT LETTER, WE DON'T GET PAID!
B-BUT HE THREATENED ME!
I WAS TOO SCARED TO SAY NO!
SO?!
YOU KNEW WHAT WOULD HAPPEN. YOU SHOULD'VE STOOD YOUR GROUND!
EEP!
I'M SORRY! HONEST, SIR!
AAAAAH!
APOLOGIES WON'T GET US OUR MONEY BACK!
CAN'T TODAY JUST END ?!

SIR, DO YOU MIND?
POKE
YOU WERE TALKING ABOUT THIS, WEREN'T YOU?
LEMME SEE THAT!
SNATCH
IT'S AN AUTHO-RIZED LETTER!
OH MY...!
??
OH...
WHY DIDN'T YOU SAY SO?
THANKS FOR THE TRANSFERS, BY THE WAY. ♡
MY FRIEND GOT 'EM.

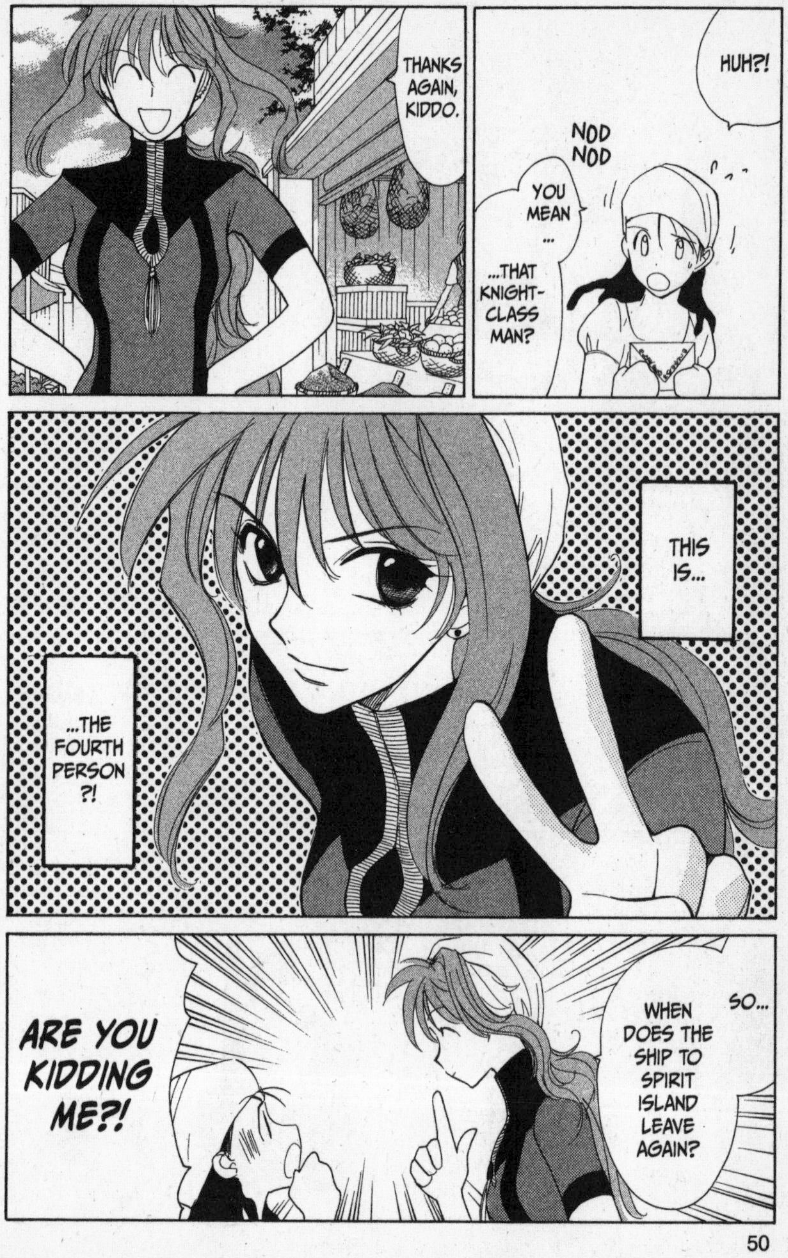
HUH?!
NOD NOD
YOU MEAN ...
...THAT KNIGHT-CLASS MAN?
THANKS AGAIN, KIDDO.
THIS IS...
...THE FOURTH PERSON?!
SO...
WHEN DOES THE SHIP TO SPIRIT ISLAND LEAVE AGAIN?
ARE YOU KIDDING ME?!

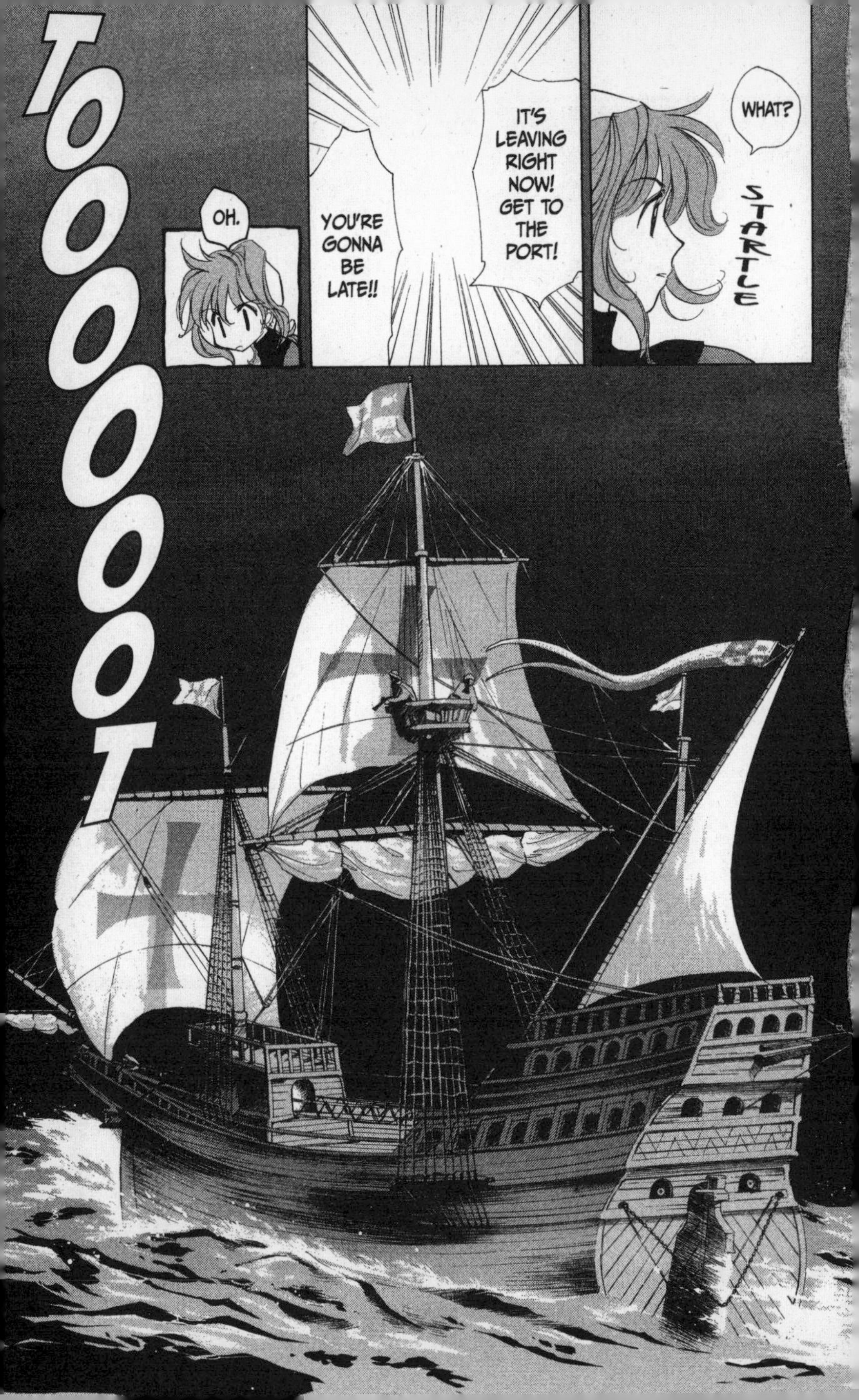
WHAT?
STARTLE
IT'S LEAVING RIGHT NOW! GET TO THE PORT!
YOU'RE GONNA BE LATE!!
OH.
TOOOOOOT

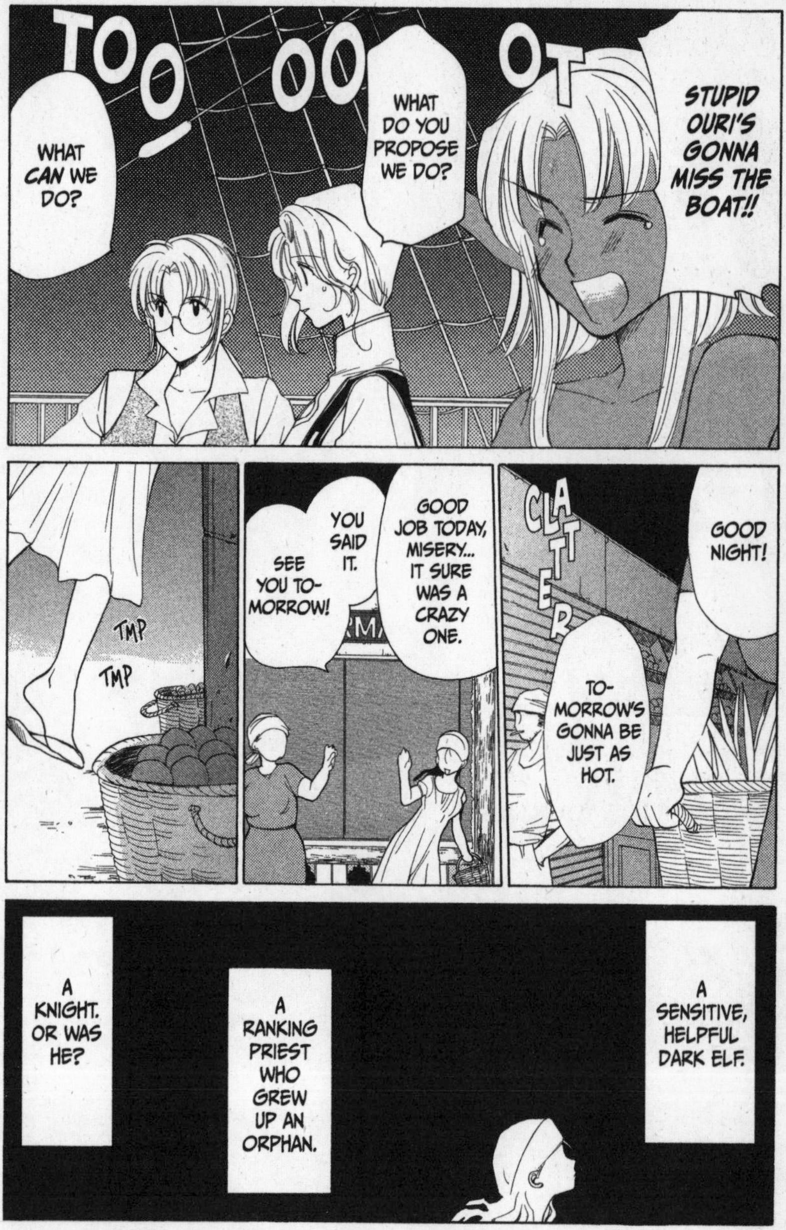
STUPID OURI'S GONNA MISS THE BOAT!!
TOO OO OT
WHAT DO YOU PROPOSE WE DO?
WHAT CAN WE DO?
GOOD NIGHT!
CLATTER
TO-MORROW'S GONNA BE JUST AS HOT.
GOOD JOB TODAY, MISERY... IT SURE WAS A CRAZY ONE.
YOU SAID IT.
SEE YOU TO-MORROW!
TMP
TMP
A SENSITIVE, HELPFUL DARK ELF.
A RANKING PRIEST WHO GREW UP AN ORPHAN.
A KNIGHT. OR WAS HE?

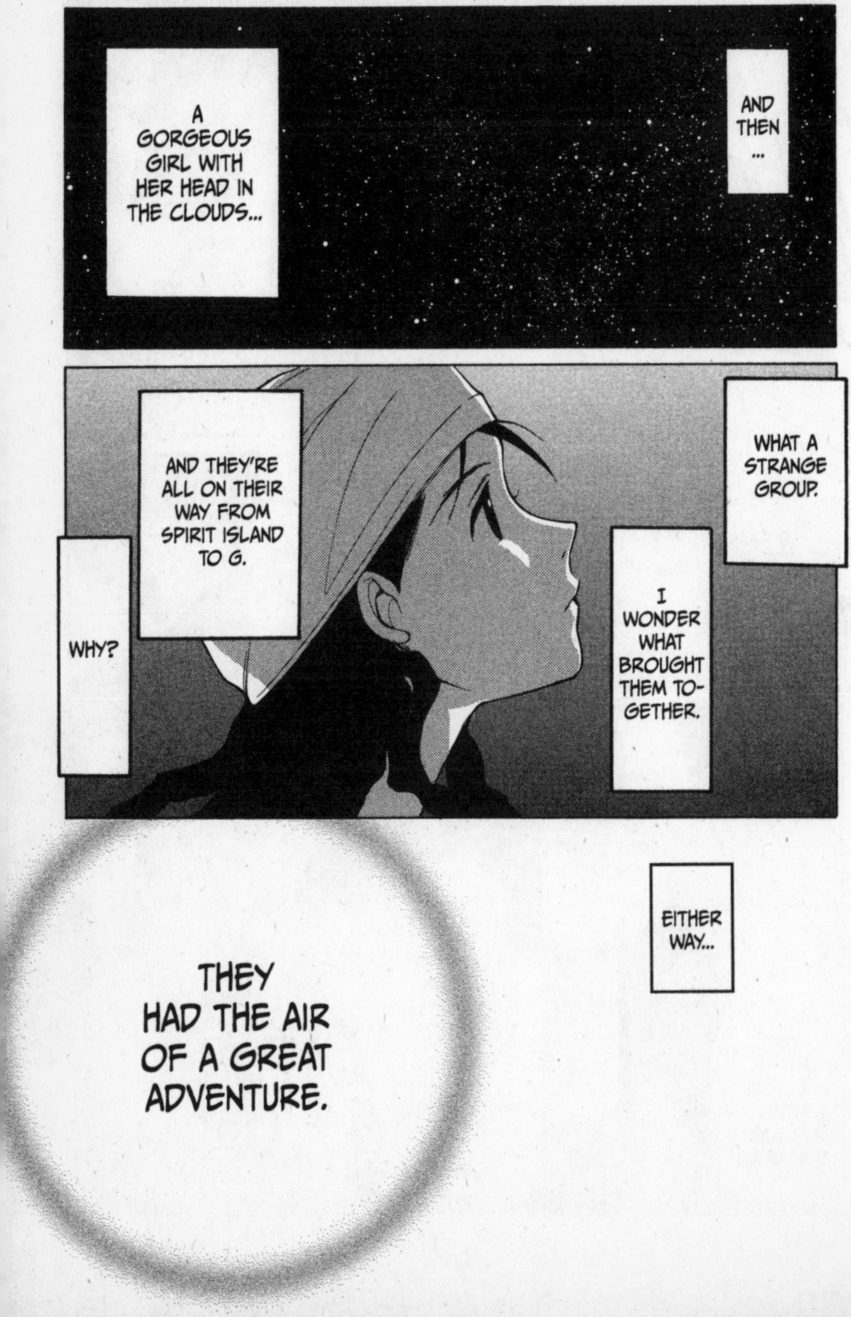
AND THEN ...
A GORGEOUS GIRL WITH HER HEAD IN THE CLOUDS...
WHAT A STRANGE GROUP.
I WONDER WHAT BROUGHT THEM TO-GETHER.
AND THEY'RE ALL ON THEIR WAY FROM SPIRIT ISLAND TO G.
WHY?
EITHER WAY...
THEY HAD THE AIR OF A GREAT ADVENTURE.

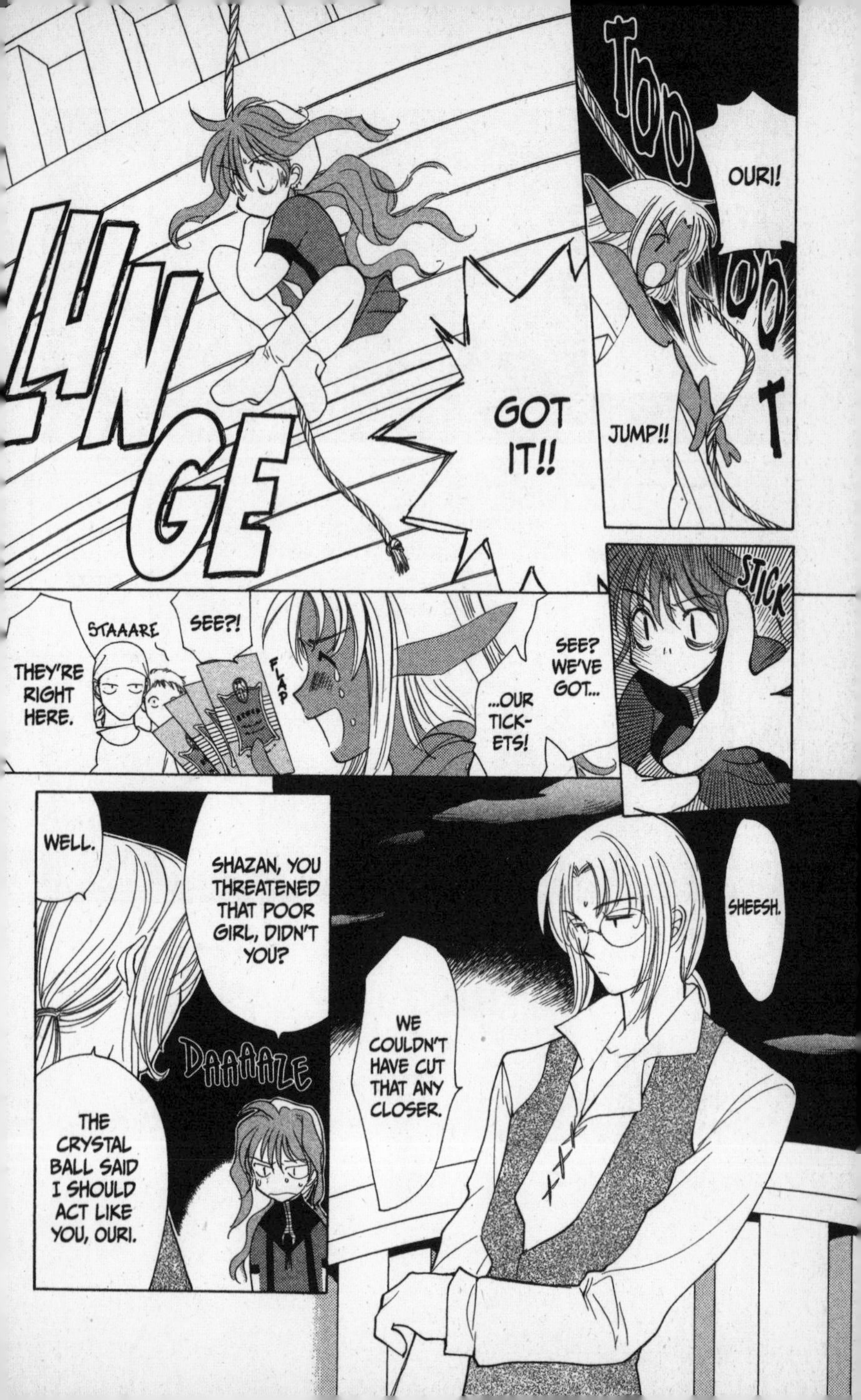
TOOO
OURI!
OOOT
JUMP!!
LUNGE
GOT IT!!
STICK
SEE? WE'VE GOT...
...OUR TICK-ETS!
FLAP
SEE?!
STAAARE
THEY'RE RIGHT HERE.
SHEESH.
WE COULDN'T HAVE CUT THAT ANY CLOSER.
SHAZAN, YOU THREATENED THAT POOR GIRL, DIDN'T YOU?
WELL.
DAAAAAZE
THE CRYSTAL BALL SAID I SHOULD ACT LIKE YOU, OURI.

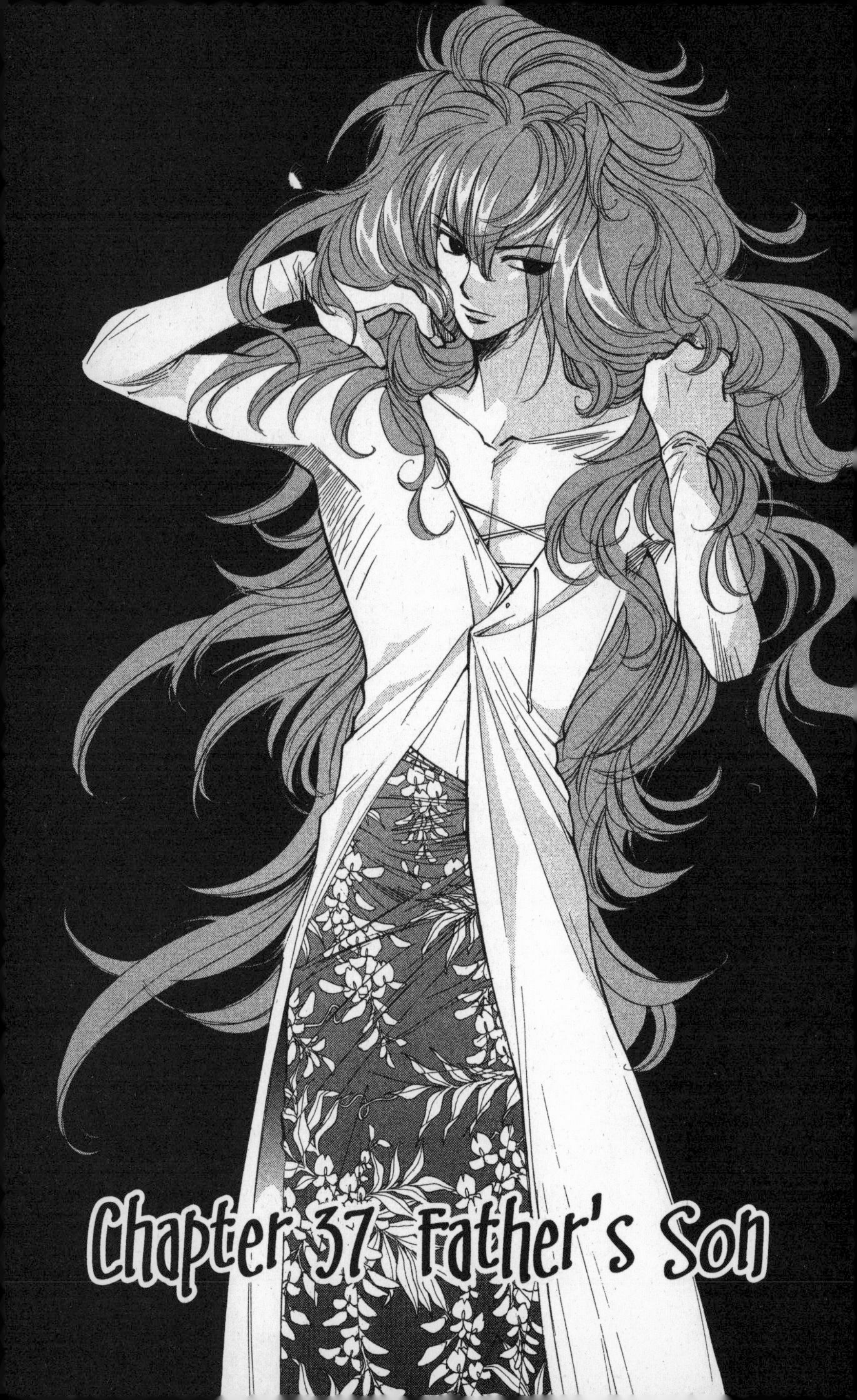

Chapter 37 Father's Son

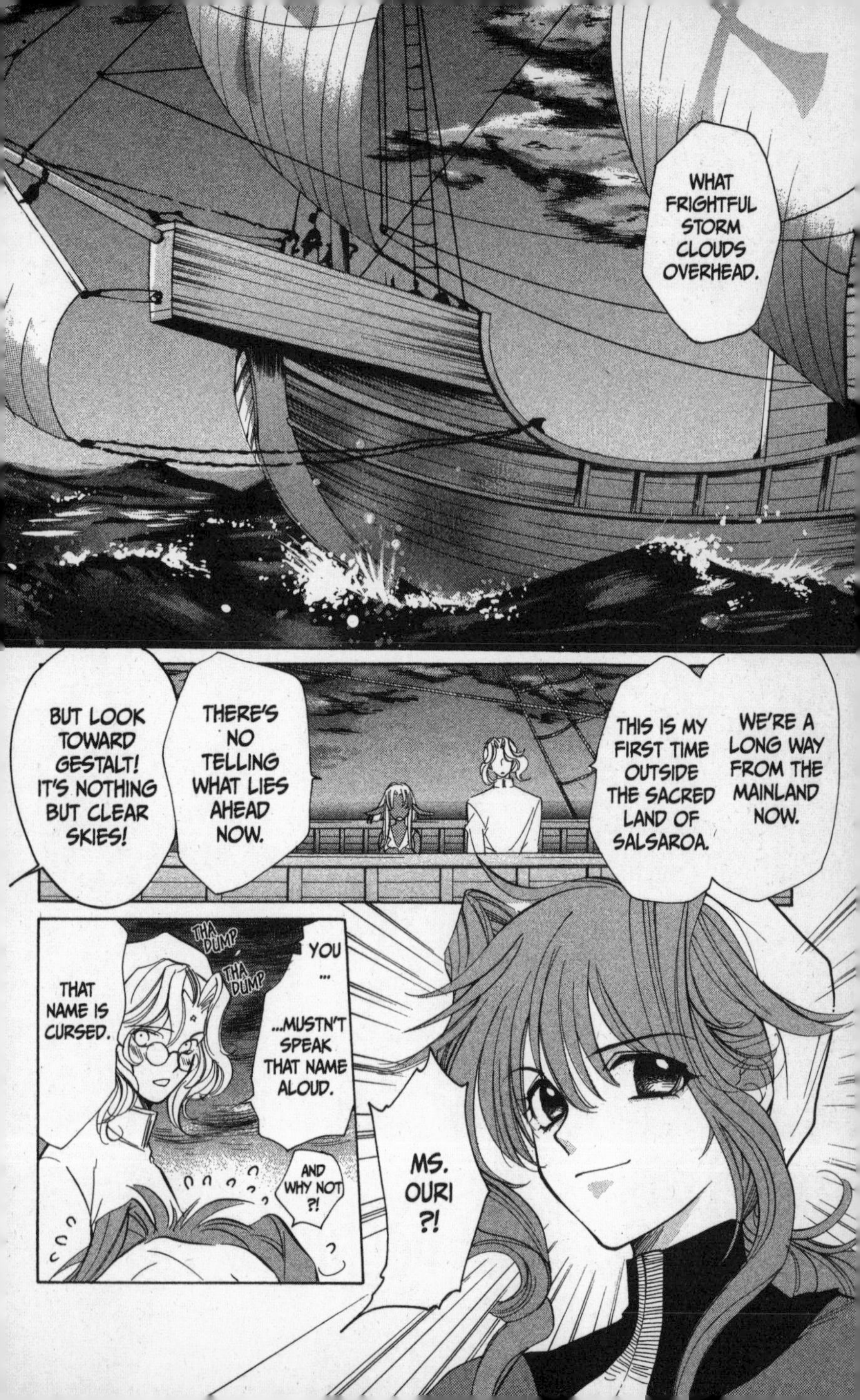
WHAT FRIGHTFUL STORM CLOUDS OVERHEAD.
WE'RE A LONG WAY FROM THE MAINLAND NOW.
THIS IS MY FIRST TIME OUTSIDE THE SACRED LAND OF SALSAROA.
THERE'S NO TELLING WHAT LIES AHEAD NOW.
BUT LOOK TOWARD GESTALT! IT'S NOTHING BUT CLEAR SKIES!
MS. OURI ?!
THA DUMP
THA DUMP
YOU ...
...MUSTN'T SPEAK THAT NAME ALOUD.
AND WHY NOT ?!
THAT NAME IS CURSED.

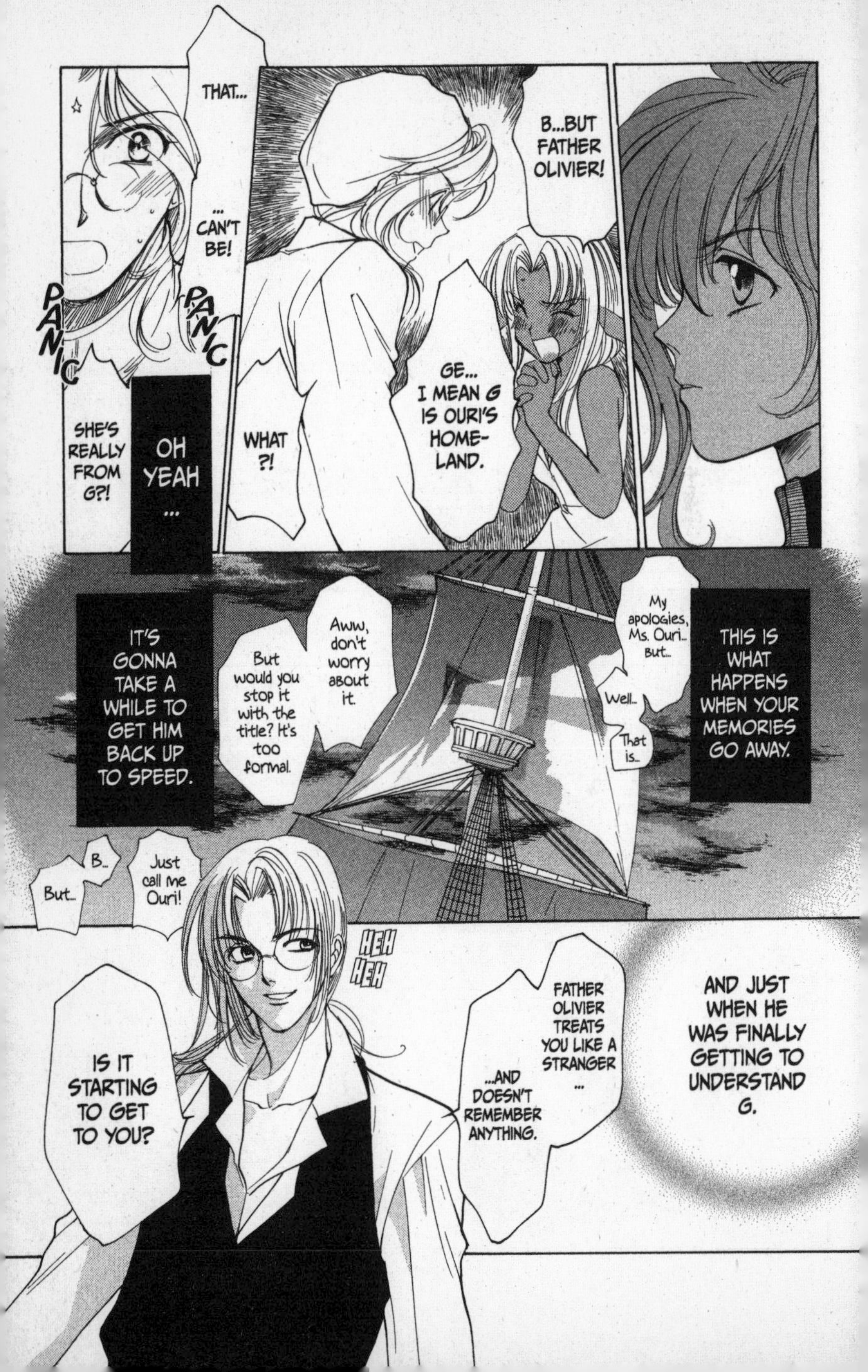
B...BUT FATHER OLIVIER!
GE... I MEAN G IS OURI'S HOME-LAND.
WHAT ?!
THAT...
... CAN'T BE!
PANIC PANIC
SHE'S REALLY FROM G?!
OH YEAH ...
THIS IS WHAT HAPPENS WHEN YOUR MEMORIES GO AWAY.
My apologies, Ms. Ouri.. but..
Well..
That is..
Aww, don't worry about it.
But would you stop it with the title? It's too formal.
IT'S GONNA TAKE A WHILE TO GET HIM BACK UP TO SPEED.
Just call me Ouri!
B..
But..
AND JUST WHEN HE WAS FINALLY GETTING TO UNDERSTAND G.
FATHER OLIVIER TREATS YOU LIKE A STRANGER ...
...AND DOESN'T REMEMBER ANYTHING.
HEH HEH
IS IT STARTING TO GET TO YOU?

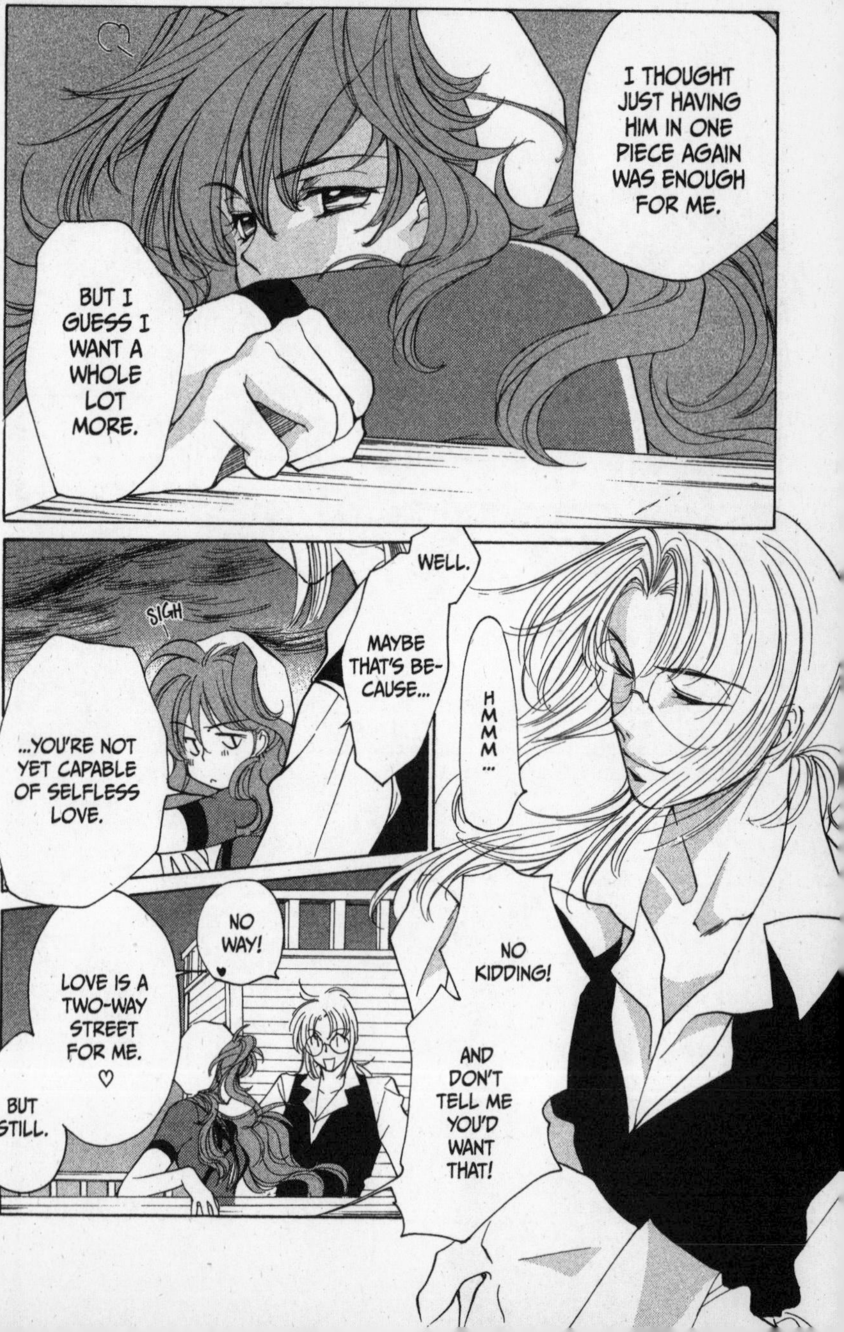
I THOUGHT JUST HAVING HIM IN ONE PIECE AGAIN WAS ENOUGH FOR ME.
BUT I GUESS I WANT A WHOLE LOT MORE.
HMMM...
SIGH
WELL.
MAYBE THAT'S BE-CAUSE...
...YOU'RE NOT YET CAPABLE OF SELFLESS LOVE.
NO WAY! ♥
LOVE IS A TWO-WAY STREET FOR ME. ♡
NO KIDDING!
AND DON'T TELL ME YOU'D WANT THAT!
BUT STILL.

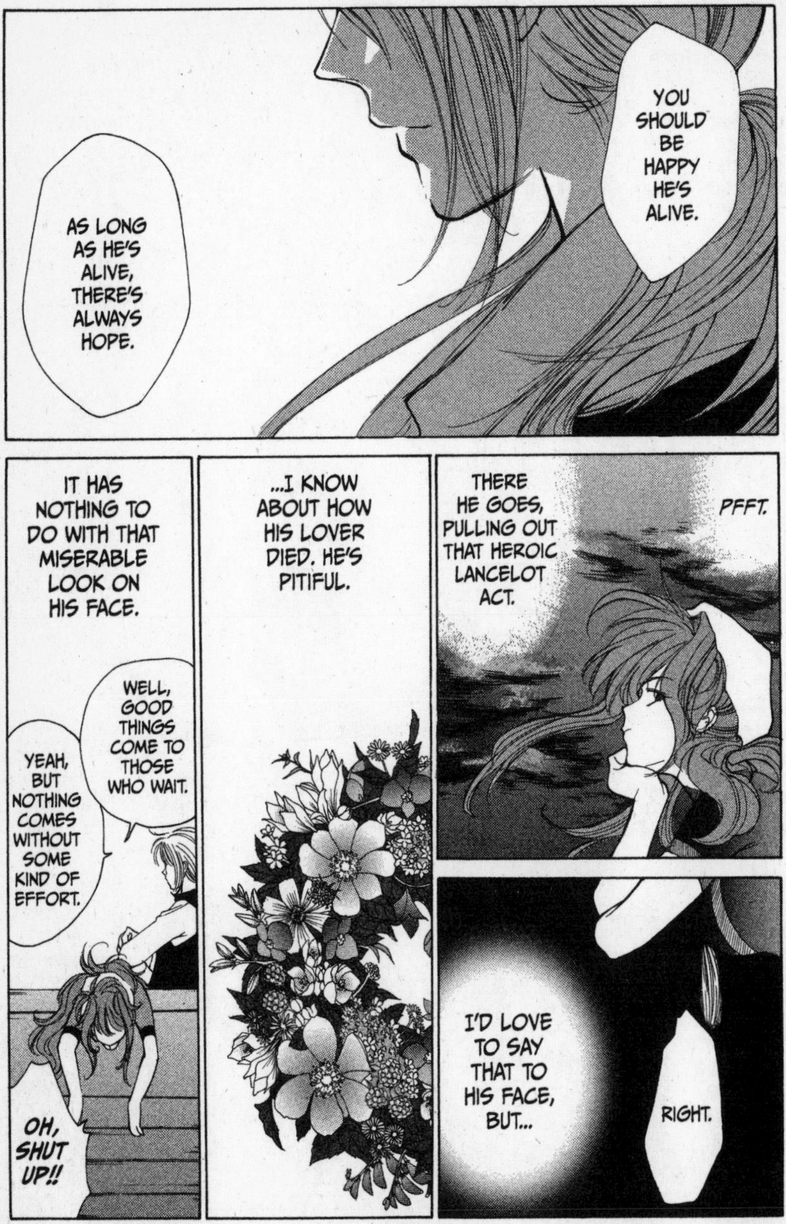
YOU SHOULD BE HAPPY HE'S ALIVE.
AS LONG AS HE'S ALIVE, THERE'S ALWAYS HOPE.
PFFT.
THERE HE GOES, PULLING OUT THAT HEROIC LANCELOT ACT.
RIGHT.
I'D LOVE TO SAY THAT TO HIS FACE, BUT...
...I KNOW ABOUT HOW HIS LOVER DIED. HE'S PITIFUL.
IT HAS NOTHING TO DO WITH THAT MISERABLE LOOK ON HIS FACE.
WELL, GOOD THINGS COME TO THOSE WHO WAIT.
YEAH, BUT NOTHING COMES WITHOUT SOME KIND OF EFFORT.
OH, SHUT UP!!

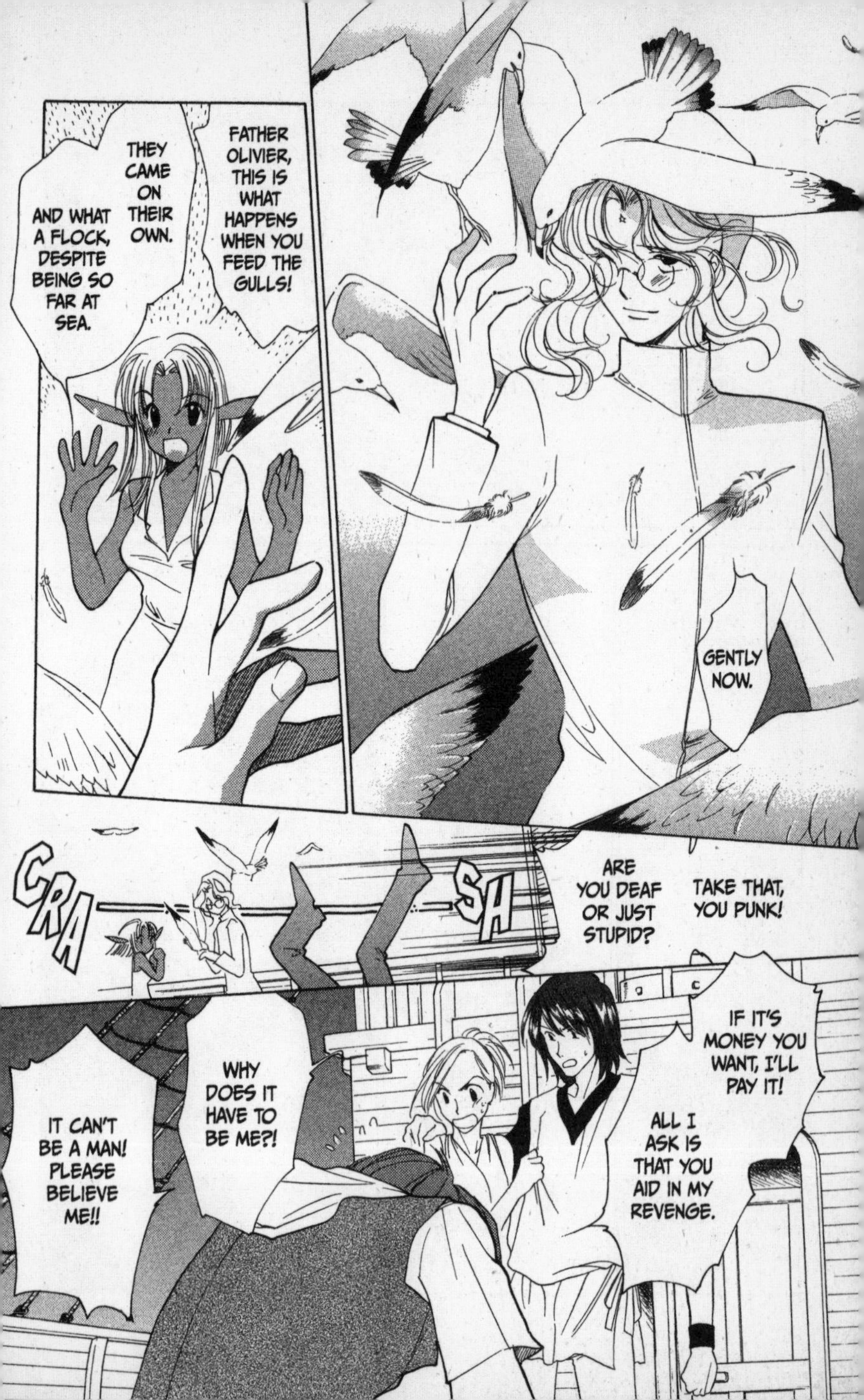
GENTLY NOW.
FATHER OLIVIER, THIS IS WHAT HAPPENS WHEN YOU FEED THE GULLS!
THEY CAME ON THEIR OWN.
AND WHAT A FLOCK, DESPITE BEING SO FAR AT SEA.
TAKE THAT, YOU PUNK!
ARE YOU DEAF OR JUST STUPID?
CRASH
IF IT'S MONEY YOU WANT, I'LL PAY IT!
ALL I ASK IS THAT YOU AID IN MY REVENGE.
WHY DOES IT HAVE TO BE ME?!
IT CAN'T BE A MAN! PLEASE BELIEVE ME!!

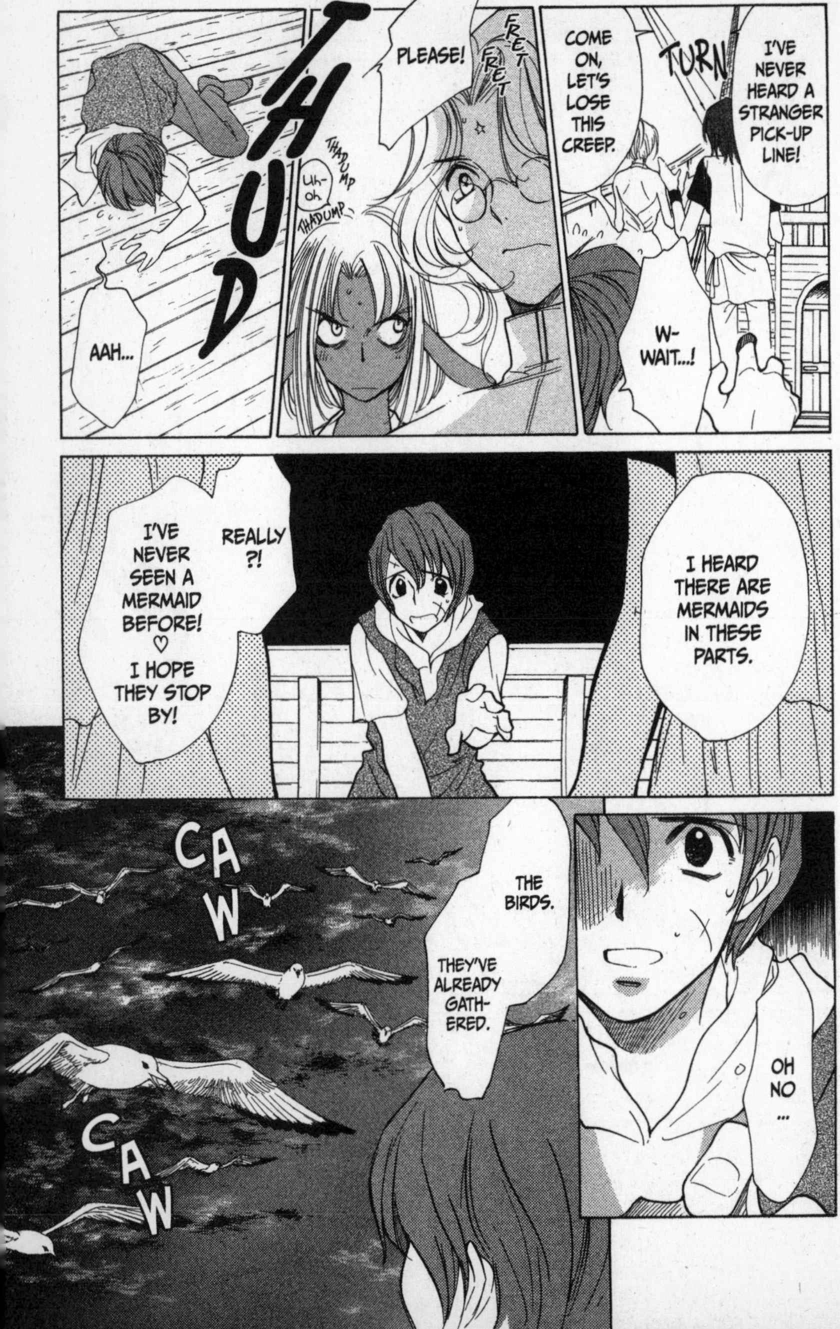
I'VE NEVER HEARD A STRANGER PICK-UP LINE!
TURN
COME ON, LET'S LOSE THIS CREEP.
W-WAIT...!
PLEASE!
FRET FRET
THADUMP THADUMP
Uh-oh
THUD
AAH...
I HEARD THERE ARE MERMAIDS IN THESE PARTS.
REALLY?!
I'VE NEVER SEEN A MERMAID BEFORE! ♡
I HOPE THEY STOP BY!
OH NO ...
THE BIRDS.
THEY'VE ALREADY GATH-ERED.
CAW
CAW

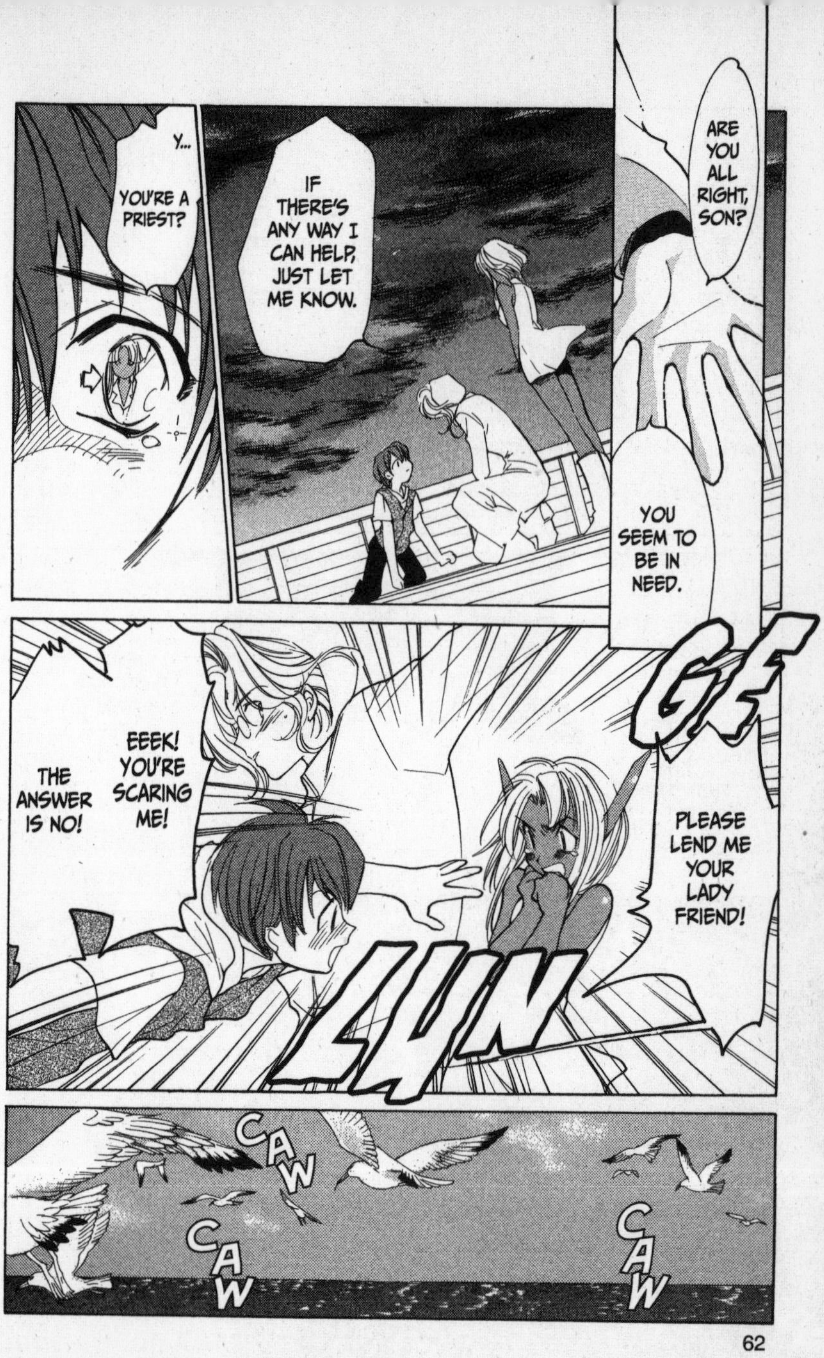
ARE YOU ALL RIGHT, SON?
YOU SEEM TO BE IN NEED.
IF THERE'S ANY WAY I CAN HELP, JUST LET ME KNOW.
Y...
YOU'RE A PRIEST?
PLEASE LEND ME YOUR LADY FRIEND!
EEEK! YOU'RE SCARING ME!
THE ANSWER IS NO!
CAW
CAW
CAW
CAW

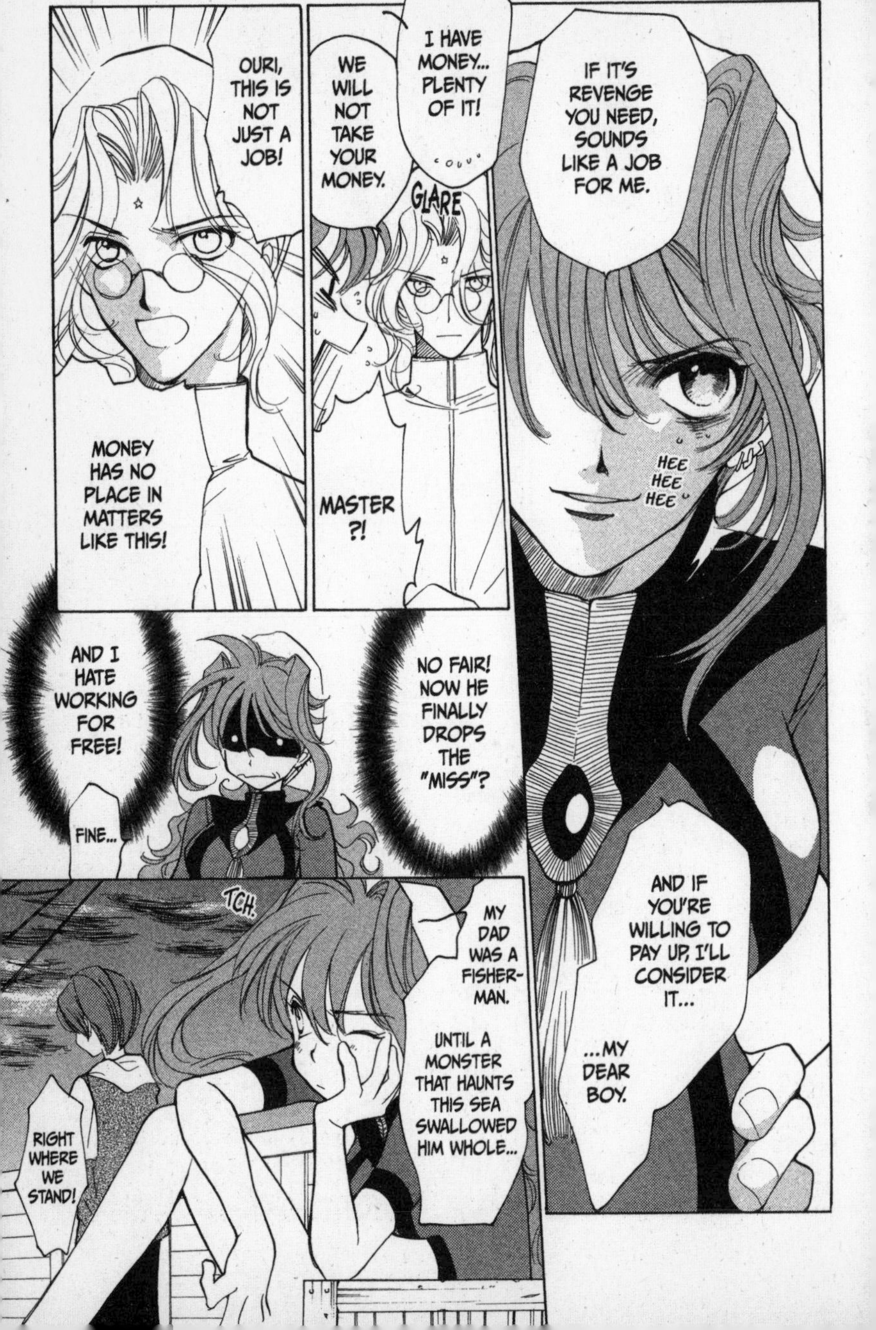
IF IT'S REVENGE YOU NEED, SOUNDS LIKE A JOB FOR ME.
HEE HEE HEE
AND IF YOU'RE WILLING TO PAY UP, I'LL CONSIDER IT...
...MY DEAR BOY.
I HAVE MONEY... PLENTY OF IT!
WE WILL NOT TAKE YOUR MONEY.
GLARE
MASTER ?!
OURI, THIS IS NOT JUST A JOB!
MONEY HAS NO PLACE IN MATTERS LIKE THIS!
NO FAIR! NOW HE FINALLY DROPS THE "MISS"?
AND I HATE WORKING FOR FREE!
FINE...
MY DAD WAS A FISHER-MAN.
UNTIL A MONSTER THAT HAUNTS THIS SEA SWALLOWED HIM WHOLE...
TCH.
RIGHT WHERE WE STAND!

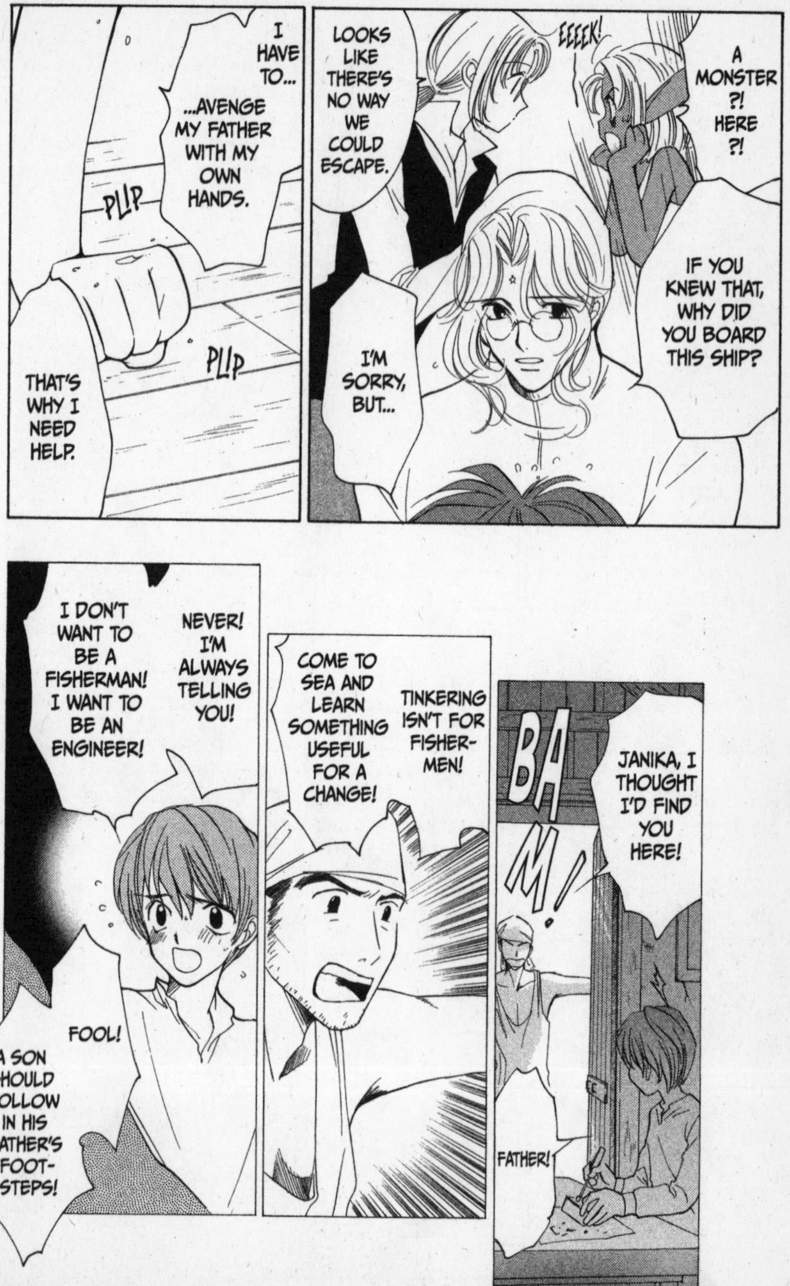
A MONSTER?! HERE?!
EEEEK!
LOOKS LIKE THERE'S NO WAY WE COULD ESCAPE.
IF YOU KNEW THAT, WHY DID YOU BOARD THIS SHIP?
I'M SORRY, BUT...
I HAVE TO...
...AVENGE MY FATHER WITH MY OWN HANDS.
PLIP
PLIP
THAT'S WHY I NEED HELP.
JANIKA, I THOUGHT I'D FIND YOU HERE!
BAM!
FATHER!
TINKERING ISN'T FOR FISHERMEN!
COME TO SEA AND LEARN SOMETHING USEFUL FOR A CHANGE!
NEVER! I'M ALWAYS TELLING YOU!
I DON'T WANT TO BE A FISHERMAN! I WANT TO BE AN ENGINEER!
FOOL!
A SON SHOULD FOLLOW IN HIS FATHER'S FOOTSTEPS!

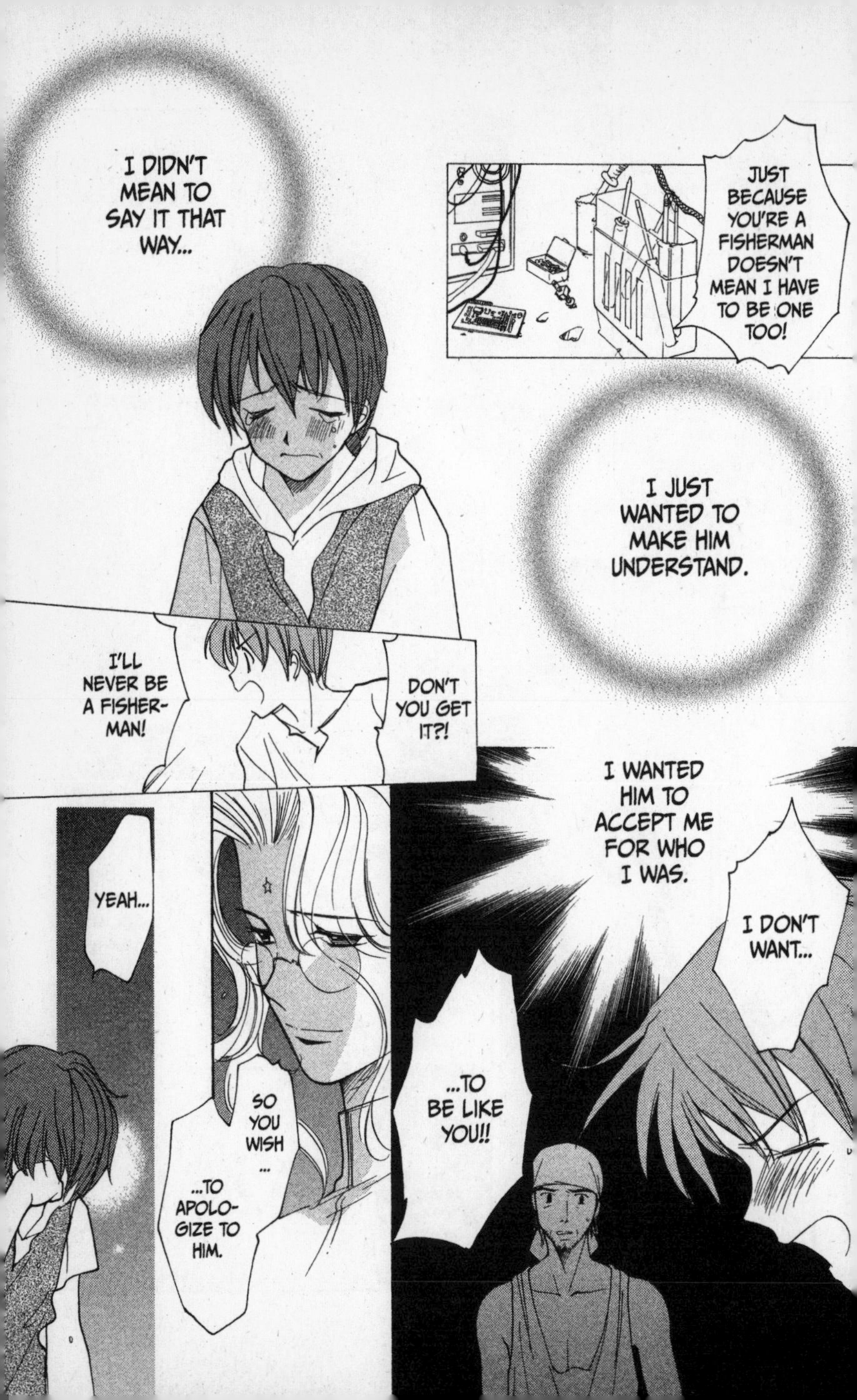
JUST BECAUSE YOU'RE A FISHERMAN DOESN'T MEAN I HAVE TO BE ONE TOO!
I DIDN'T MEAN TO SAY IT THAT WAY...
I JUST WANTED TO MAKE HIM UNDERSTAND.
DON'T YOU GET IT?!
I'LL NEVER BE A FISHER-MAN!
I WANTED HIM TO ACCEPT ME FOR WHO I WAS.
I DON'T WANT...
...TO BE LIKE YOU!!
SO YOU WISH...
...TO APOLO-GIZE TO HIM.
YEAH...

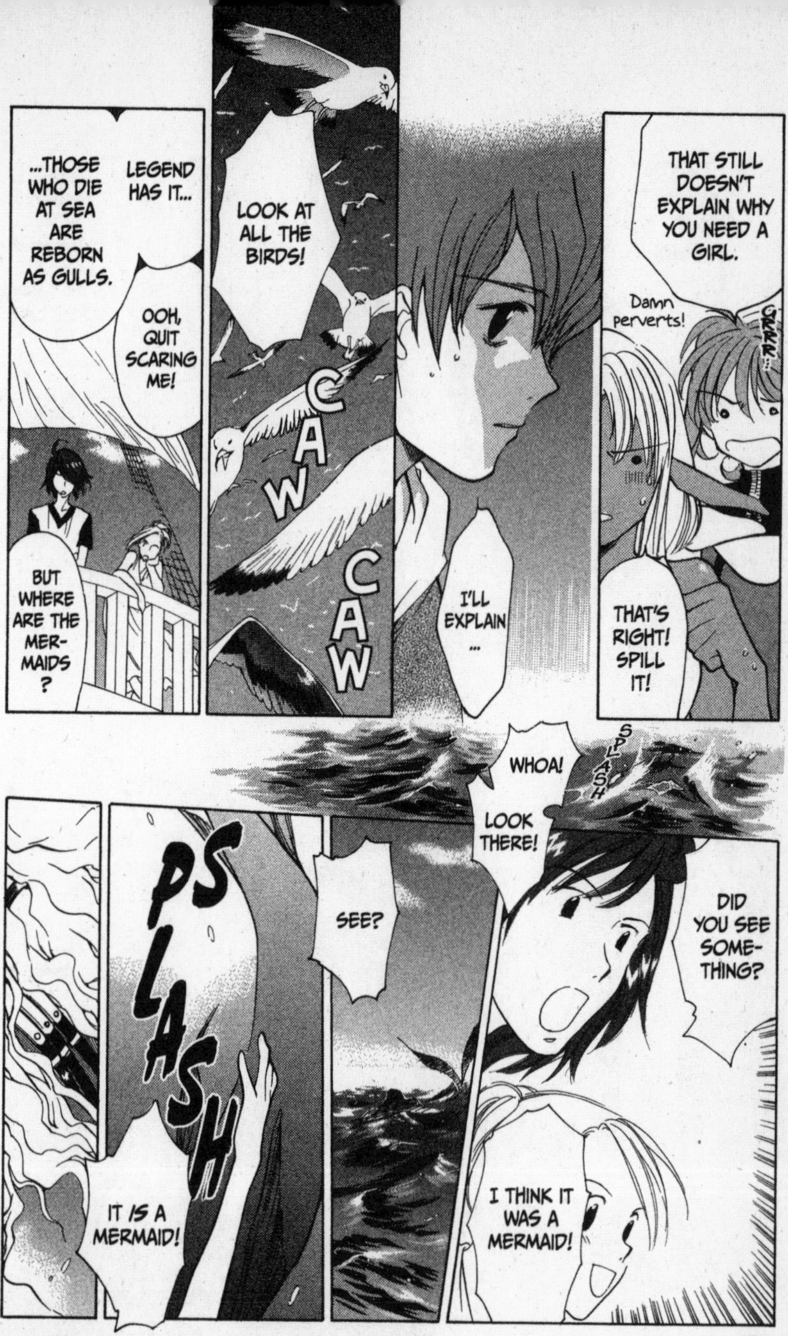
THAT STILL DOESN'T EXPLAIN WHY YOU NEED A GIRL.
Damn perverts!
GRRRR!!
THAT'S RIGHT! SPILL IT!
I'LL EXPLAIN...
LOOK AT ALL THE BIRDS!
CAW CAW
CAW CAW
LEGEND HAS IT...
...THOSE WHO DIE AT SEA ARE REBORN AS GULLS.
OOH, QUIT SCARING ME!
BUT WHERE ARE THE MERMAIDS?
SPLASH
WHOA!
LOOK THERE!
DID YOU SEE SOMETHING?
I THINK IT WAS A MERMAID!
SEE?
PSPLASH
IT *IS* A MERMAID!

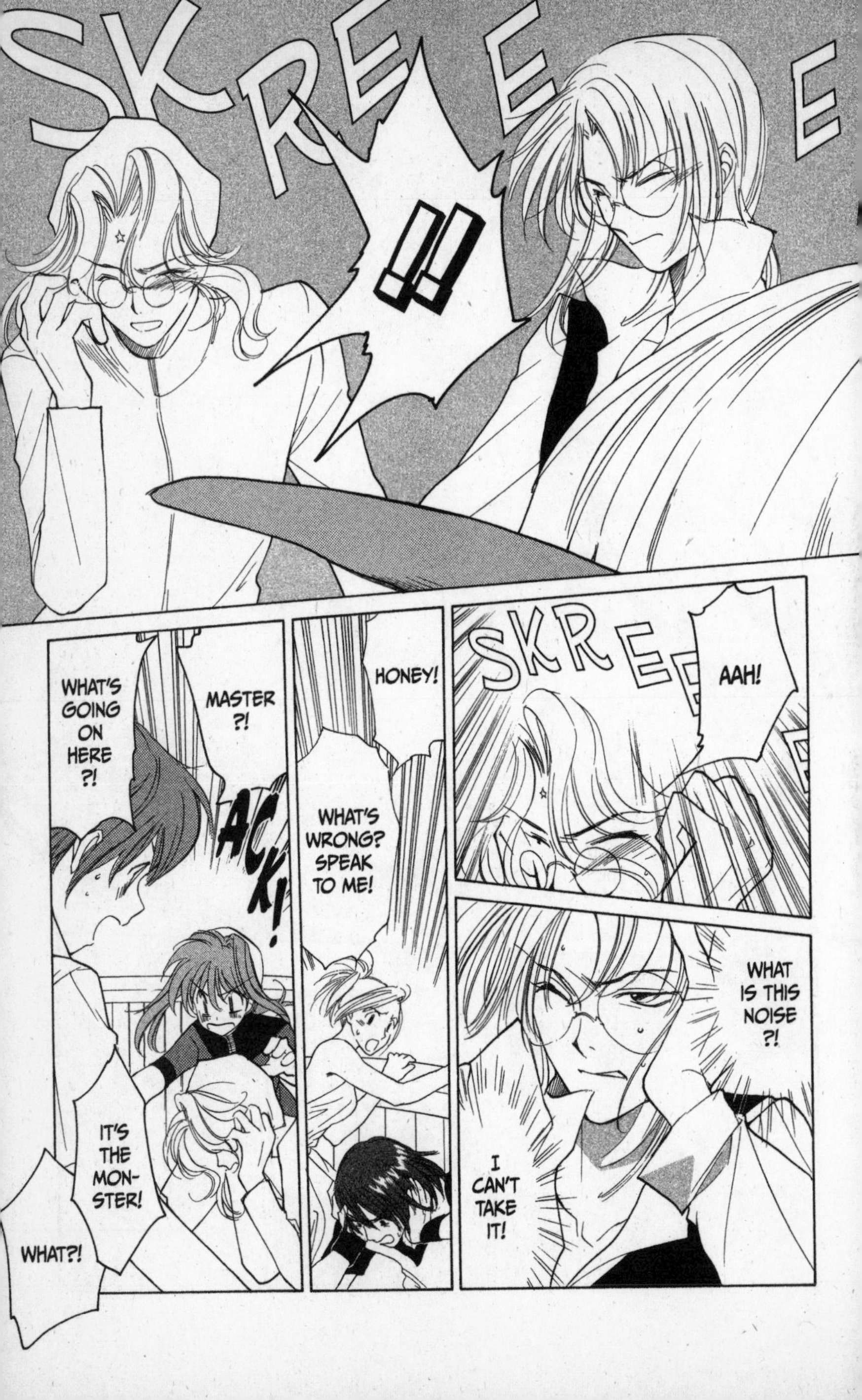
SKREEEE
!!
SKREEEE
AAH!
WHAT IS THIS NOISE?!
I CAN'T TAKE IT!
HONEY!
WHAT'S WRONG? SPEAK TO ME!
MASTER?!
WHAT'S GOING ON HERE?!
ACK!
IT'S THE MON-STER!
WHAT?!

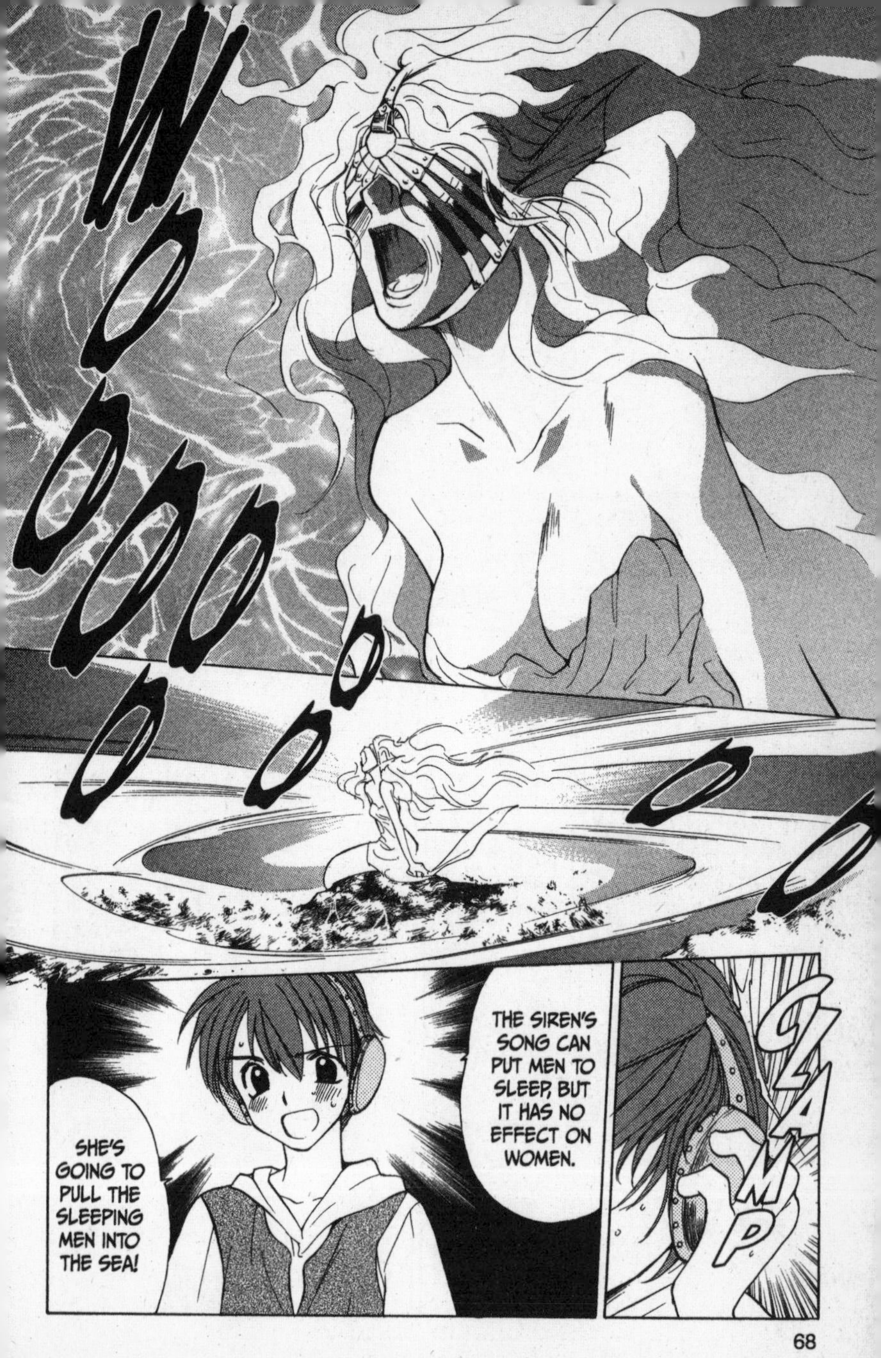
WOOOOOOOOOOOOOO
CLAMP
THE SIREN'S SONG CAN PUT MEN TO SLEEP, BUT IT HAS NO EFFECT ON WOMEN.
SHE'S GOING TO PULL THE SLEEPING MEN INTO THE SEA!

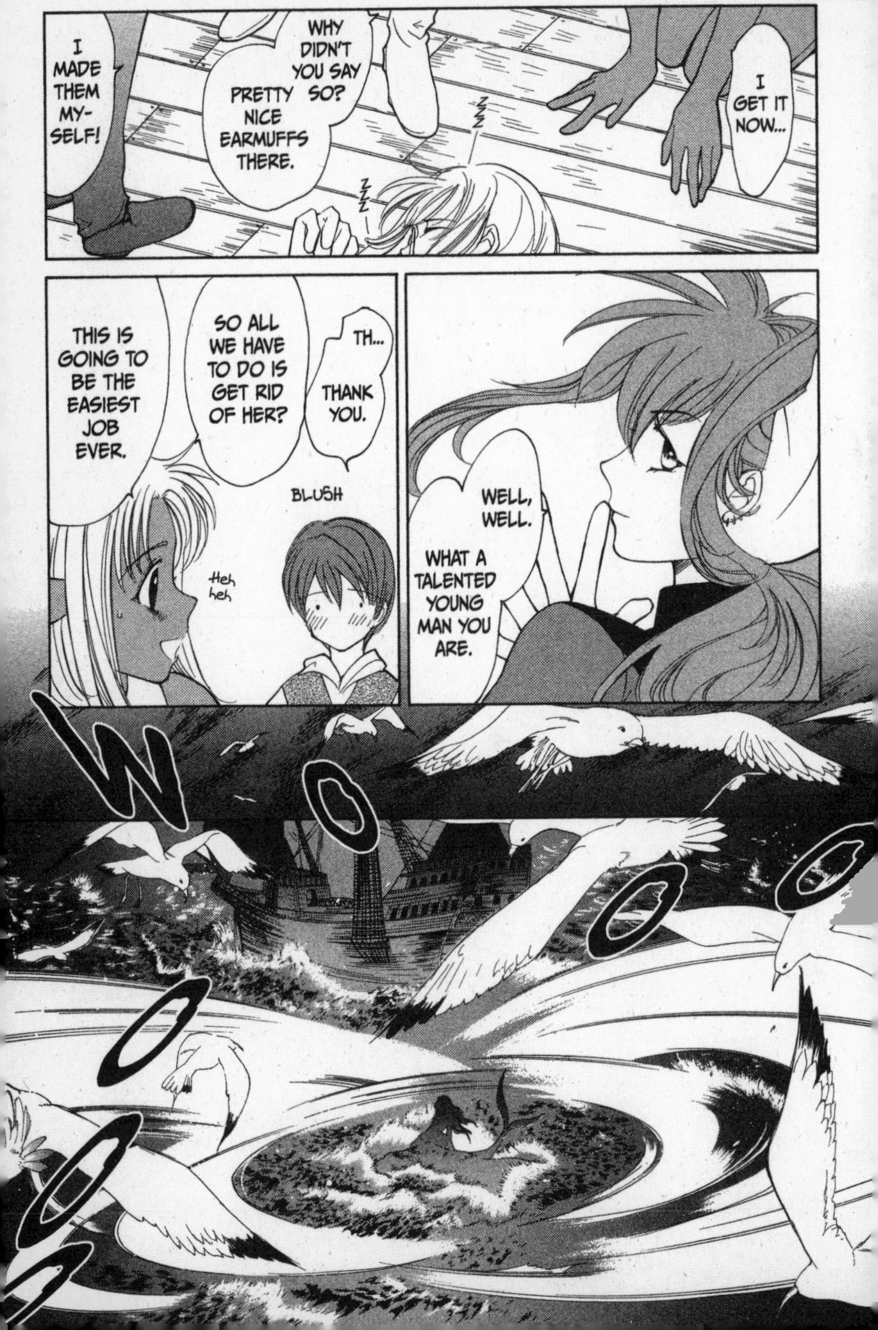
I GET IT NOW...
WHY DIDN'T YOU SAY SO?
PRETTY NICE EARMUFFS THERE.
Z Z Z
Z Z Z
I MADE THEM MY-SELF!
WELL, WELL.
WHAT A TALENTED YOUNG MAN YOU ARE.
TH...
THANK YOU.
SO ALL WE HAVE TO DO IS GET RID OF HER?
THIS IS GOING TO BE THE EASIEST JOB EVER.
BLUSH
Heh heh
WOOOOOOO

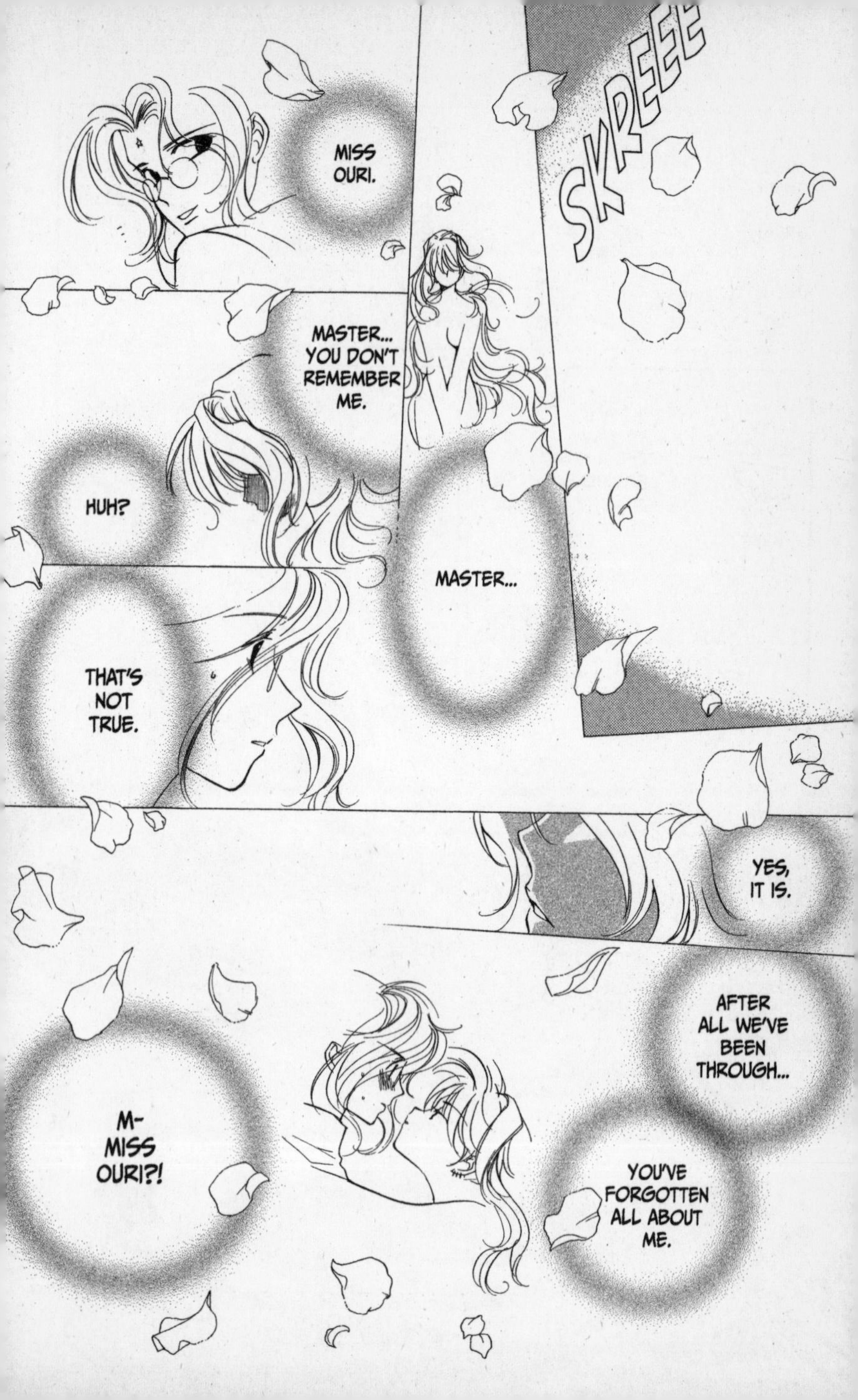
SKREEE
MASTER...
MISS OURI.
MASTER... YOU DON'T REMEMBER ME.
HUH?
THAT'S NOT TRUE.
YES, IT IS.
AFTER ALL WE'VE BEEN THROUGH...
YOU'VE FORGOTTEN ALL ABOUT ME.
M-MISS OURI?!

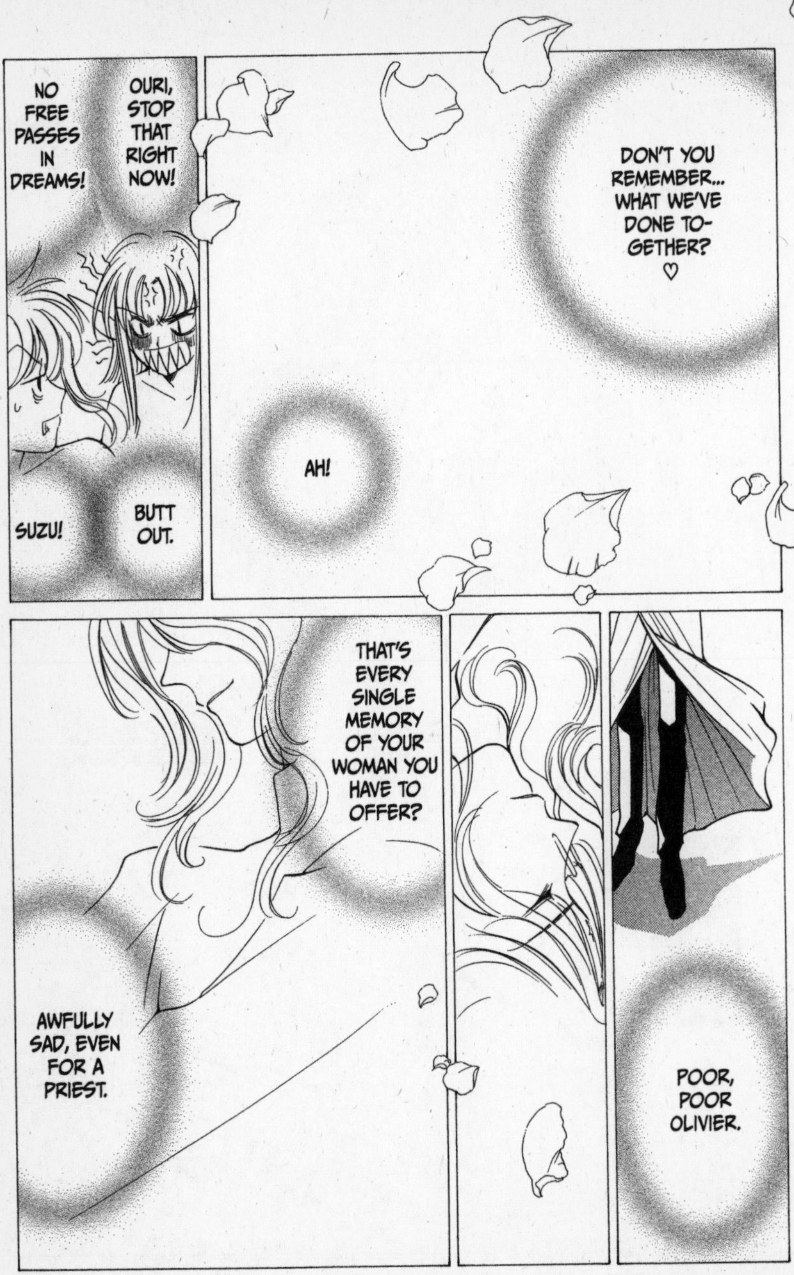
DON'T YOU REMEMBER... WHAT WE'VE DONE TO-GETHER? ♡
AH!
OURI, STOP THAT RIGHT NOW!
NO FREE PASSES IN DREAMS!
BUTT OUT.
SUZU!
POOR, POOR OLIVIER.
THAT'S EVERY SINGLE MEMORY OF YOUR WOMAN YOU HAVE TO OFFER?
AWFULLY SAD, EVEN FOR A PRIEST.

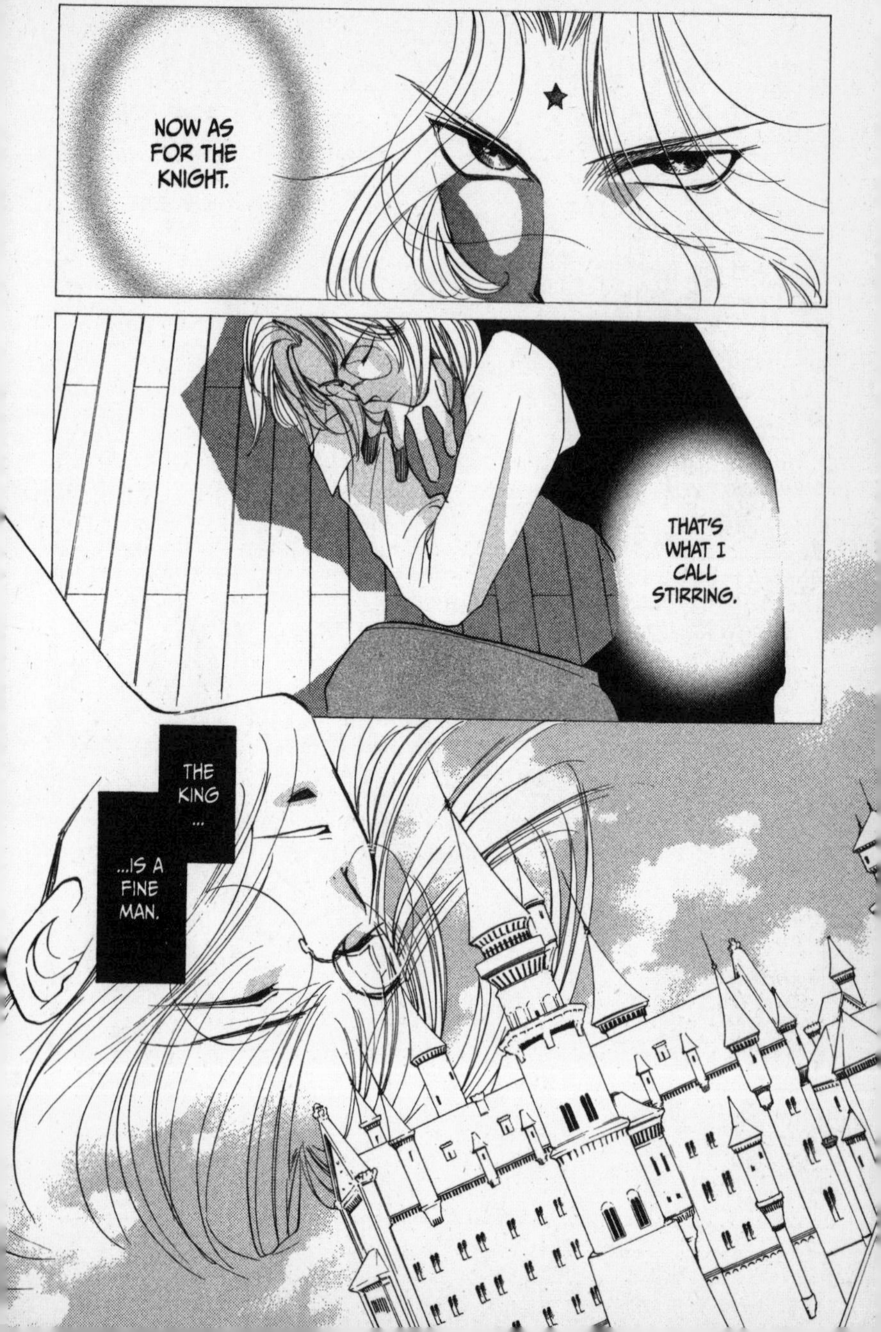
NOW AS FOR THE KNIGHT.
THAT'S WHAT I CALL STIRRING.
THE KING ...
...IS A FINE MAN.

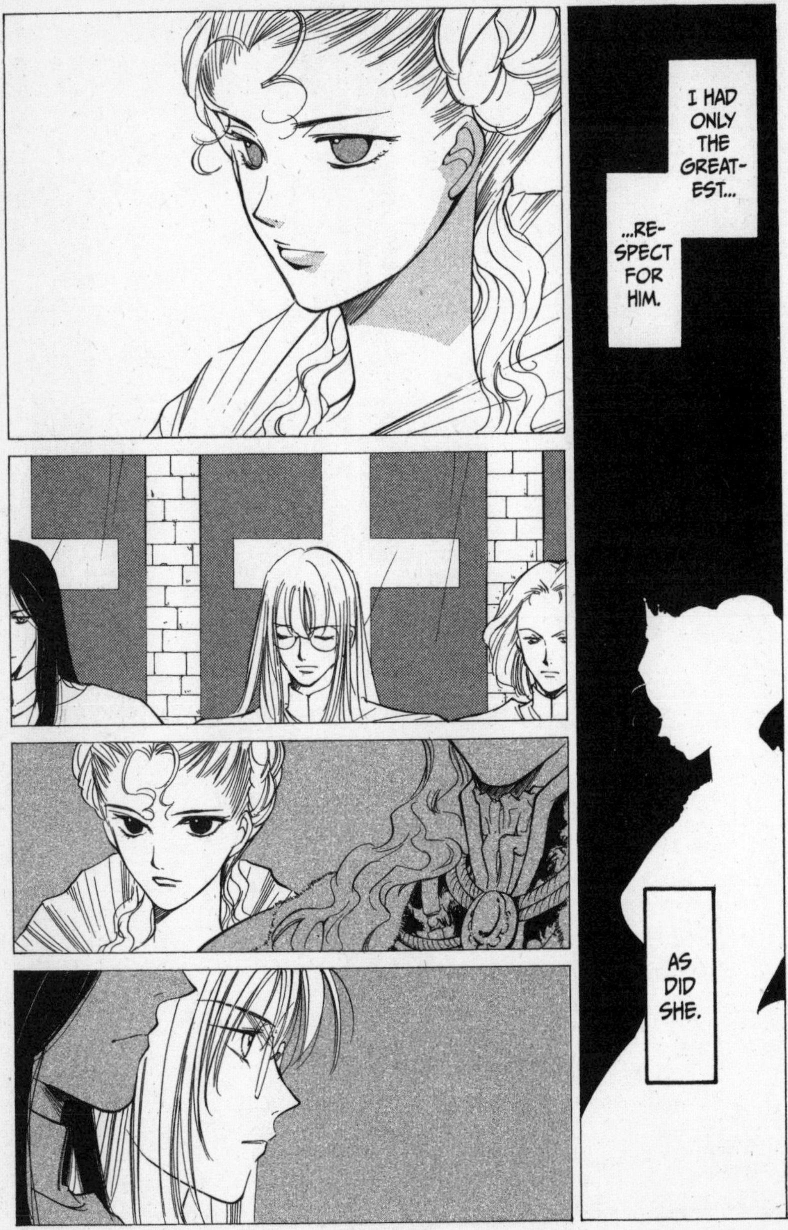
I HAD ONLY THE GREAT-EST...
...RE-SPECT FOR HIM.
AS DID SHE.

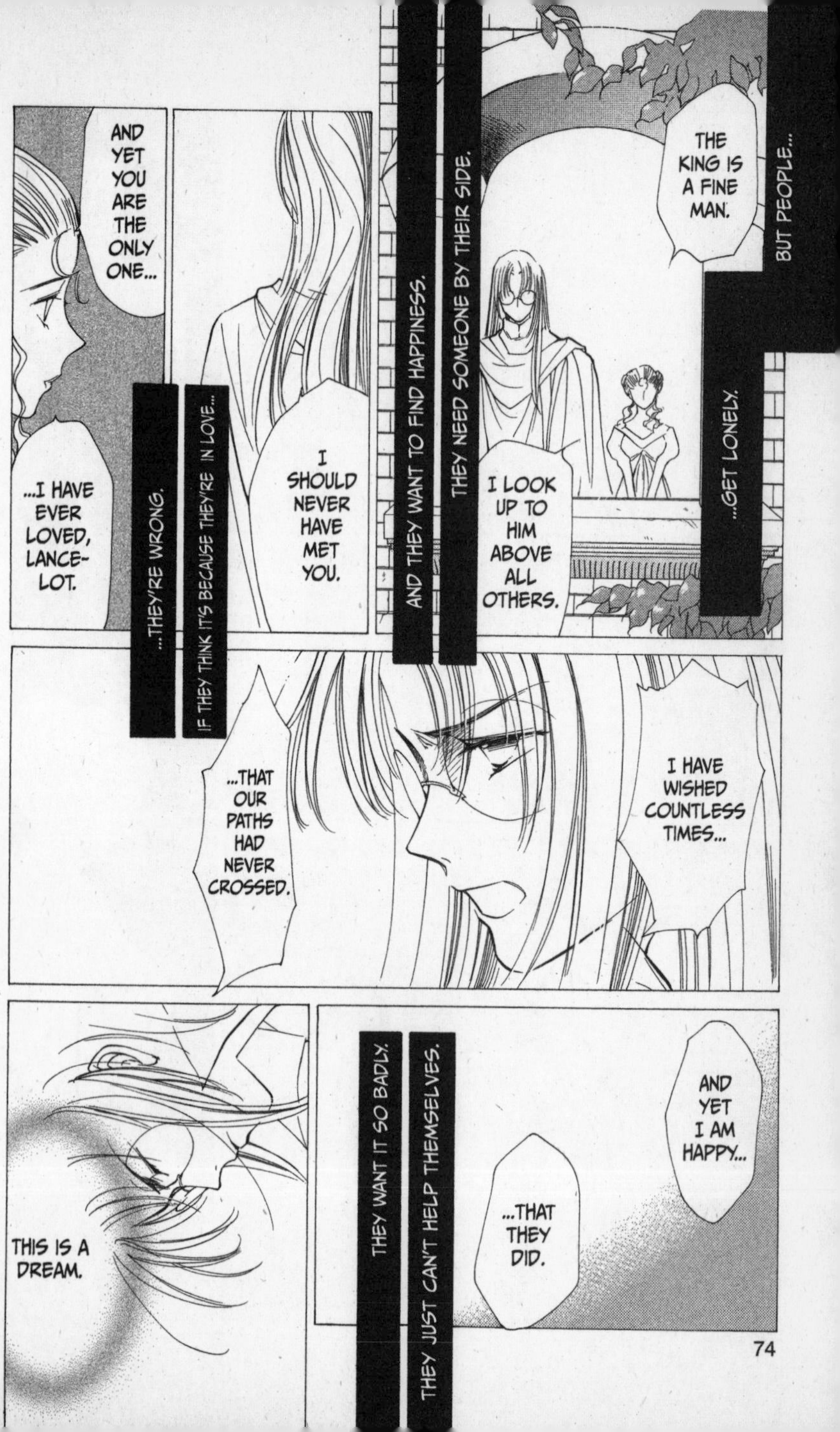
THE KING IS A FINE MAN.
BUT PEOPLE...
...GET LONELY.
I LOOK UP TO HIM ABOVE ALL OTHERS.
THEY NEED SOMEONE BY THEIR SIDE.
AND THEY WANT TO FIND HAPPINESS.
I SHOULD NEVER HAVE MET YOU.
IF THEY THINK IT'S BECAUSE THEY'RE IN LOVE...
...THEY'RE WRONG.
AND YET YOU ARE THE ONLY ONE...
...I HAVE EVER LOVED, LANCELOT.
I HAVE WISHED COUNTLESS TIMES...
...THAT OUR PATHS HAD NEVER CROSSED.
AND YET I AM HAPPY...
...THAT THEY DID.
THEY JUST CAN'T HELP THEMSELVES.
THEY WANT IT SO BADLY.
THIS IS A DREAM.

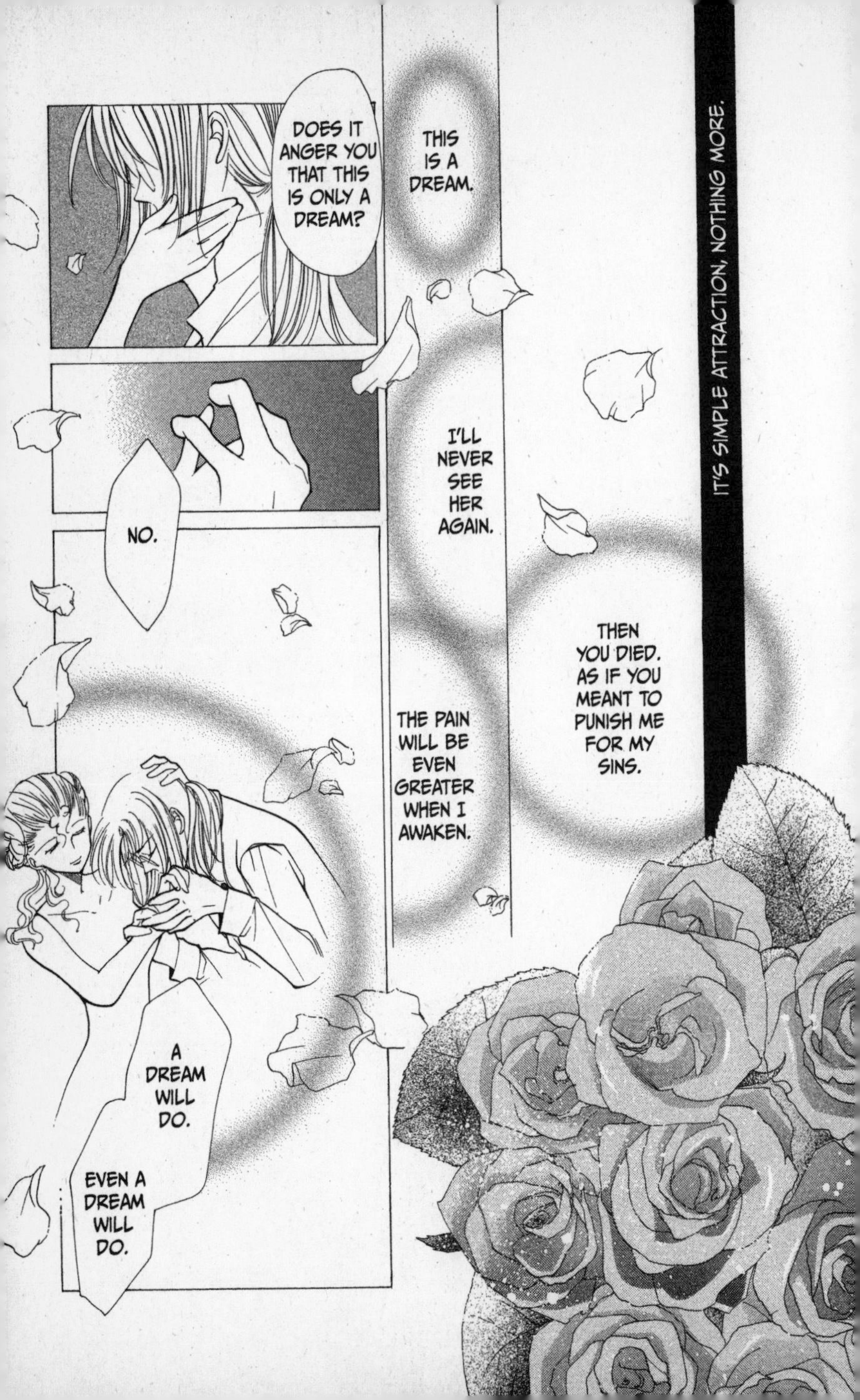
IT'S SIMPLE ATTRACTION, NOTHING MORE.
THEN YOU DIED. AS IF YOU MEANT TO PUNISH ME FOR MY SINS.
THIS IS A DREAM.
I'LL NEVER SEE HER AGAIN.
THE PAIN WILL BE EVEN GREATER WHEN I AWAKEN.
DOES IT ANGER YOU THAT THIS IS ONLY A DREAM?
NO.
A DREAM WILL DO.
EVEN A DREAM WILL DO.

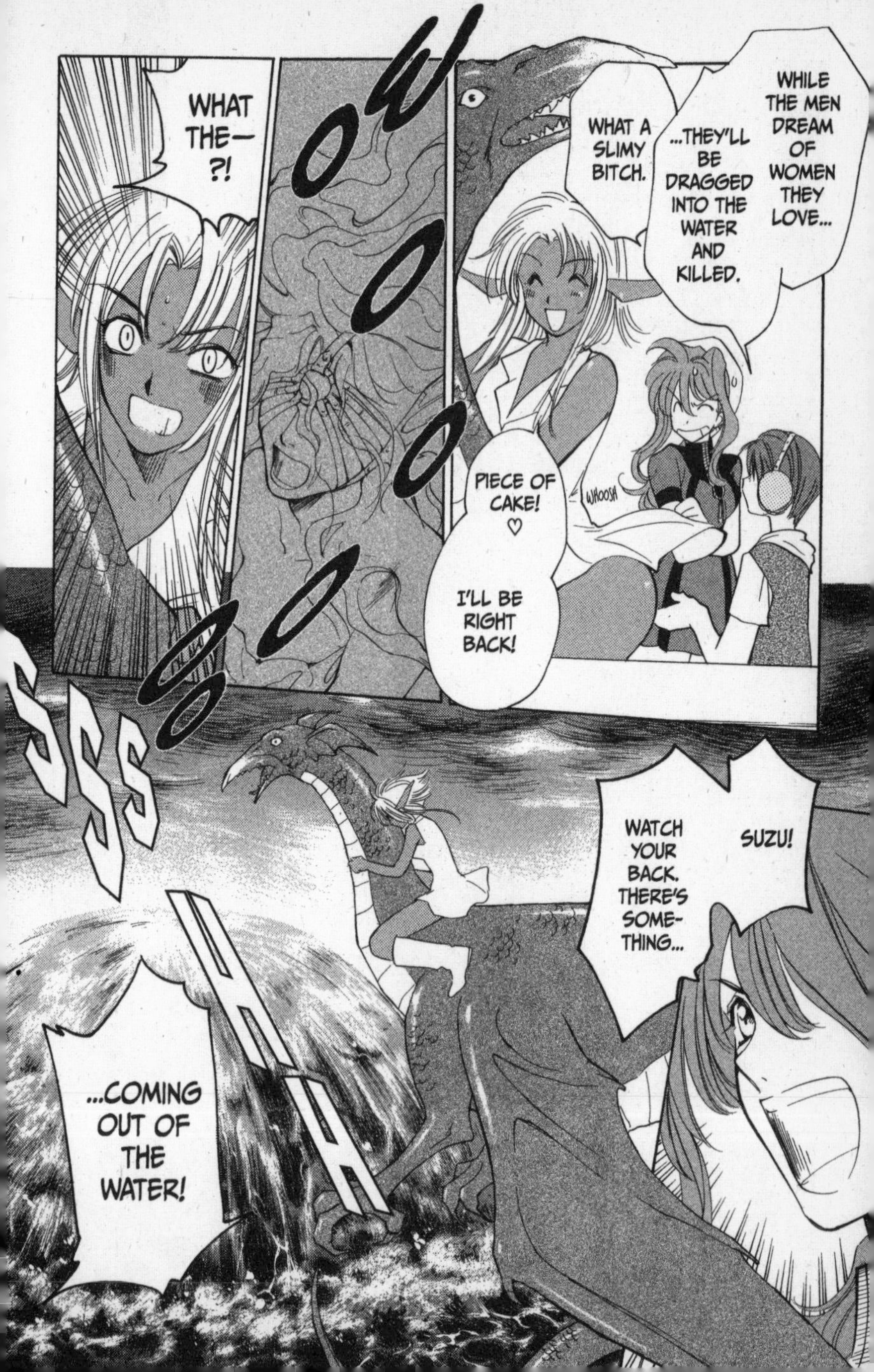
WHILE THE MEN DREAM OF WOMEN THEY LOVE...
...THEY'LL BE DRAGGED INTO THE WATER AND KILLED.
WHAT A SLIMY BITCH.
PIECE OF CAKE! ♡
WHOOSH
I'LL BE RIGHT BACK!
WHAT THE— ?!
SUZU!
WATCH YOUR BACK. THERE'S SOME-THING...
...COMING OUT OF THE WATER!
SSS

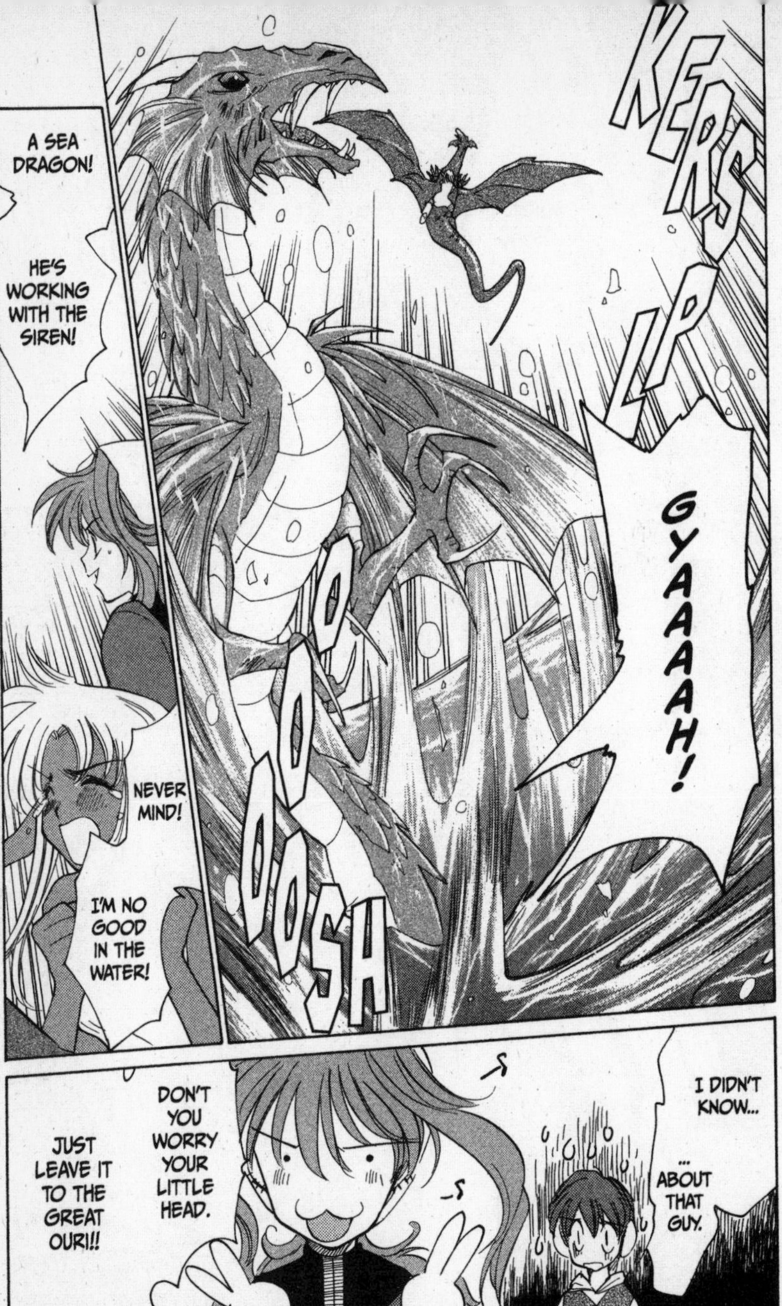
KERSPLURP
GYAAAAAH!
OOOOSH
A SEA DRAGON!
HE'S WORKING WITH THE SIREN!
NEVER MIND!
I'M NO GOOD IN THE WATER!
High-tailed it right back
I DIDN'T KNOW...
... ABOUT THAT GUY.
DON'T YOU WORRY YOUR LITTLE HEAD.
JUST LEAVE IT TO THE GREAT OURI!!

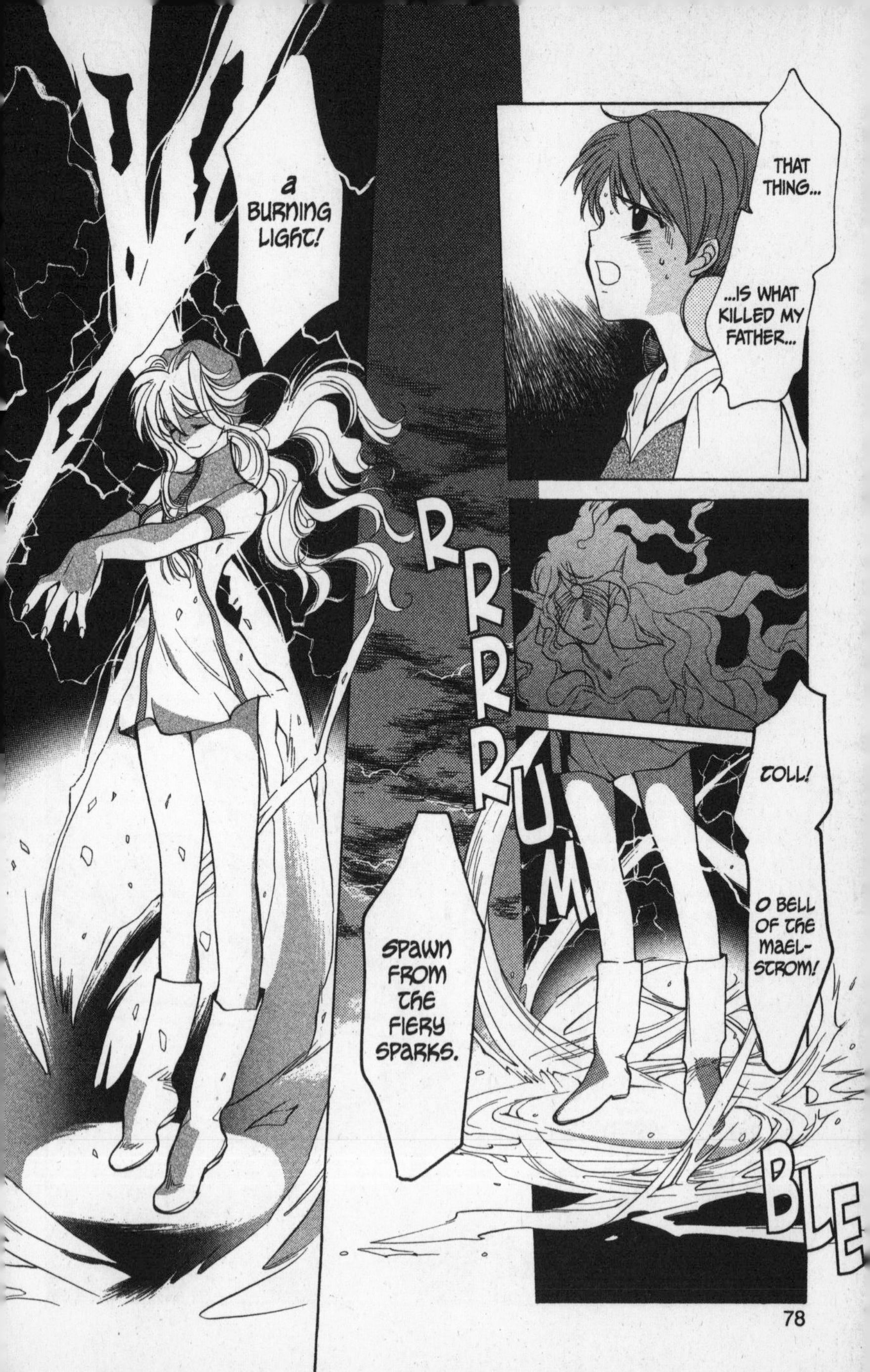
THAT THING...
...IS WHAT KILLED MY FATHER...
RRRRUMBLE
TOLL!
O BELL OF THE MAEL-STROM!
a BURNING LIGHT!
SPAWN FROM THE FIERY SPARKS.

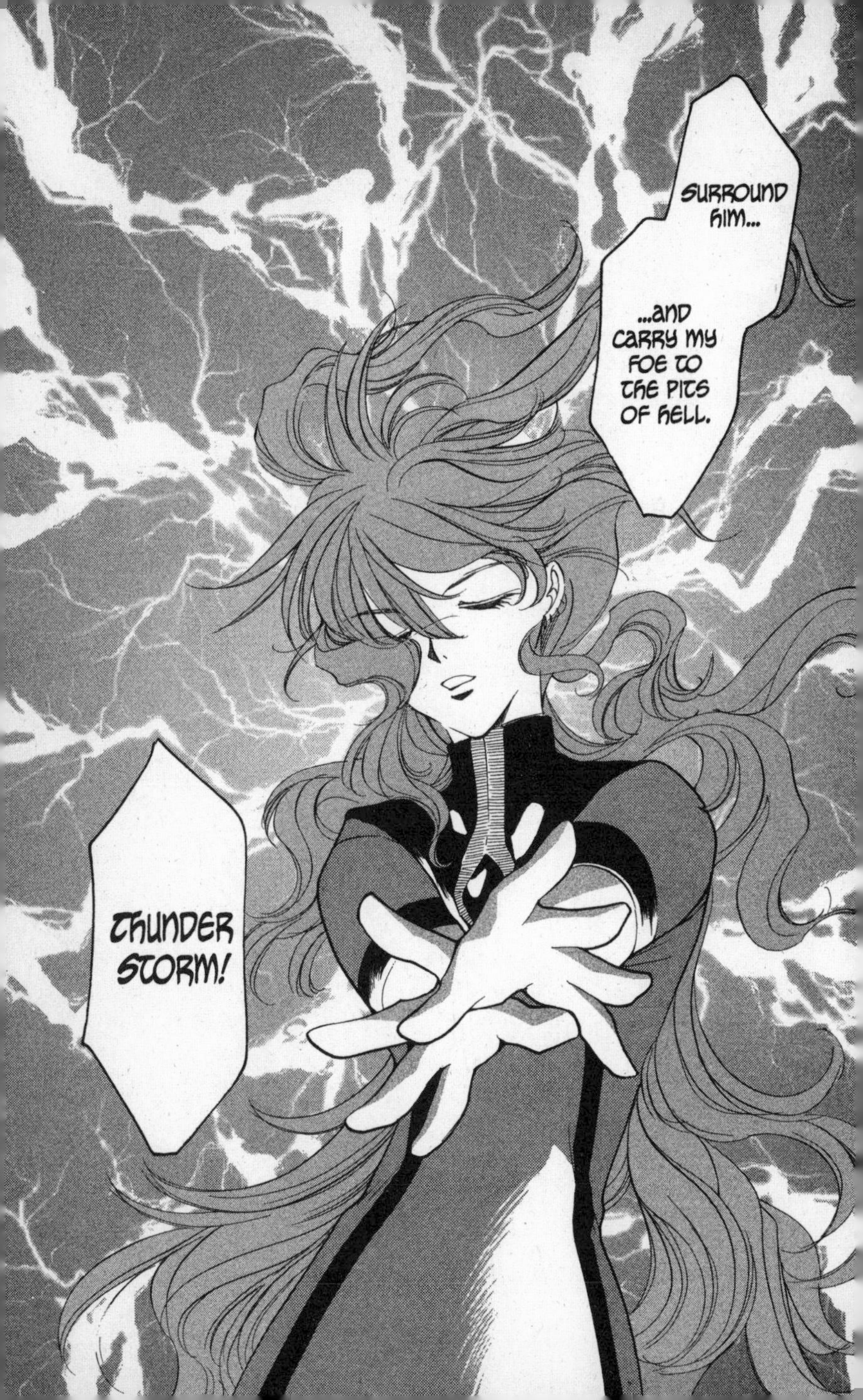
SURROUND HIM...
...AND CARRY MY FOE TO THE PITS OF HELL.
THUNDER STORM!

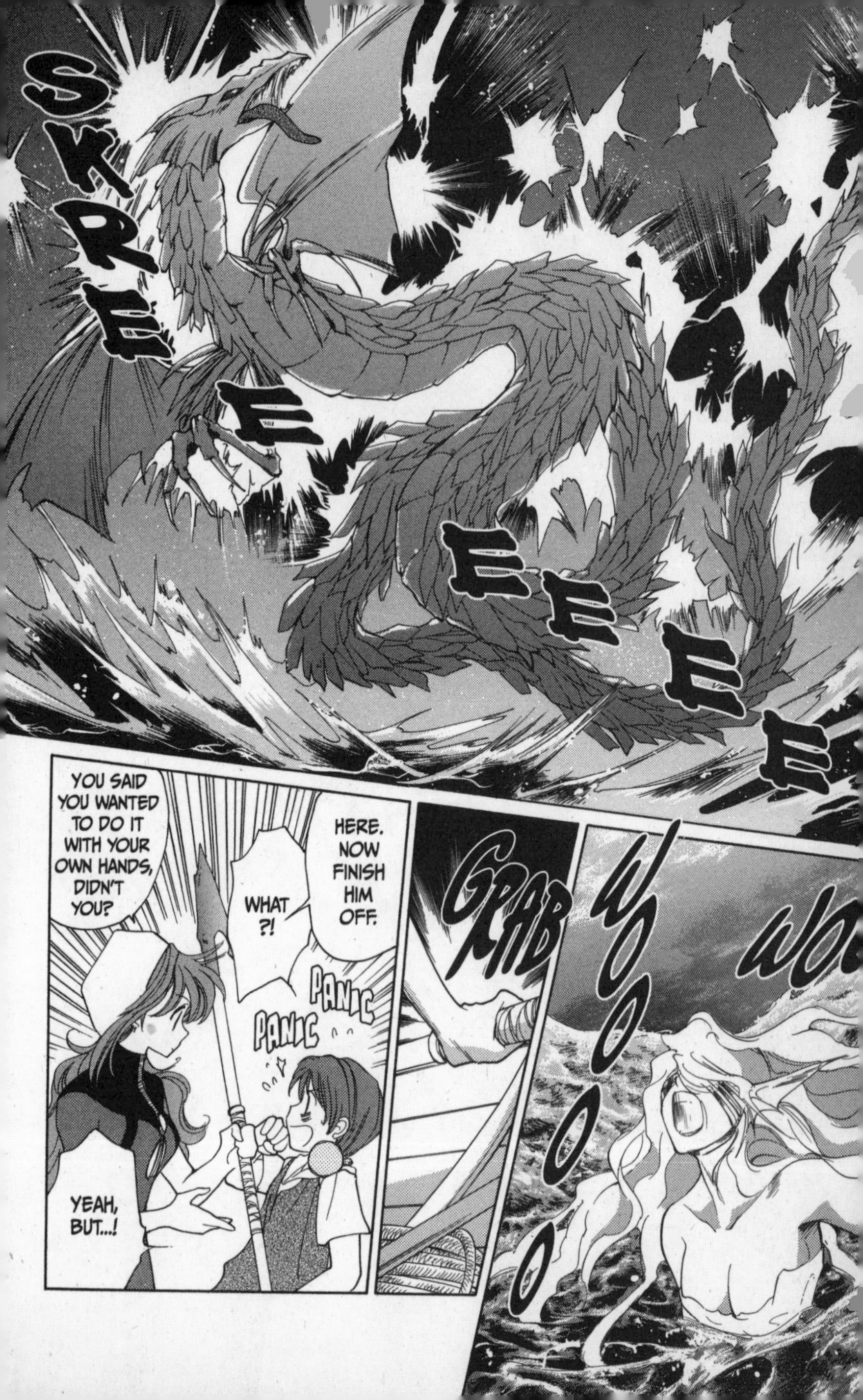

SKREEEEEEEE
WOO
WOOOOOO
GRAB
HERE. NOW FINISH HIM OFF.
WHAT?!
YOU SAID YOU WANTED TO DO IT WITH YOUR OWN HANDS, DIDN'T YOU?
PANIC
PANIC
YEAH, BUT...!

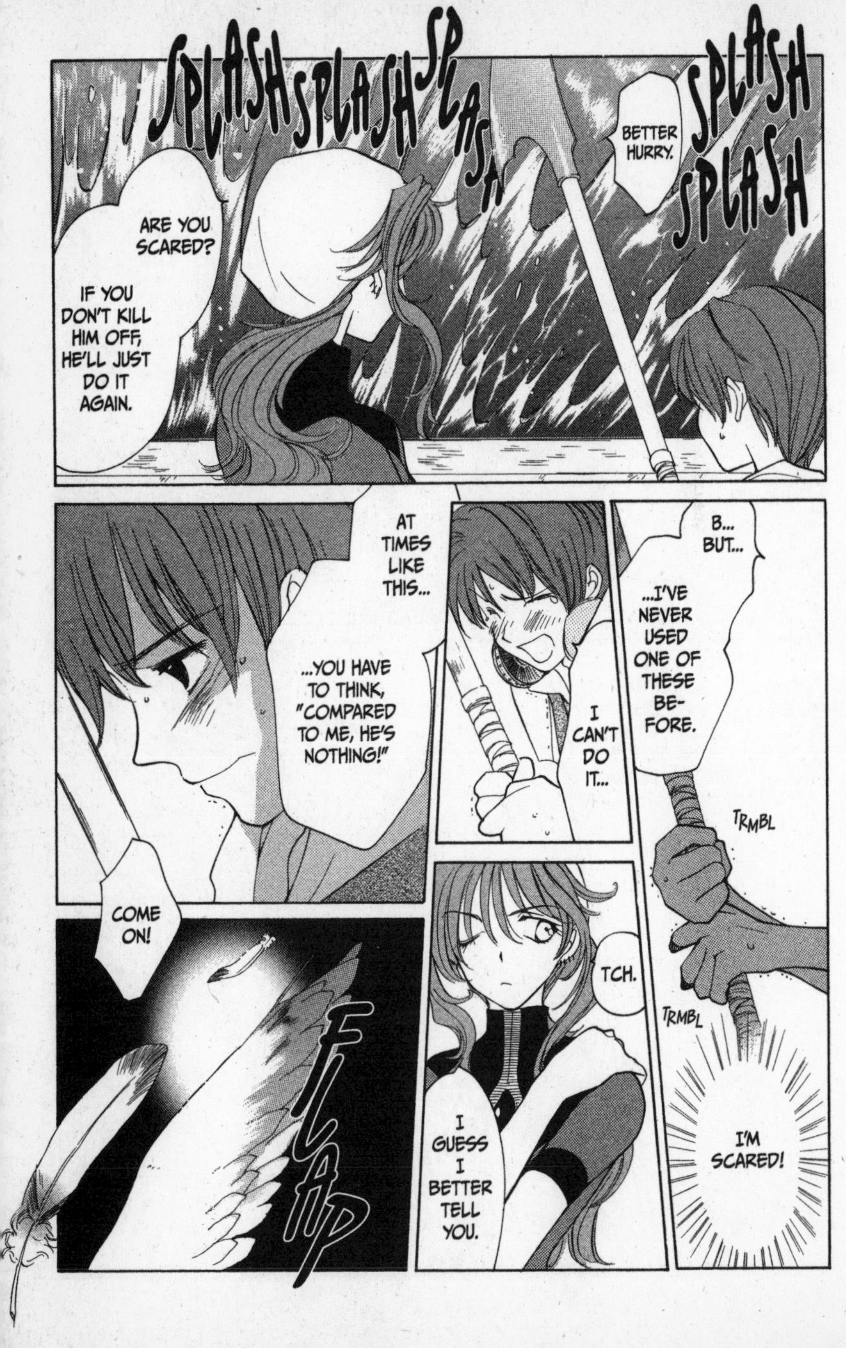
SPLASH SPLASH
BETTER HURRY.
SPLASH
SPLASH SPLASH
ARE YOU SCARED?
IF YOU DON'T KILL HIM OFF, HE'LL JUST DO IT AGAIN.
B... BUT...
...I'VE NEVER USED ONE OF THESE BE-FORE.
TRMBL
TRMBL
I'M SCARED!
I CAN'T DO IT...
AT TIMES LIKE THIS...
...YOU HAVE TO THINK, "COMPARED TO ME, HE'S NOTHING!"
TCH.
I GUESS I BETTER TELL YOU.
COME ON!
FLAP

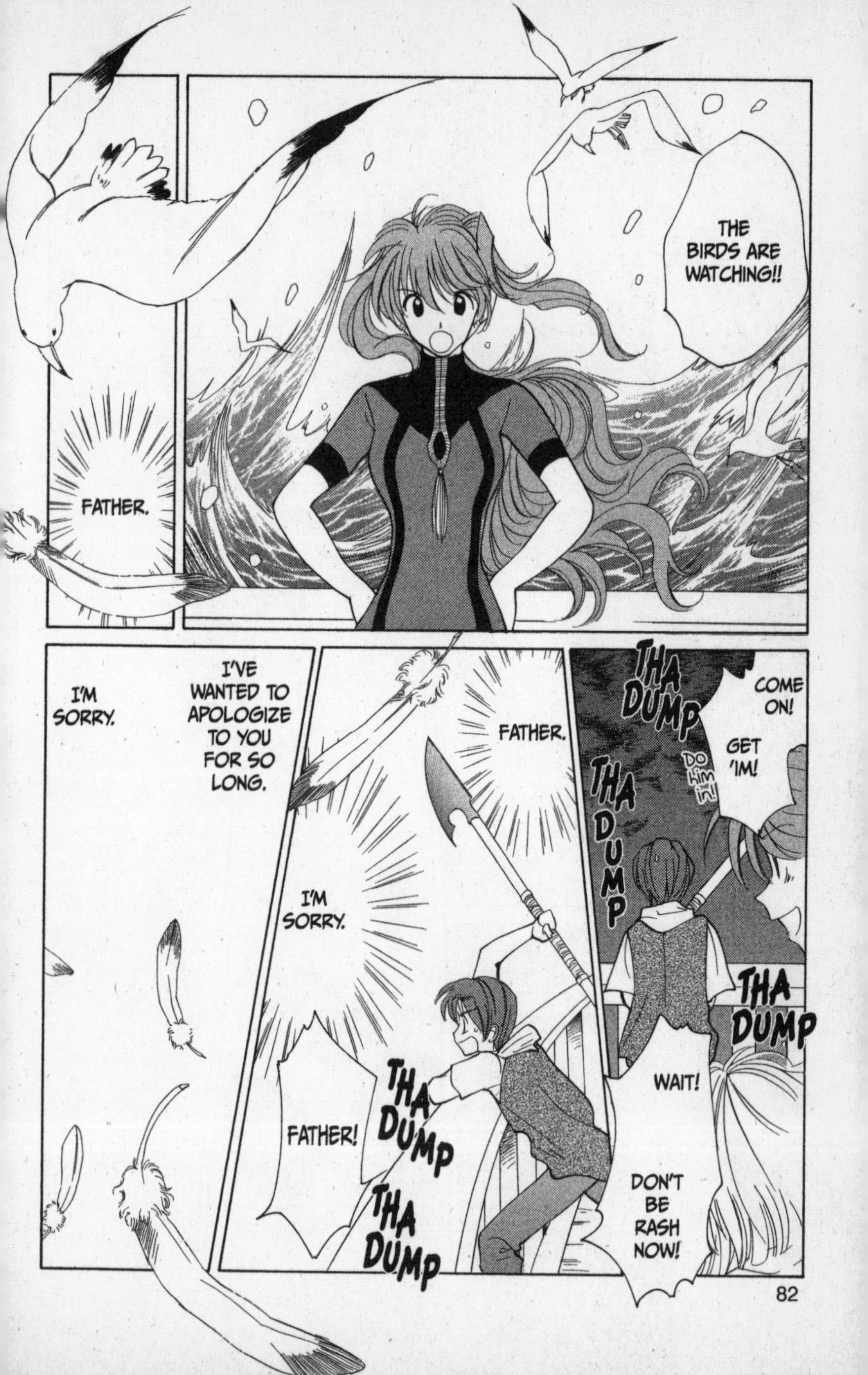
THE BIRDS ARE WATCHING!!
FATHER.
THA DUMP
COME ON!
THA DUMP
Do him in!
GET 'IM!
THA DUMP
WAIT!
DON'T BE RASH NOW!
FATHER.
I'M SORRY.
FATHER!
THA DUMP
THA DUMP
I'VE WANTED TO APOLOGIZE TO YOU FOR SO LONG.
I'M SORRY.

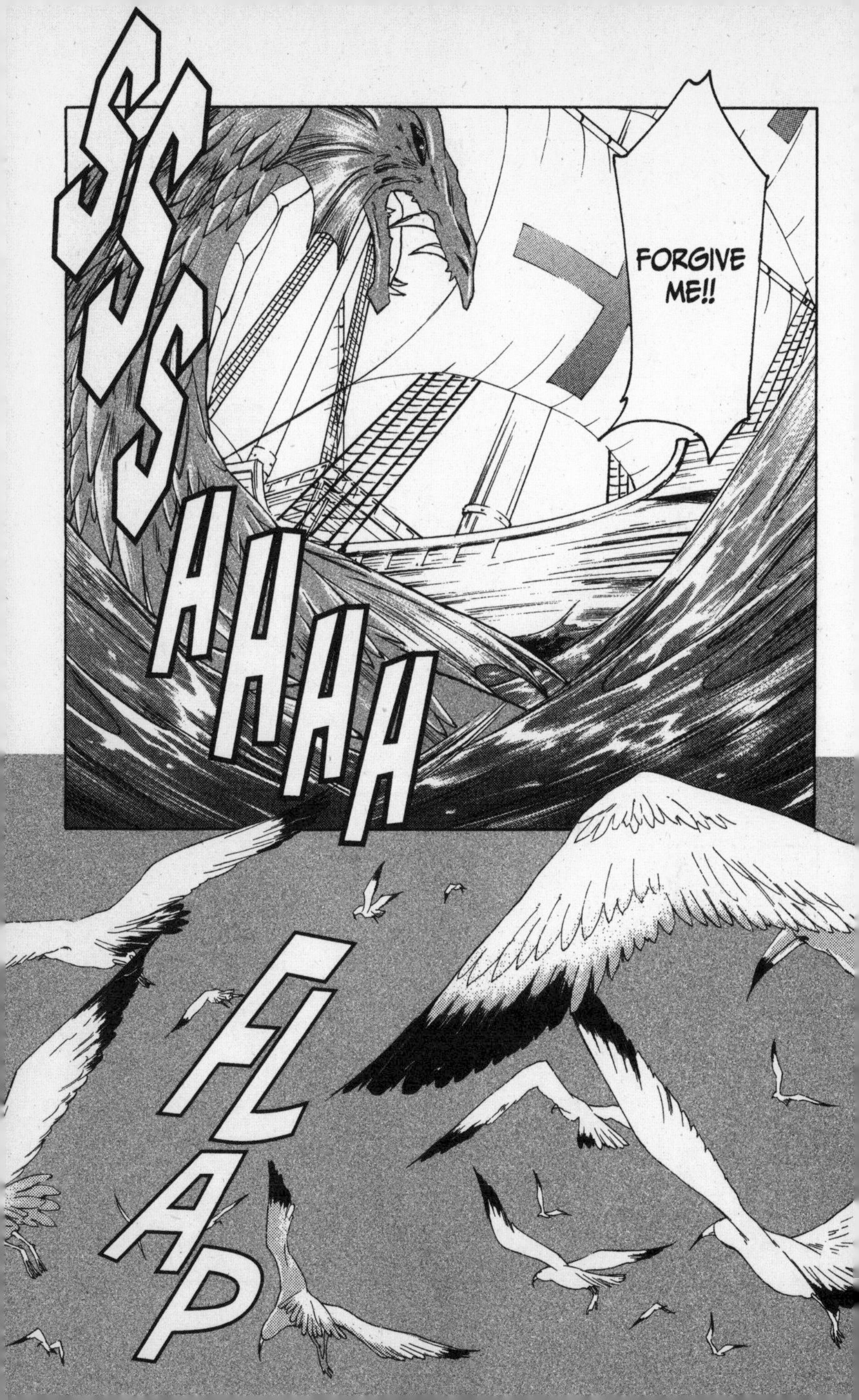
FORGIVE ME!!
SSSAAAAA
FLAP

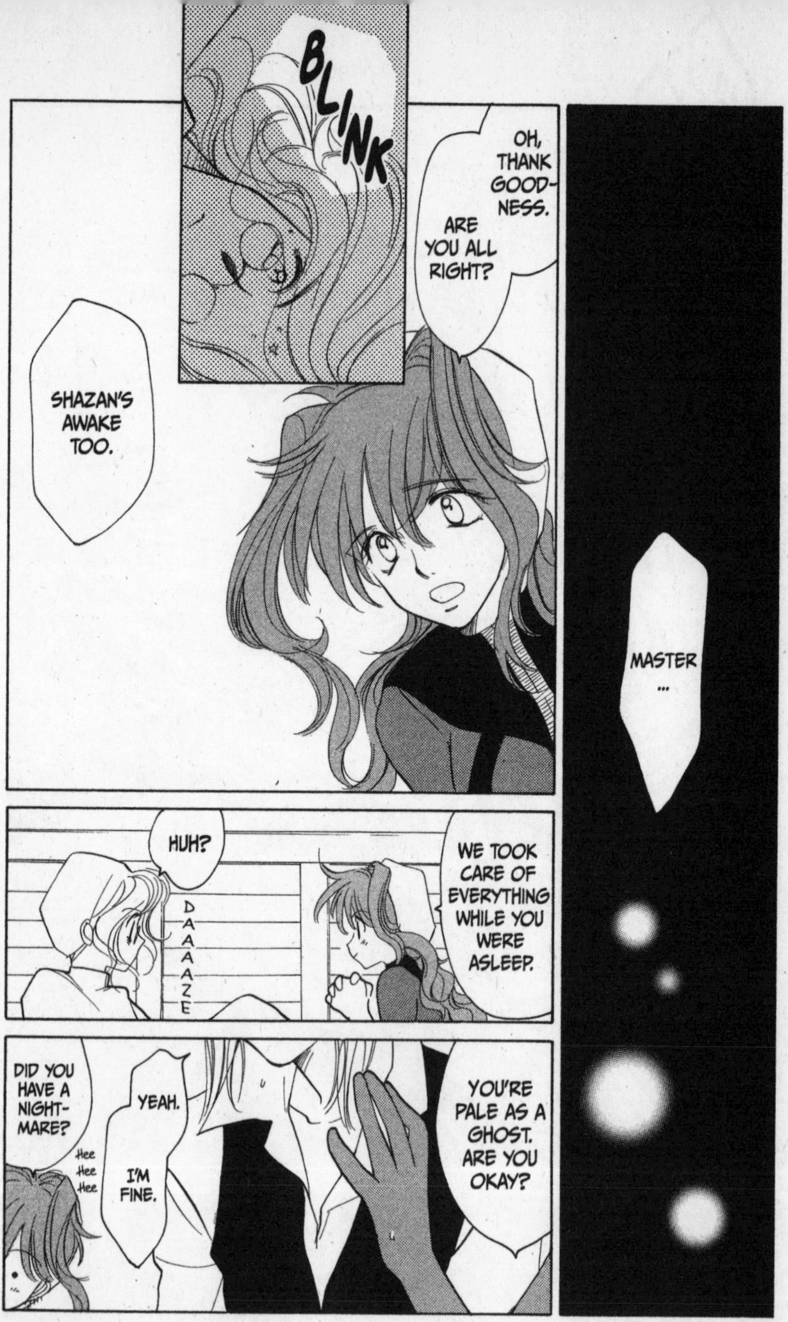
MASTER ...
BLINK
OH, THANK GOODNESS. ARE YOU ALL RIGHT?
SHAZAN'S AWAKE TOO.
WE TOOK CARE OF EVERYTHING WHILE YOU WERE ASLEEP.
HUH?
DAAAAAZE
YOU'RE PALE AS A GHOST. ARE YOU OKAY?
YEAH.
I'M FINE.
DID YOU HAVE A NIGHTMARE?
Hee Hee Hee

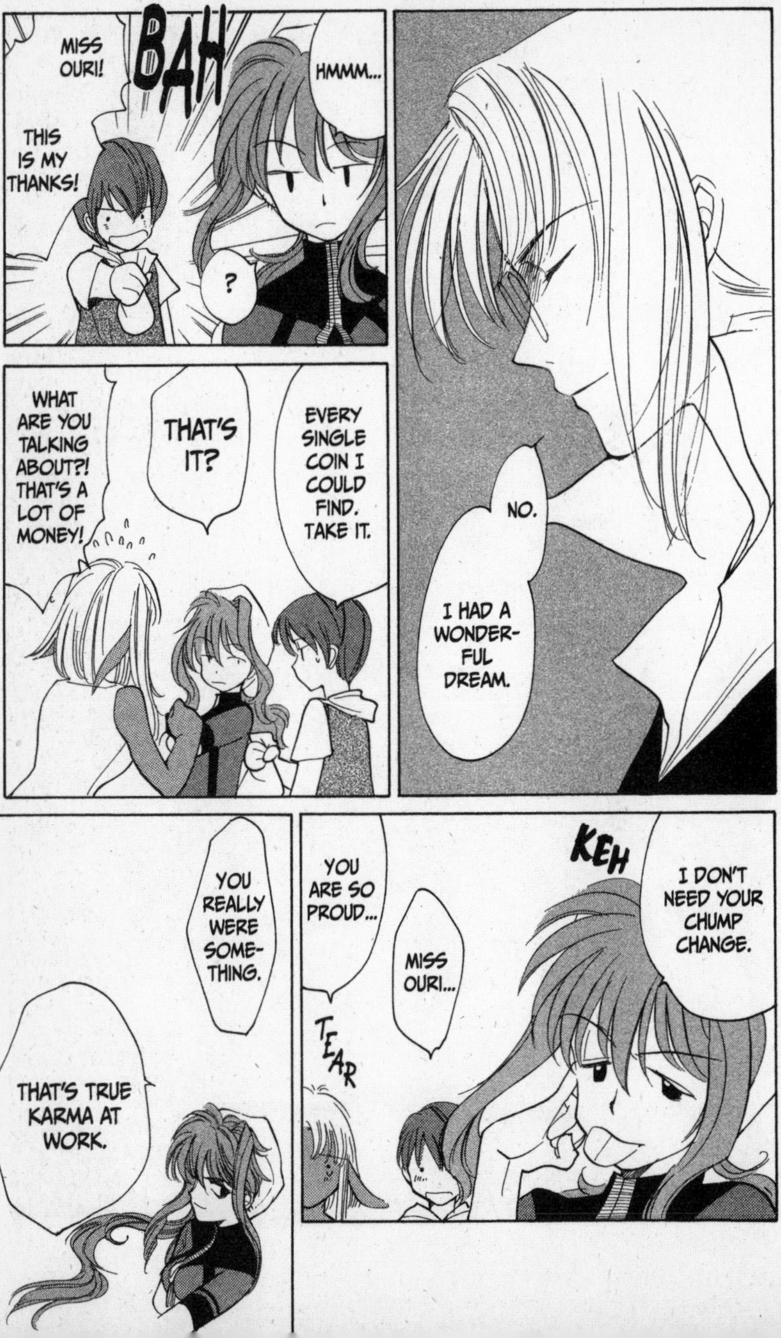
NO.
I HAD A WONDERFUL-FUL DREAM.
HMMM...
BAH
MISS OURI!
THIS IS MY THANKS!
?
EVERY SINGLE COIN I COULD FIND. TAKE IT.
THAT'S IT?
WHAT ARE YOU TALKING ABOUT?! THAT'S A LOT OF MONEY!
KEH
I DON'T NEED YOUR CHUMP CHANGE.
MISS OURI...
YOU ARE SO PROUD...
TEAR
YOU REALLY WERE SOME-THING.
THAT'S TRUE KARMA AT WORK.

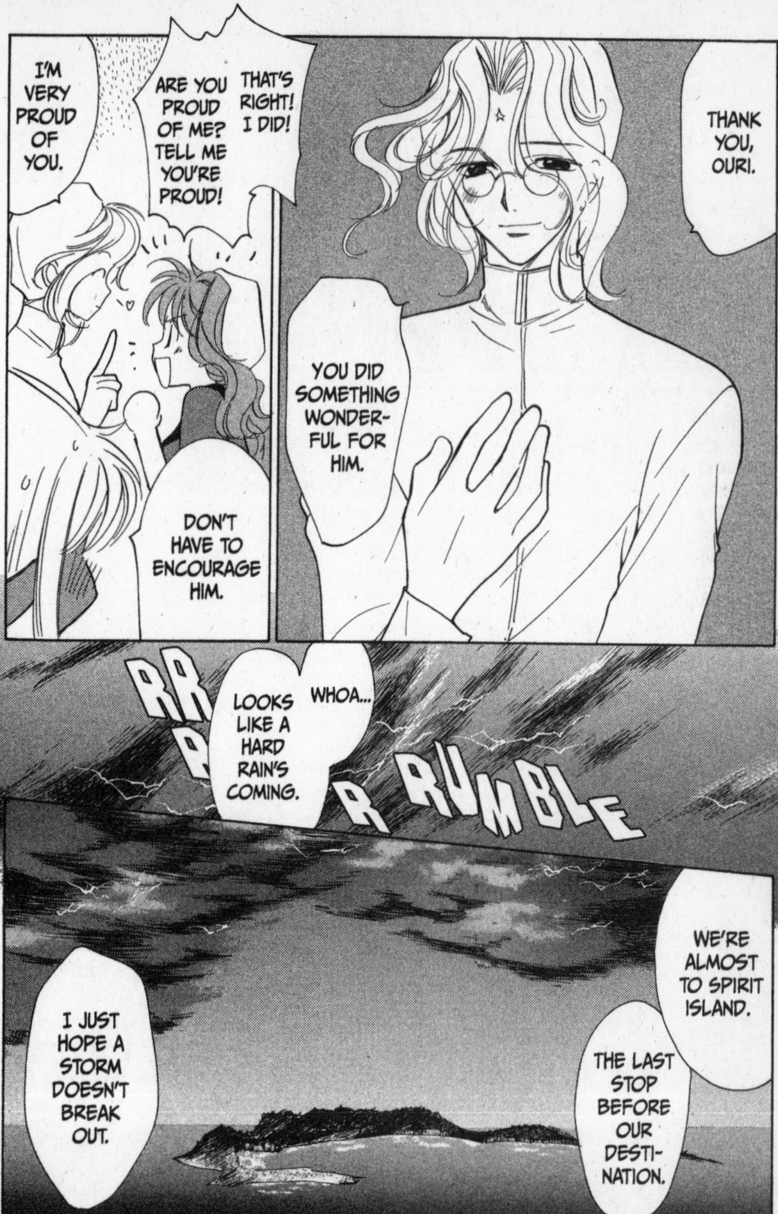
THANK YOU, OURI.
YOU DID SOMETHING WONDERFUL FOR HIM.
THAT'S RIGHT! I DID!
ARE YOU PROUD OF ME? TELL ME YOU'RE PROUD!
I'M VERY PROUD OF YOU.
DON'T HAVE TO ENCOURAGE HIM.
RRRR RUMBLE
WHOA...
LOOKS LIKE A HARD RAIN'S COMING.
WE'RE ALMOST TO SPIRIT ISLAND.
THE LAST STOP BEFORE OUR DESTINATION.
I JUST HOPE A STORM DOESN'T BREAK OUT.

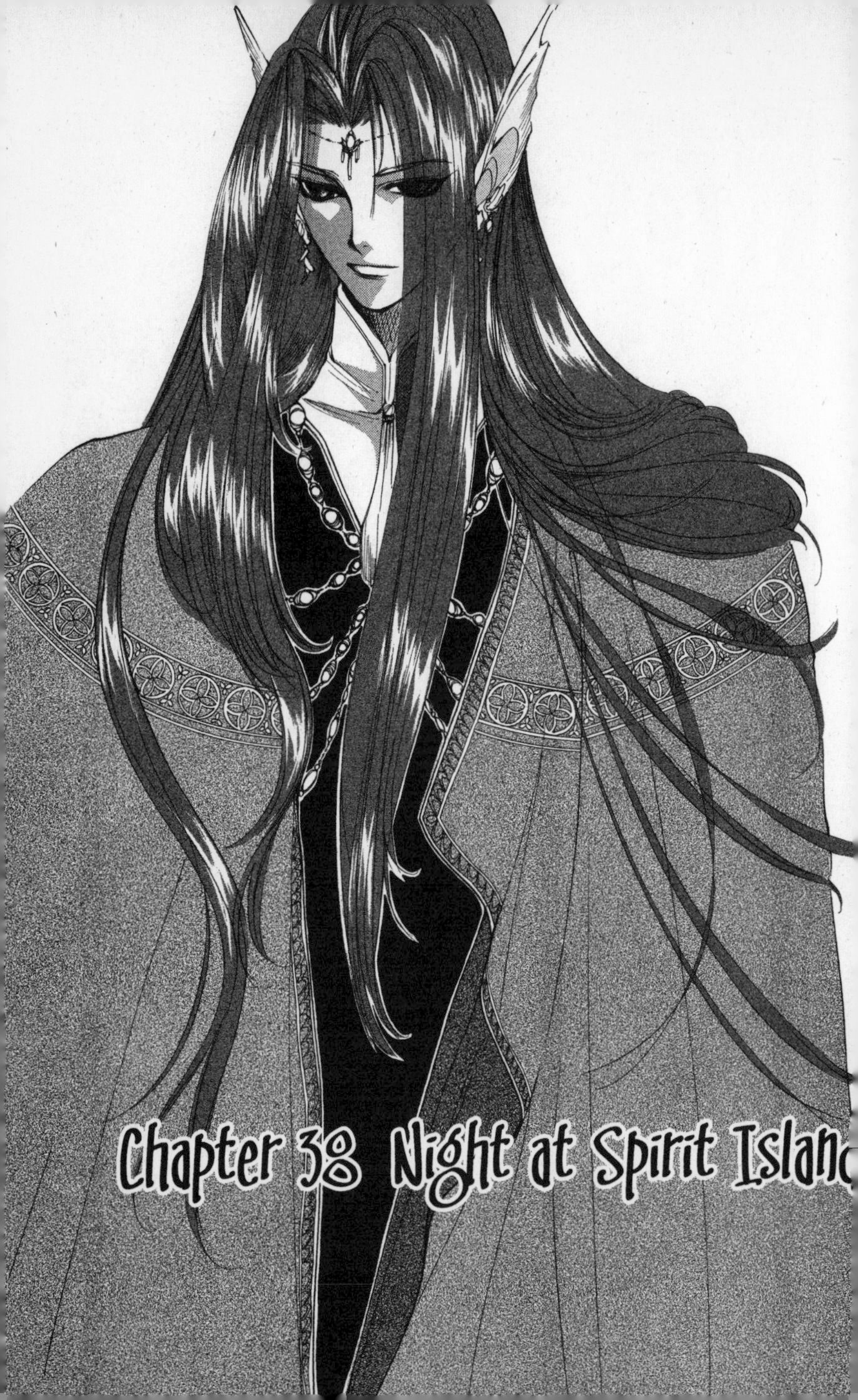
Chapter 38 Night at Spirit Island

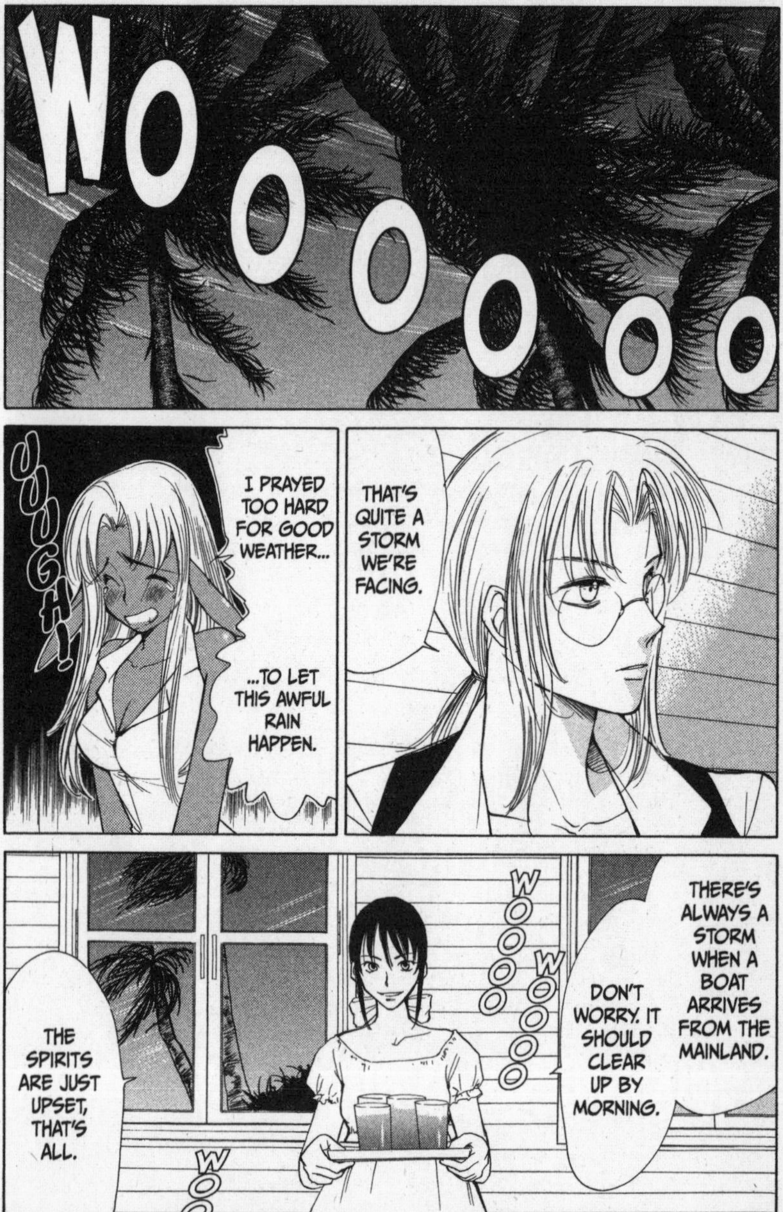
WOOOOOOO
THAT'S QUITE A STORM WE'RE FACING.
UUUGH!
I PRAYED TOO HARD FOR GOOD WEATHER...
...TO LET THIS AWFUL RAIN HAPPEN.
THERE'S ALWAYS A STORM WHEN A BOAT ARRIVES FROM THE MAINLAND.
DON'T WORRY. IT SHOULD CLEAR UP BY MORNING.
WOOOOO
WOOOOO
THE SPIRITS ARE JUST UPSET, THAT'S ALL.
WOOOOO

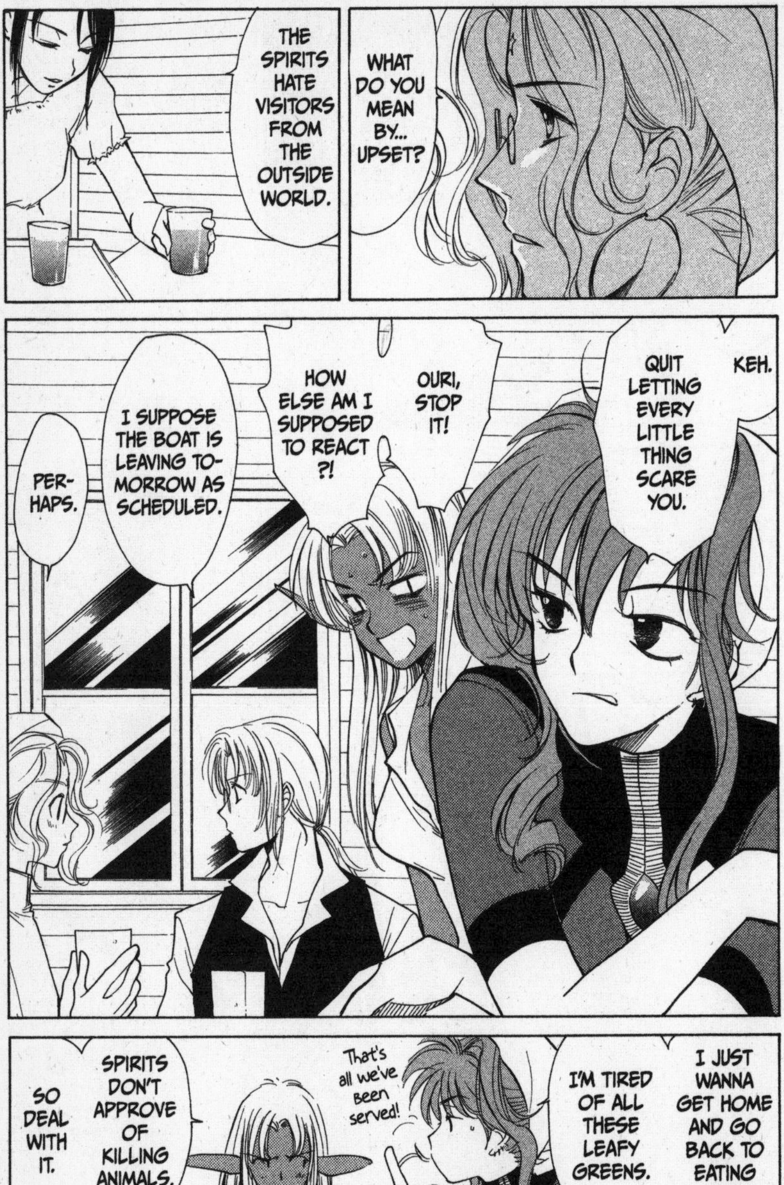
WHAT DO YOU MEAN BY... UPSET?
THE SPIRITS HATE VISITORS FROM THE OUTSIDE WORLD.
KEH.
QUIT LETTING EVERY LITTLE THING SCARE YOU.
OURI, STOP IT!
HOW ELSE AM I SUPPOSED TO REACT?!
I SUPPOSE THE BOAT IS LEAVING TOMORROW AS SCHEDULED.
PERHAPS.
I JUST WANNA GET HOME AND GO BACK TO EATING MEAT.
I'M TIRED OF ALL THESE LEAFY GREENS.
That's all we've been served!
SPIRITS DON'T APPROVE OF KILLING ANIMALS.
SO DEAL WITH IT.

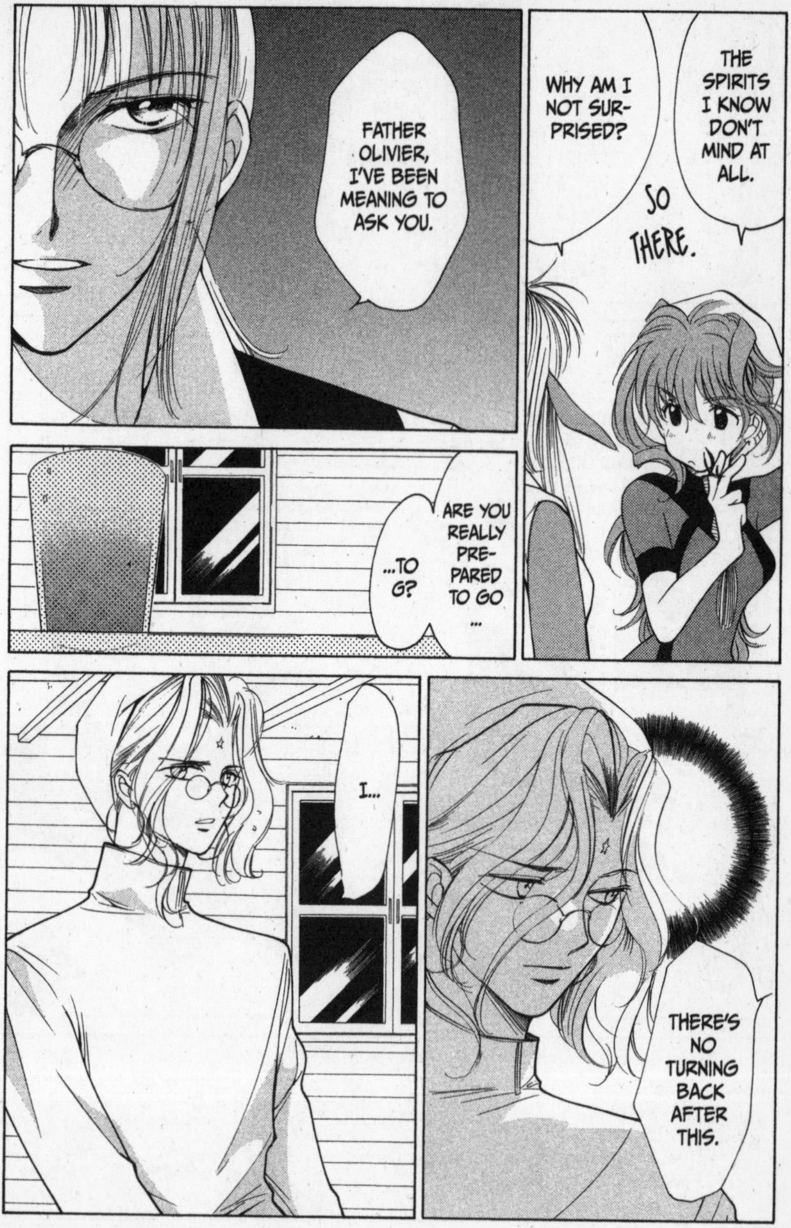
THE SPIRITS I KNOW DON'T MIND AT ALL.
WHY AM I NOT SUR-PRISED?
SO THERE.
FATHER OLIVIER, I'VE BEEN MEANING TO ASK YOU.
ARE YOU REALLY PRE-PARED TO GO ...
...TO G?
THERE'S NO TURNING BACK AFTER THIS.
I...

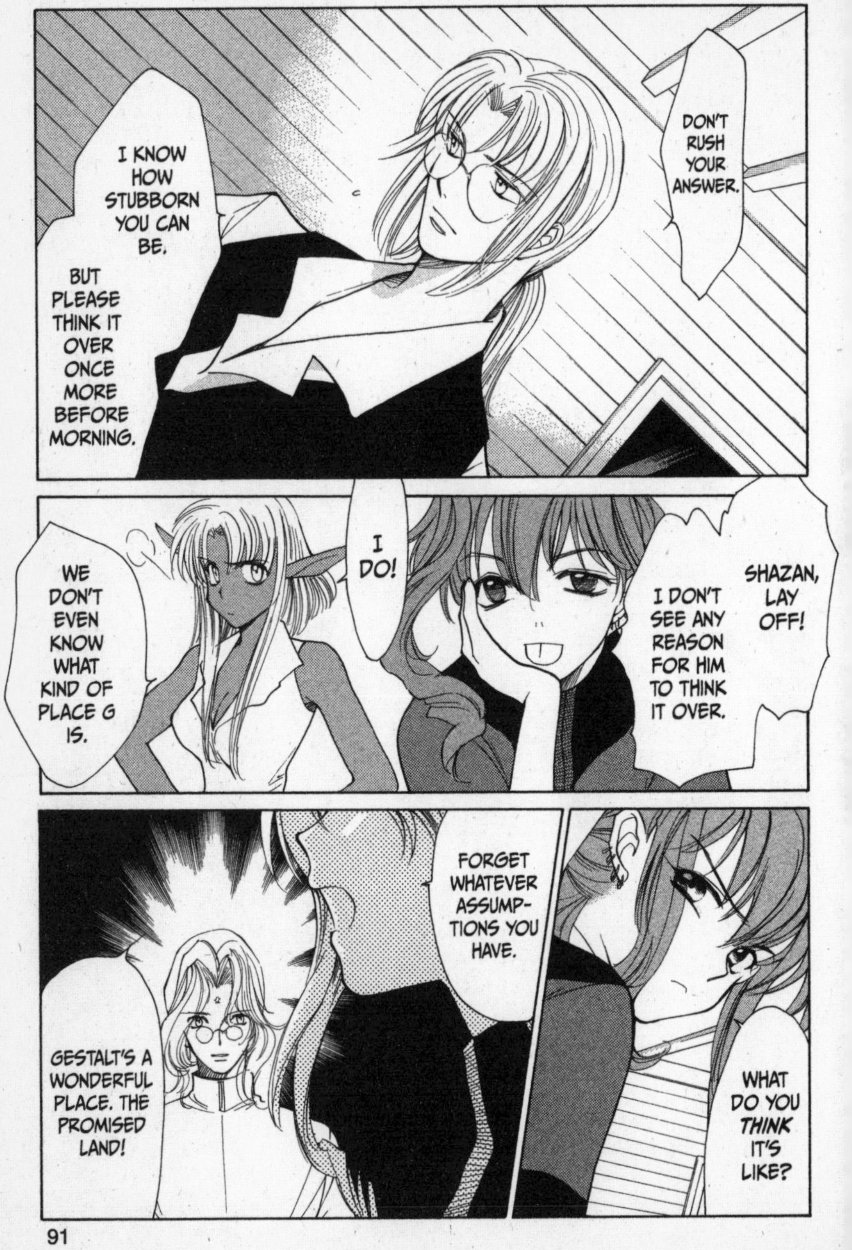
DON'T RUSH YOUR ANSWER.
I KNOW HOW STUBBORN YOU CAN BE.
BUT PLEASE THINK IT OVER ONCE MORE BEFORE MORNING.
SHAZAN, LAY OFF!
I DON'T SEE ANY REASON FOR HIM TO THINK IT OVER.
I DO!
WE DON'T EVEN KNOW WHAT KIND OF PLACE G IS.
WHAT DO YOU *THINK* IT'S LIKE?
FORGET WHATEVER ASSUMP-TIONS YOU HAVE.
GESTALT'S A WONDERFUL PLACE. THE PROMISED LAND!

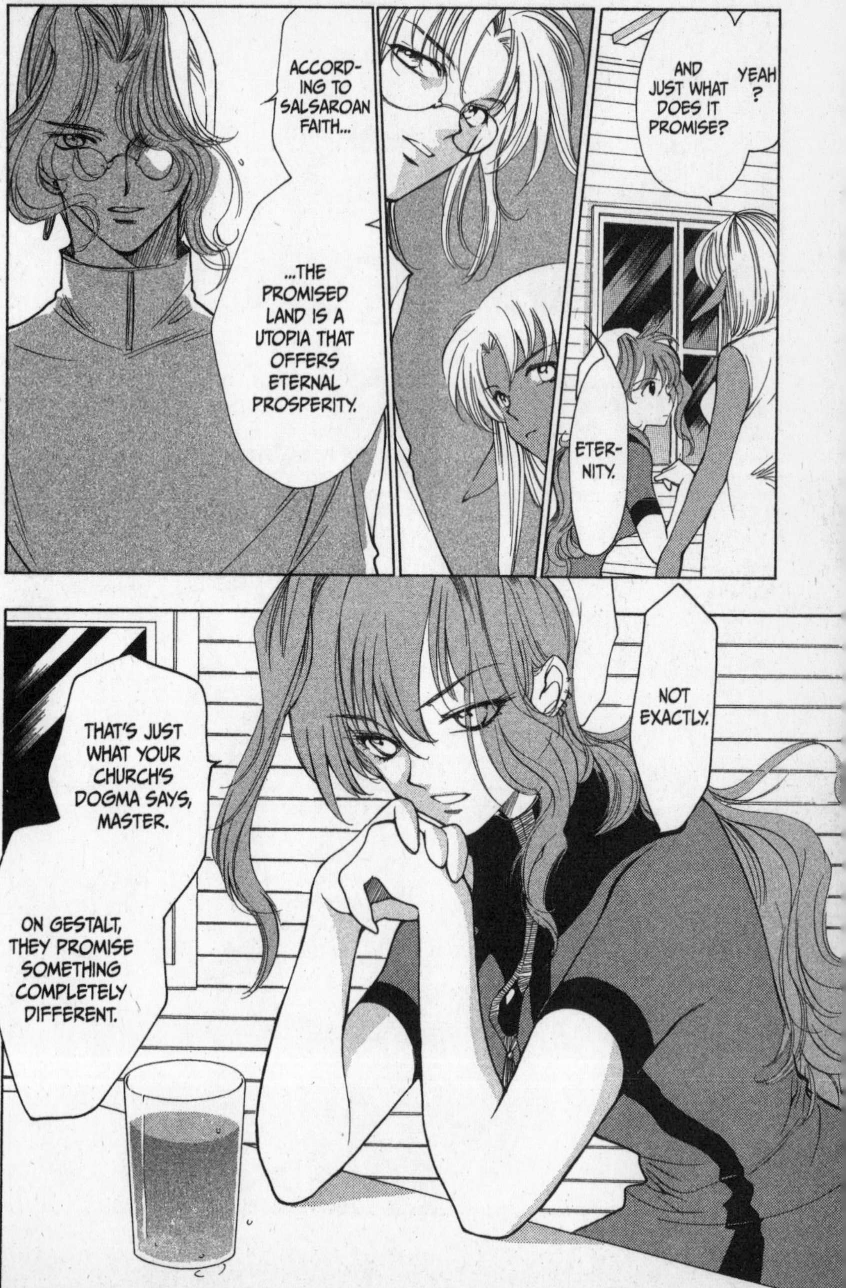
YEAH?
AND JUST WHAT DOES IT PROMISE?
ETERNITY.
ACCORDING TO SALSAROAN FAITH...
...THE PROMISED LAND IS A UTOPIA THAT OFFERS ETERNAL PROSPERITY.
NOT EXACTLY.
THAT'S JUST WHAT YOUR CHURCH'S DOGMA SAYS, MASTER.
ON GESTALT, THEY PROMISE SOMETHING COMPLETELY DIFFERENT.

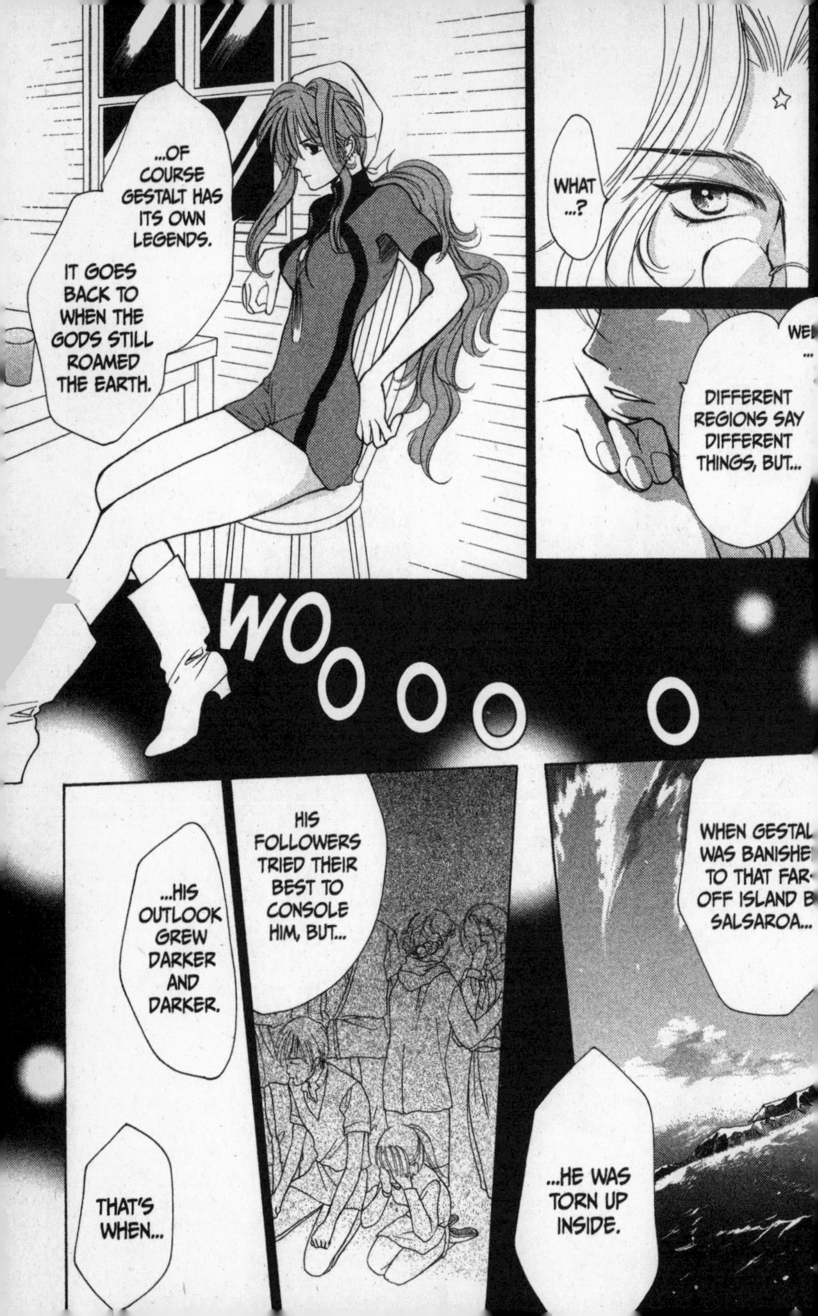
WHAT ...?
WEL ...
DIFFERENT REGIONS SAY DIFFERENT THINGS, BUT...
...OF COURSE GESTALT HAS ITS OWN LEGENDS.
IT GOES BACK TO WHEN THE GODS STILL ROAMED THE EARTH.
WOOOOO
WHEN GESTAL WAS BANISHE TO THAT FAR-OFF ISLAND B SALSAROA...
...HE WAS TORN UP INSIDE.
HIS FOLLOWERS TRIED THEIR BEST TO CONSOLE HIM, BUT...
...HIS OUTLOOK GREW DARKER AND DARKER.
THAT'S WHEN...

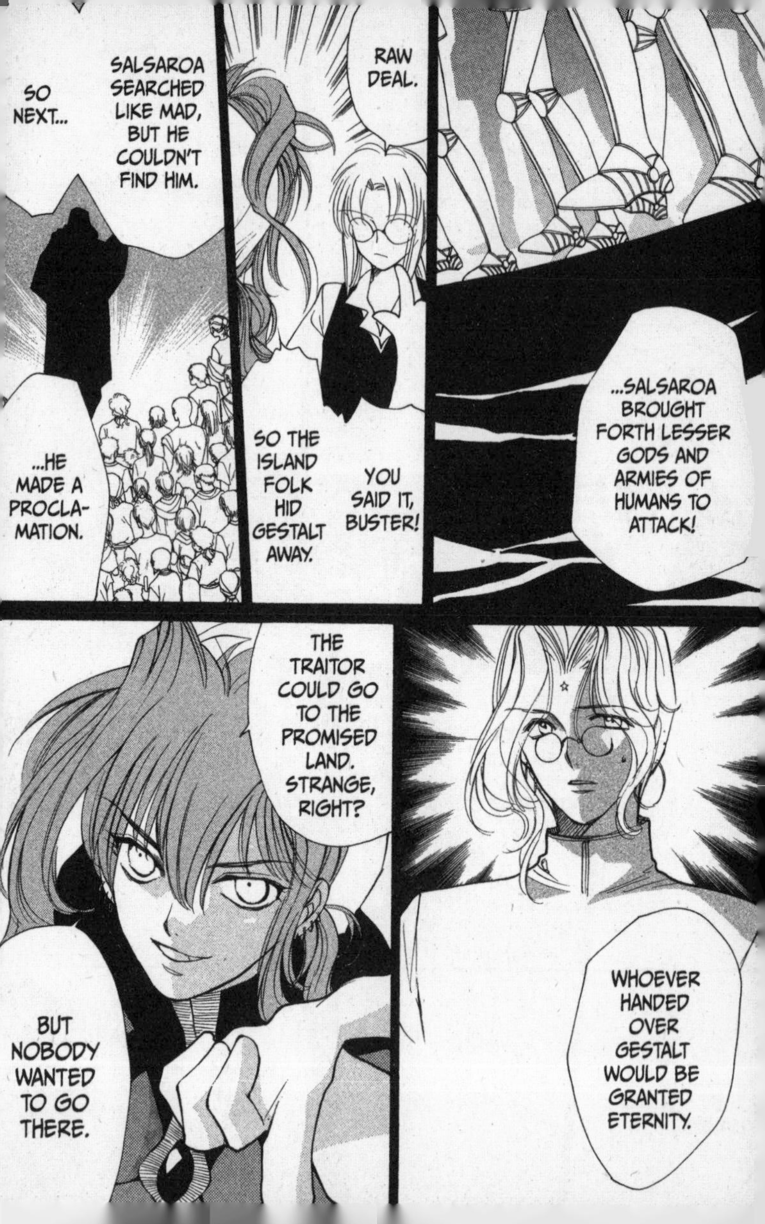
...SALSAROA BROUGHT FORTH LESSER GODS AND ARMIES OF HUMANS TO ATTACK!
RAW DEAL.
SO THE ISLAND FOLK HID GESTALT AWAY.
YOU SAID IT, BUSTER!
SALSAROA SEARCHED LIKE MAD, BUT HE COULDN'T FIND HIM.
SO NEXT...
...HE MADE A PROCLAMATION.
WHOEVER HANDED OVER GESTALT WOULD BE GRANTED ETERNITY.
THE TRAITOR COULD GO TO THE PROMISED LAND. STRANGE, RIGHT?
BUT NOBODY WANTED TO GO THERE.

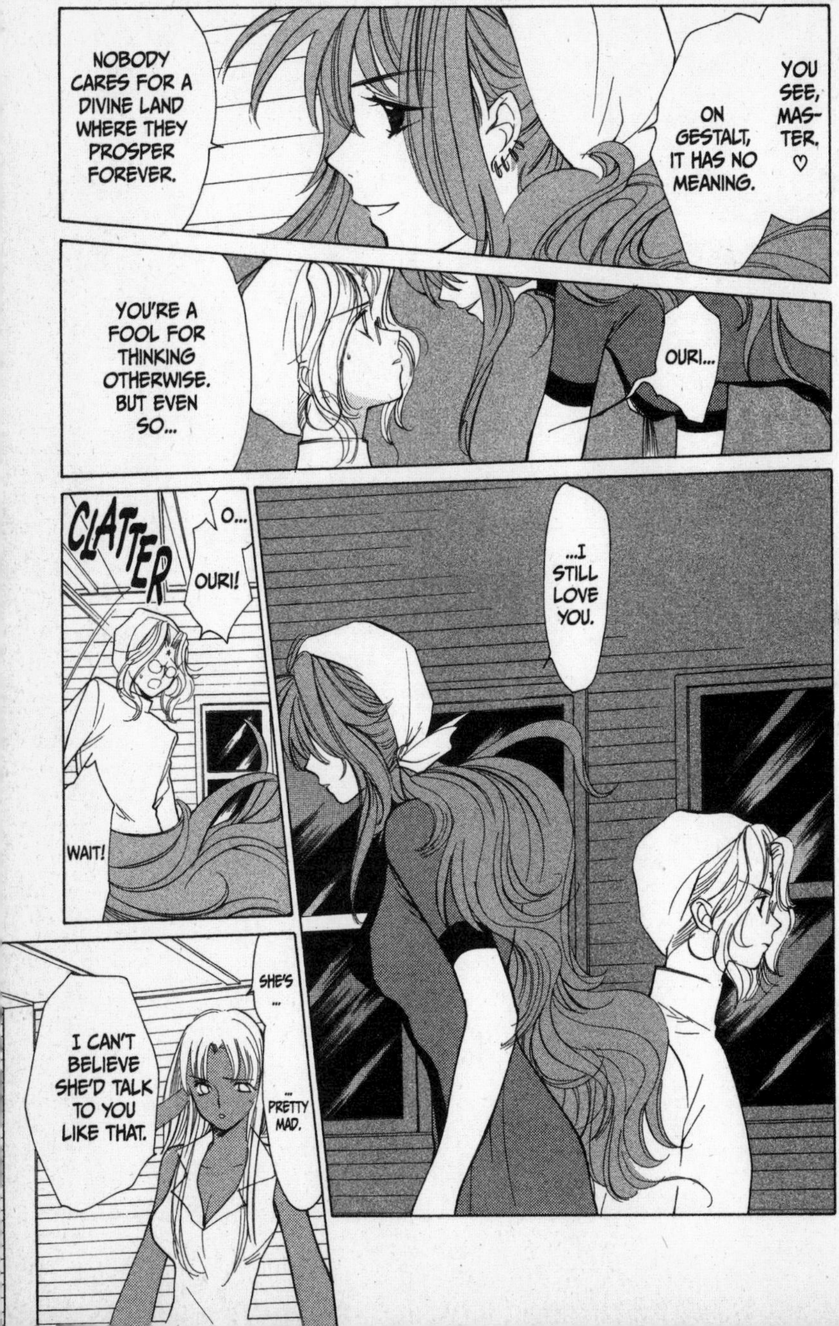
YOU SEE, MASTER. ♡
ON GESTALT, IT HAS NO MEANING.
NOBODY CARES FOR A DIVINE LAND WHERE THEY PROSPER FOREVER.
OURI...
YOU'RE A FOOL FOR THINKING OTHERWISE. BUT EVEN SO...
...I STILL LOVE YOU.
CLATTER
O...
OURI!
WAIT!
SHE'S ...
... PRETTY MAD.
I CAN'T BELIEVE SHE'D TALK TO YOU LIKE THAT.

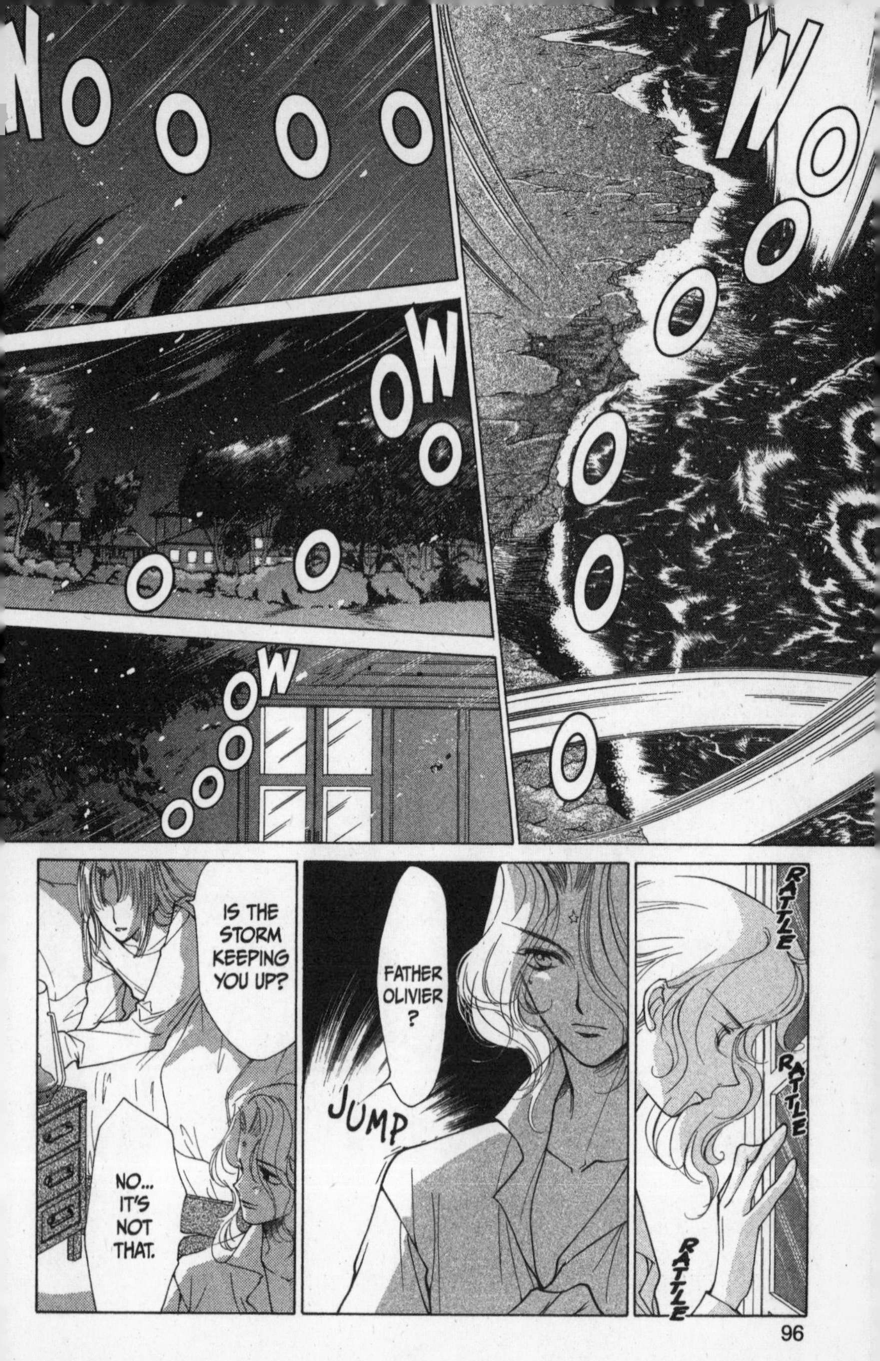
WOOOOOO
NOOOO
OOOOW
OOOOW
RATTLE
RATTLE
RATTLE
FATHER OLIVIER ?
JUMP
IS THE STORM KEEPING YOU UP?
NO... IT'S NOT THAT.

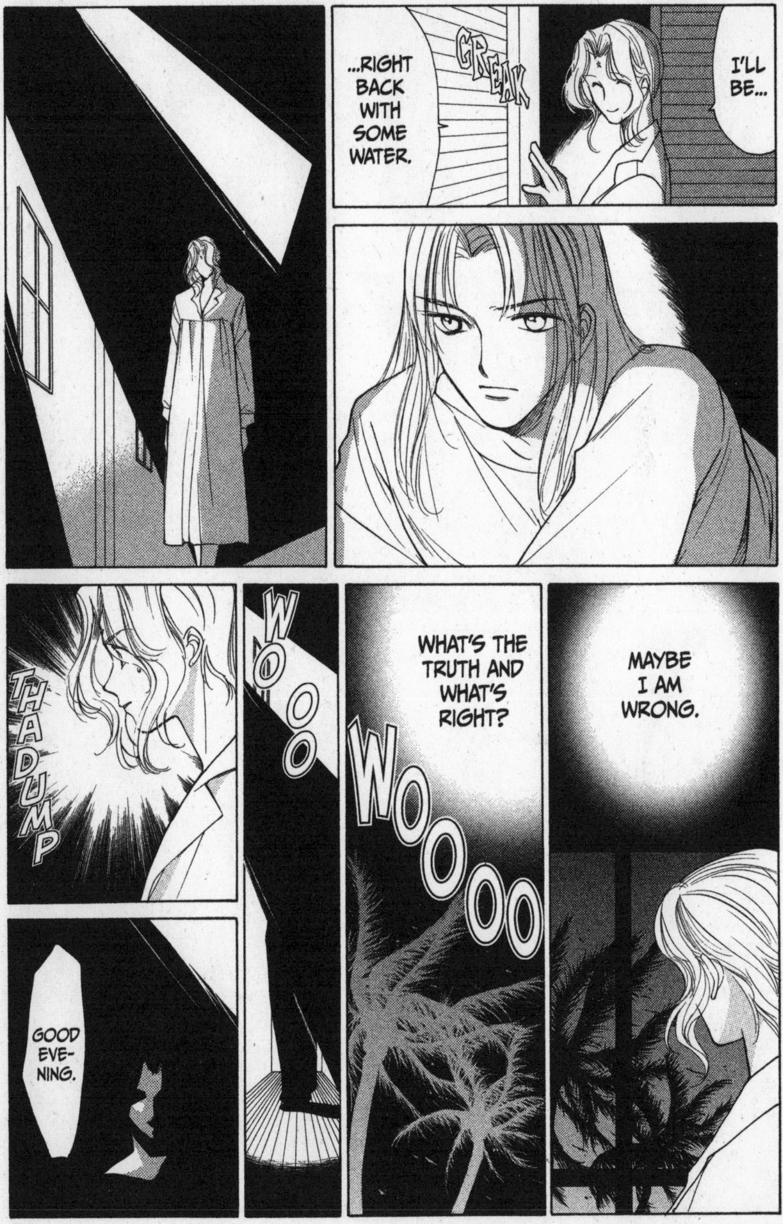
I'LL BE...
CREAK
...RIGHT BACK WITH SOME WATER.
MAYBE I AM WRONG.
WHAT'S THE TRUTH AND WHAT'S RIGHT?
WOOOOO
WOOO
THADUMP
GOOD EVE-NING.

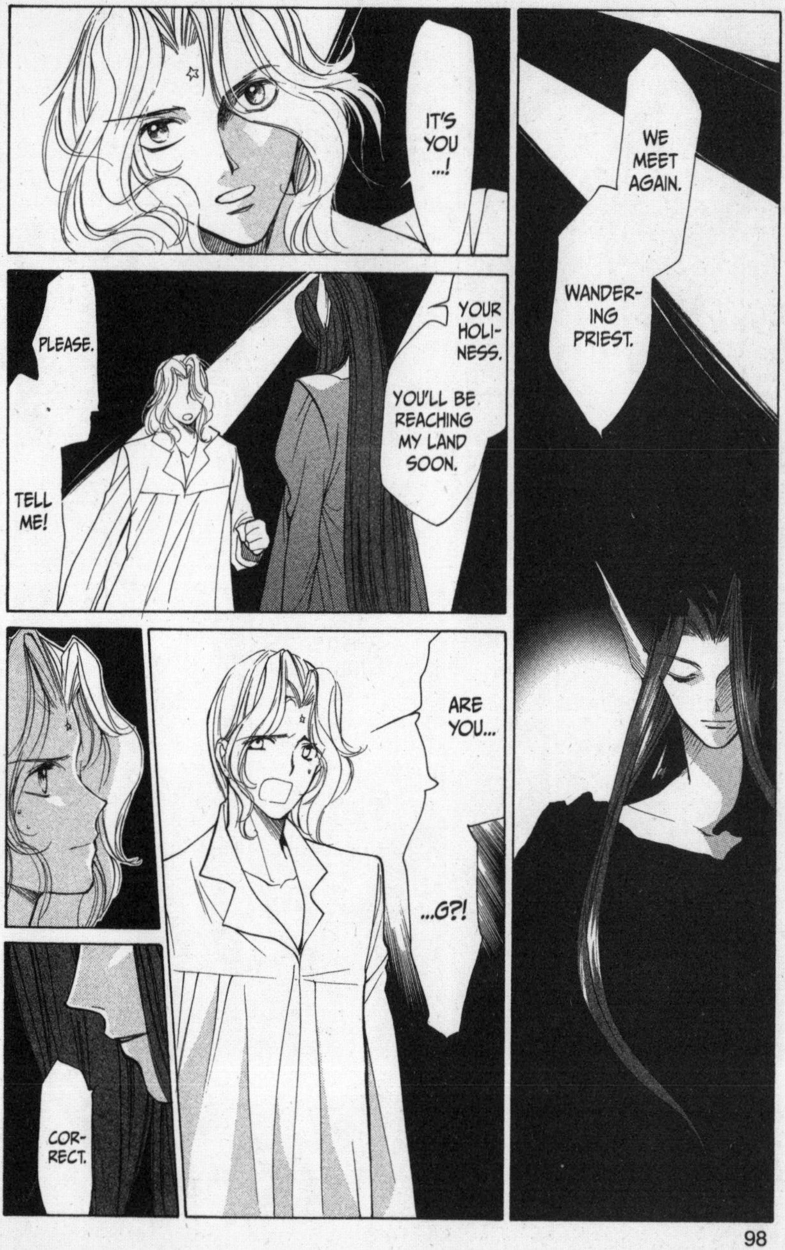

WE MEET AGAIN.
WANDER-ING PRIEST.
IT'S YOU ...!
YOUR HOLI-NESS.
YOU'LL BE REACHING MY LAND SOON.
PLEASE.
TELL ME!
ARE YOU...
...G?!
COR-RECT.

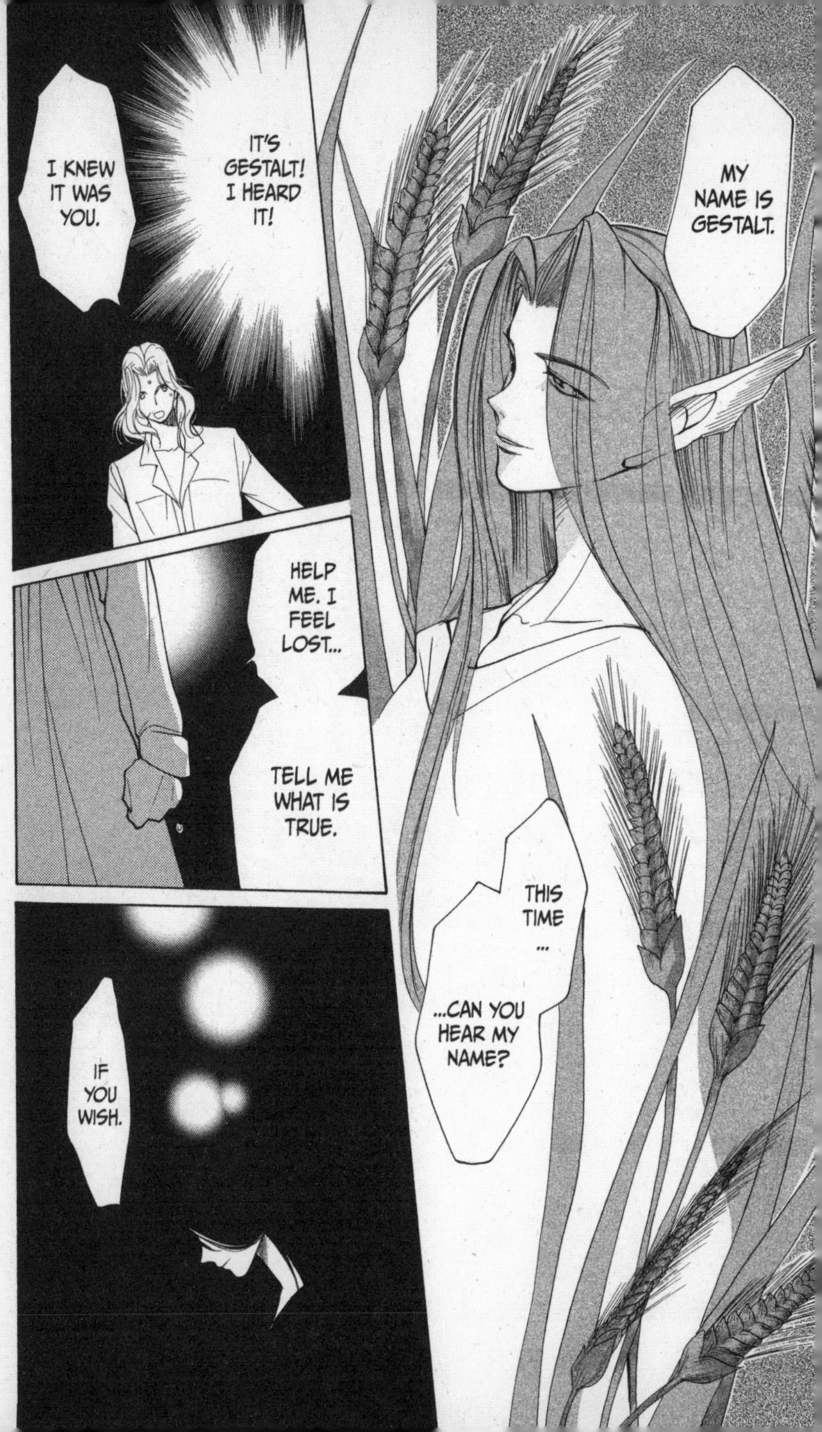
MY NAME IS GESTALT.
THIS TIME ...
...CAN YOU HEAR MY NAME?
IT'S GESTALT! I HEARD IT!
I KNEW IT WAS YOU.
HELP ME. I FEEL LOST...
TELL ME WHAT IS TRUE.
IF YOU WISH.

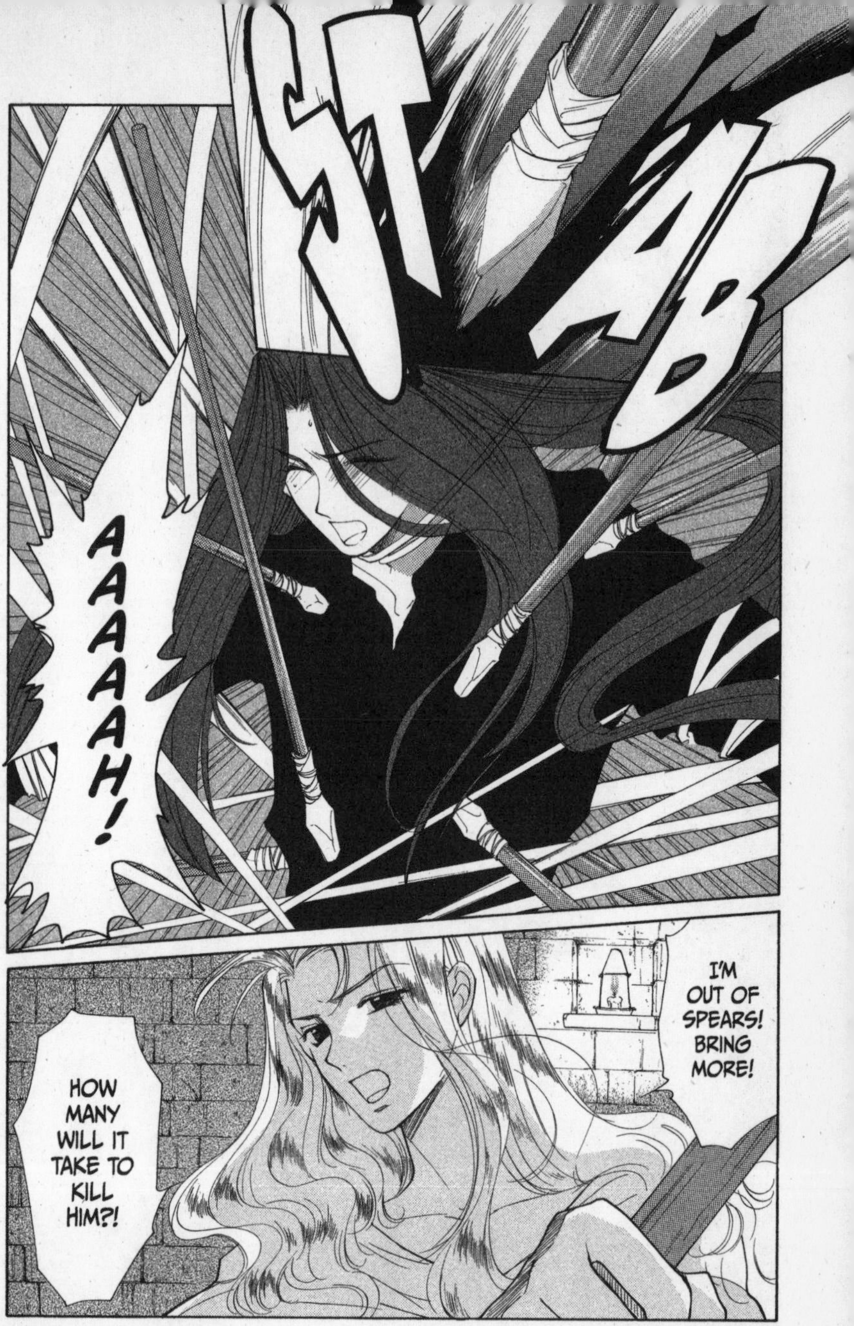
STAB
AAAAAAH!
I'M OUT OF SPEARS! BRING MORE!
HOW MANY WILL IT TAKE TO KILL HIM?!

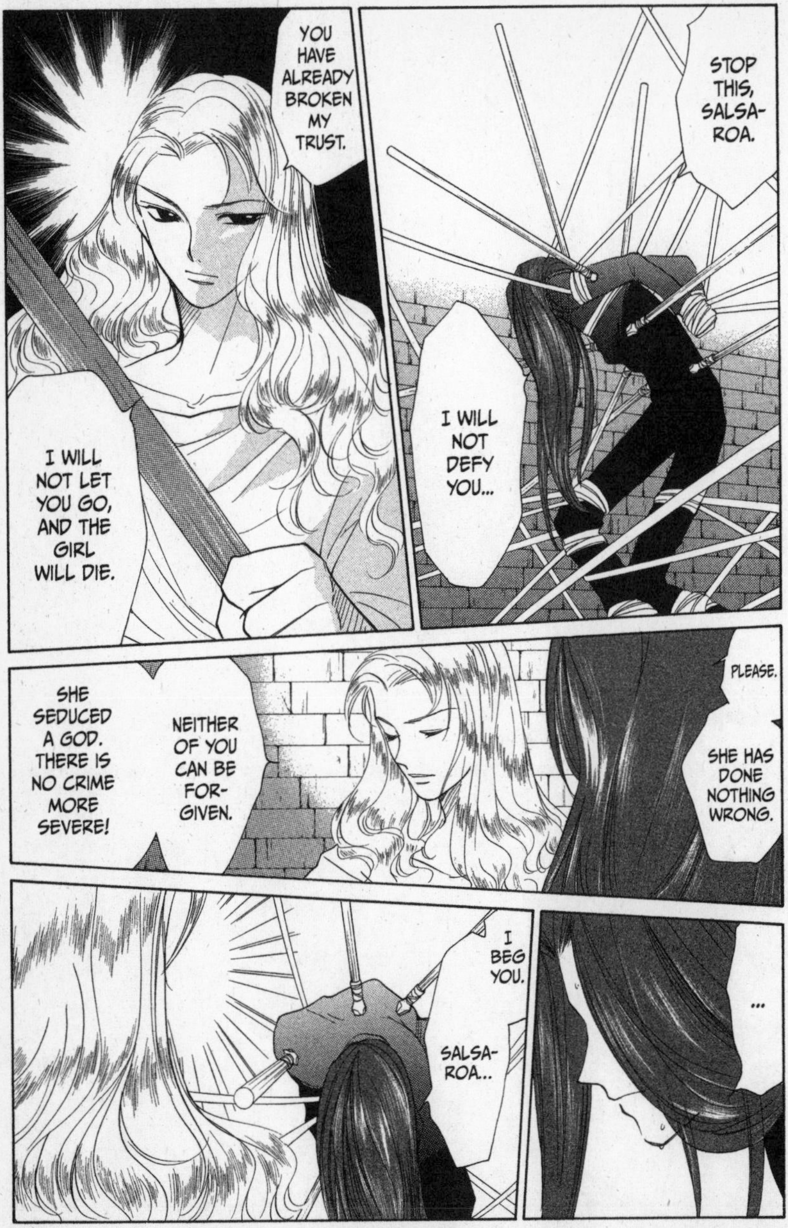
STOP THIS, SALSA-ROA.
I WILL NOT DEFY YOU...
YOU HAVE ALREADY BROKEN MY TRUST.
I WILL NOT LET YOU GO, AND THE GIRL WILL DIE.
PLEASE.
SHE HAS DONE NOTHING WRONG.
NEITHER OF YOU CAN BE FOR-GIVEN.
SHE SEDUCED A GOD. THERE IS NO CRIME MORE SEVERE!
...
I BEG YOU.
SALSA-ROA...

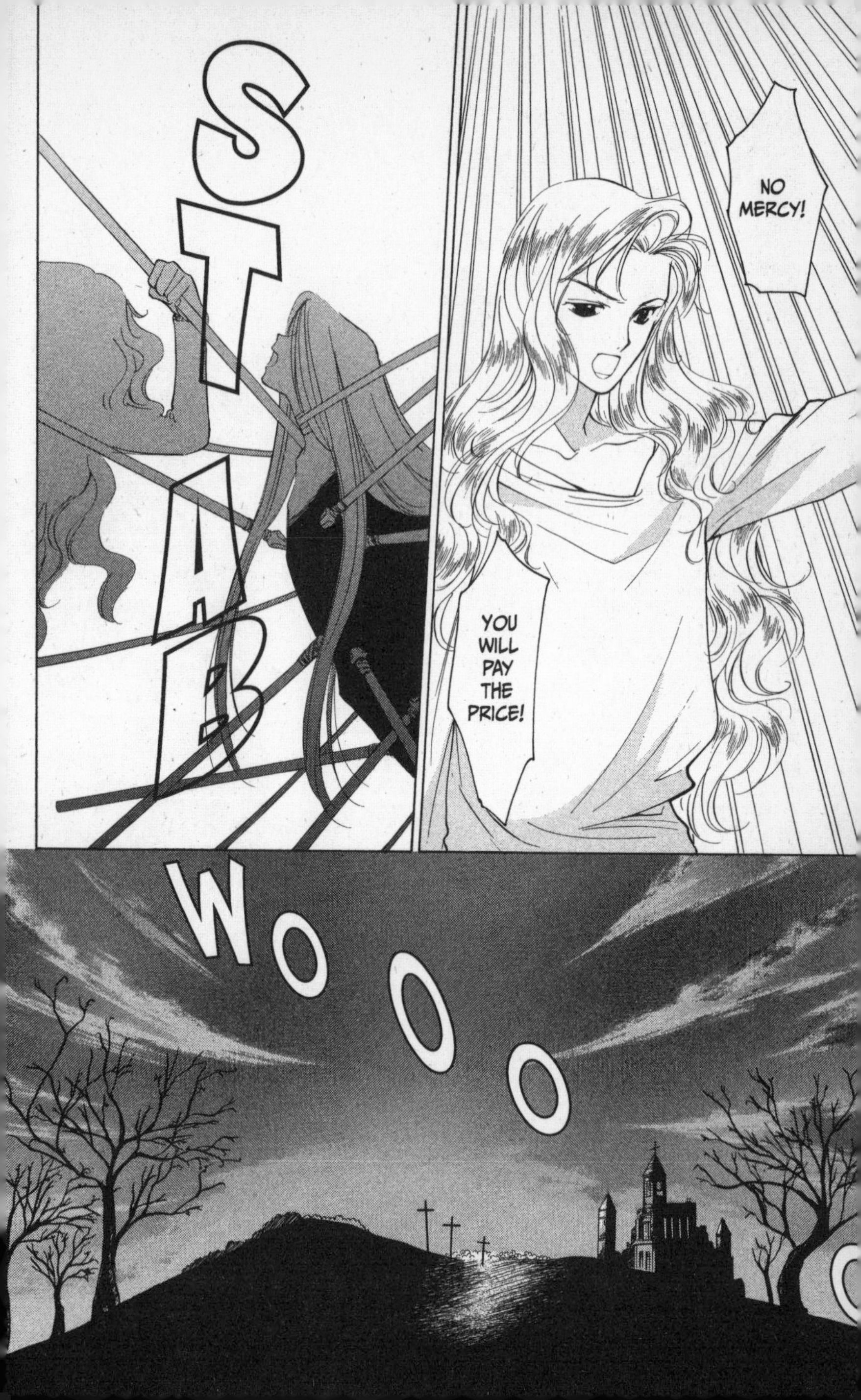
NO MERCY!
YOU WILL PAY THE PRICE!
STAB
WOOOO

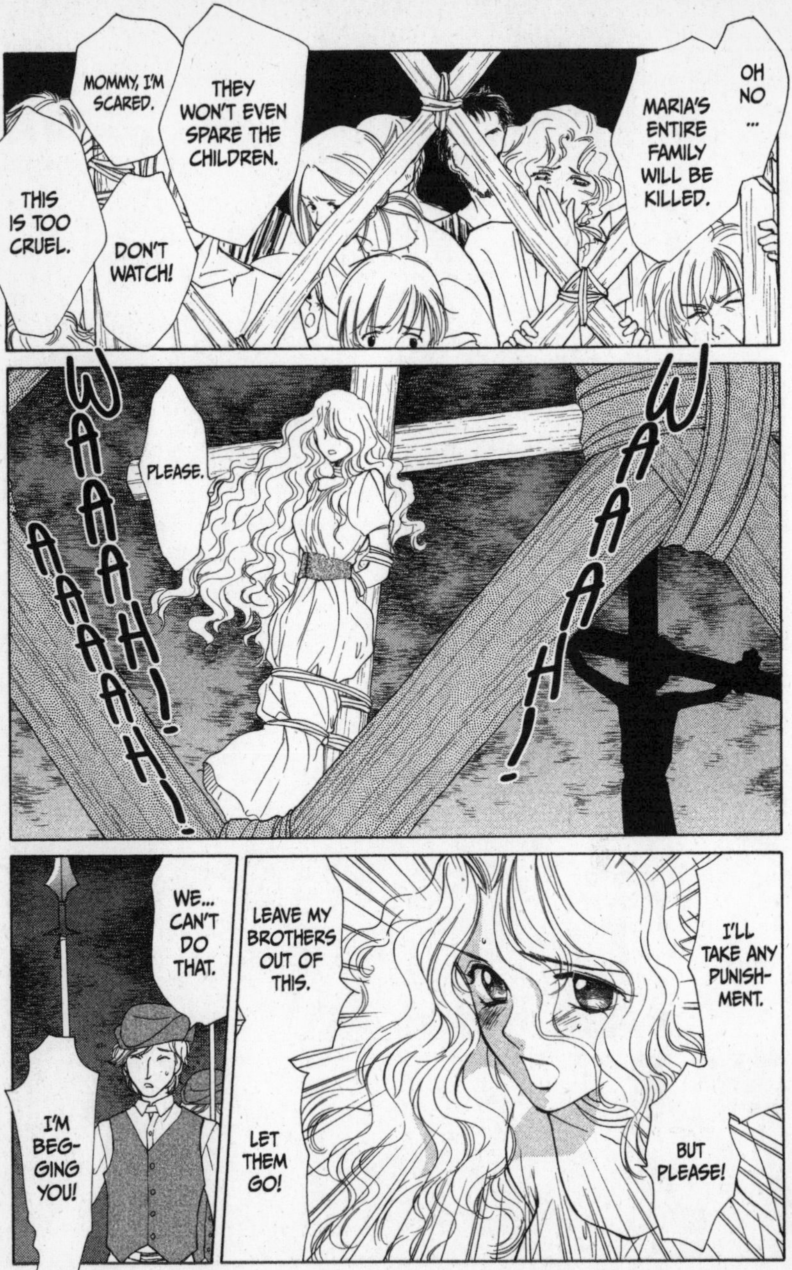
OH NO ...
MARIA'S ENTIRE FAMILY WILL BE KILLED.
THEY WON'T EVEN SPARE THE CHILDREN.
MOMMY, I'M SCARED.
DON'T WATCH!
THIS IS TOO CRUEL.
WAAAAH!
PLEASE.
WAAAAAH!
AAAAAAH!
I'LL TAKE ANY PUNISH-MENT.
LEAVE MY BROTHERS OUT OF THIS.
BUT PLEASE!
LET THEM GO!
I'M BEG-GING YOU!
WE... CAN'T DO THAT.

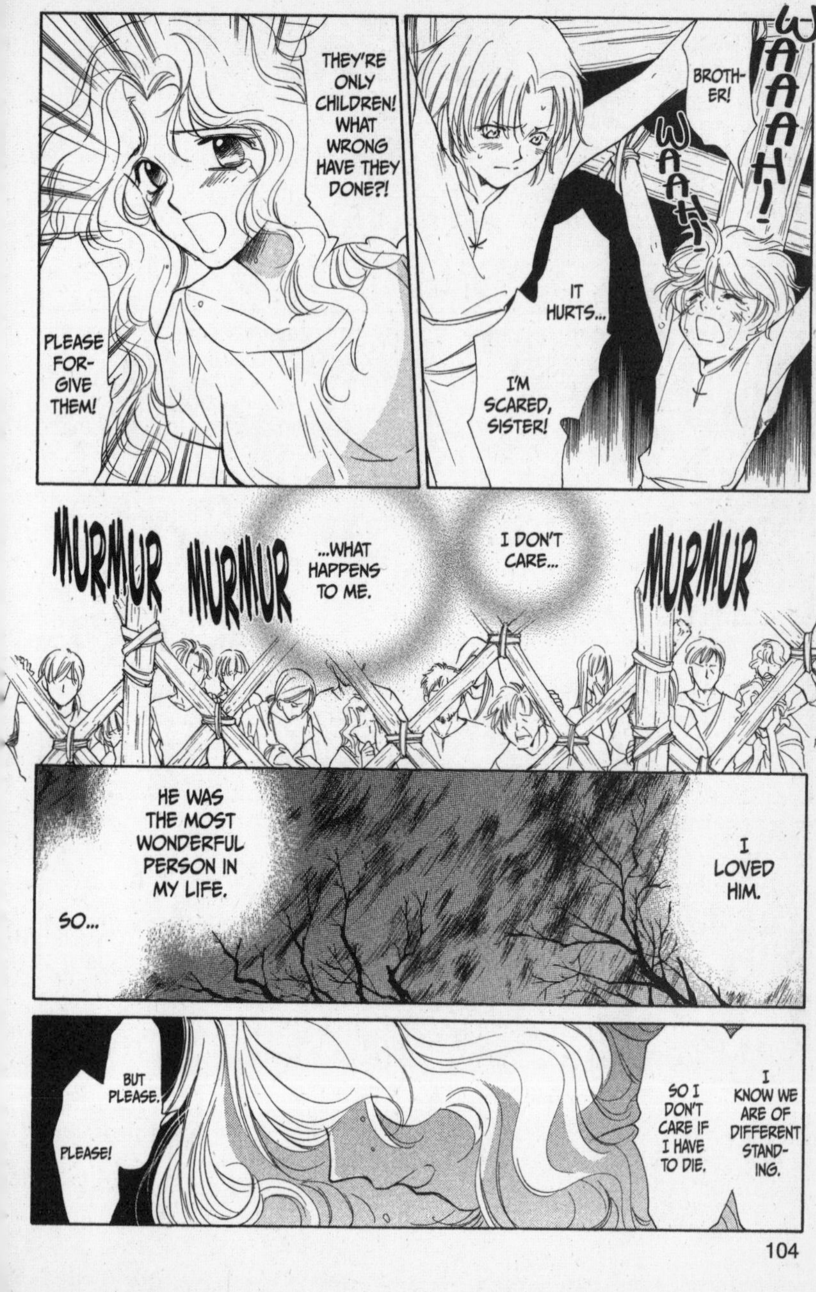
WAAAAH!
BROTHER!
WAAH!
IT HURTS...
I'M SCARED, SISTER!
THEY'RE ONLY CHILDREN! WHAT WRONG HAVE THEY DONE?!
PLEASE FOR-GIVE THEM!
MURMUR
I DON'T CARE...
...WHAT HAPPENS TO ME.
MURMUR
MURMUR
I LOVED HIM.
HE WAS THE MOST WONDERFUL PERSON IN MY LIFE.
SO...
I KNOW WE ARE OF DIFFERENT STAND-ING.
SO I DON'T CARE IF I HAVE TO DIE.
BUT PLEASE.
PLEASE!

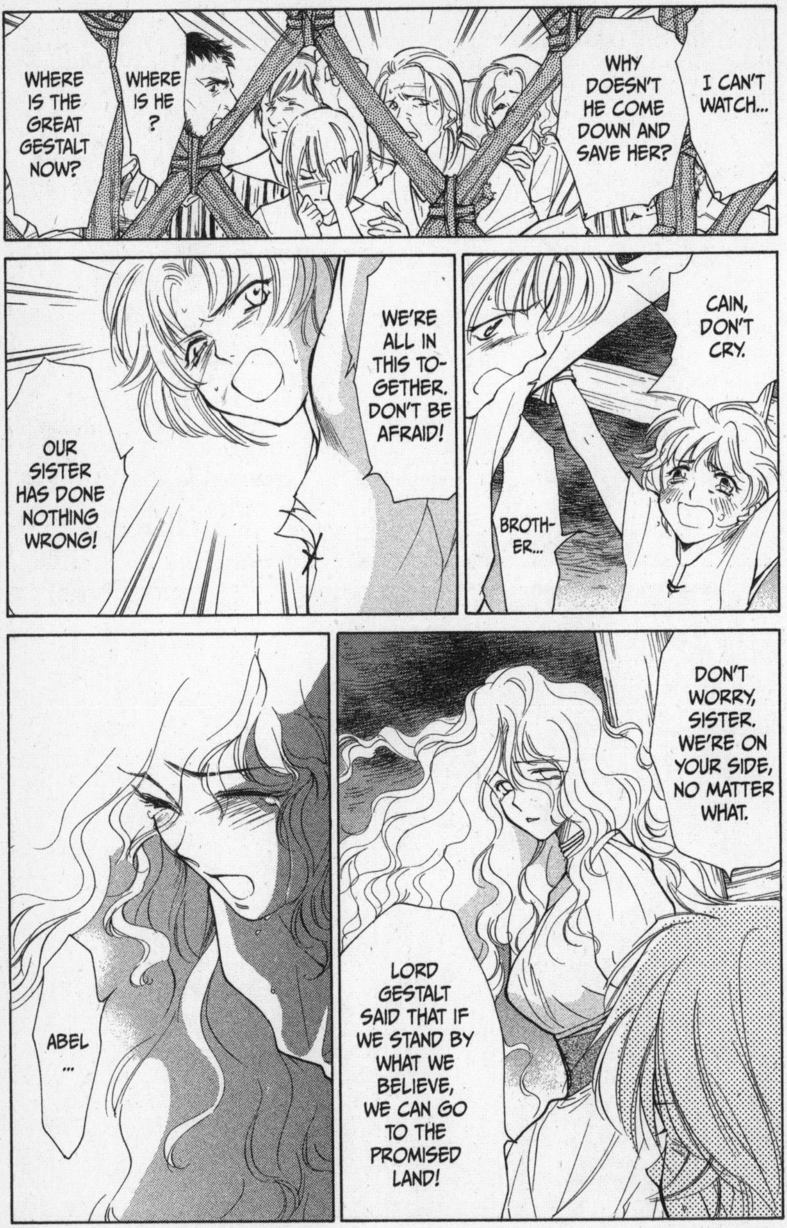
I CAN'T WATCH...
WHY DOESN'T HE COME DOWN AND SAVE HER?
WHERE IS HE ?
WHERE IS THE GREAT GESTALT NOW?
CAIN, DON'T CRY.
BROTHER...
WE'RE ALL IN THIS TOGETHER. DON'T BE AFRAID!
OUR SISTER HAS DONE NOTHING WRONG!
DON'T WORRY, SISTER. WE'RE ON YOUR SIDE, NO MATTER WHAT.
LORD GESTALT SAID THAT IF WE STAND BY WHAT WE BELIEVE, WE CAN GO TO THE PROMISED LAND!
ABEL ...

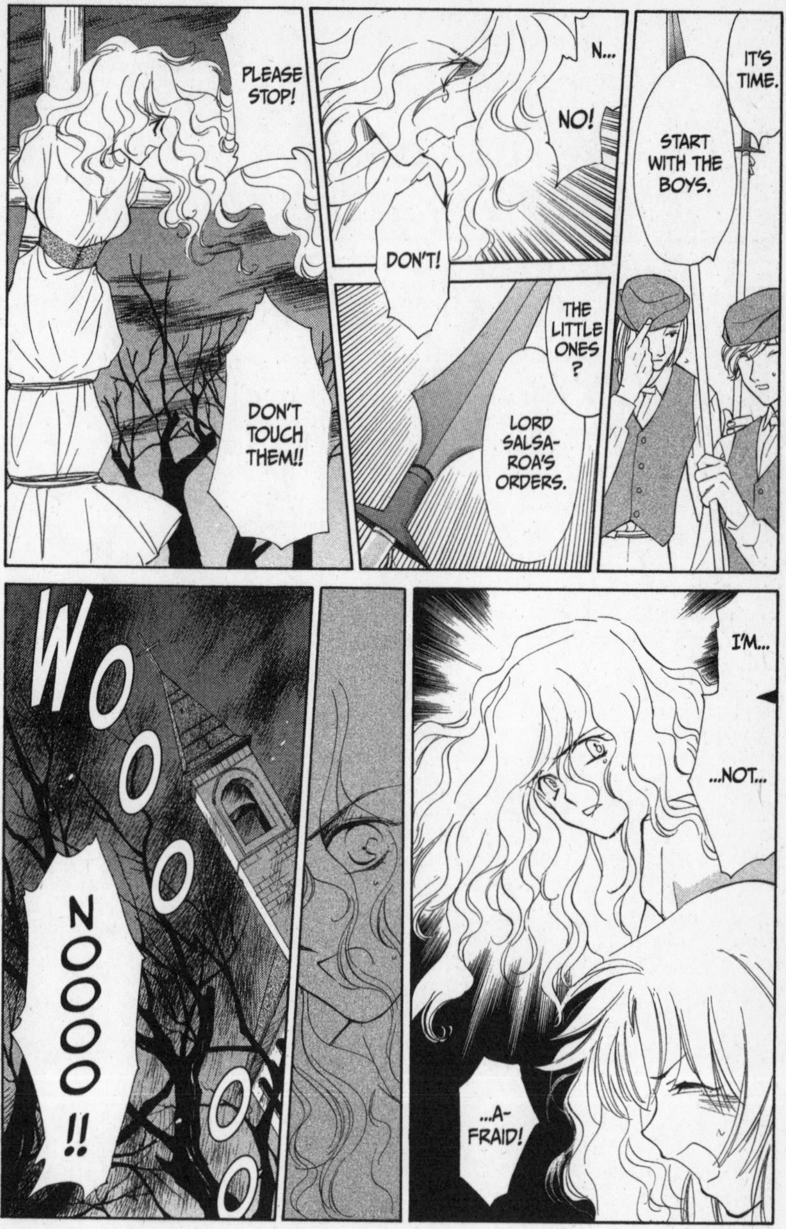
IT'S TIME.
START WITH THE BOYS.
N...
NO!
DON'T!
THE LITTLE ONES?
LORD SALSA-ROA'S ORDERS.
PLEASE STOP!
DON'T TOUCH THEM!!
I'M...
...NOT...
...A-FRAID!
WOOOOOO
NOOOO!!

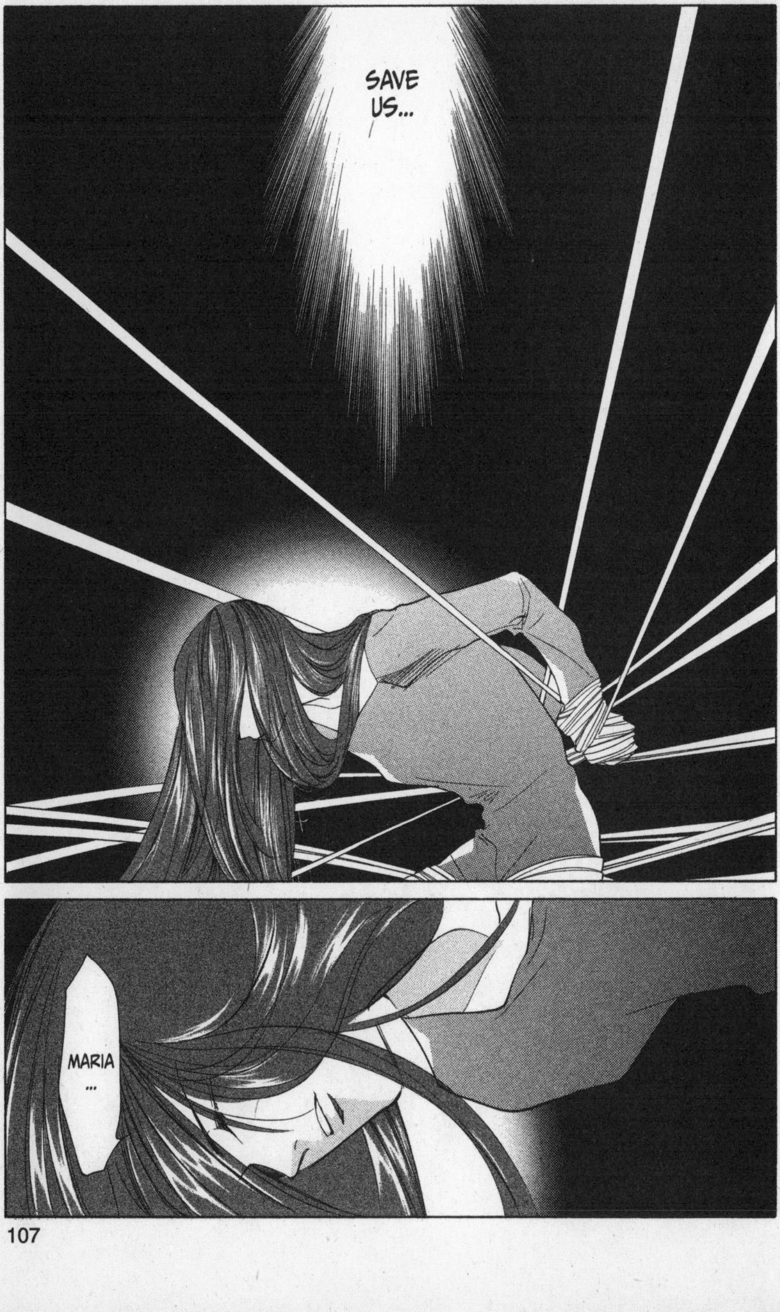
SAVE US...
MARIA
...

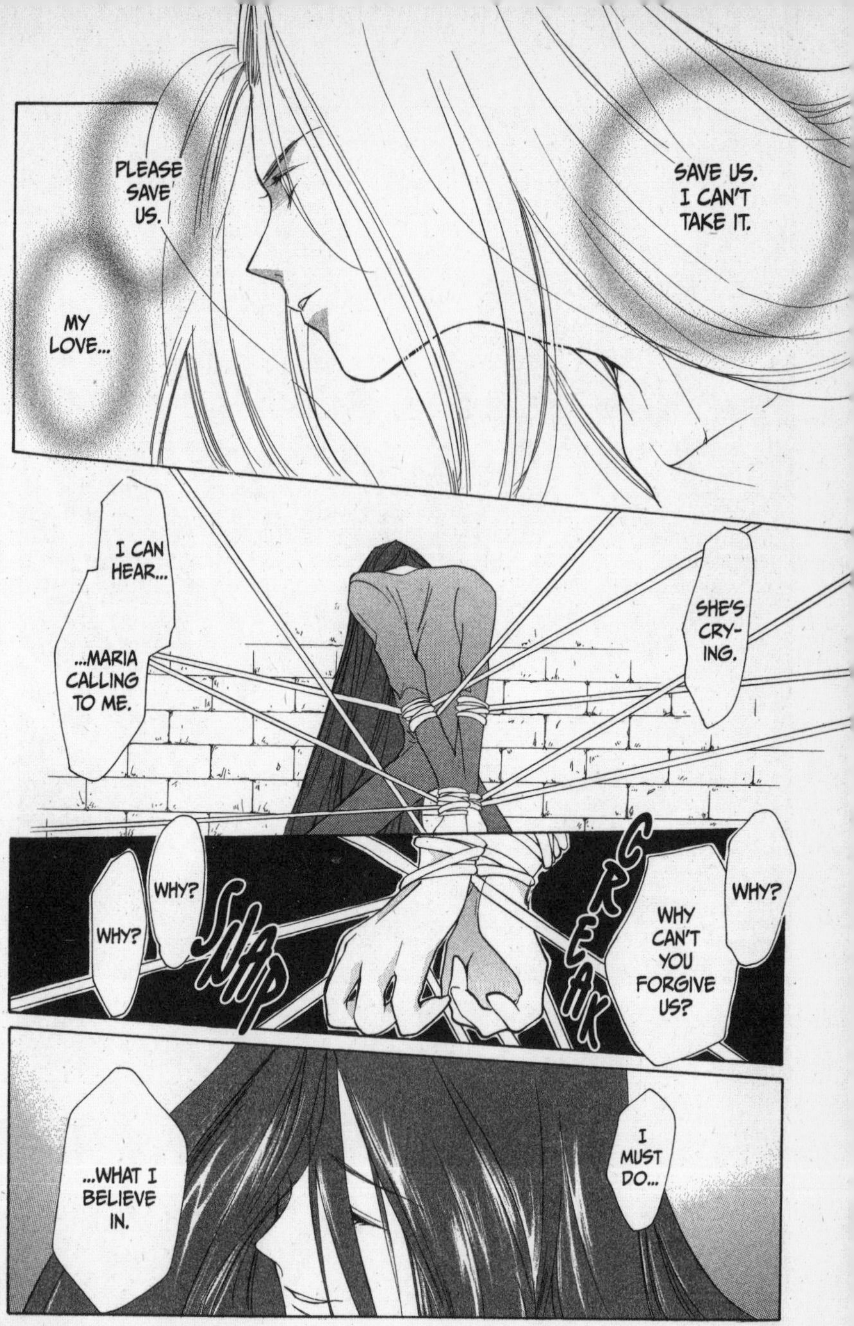
SAVE US. I CAN'T TAKE IT.
PLEASE SAVE US.
MY LOVE...
SHE'S CRY-ING.
I CAN HEAR...
...MARIA CALLING TO ME.
WHY?
WHY CAN'T YOU FORGIVE US?
CREAK
SNAP
WHY?
WHY?
I MUST DO...
...WHAT I BELIEVE IN.

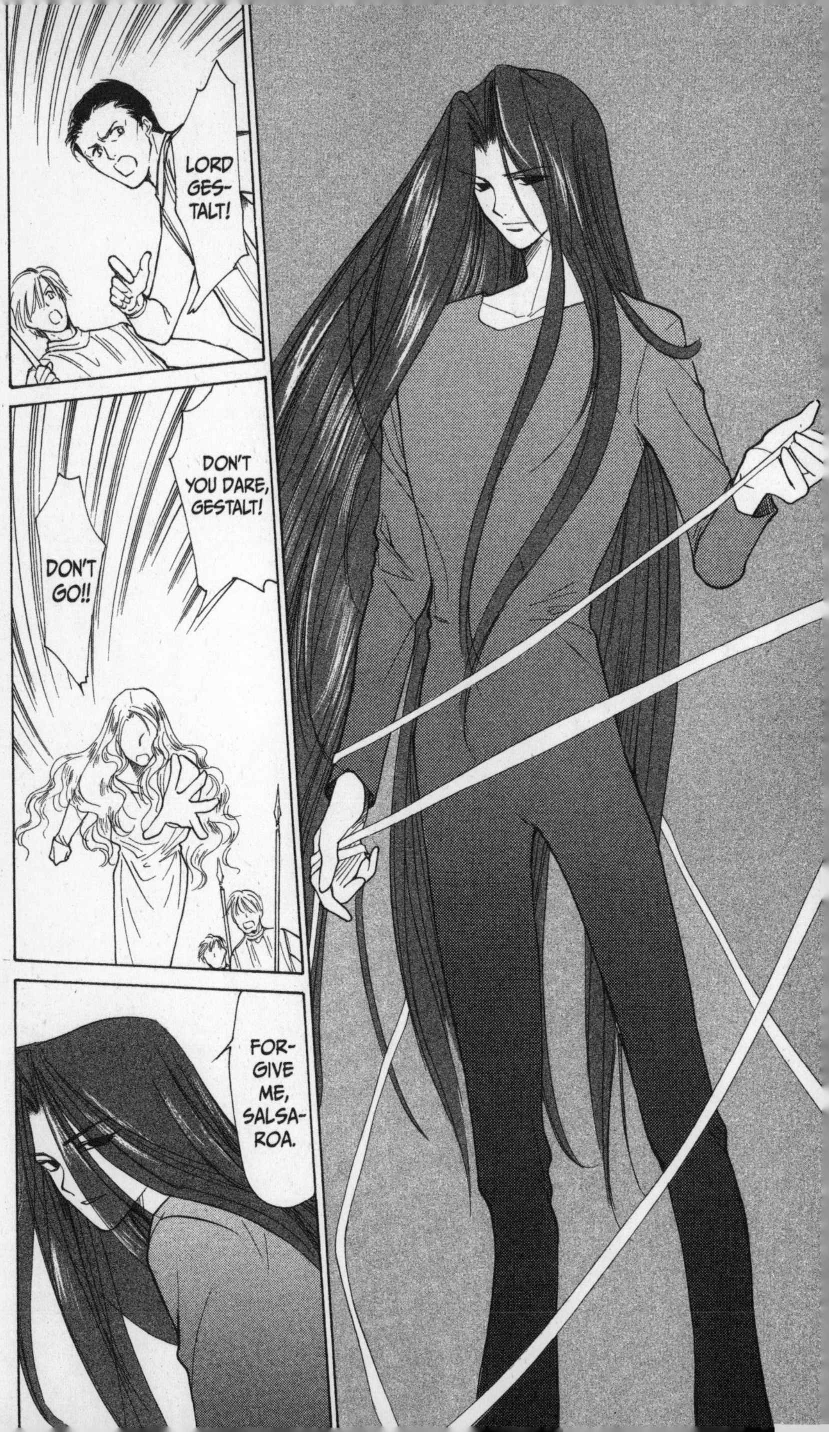
LORD GES-TALT!
DON'T YOU DARE, GESTALT!
DON'T GO!!
FOR-GIVE ME, SALSA-ROA.

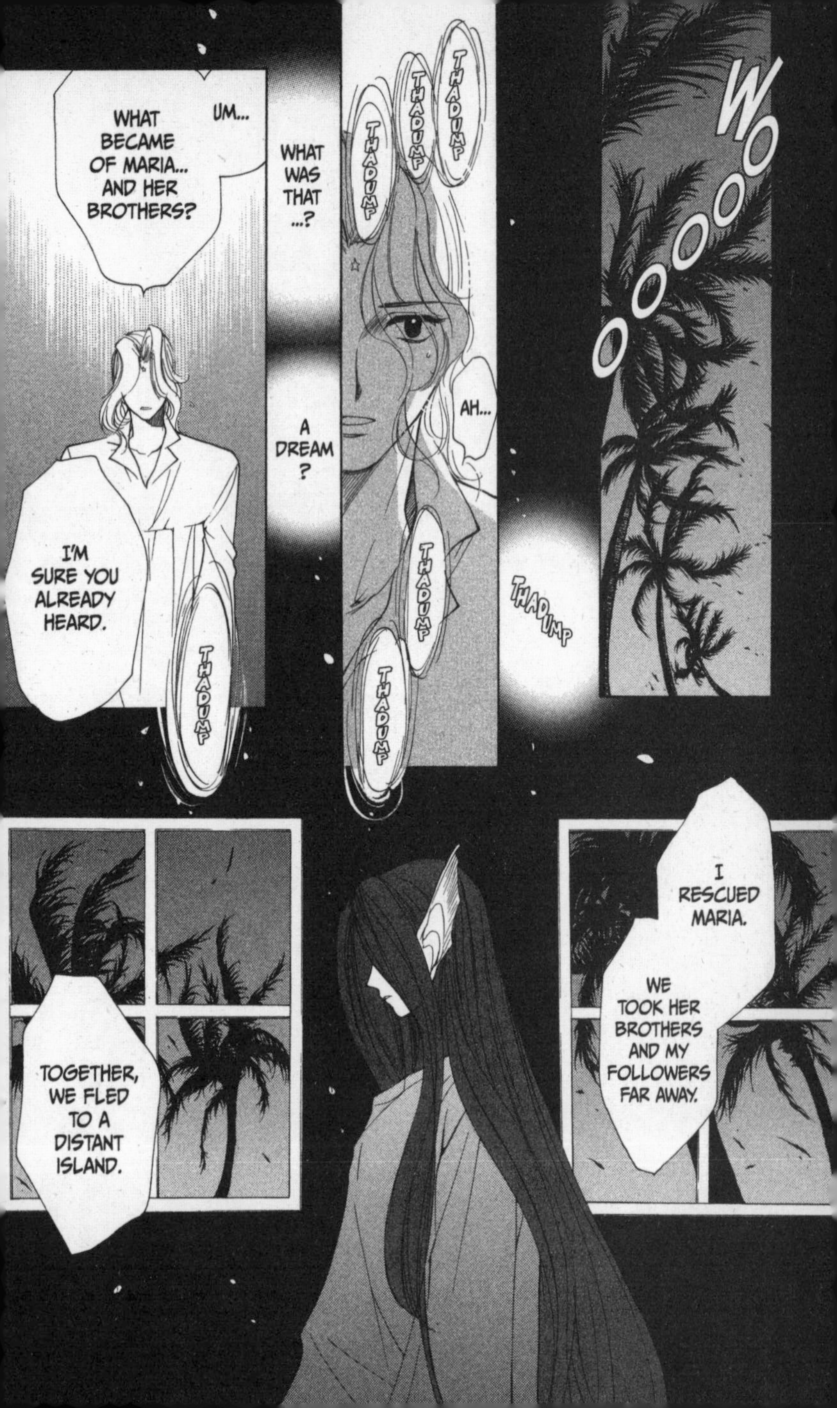
WOOOOOOO
THADUMP
THADUMP
THADUMP
AH...
THADUMP
THADUMP
THADUMP
WHAT WAS THAT ...?
A DREAM ?
UM...
WHAT BECAME OF MARIA... AND HER BROTHERS?
I'M SURE YOU ALREADY HEARD.
THADUMP
I RESCUED MARIA.
WE TOOK HER BROTHERS AND MY FOLLOWERS FAR AWAY.
TOGETHER, WE FLED TO A DISTANT ISLAND.

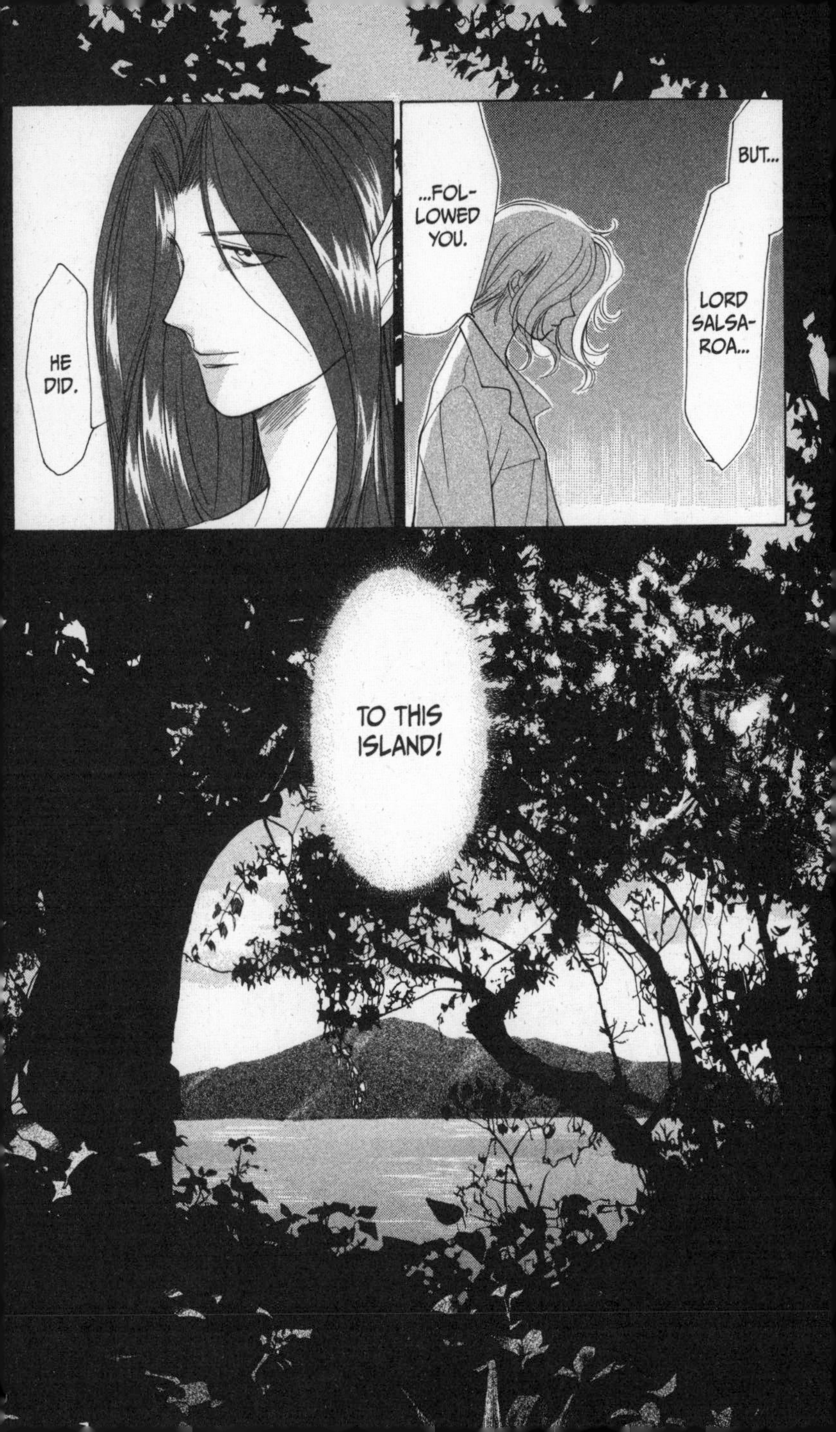
BUT... LORD SALSA-ROA...
...FOL-LOWED YOU.
HE DID.
TO THIS ISLAND!

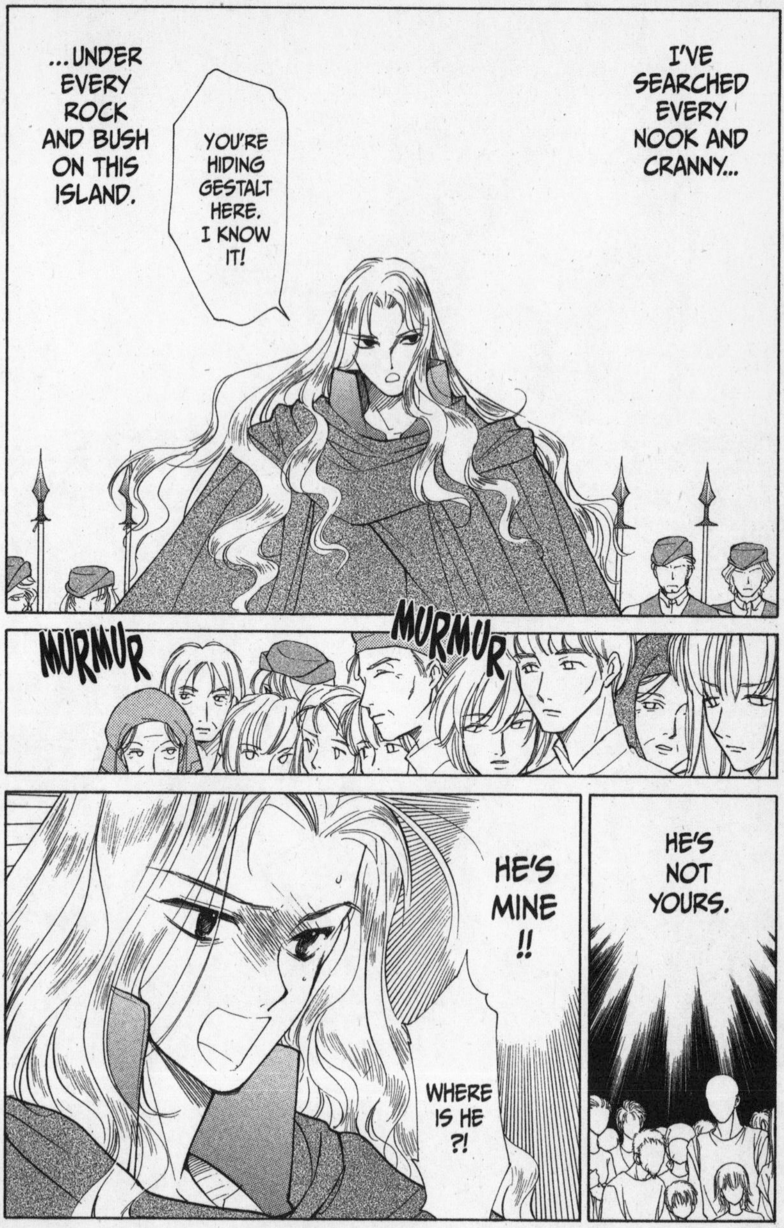
I'VE SEARCHED EVERY NOOK AND CRANNY...
...UNDER EVERY ROCK AND BUSH ON THIS ISLAND.
YOU'RE HIDING GESTALT HERE. I KNOW IT!
MURMUR
MURMUR
HE'S NOT YOURS.
HE'S MINE!!
WHERE IS HE?!

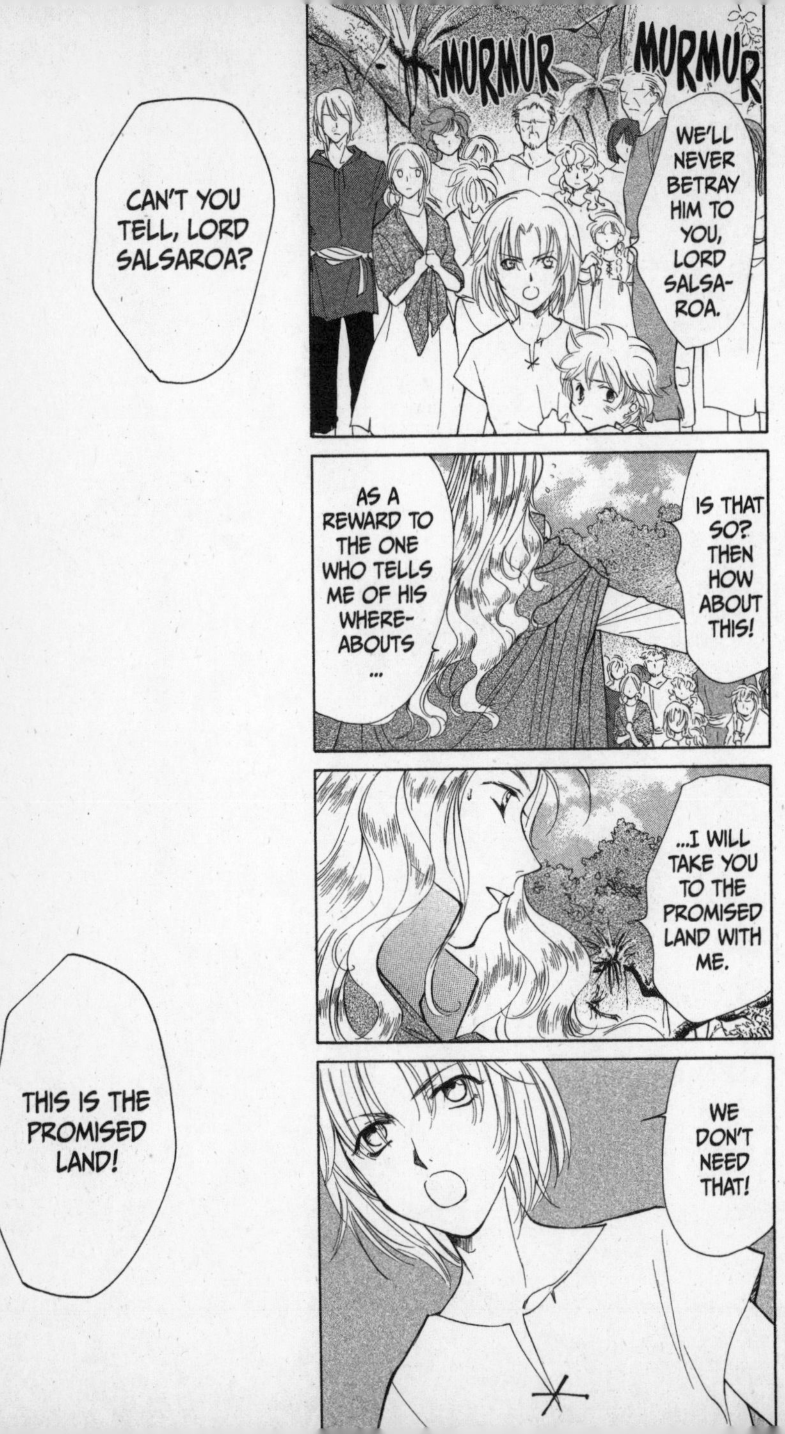
MURMUR
MURMUR
WE'LL NEVER BETRAY HIM TO YOU, LORD SALSA-ROA.
CAN'T YOU TELL, LORD SALSAROA?
IS THAT SO? THEN HOW ABOUT THIS!
AS A REWARD TO THE ONE WHO TELLS ME OF HIS WHERE-ABOUTS ...
...I WILL TAKE YOU TO THE PROMISED LAND WITH ME.
WE DON'T NEED THAT!
THIS IS THE PROMISED LAND!

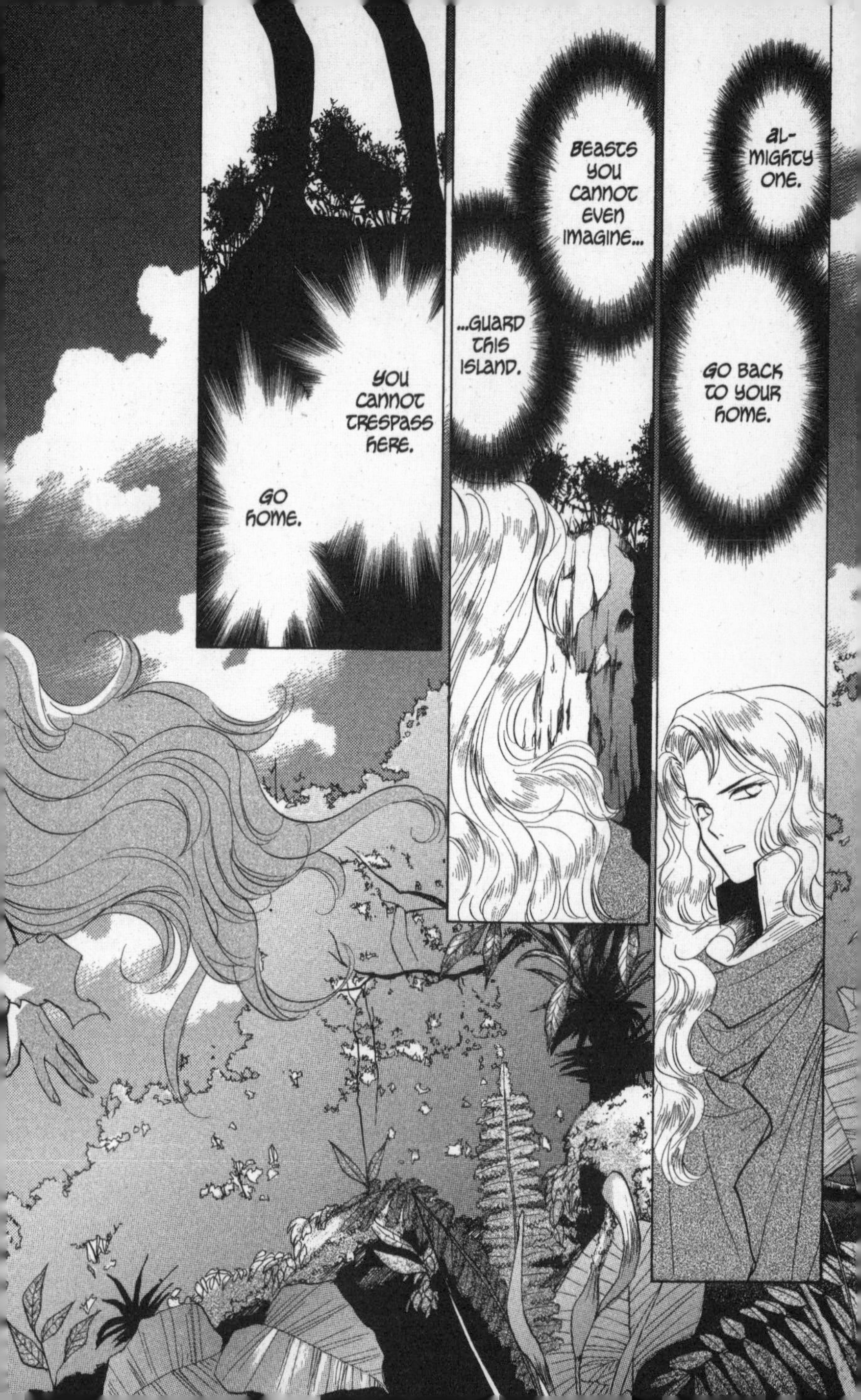
AL-MIGHTY ONE.
GO BACK TO YOUR HOME.
BEASTS YOU CANNOT EVEN IMAGINE...
...GUARD THIS ISLAND.
YOU CANNOT TRESPASS HERE.
GO HOME.

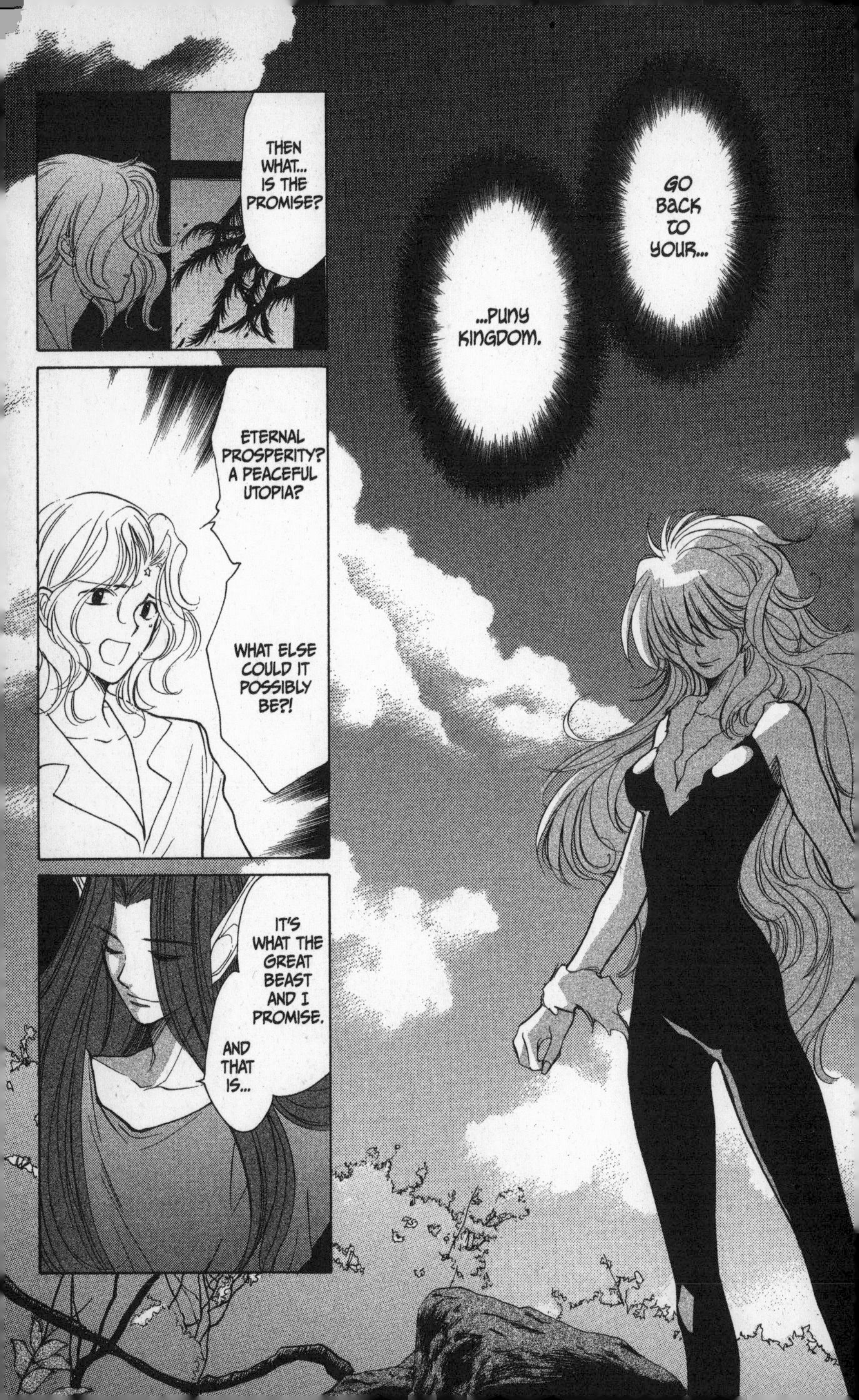
GO BACK TO YOUR...
...PUNY KINGDOM.
THEN WHAT... IS THE PROMISE?
ETERNAL PROSPERITY? A PEACEFUL UTOPIA?
WHAT ELSE COULD IT POSSIBLY BE?!
IT'S WHAT THE GREAT BEAST AND I PROMISE.
AND THAT IS...

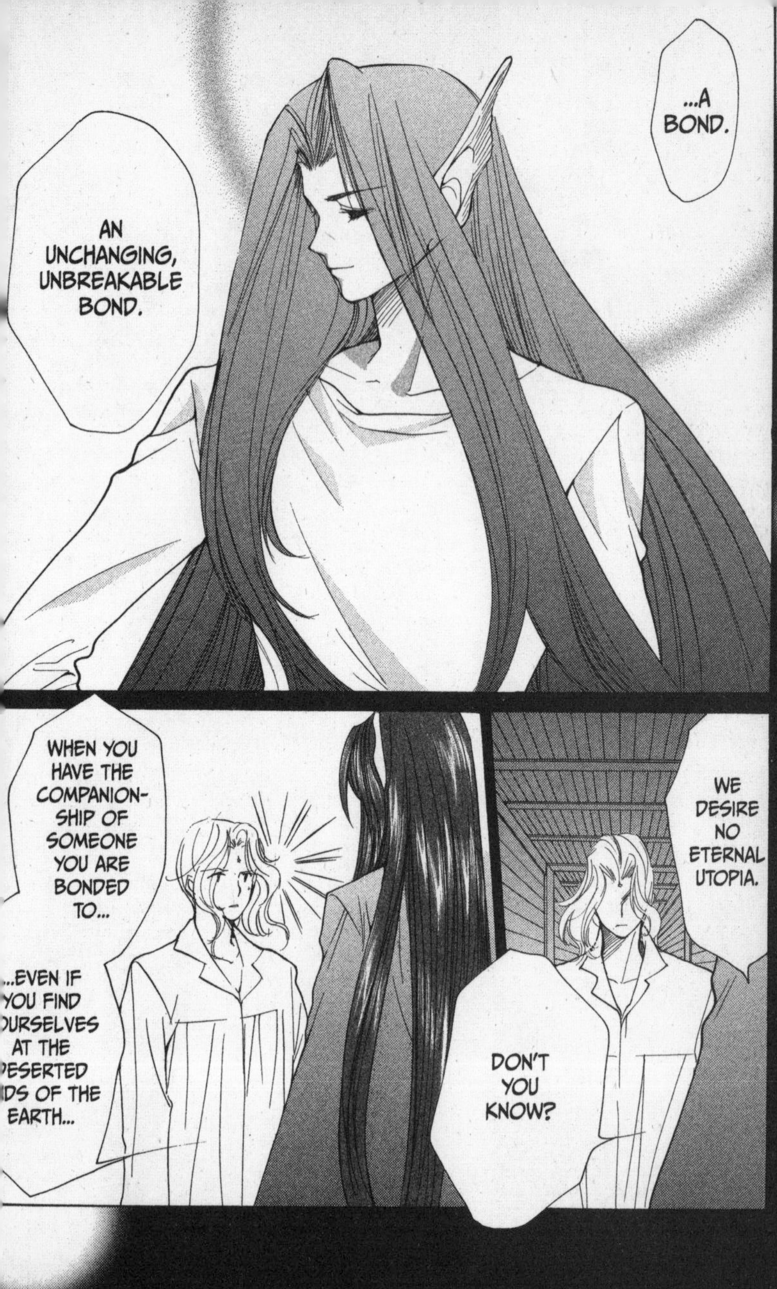
...A BOND.
AN UNCHANGING, UNBREAKABLE BOND.
WE DESIRE NO ETERNAL UTOPIA.
DON'T YOU KNOW?
WHEN YOU HAVE THE COMPANION-SHIP OF SOMEONE YOU ARE BONDED TO...
...EVEN IF YOU FIND OURSELVES AT THE ESERTED DS OF THE EARTH...

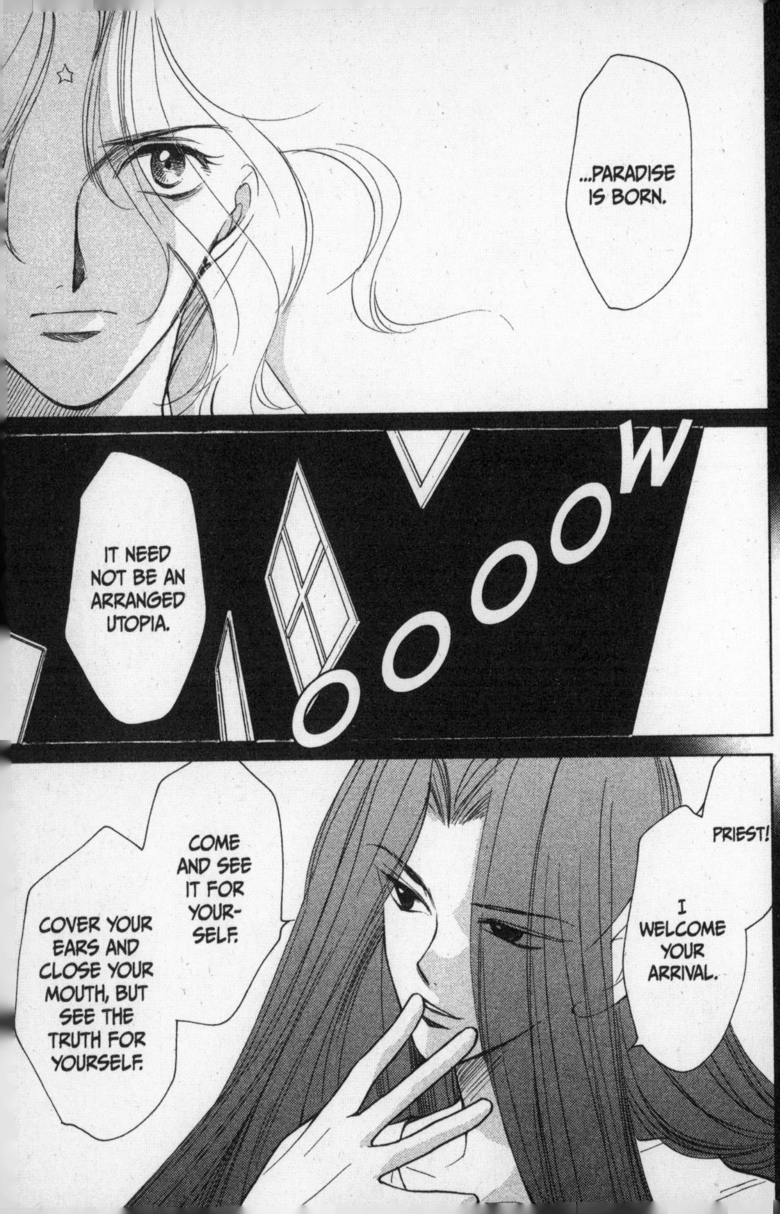
...PARADISE IS BORN.
IT NEED NOT BE AN ARRANGED UTOPIA.
OOOOOOW
PRIEST!
I WELCOME YOUR ARRIVAL.
COME AND SEE IT FOR YOUR-SELF.
COVER YOUR EARS AND CLOSE YOUR MOUTH, BUT SEE THE TRUTH FOR YOURSELF.

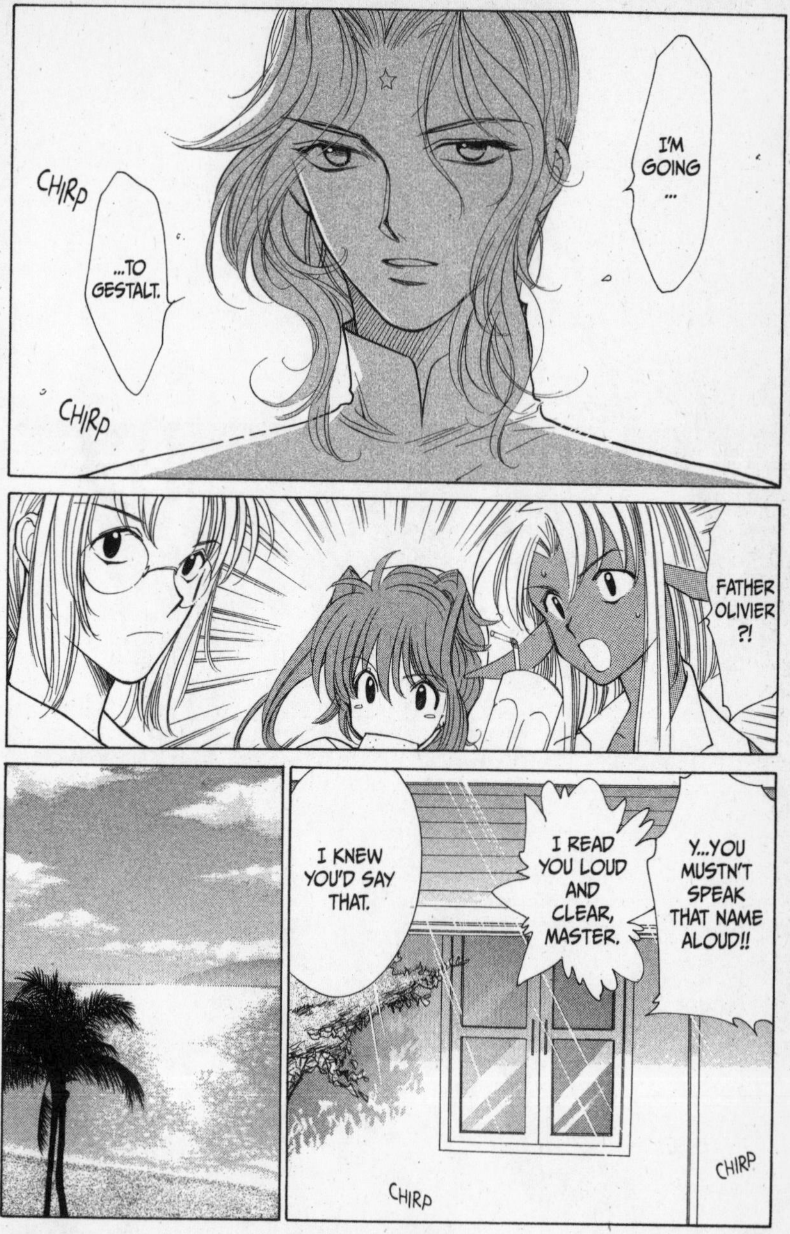
I'M GOING ...
...TO GESTALT.
CHIRP
CHIRP
FATHER OLIVIER ?!
Y...YOU MUSTN'T SPEAK THAT NAME ALOUD!!
I READ YOU LOUD AND CLEAR, MASTER.
I KNEW YOU'D SAY THAT.
CHIRP
CHIRP

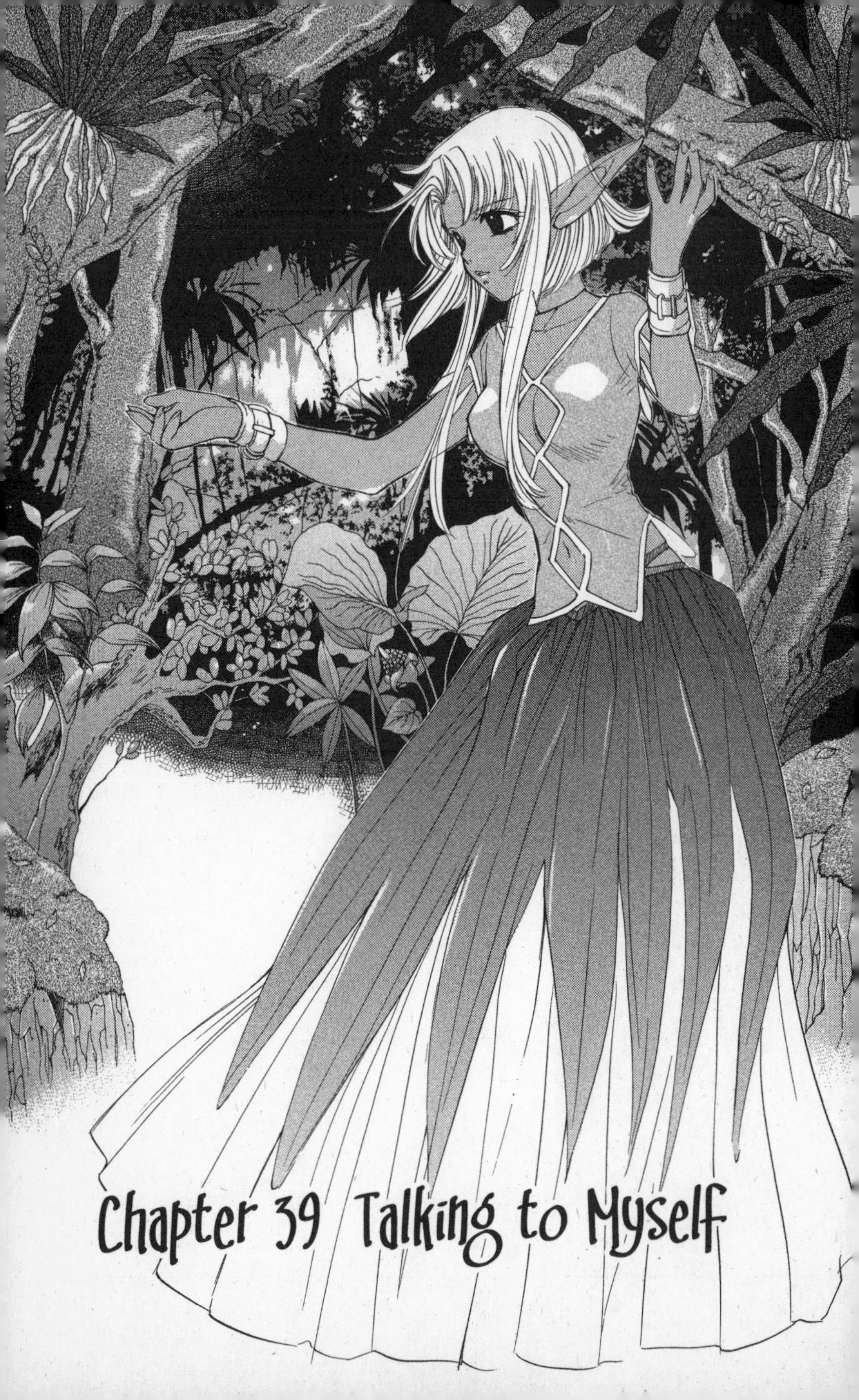
Chapter 39 Talking to Myself

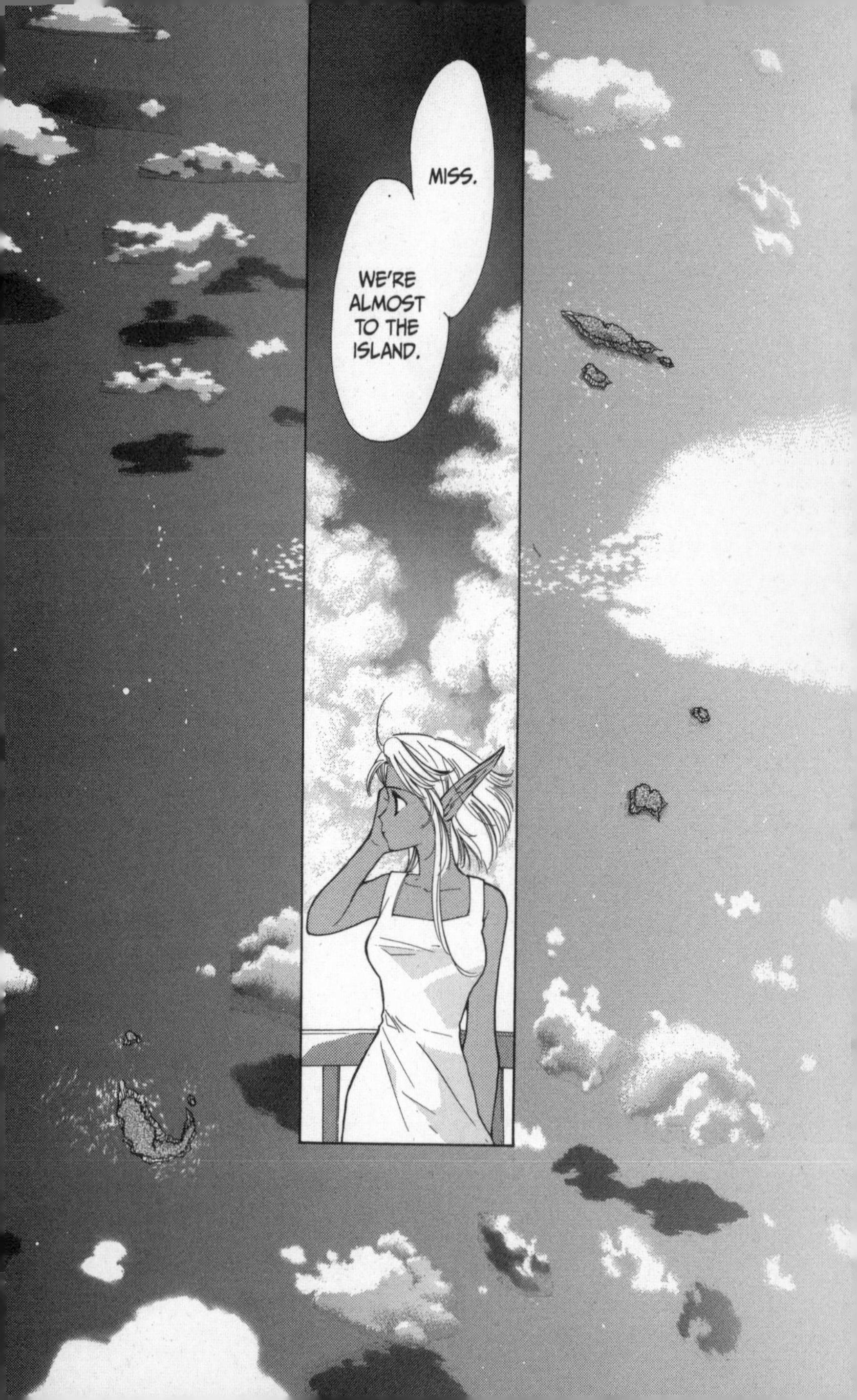
MISS.
WE'RE ALMOST TO THE ISLAND.

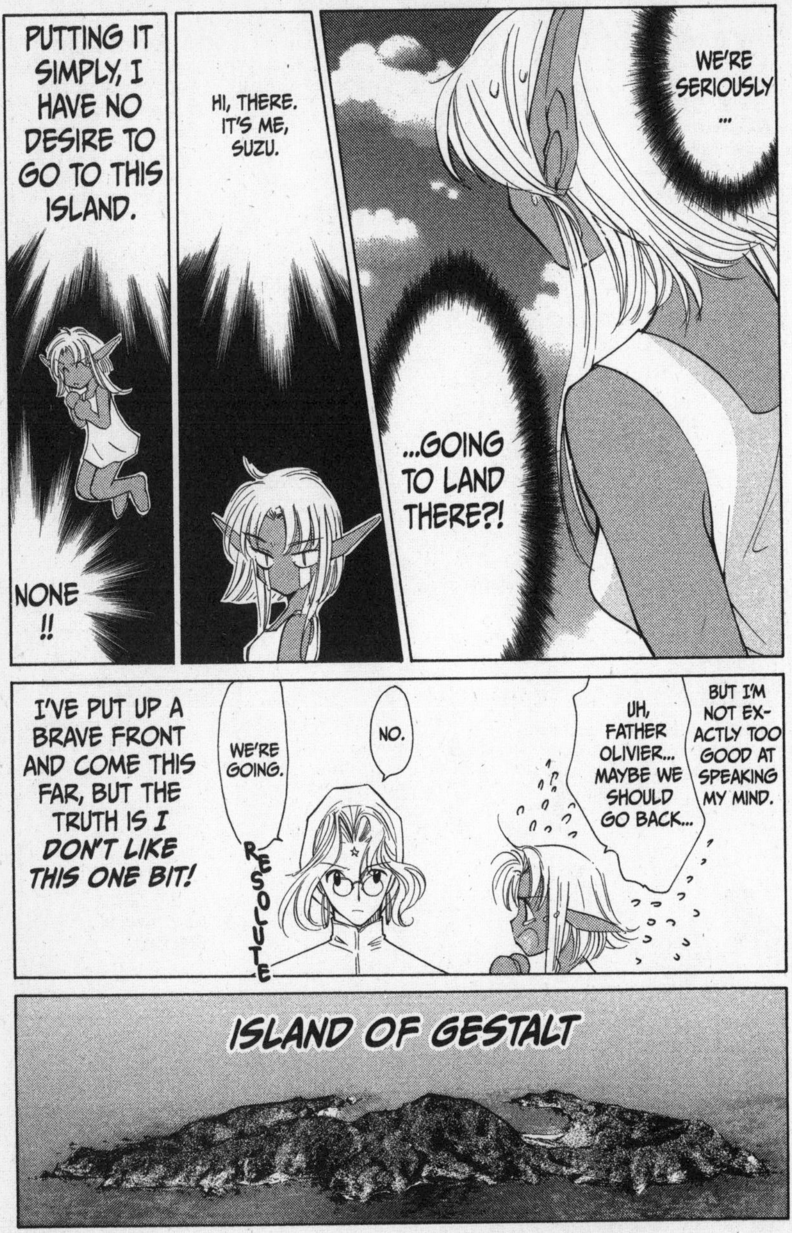
WE'RE SERIOUSLY ...
...GOING TO LAND THERE?!
HI, THERE. IT'S ME, SUZU.
PUTTING IT SIMPLY, I HAVE NO DESIRE TO GO TO THIS ISLAND.
NONE !!
BUT I'M NOT EX-ACTLY TOO GOOD AT SPEAKING MY MIND.
UH, FATHER OLIVIER... MAYBE WE SHOULD GO BACK...
NO.
WE'RE GOING.
RESOLUTE
I'VE PUT UP A BRAVE FRONT AND COME THIS FAR, BUT THE TRUTH IS I DON'T LIKE THIS ONE BIT!
ISLAND OF GESTALT

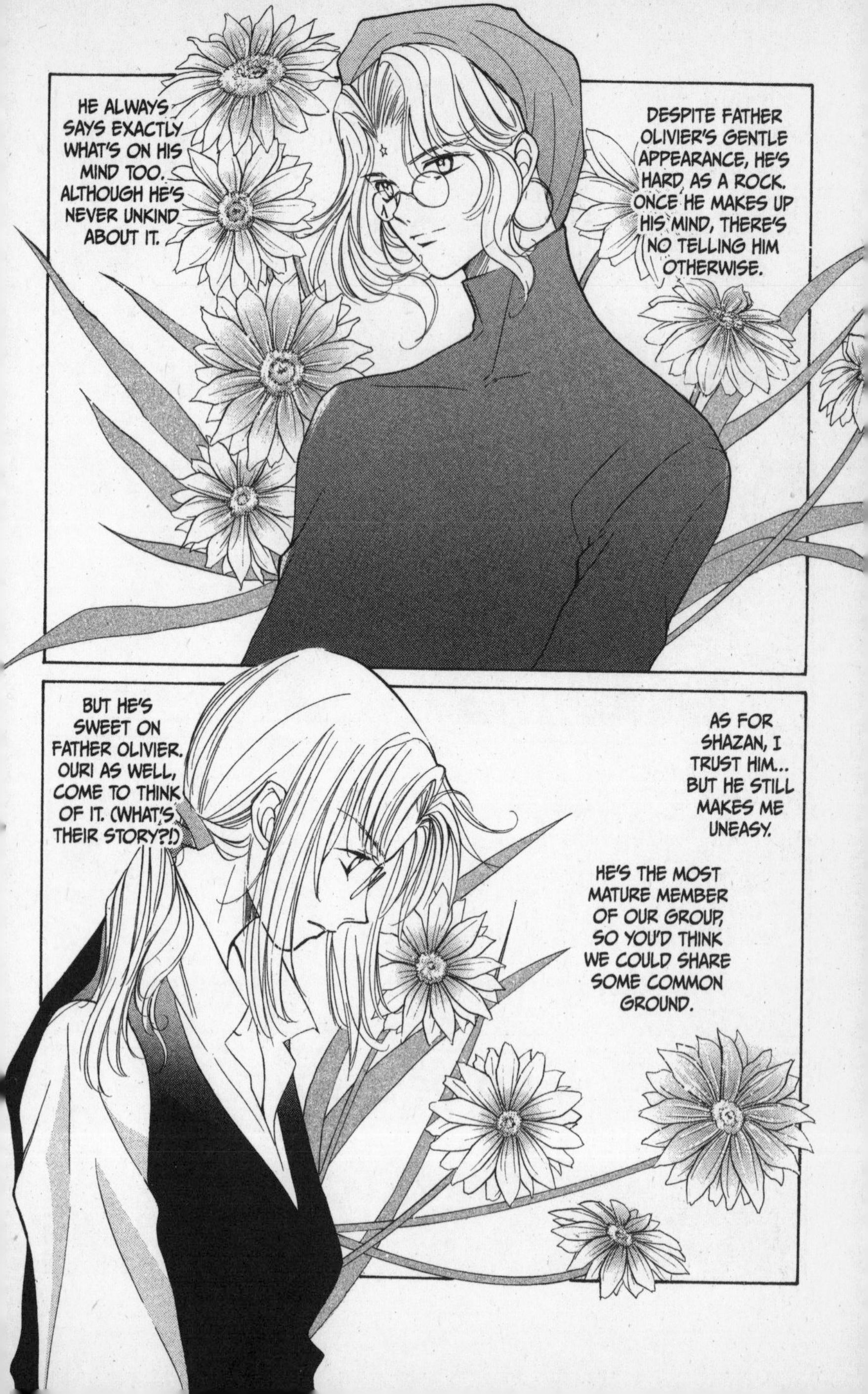
DESPITE FATHER OLIVIER'S GENTLE APPEARANCE, HE'S HARD AS A ROCK. ONCE HE MAKES UP HIS MIND, THERE'S NO TELLING HIM OTHERWISE.
HE ALWAYS SAYS EXACTLY WHAT'S ON HIS MIND TOO. ALTHOUGH HE'S NEVER UNKIND ABOUT IT.
AS FOR SHAZAN, I TRUST HIM... BUT HE STILL MAKES ME UNEASY.
HE'S THE MOST MATURE MEMBER OF OUR GROUP, SO YOU'D THINK WE COULD SHARE SOME COMMON GROUND.
BUT HE'S SWEET ON FATHER OLIVIER. OURI AS WELL, COME TO THINK OF IT. (WHAT'S THEIR STORY?!)

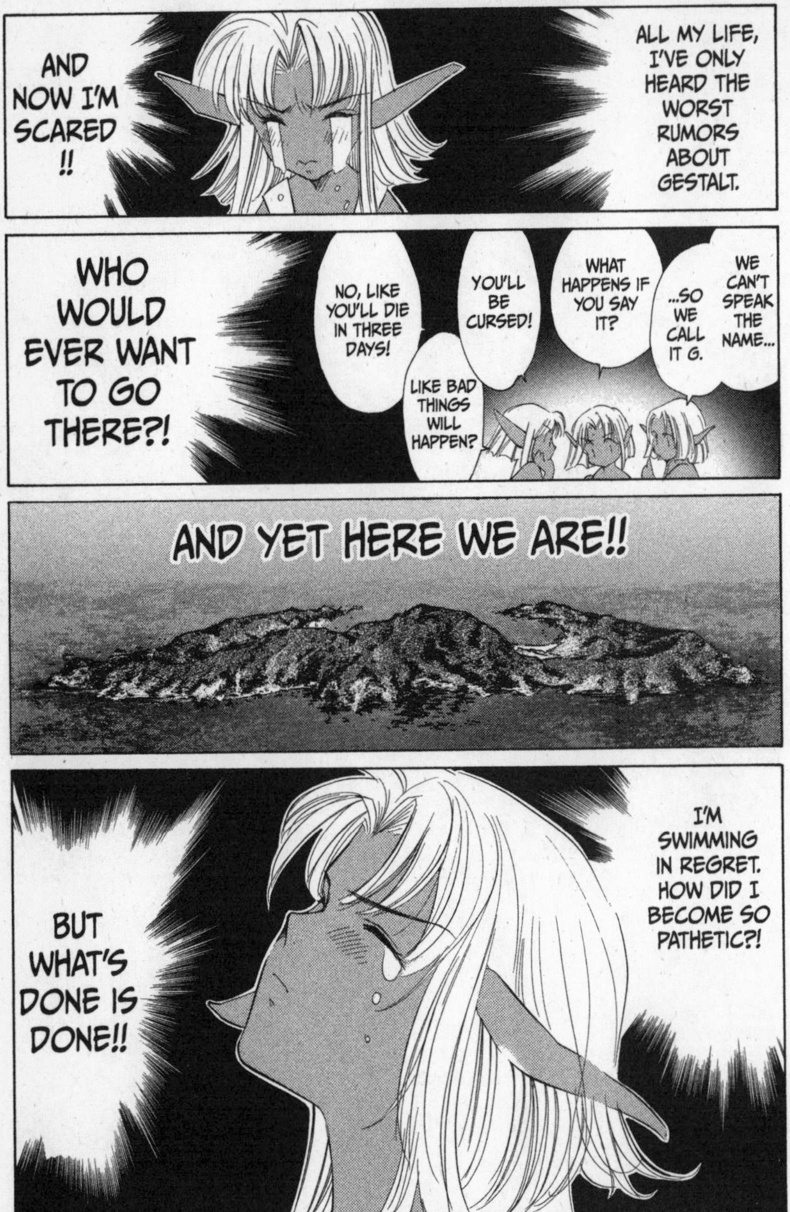
ALL MY LIFE, I'VE ONLY HEARD THE WORST RUMORS ABOUT GESTALT.
AND NOW I'M SCARED!!
WE CAN'T SPEAK THE NAME...
...SO WE CALL IT G.
WHAT HAPPENS IF YOU SAY IT?
YOU'LL BE CURSED!
LIKE BAD THINGS WILL HAPPEN?
NO, LIKE YOU'LL DIE IN THREE DAYS!
WHO WOULD EVER WANT TO GO THERE?!
AND YET HERE WE ARE!!
I'M SWIMMING IN REGRET. HOW DID I BECOME SO PATHETIC?!
BUT WHAT'S DONE IS DONE!!

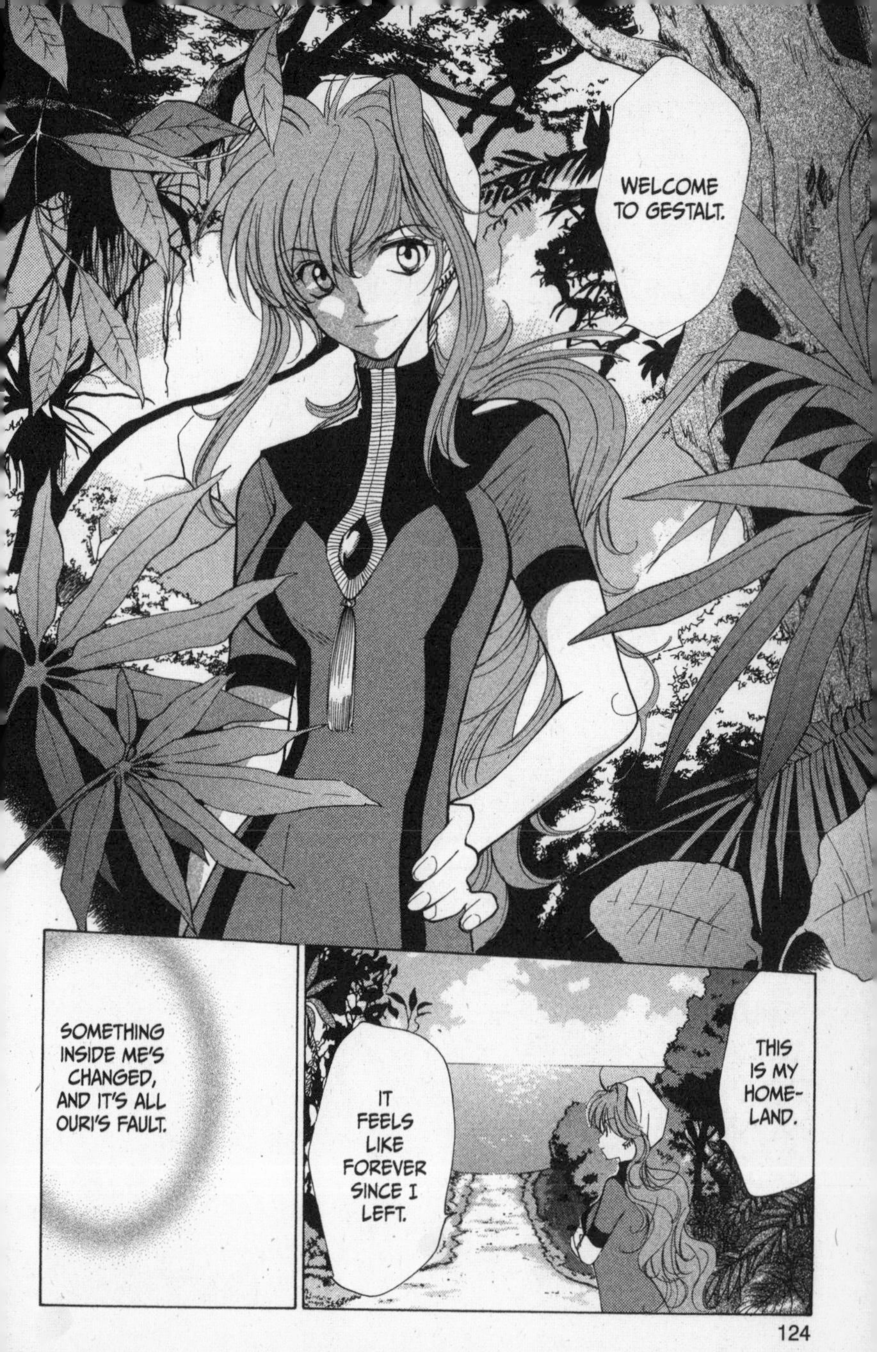
WELCOME TO GESTALT.
THIS IS MY HOME-LAND.
IT FEELS LIKE FOREVER SINCE I LEFT.
SOMETHING INSIDE ME'S CHANGED, AND IT'S ALL OURI'S FAULT.

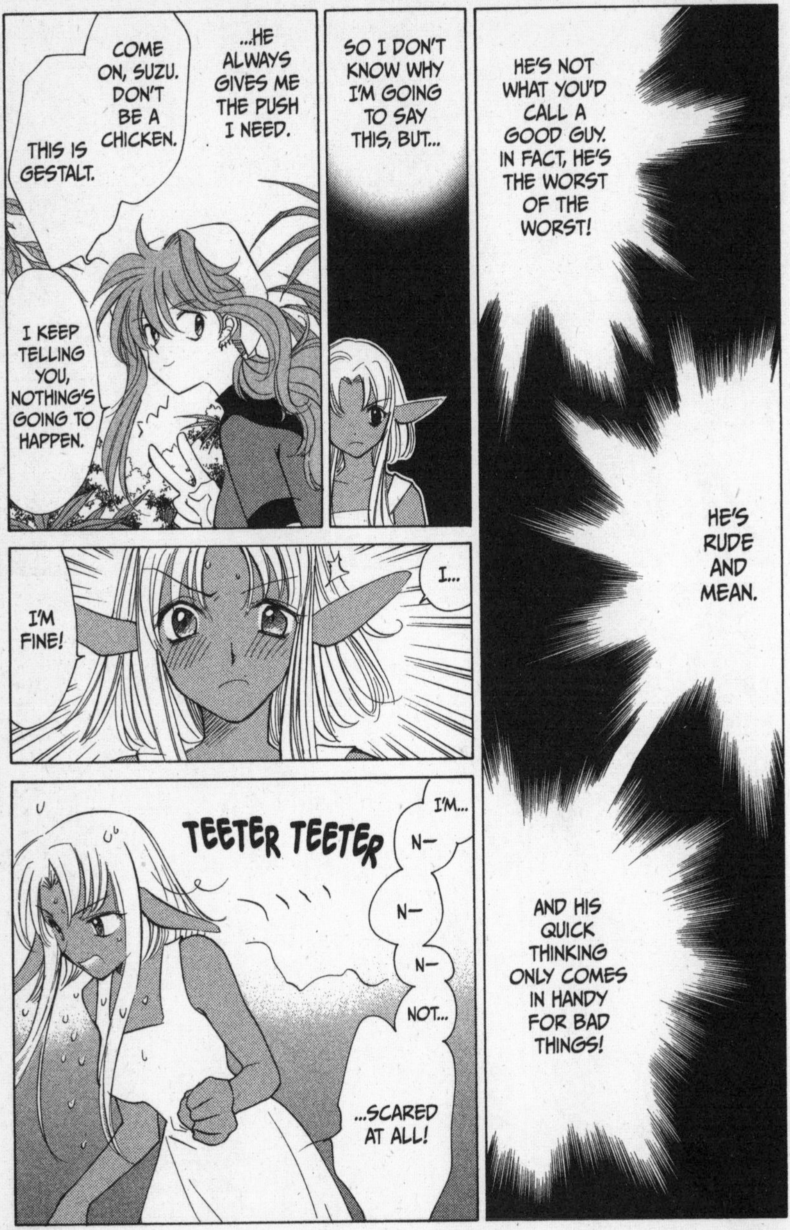
HE'S NOT WHAT YOU'D CALL A GOOD GUY. IN FACT, HE'S THE WORST OF THE WORST!
HE'S RUDE AND MEAN.
AND HIS QUICK THINKING ONLY COMES IN HANDY FOR BAD THINGS!
SO I DON'T KNOW WHY I'M GOING TO SAY THIS, BUT...
...HE ALWAYS GIVES ME THE PUSH I NEED.
COME ON, SUZU. DON'T BE A CHICKEN.
THIS IS GESTALT.
I KEEP TELLING YOU, NOTHING'S GOING TO HAPPEN.
I...
I'M FINE!
I'M...
N—
N—
N—
NOT...
...SCARED AT ALL!
TEETER TEETER

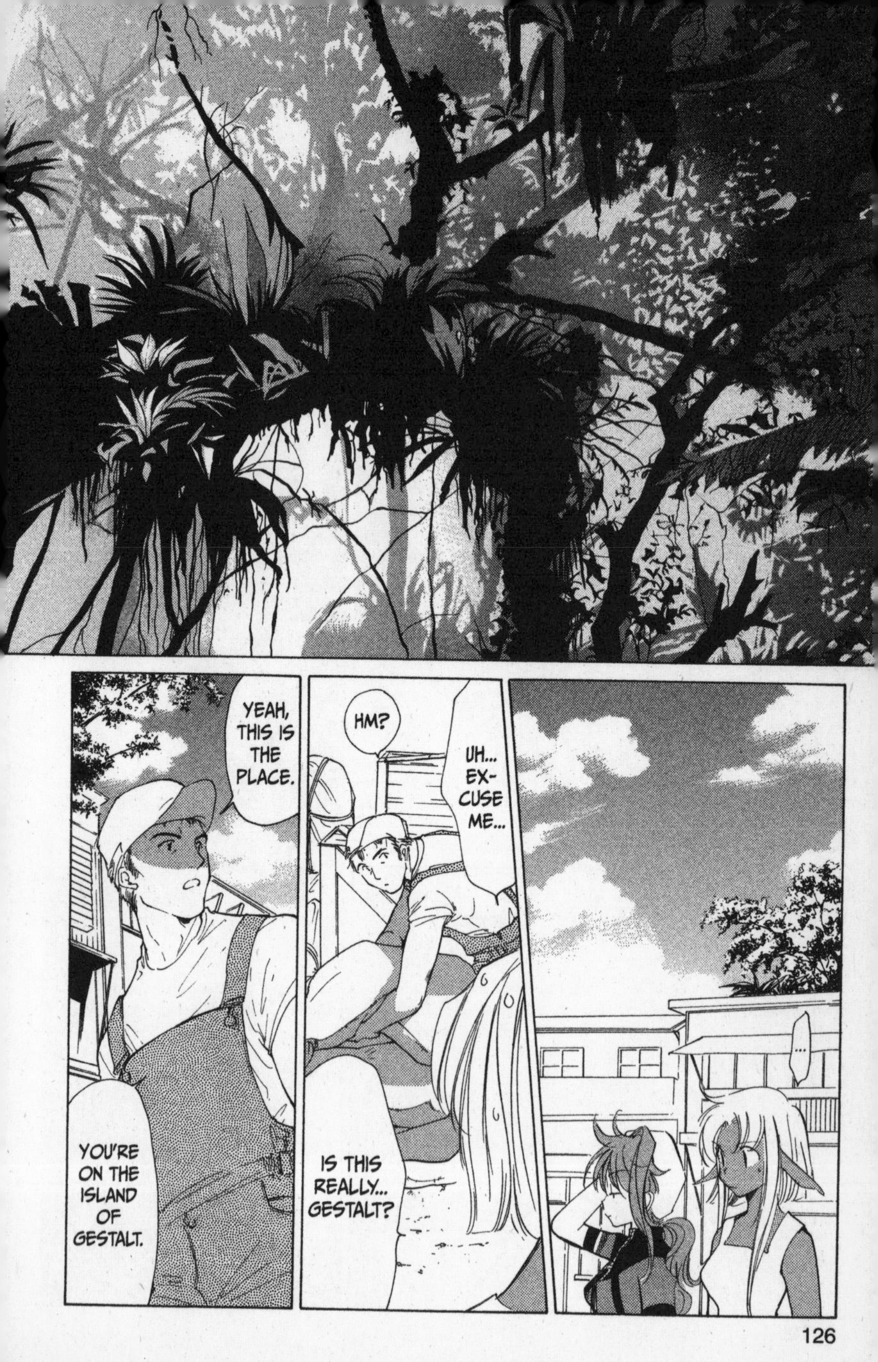
...
UH... EX-CUSE ME...
HM?
IS THIS REALLY... GESTALT?
YEAH, THIS IS THE PLACE.
YOU'RE ON THE ISLAND OF GESTALT.

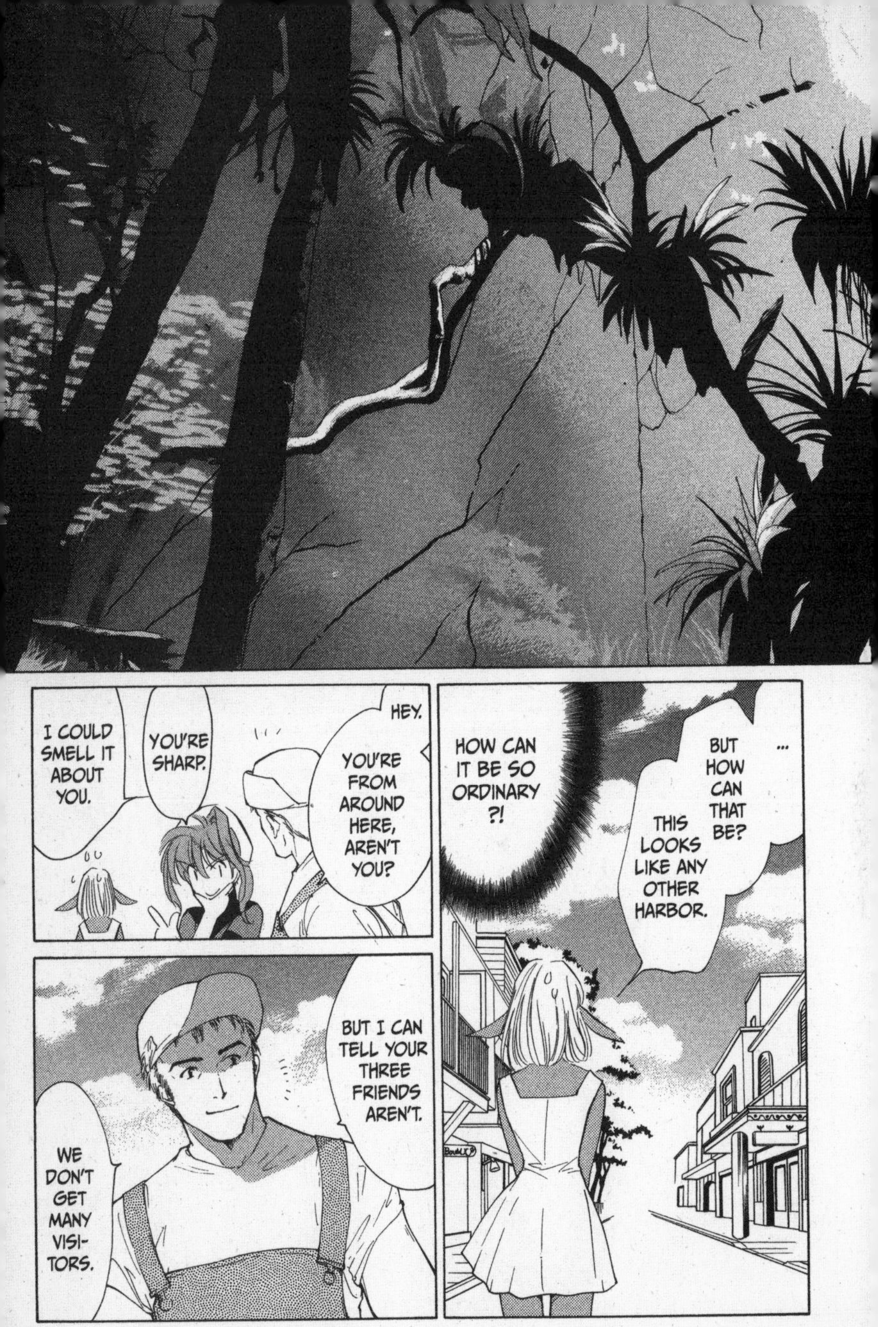
...
BUT HOW CAN THAT BE?
THIS LOOKS LIKE ANY OTHER HARBOR.
HOW CAN IT BE SO ORDINARY ?!
HEY. YOU'RE FROM AROUND HERE, AREN'T YOU?
YOU'RE SHARP.
I COULD SMELL IT ABOUT YOU.
BUT I CAN TELL YOUR THREE FRIENDS AREN'T.
WE DON'T GET MANY VISI-TORS.

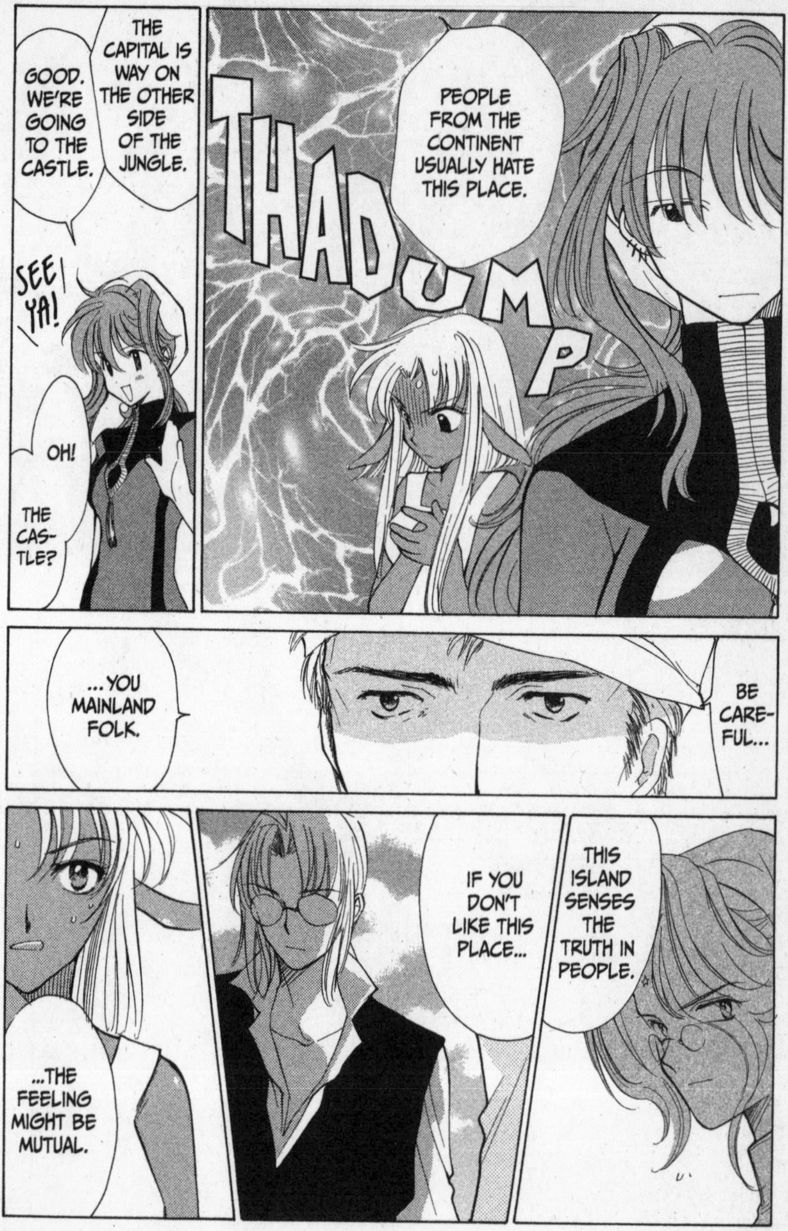
PEOPLE FROM THE CONTINENT USUALLY HATE THIS PLACE.
THADUMP
THE CAPITAL IS WAY ON THE OTHER SIDE OF THE JUNGLE.
GOOD. WE'RE GOING TO THE CASTLE.
SEE YA!
OH!
THE CAS-TLE?
BE CARE-FUL...
...YOU MAINLAND FOLK.
THIS ISLAND SENSES THE TRUTH IN PEOPLE.
IF YOU DON'T LIKE THIS PLACE...
...THE FEELING MIGHT BE MUTUAL.

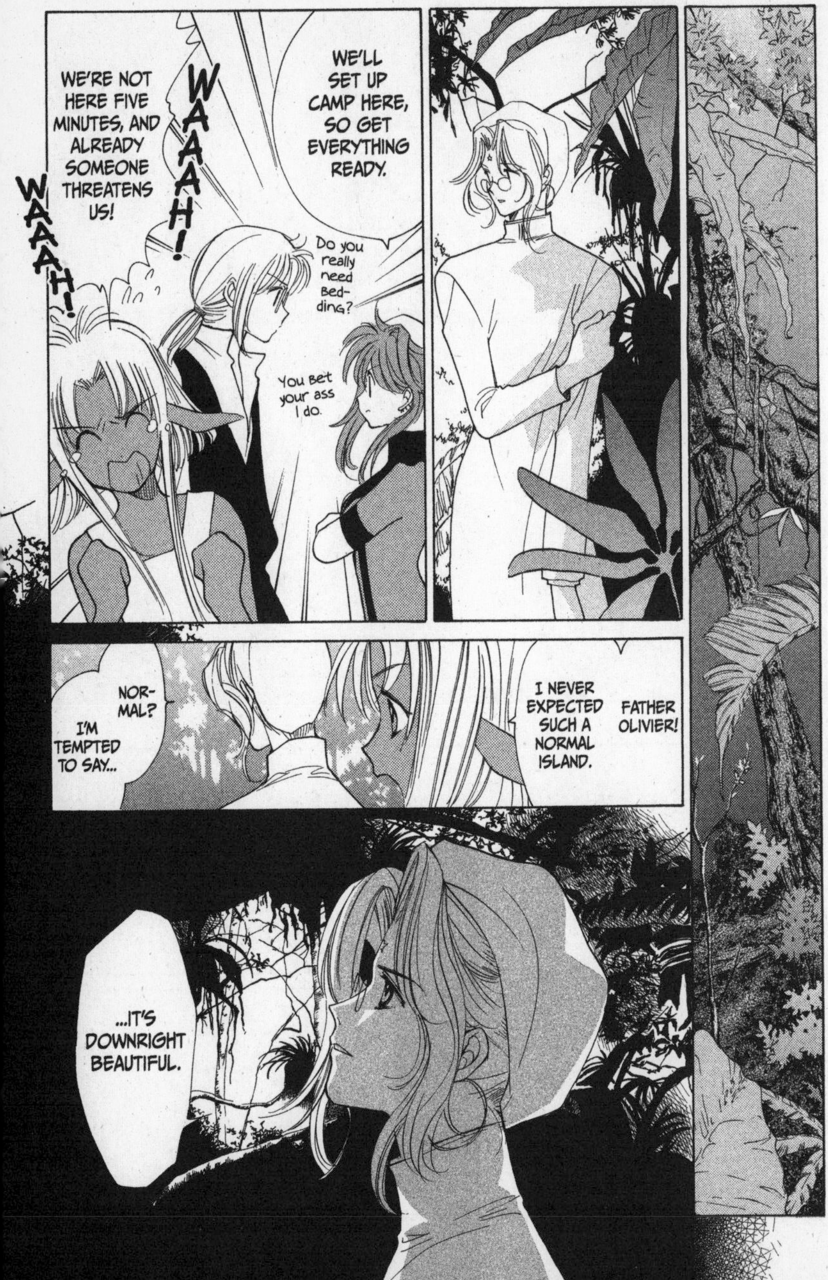
WE'LL SET UP CAMP HERE, SO GET EVERYTHING READY.
WAAAH!
WE'RE NOT HERE FIVE MINUTES, AND ALREADY SOMEONE THREATENS US!
WAAAH!
Do you really need Bed-ding?
You bet your ass I do.
FATHER OLIVIER!
I NEVER EXPECTED SUCH A NORMAL ISLAND.
NOR-MAL? I'M TEMPTED TO SAY...
...IT'S DOWNRIGHT BEAUTIFUL.

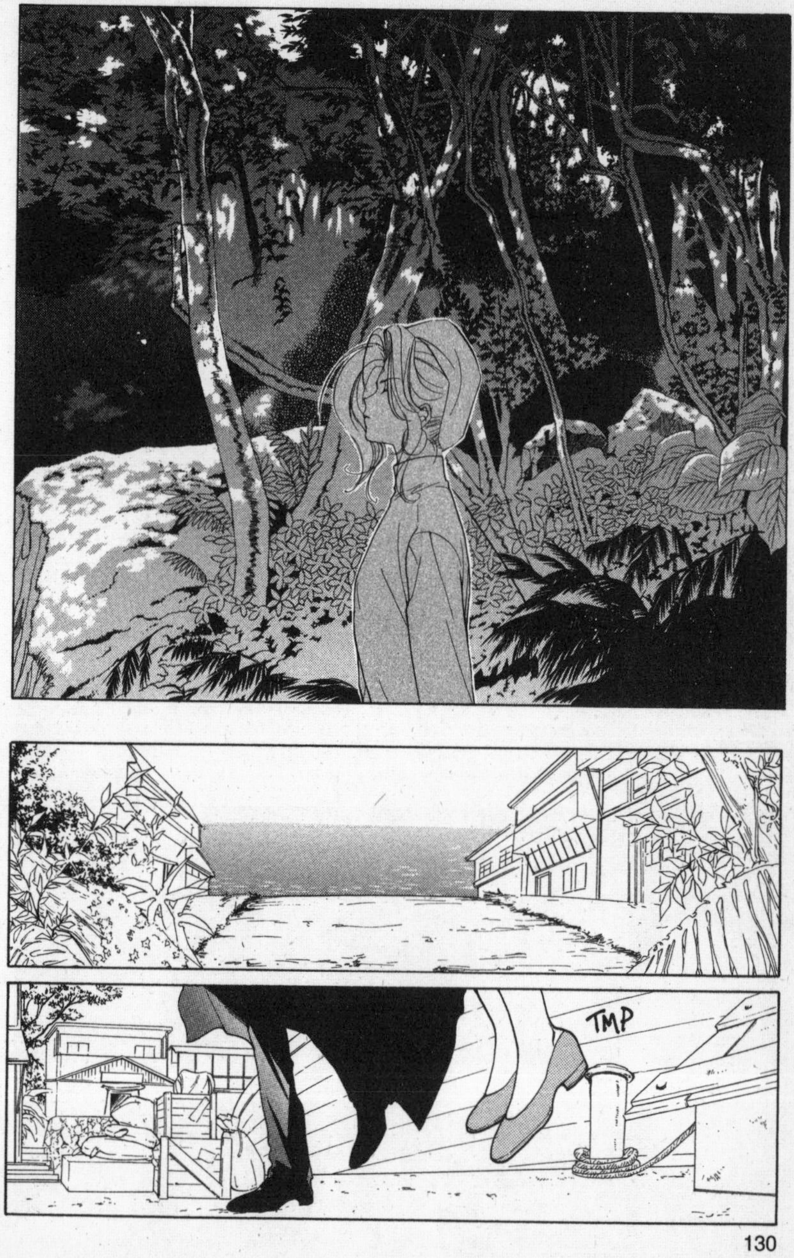
TMP

PHEW!
GOO!
WE FINALLY MADE IT.
SIR, WOULD YOU POINT ME TO THE CAPITAL OF THE ISLAND?
THE CAPITAL?
JUST GO STRAIGHT THATAWAY.
TMP TMP
TMP
IS THE CAPITAL UP AHEAD?
HM?
YEAH, BUT YOU'VE STILL A WAYS TO GO.
SKFF
SKFF
SKFF
THANKS.
WOW...
MUST BE A BLUE MOON OUT.
WE'VE NEVER HAD SO MANY VISITORS IN TOWN.

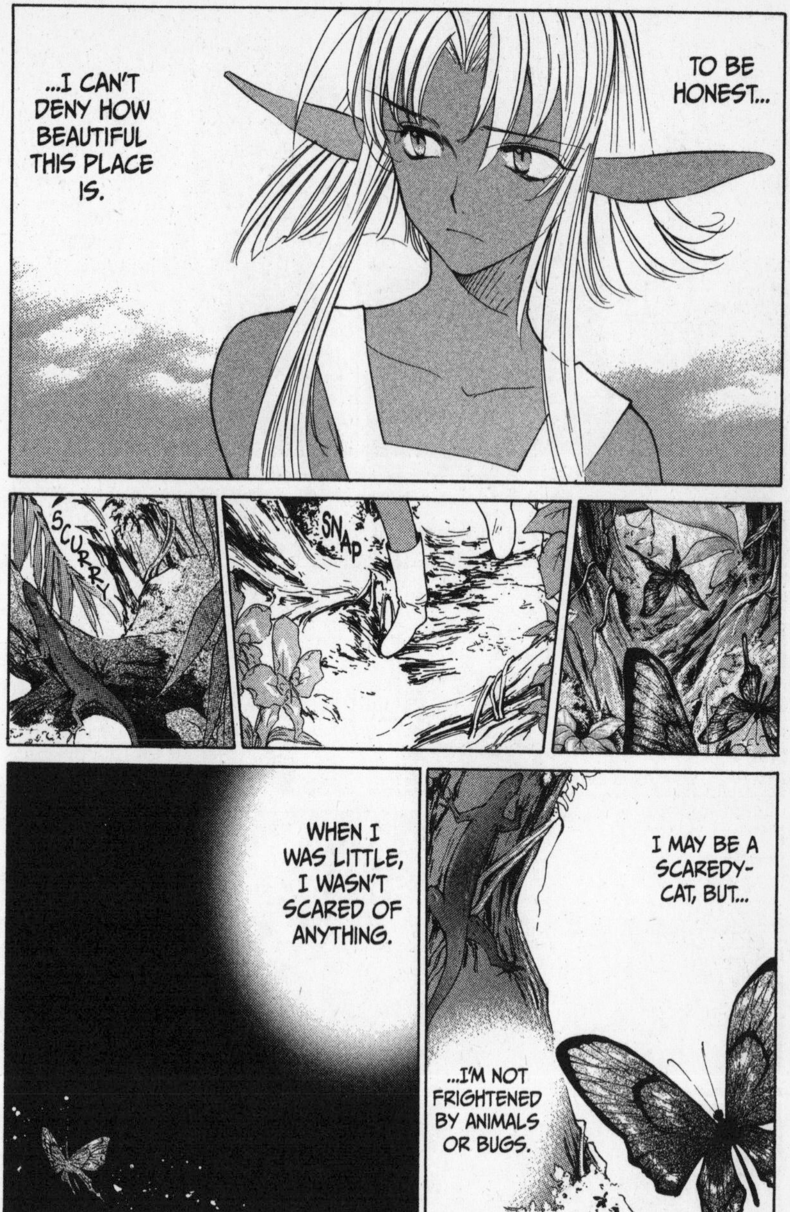
TO BE HONEST...
...I CAN'T DENY HOW BEAUTIFUL THIS PLACE IS.
SNAP
SCURRY
I MAY BE A SCAREDY-CAT, BUT...
...I'M NOT FRIGHTENED BY ANIMALS OR BUGS.
WHEN I WAS LITTLE, I WASN'T SCARED OF ANYTHING.

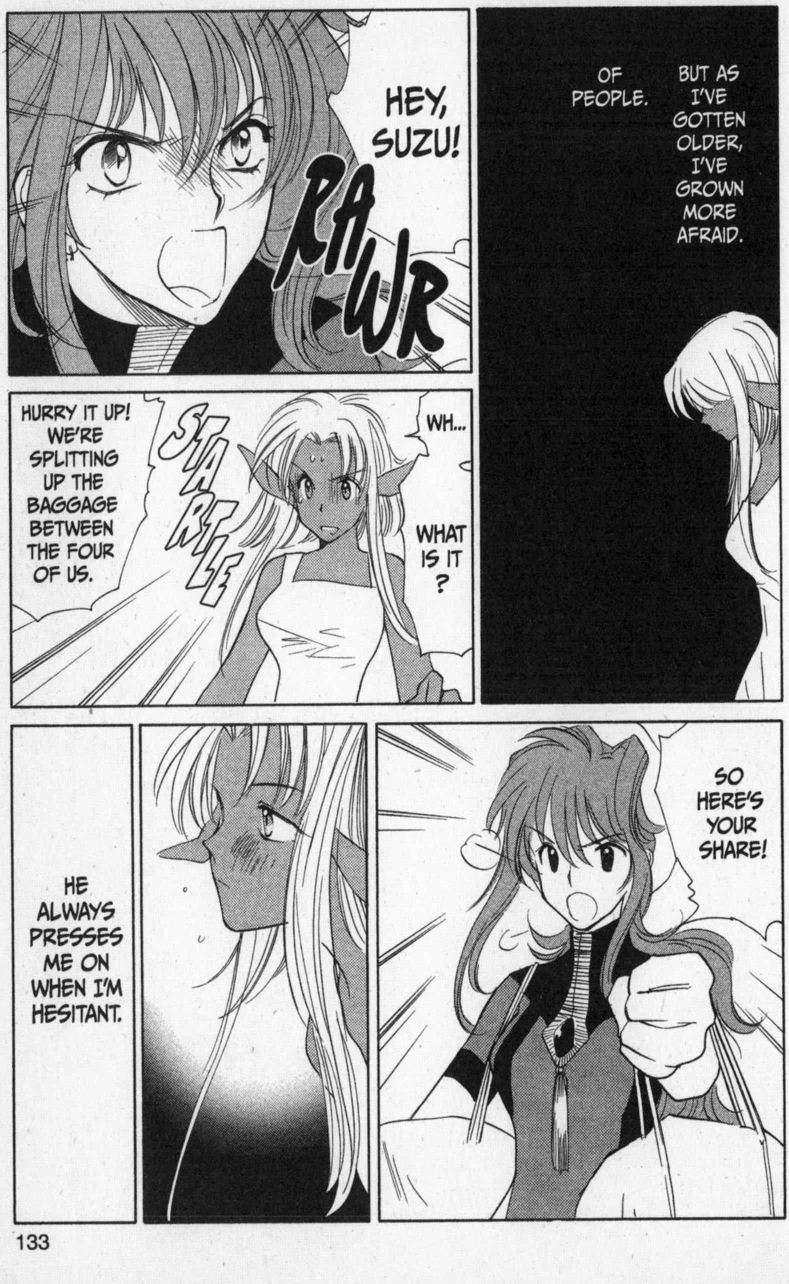
BUT AS I'VE GOTTEN OLDER, I'VE GROWN MORE AFRAID
OF PEOPLE.
HEY, SUZU!
RAWR
WH...
WHAT IS IT?
STARTLE
HURRY IT UP! WE'RE SPLITTING UP THE BAGGAGE BETWEEN THE FOUR OF US.
SO HERE'S YOUR SHARE!
HE ALWAYS PRESSES ME ON WHEN I'M HESITANT.

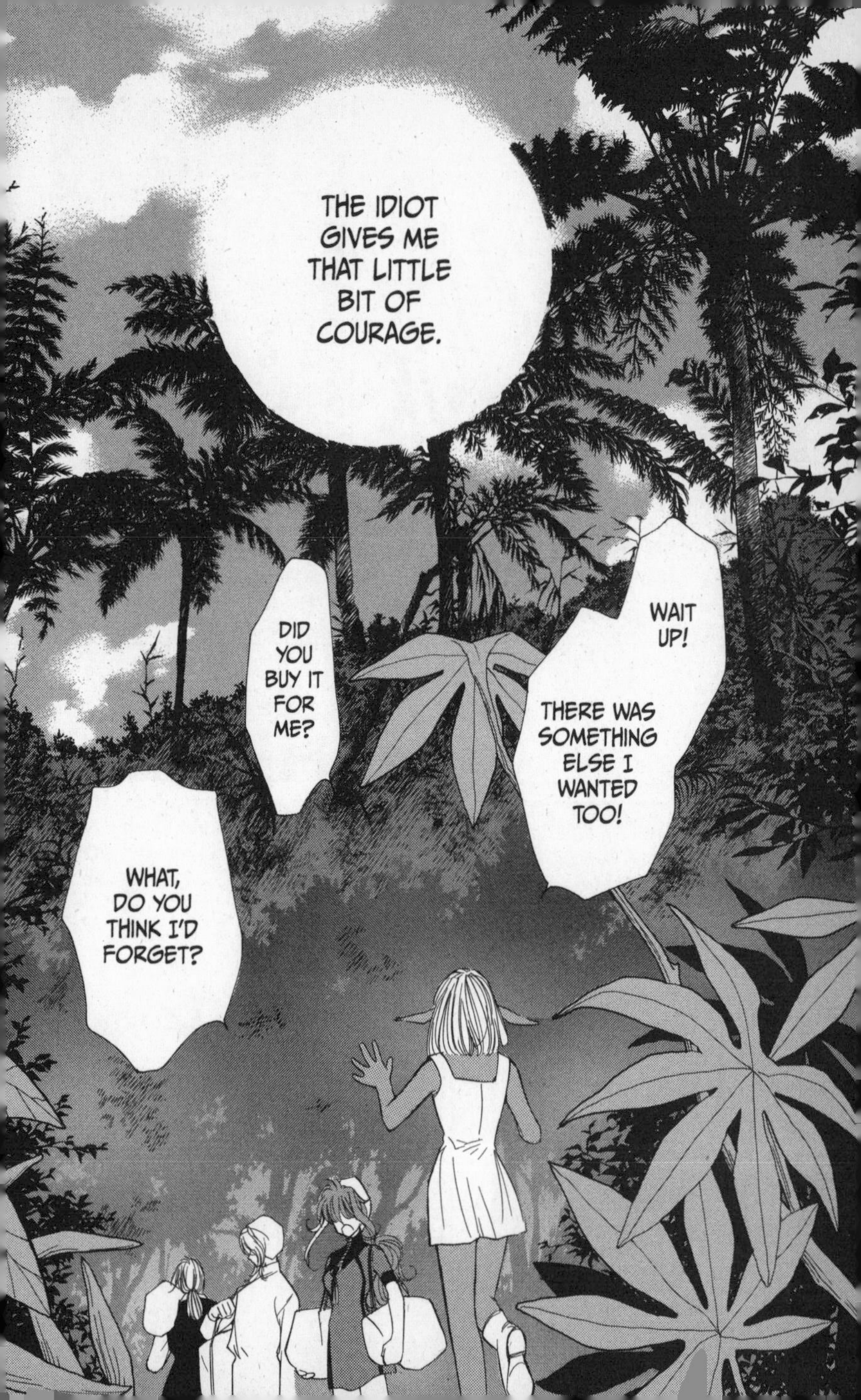
THE IDIOT GIVES ME THAT LITTLE BIT OF COURAGE.
WAIT UP!
THERE WAS SOMETHING ELSE I WANTED TOO!
DID YOU BUY IT FOR ME?
WHAT, DO YOU THINK I'D FORGET?

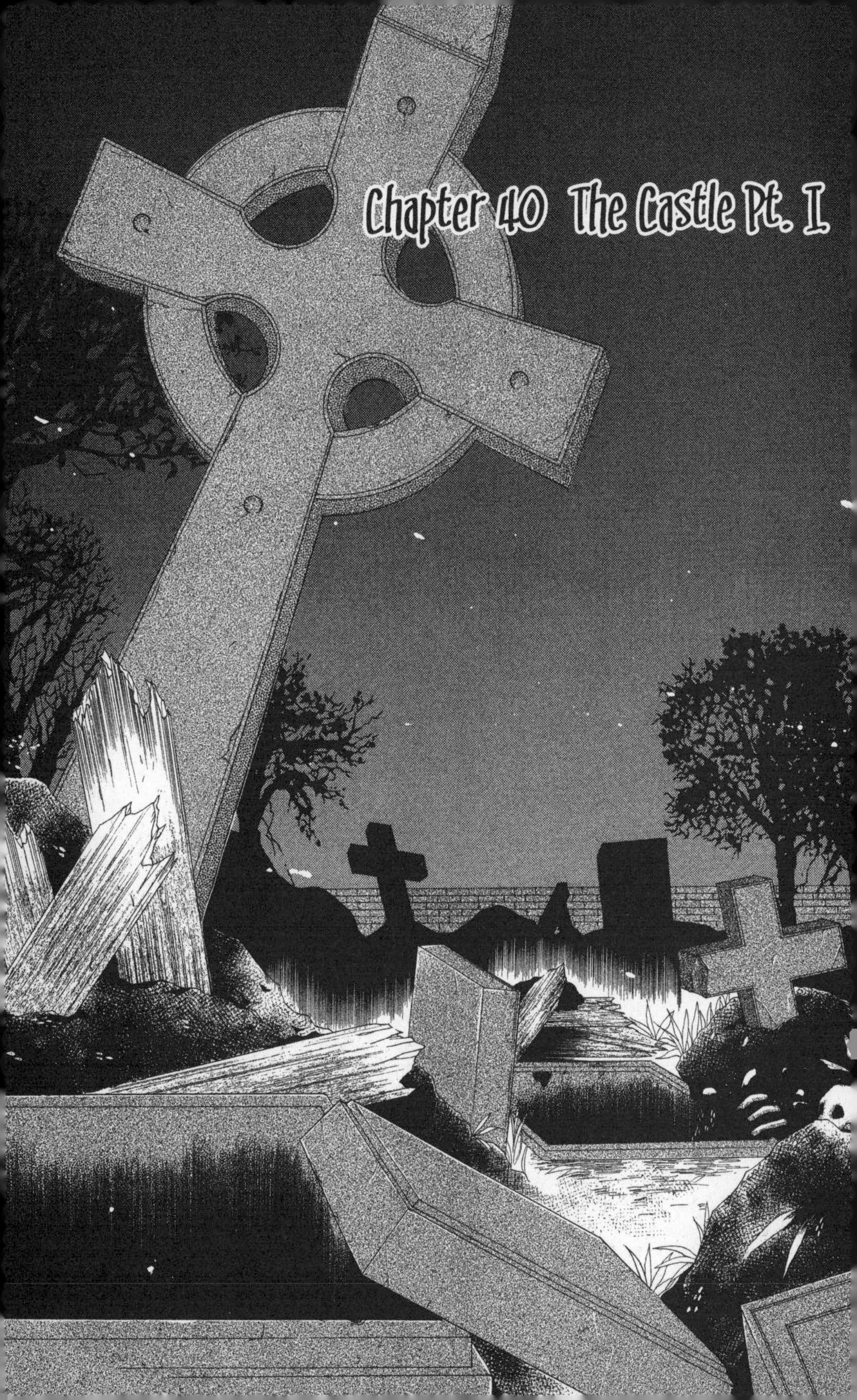
Chapter 40 The Castle Pt. I.

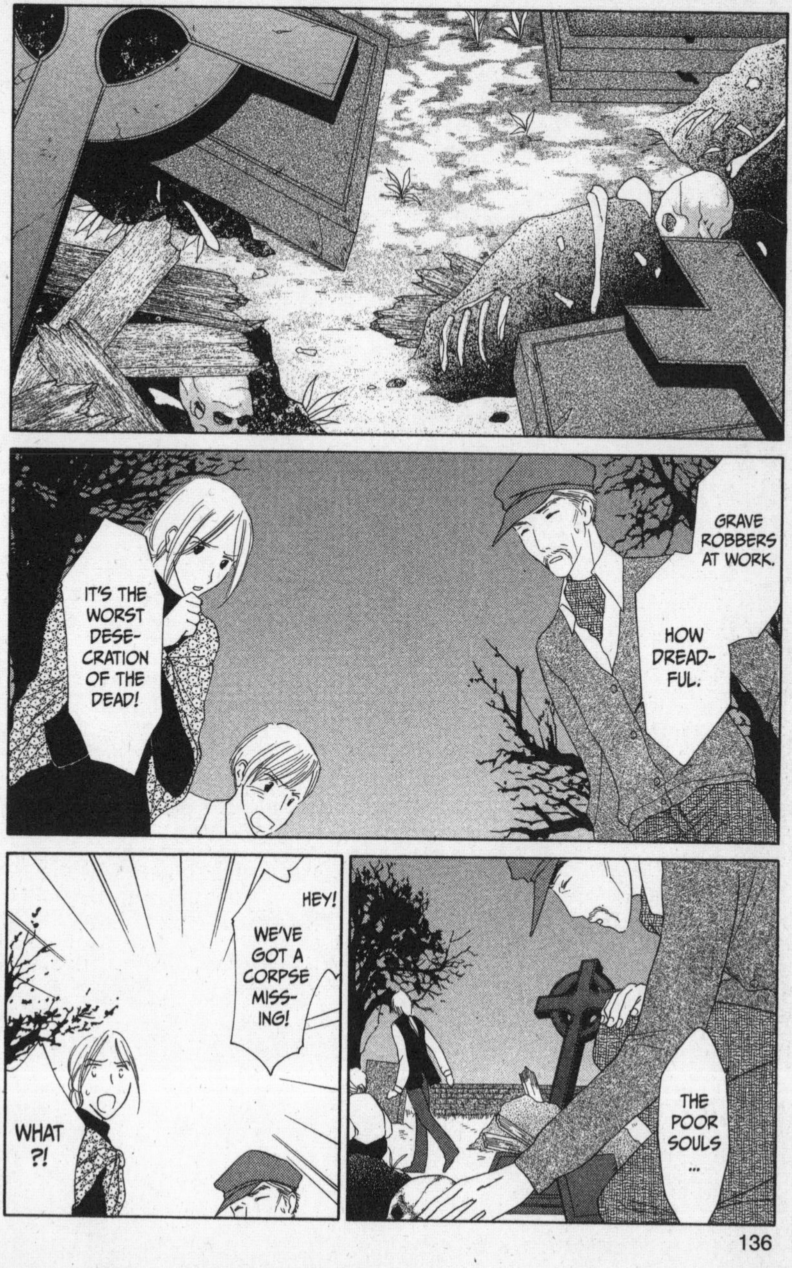
GRAVE ROBBERS AT WORK.
HOW DREAD-FUL.
IT'S THE WORST DESE-CRATION OF THE DEAD!
THE POOR SOULS ...
HEY!
WE'VE GOT A CORPSE MISS-ING!
WHAT ?!

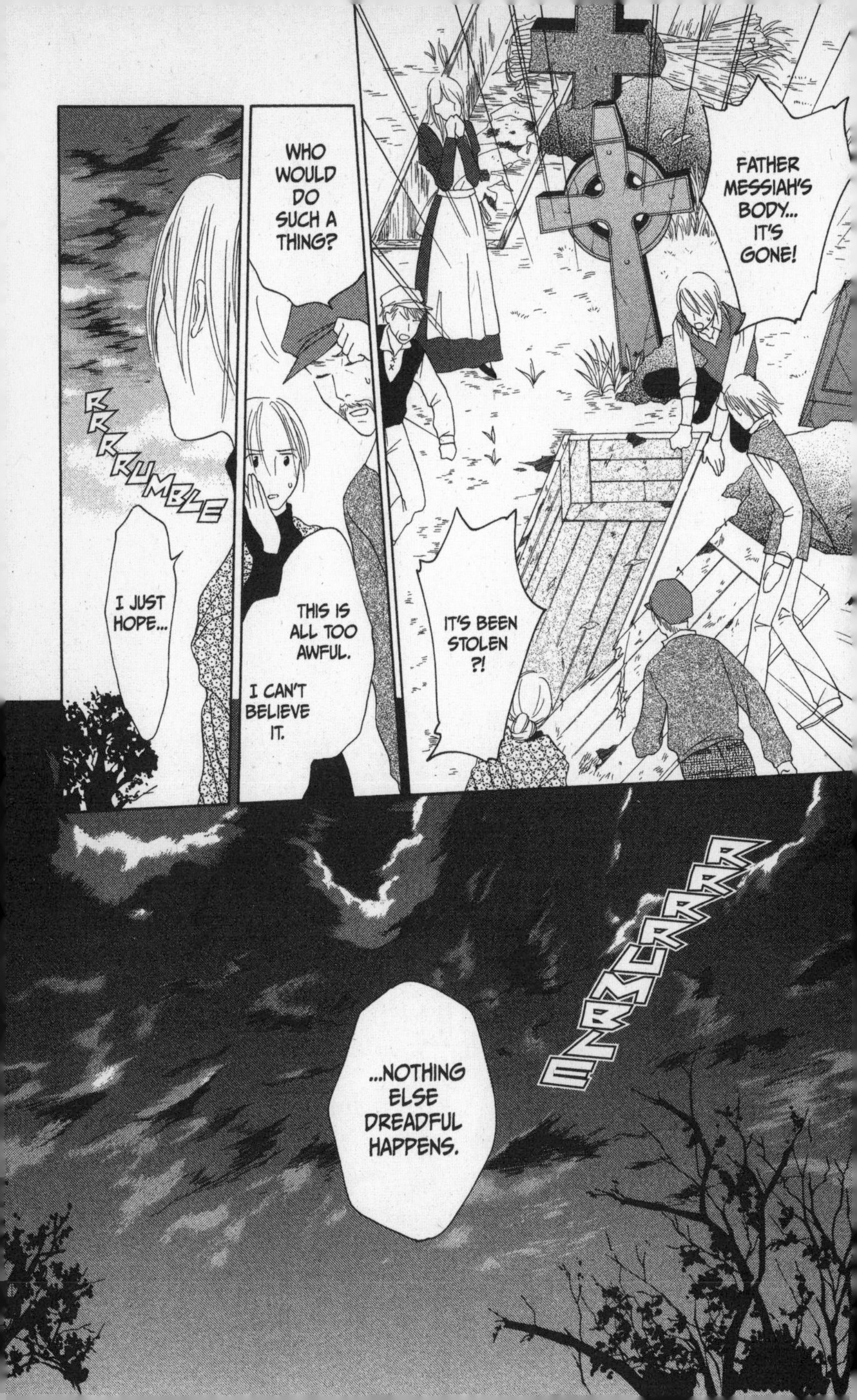
FATHER MESSIAH'S BODY... IT'S GONE!
IT'S BEEN STOLEN ?!
WHO WOULD DO SUCH A THING?
THIS IS ALL TOO AWFUL.
I CAN'T BELIEVE IT.
RRRUMBLE
I JUST HOPE...
RRRRUMBLE
...NOTHING ELSE DREADFUL HAPPENS.

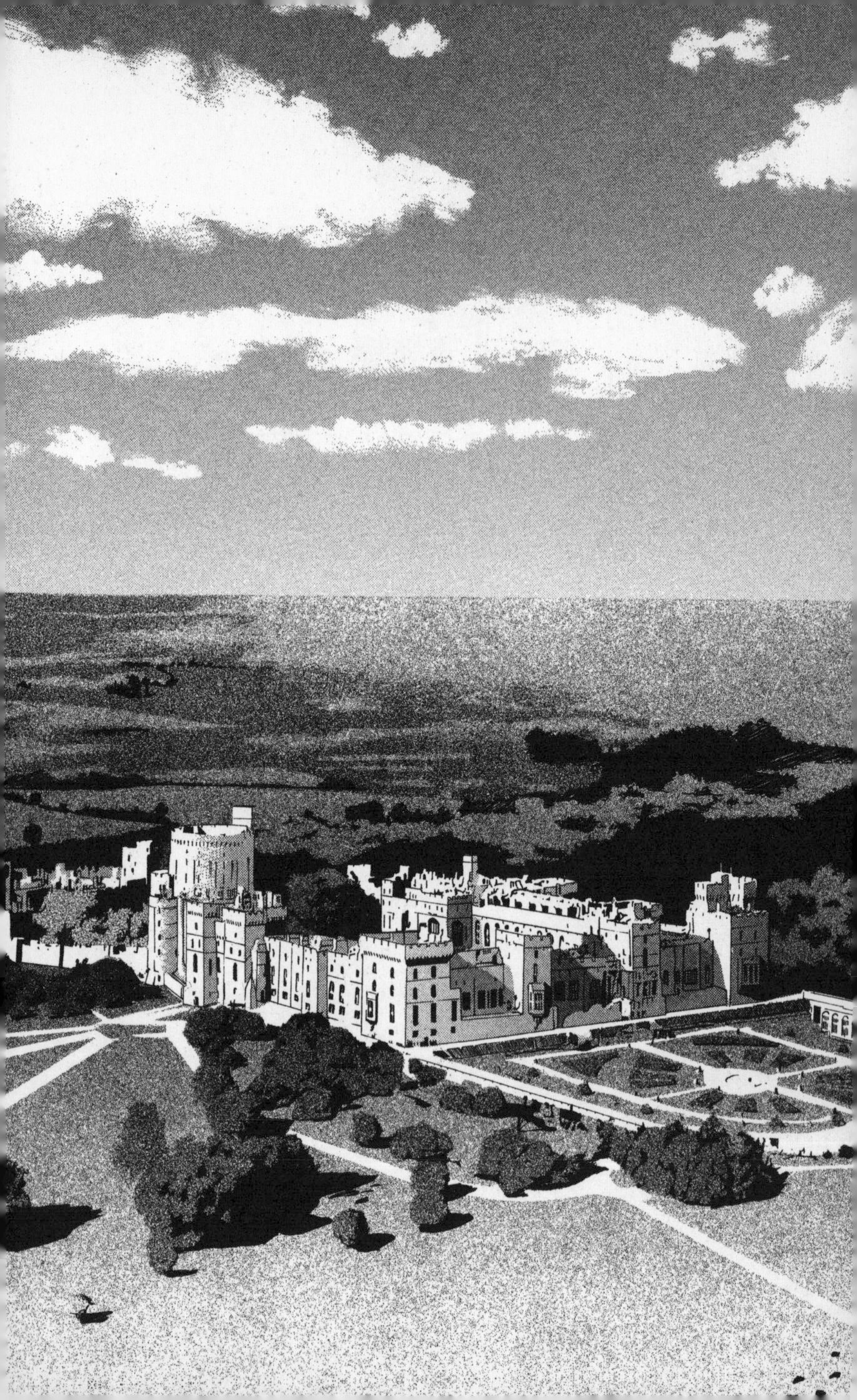

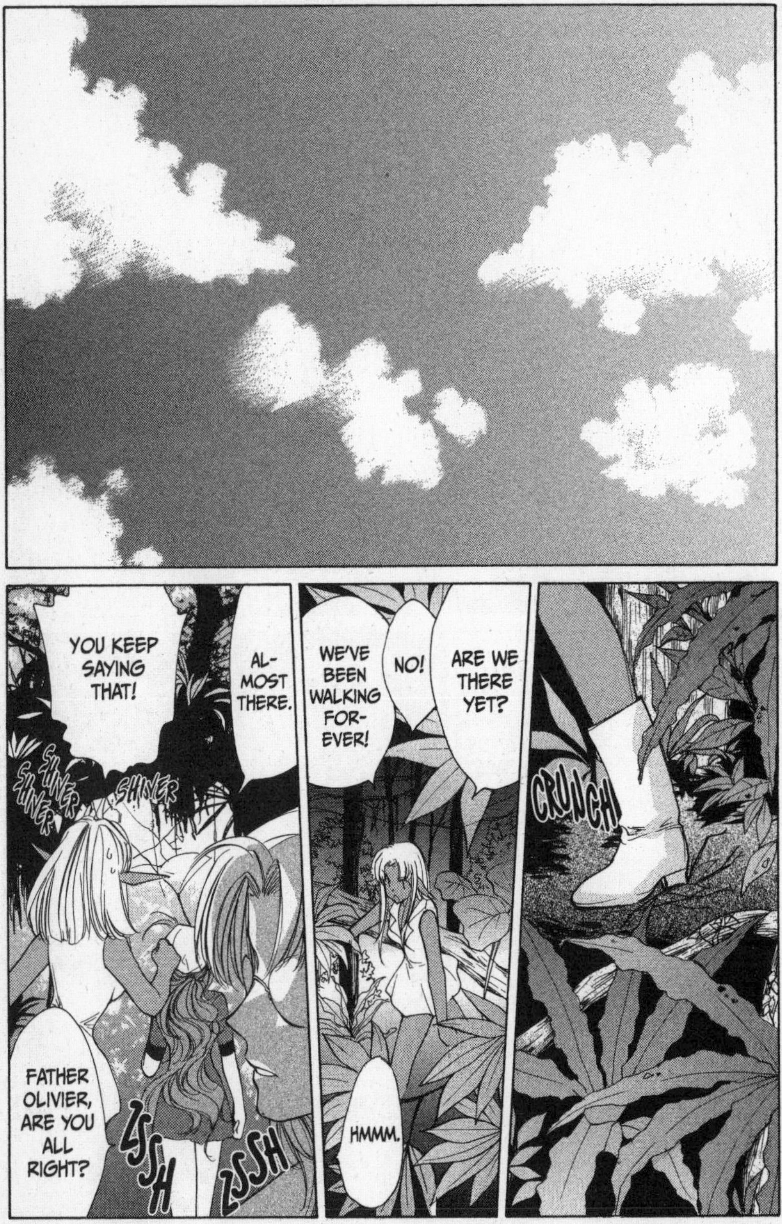
CRUNCH
ARE WE THERE YET?
NO!
WE'VE BEEN WALKING FOR-EVER!
HMMM.
AL-MOST THERE.
YOU KEEP SAYING THAT!
SHIVER
SHIVER
SHIVER
FATHER OLIVIER, ARE YOU ALL RIGHT?
ZSSH
ZSSH

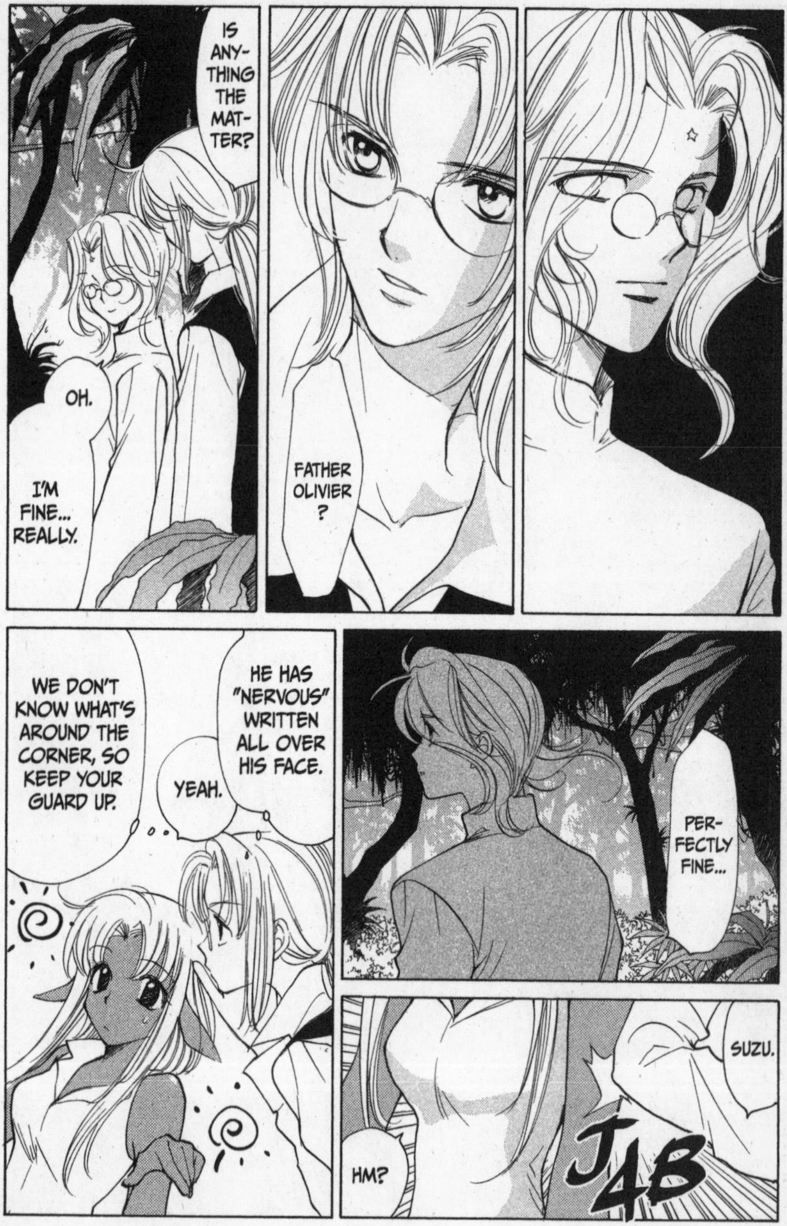
FATHER OLIVIER?
IS ANYTHING THE MATTER?
OH.
I'M FINE... REALLY.
PERFECTLY FINE...
SUZU.
JAB
HM?
HE HAS "NERVOUS" WRITTEN ALL OVER HIS FACE.
YEAH.
WE DON'T KNOW WHAT'S AROUND THE CORNER, SO KEEP YOUR GUARD UP.

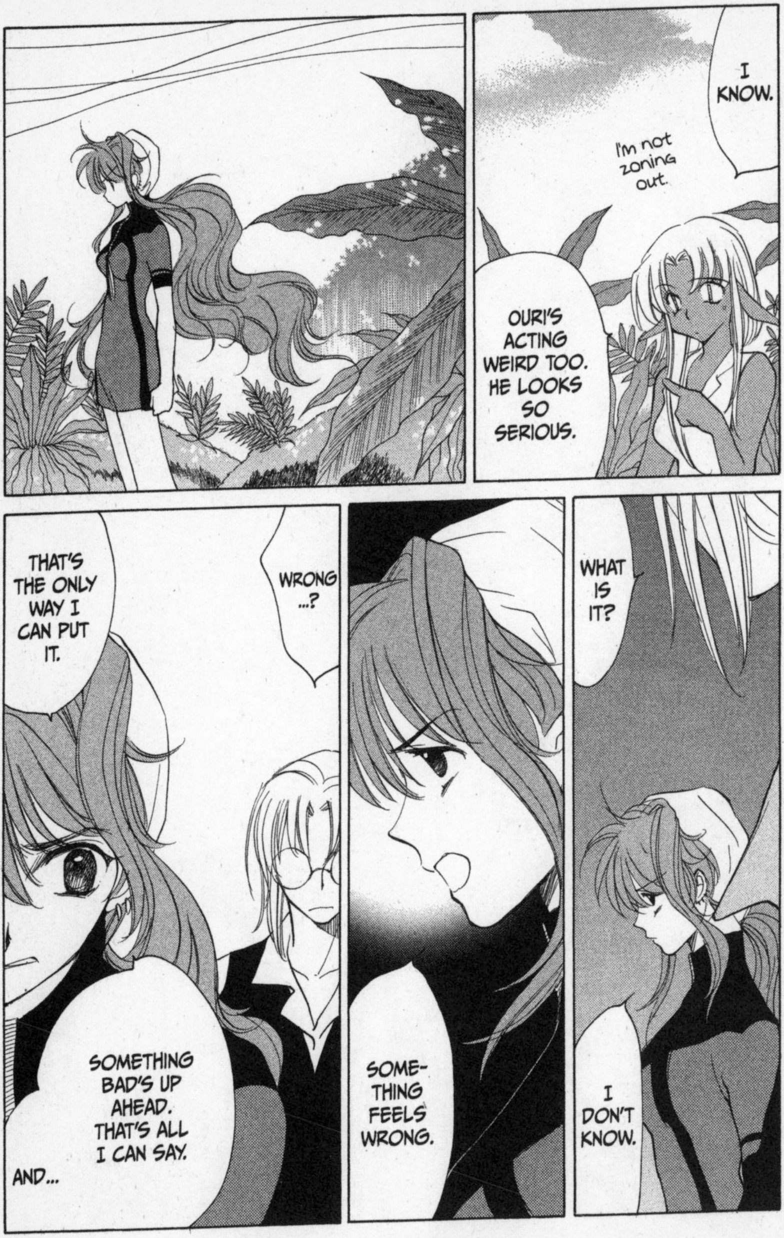
I KNOW.
I'm not zoning out.
OURI'S ACTING WEIRD TOO. HE LOOKS SO SERIOUS.
WHAT IS IT?
I DON'T KNOW.
SOME-THING FEELS WRONG.
WRONG ...?
THAT'S THE ONLY WAY I CAN PUT IT.
SOMETHING BAD'S UP AHEAD. THAT'S ALL I CAN SAY.
AND...

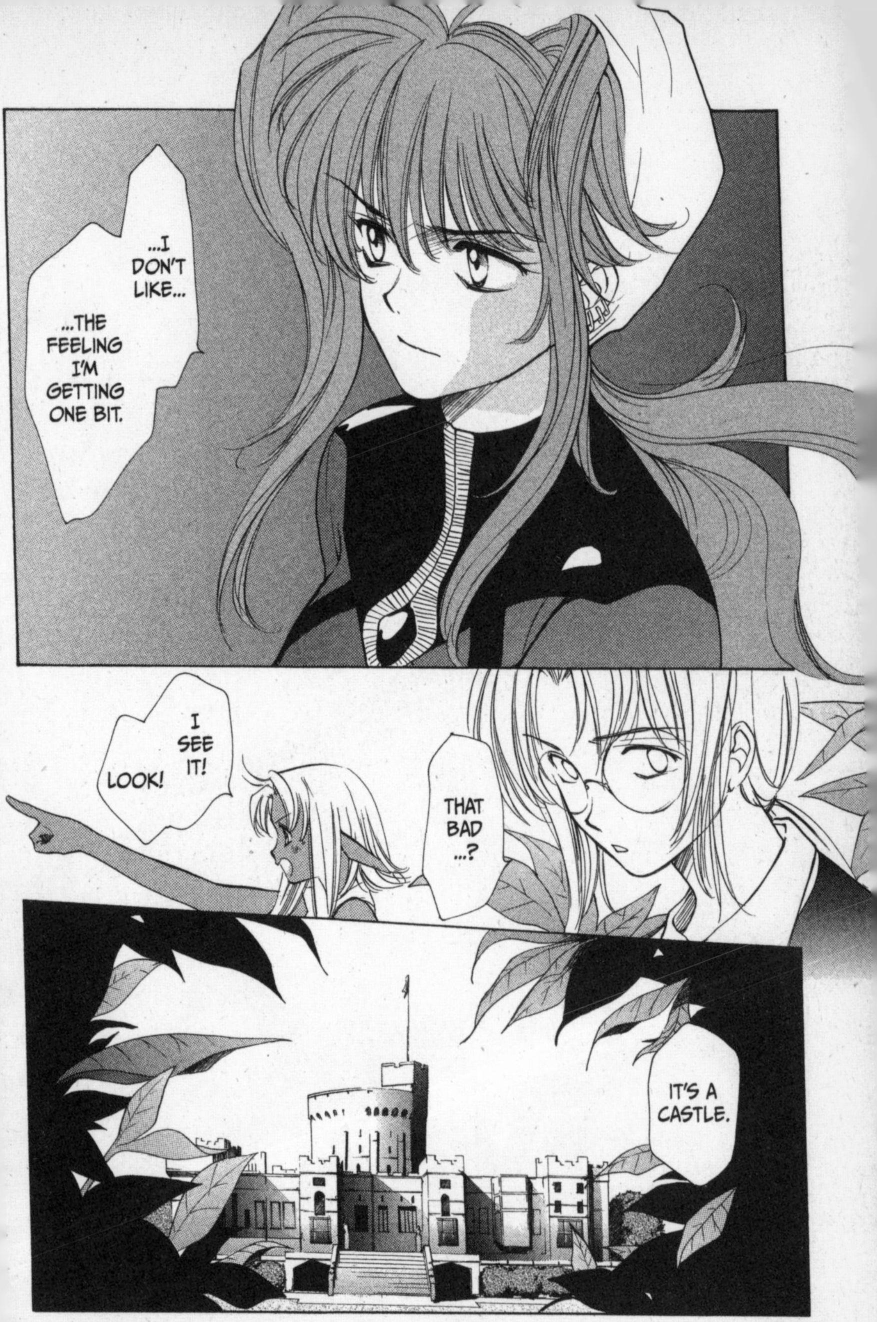
...I DON'T LIKE...
...THE FEELING I'M GETTING ONE BIT.
THAT BAD ...?
I SEE IT!
LOOK!
IT'S A CASTLE.

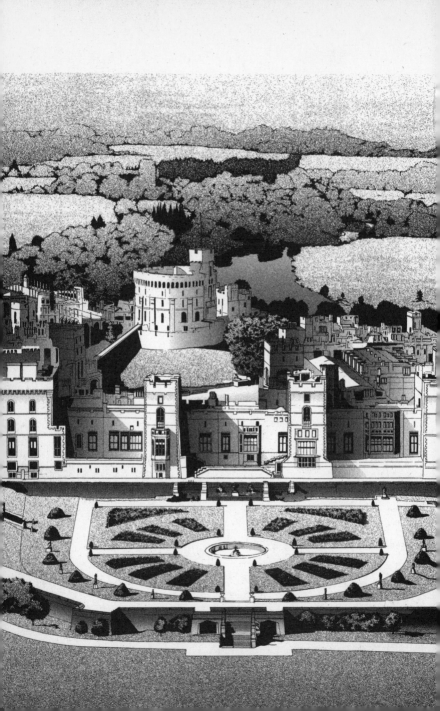

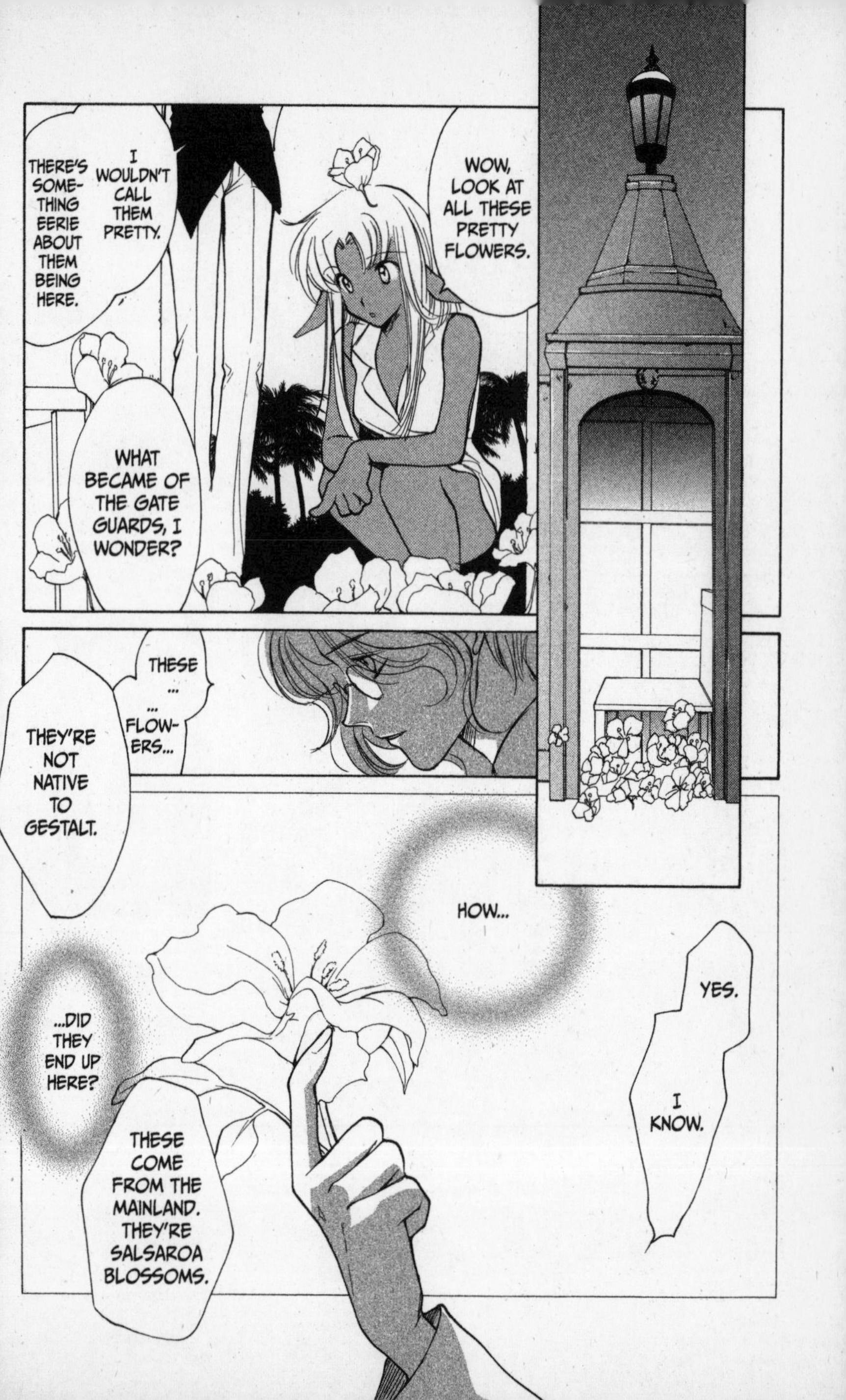
WOW, LOOK AT ALL THESE PRETTY FLOWERS.
I WOULDN'T CALL THEM PRETTY.
THERE'S SOME-THING EERIE ABOUT THEM BEING HERE.
WHAT BECAME OF THE GATE GUARDS, I WONDER?
THESE ... ... FLOW-ERS...
THEY'RE NOT NATIVE TO GESTALT.
HOW...
YES.
I KNOW.
...DID THEY END UP HERE?
THESE COME FROM THE MAINLAND. THEY'RE SALSAROA BLOSSOMS.

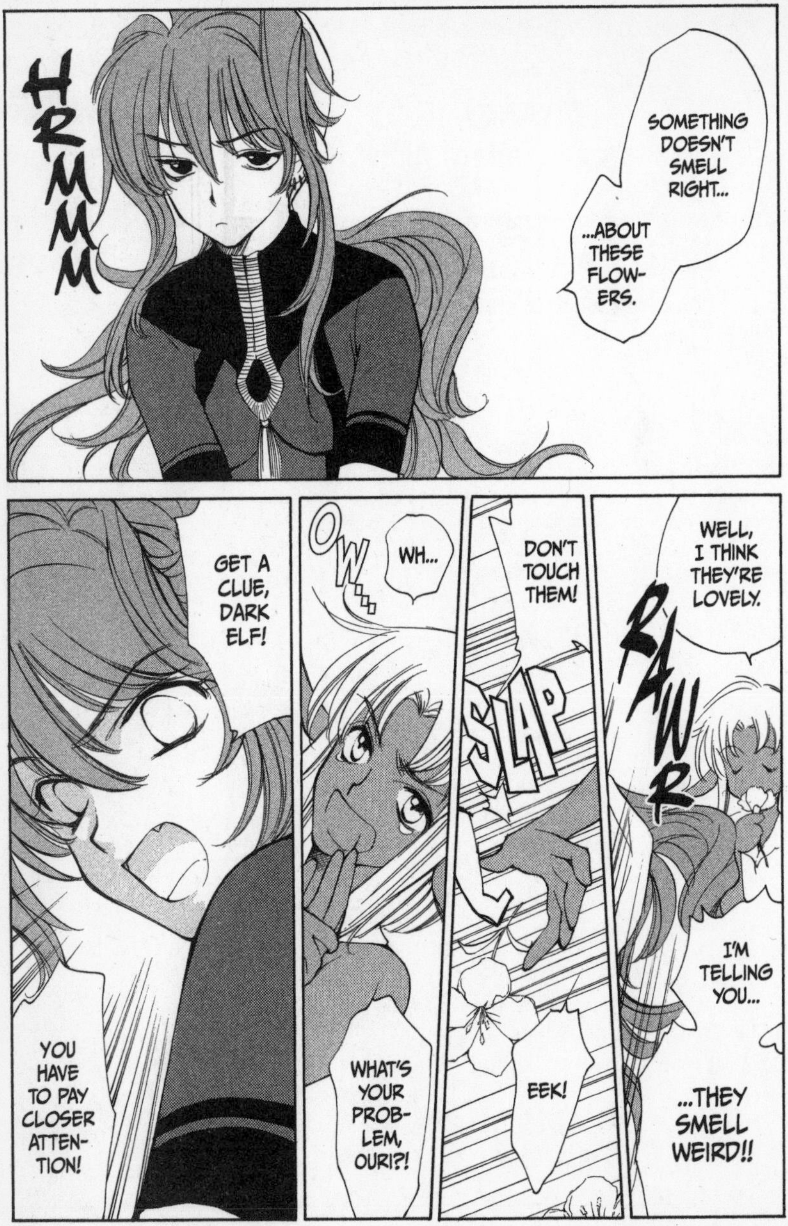
SOMETHING DOESN'T SMELL RIGHT...
...ABOUT THESE FLOW-ERS.
HRMMM
WELL, I THINK THEY'RE LOVELY.
RAWR
I'M TELLING YOU...
...THEY SMELL WEIRD!!
DON'T TOUCH THEM!
SLAP
EEK!
WH...
OW...
WHAT'S YOUR PROB-LEM, OURI?!
GET A CLUE, DARK ELF!
YOU HAVE TO PAY CLOSER ATTEN-TION!

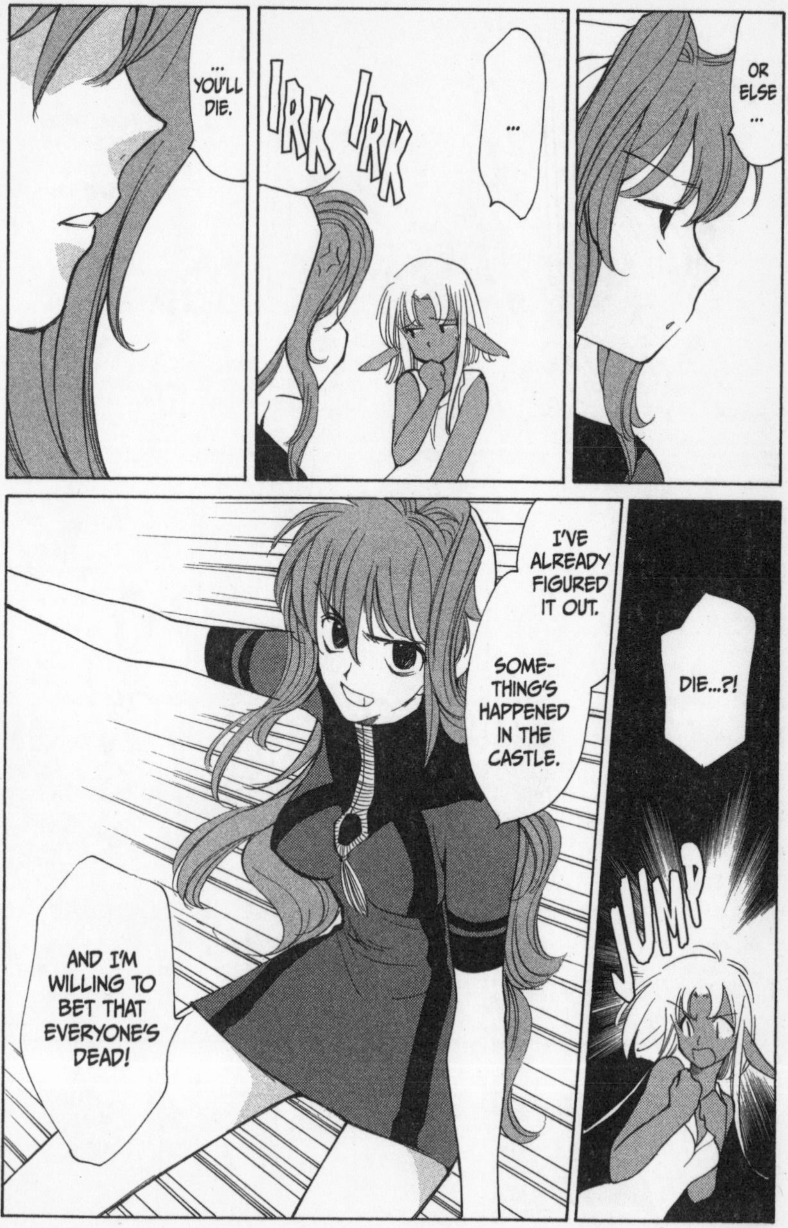
OR ELSE ...
...
IRK IRK
... YOU'LL DIE.
DIE...?!
JUMP
I'VE ALREADY FIGURED IT OUT.
SOME-THING'S HAPPENED IN THE CASTLE.
AND I'M WILLING TO BET THAT EVERYONE'S DEAD!

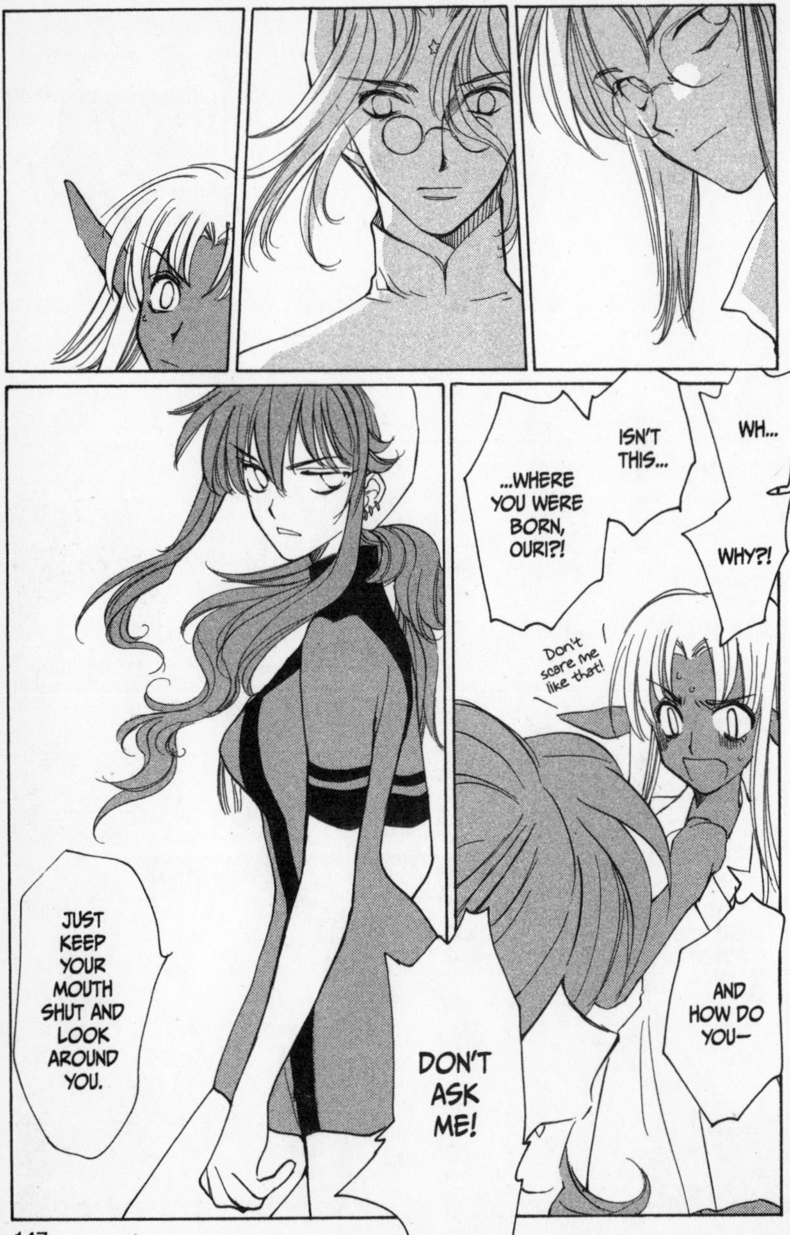
WH...
WHY?!
ISN'T THIS...
...WHERE YOU WERE BORN, OURI?!
Don't scare me like that!
AND HOW DO YOU—
DON'T ASK ME!
JUST KEEP YOUR MOUTH SHUT AND LOOK AROUND YOU.

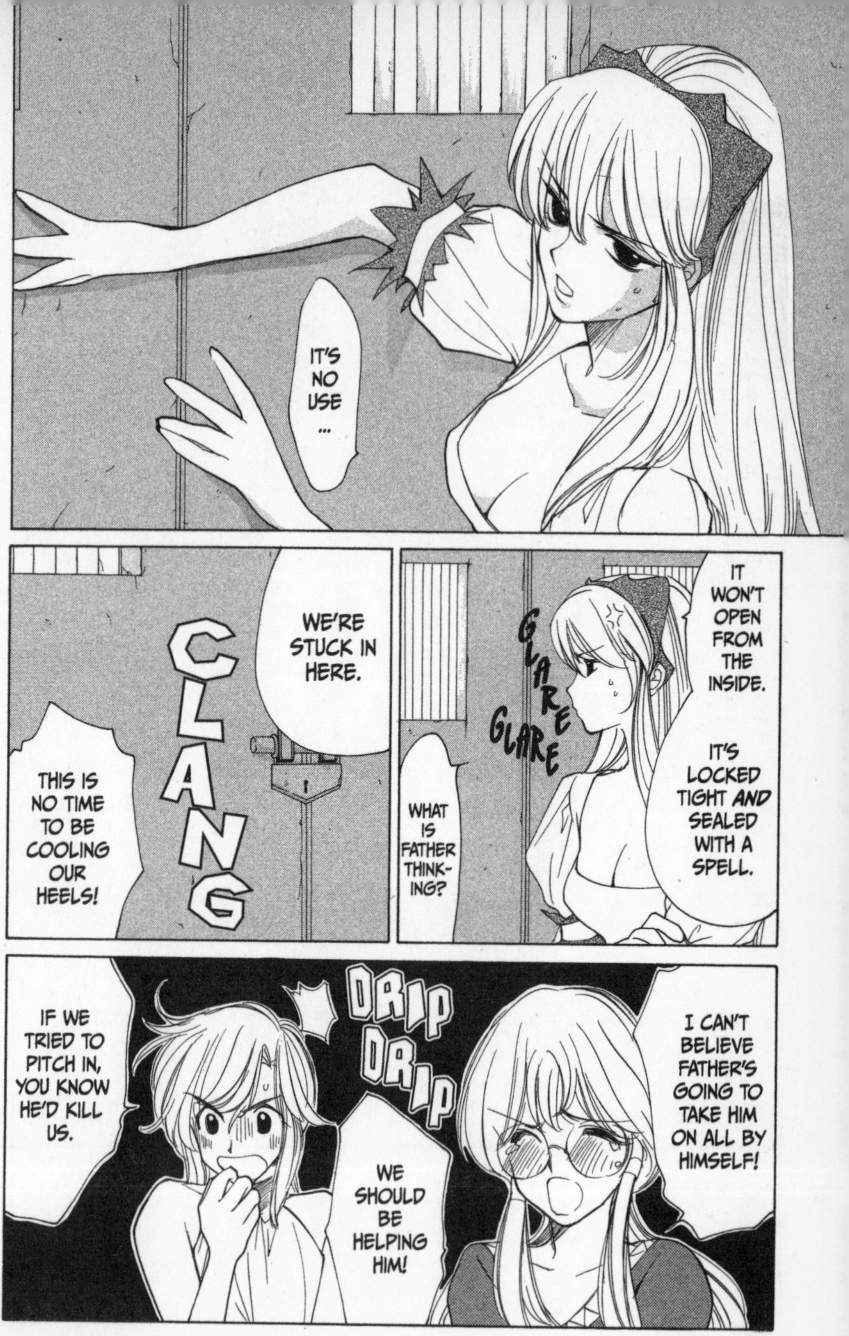
IT'S NO USE ...
IT WON'T OPEN FROM THE INSIDE.
IT'S LOCKED TIGHT *AND* SEALED WITH A SPELL.
GLARE GLARE
WHAT IS FATHER THINK-ING?
WE'RE STUCK IN HERE.
CLANG
THIS IS NO TIME TO BE COOLING OUR HEELS!
I CAN'T BELIEVE FATHER'S GOING TO TAKE HIM ON ALL BY HIMSELF!
DRIP DRIP
WE SHOULD BE HELPING HIM!
IF WE TRIED TO PITCH IN, YOU KNOW HE'D KILL US.

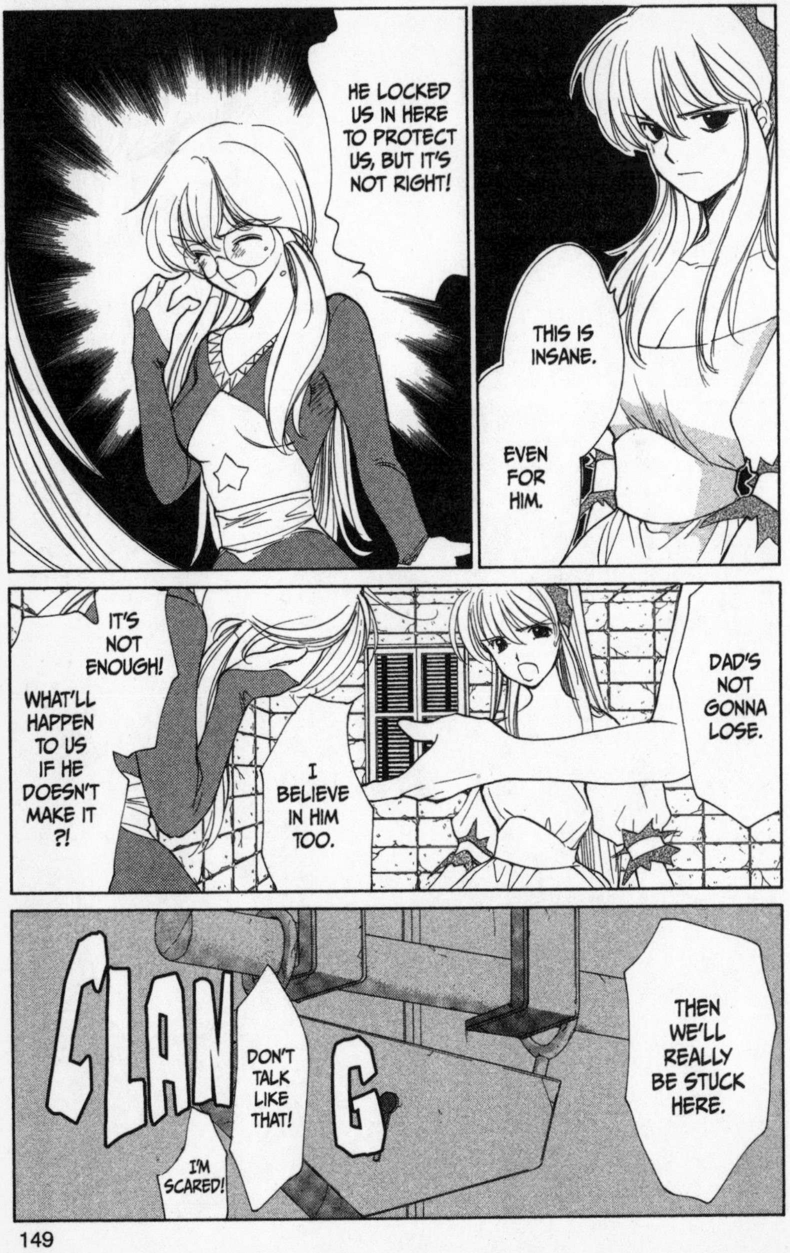
THIS IS INSANE.
EVEN FOR HIM.
HE LOCKED US IN HERE TO PROTECT US, BUT IT'S NOT RIGHT!
DAD'S NOT GONNA LOSE.
I BELIEVE IN HIM TOO.
IT'S NOT ENOUGH!
WHAT'LL HAPPEN TO US IF HE DOESN'T MAKE IT?!
THEN WE'LL REALLY BE STUCK HERE.
CLANG
DON'T TALK LIKE THAT!
I'M SCARED!

CREAK
WHO'S THERE ?!
DAD?
FATHER ?!
GASP!
NO.
YOUR DADDY'S. SLEEPING NOW.

Chapter 41 The Castle Pt. II

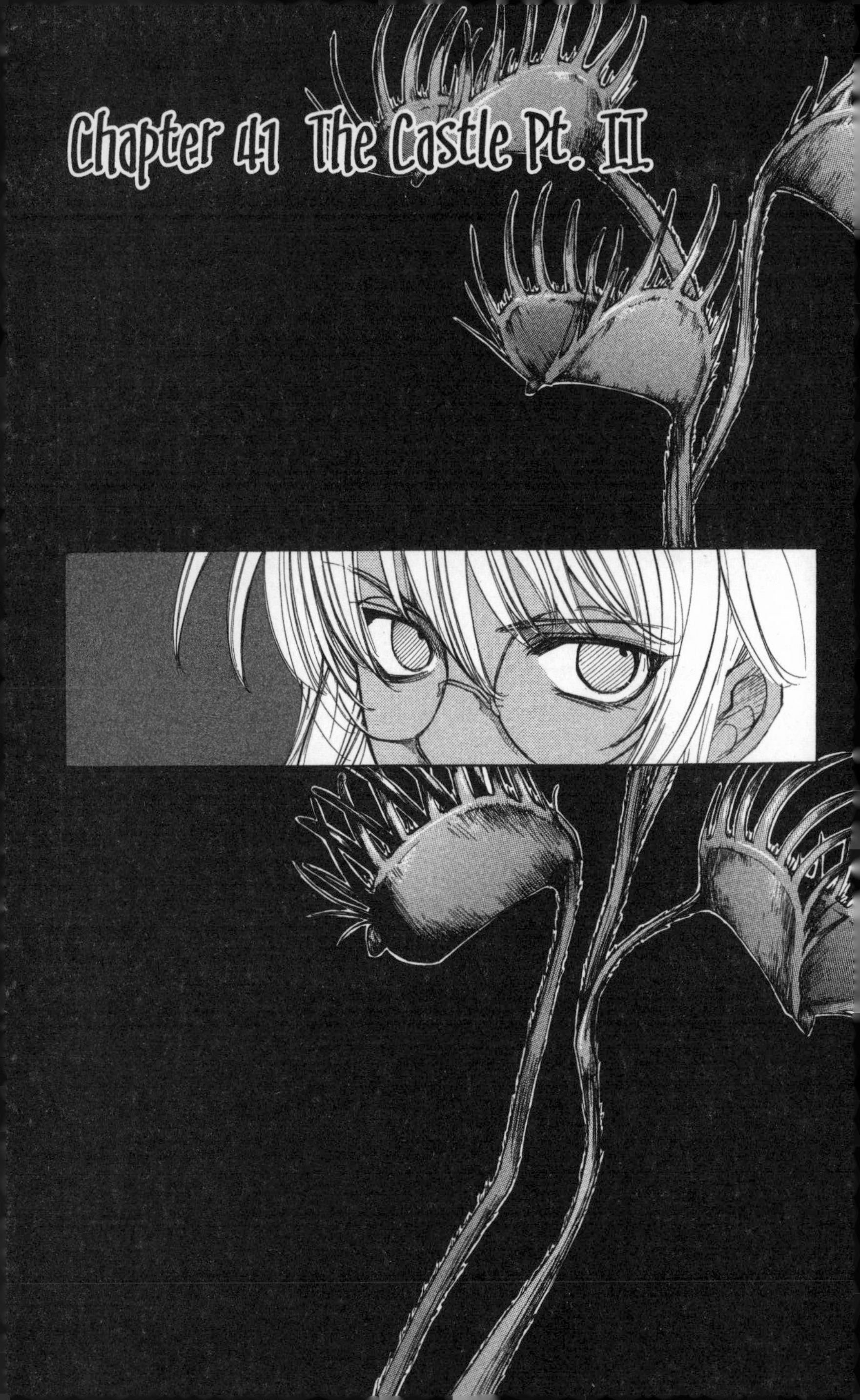

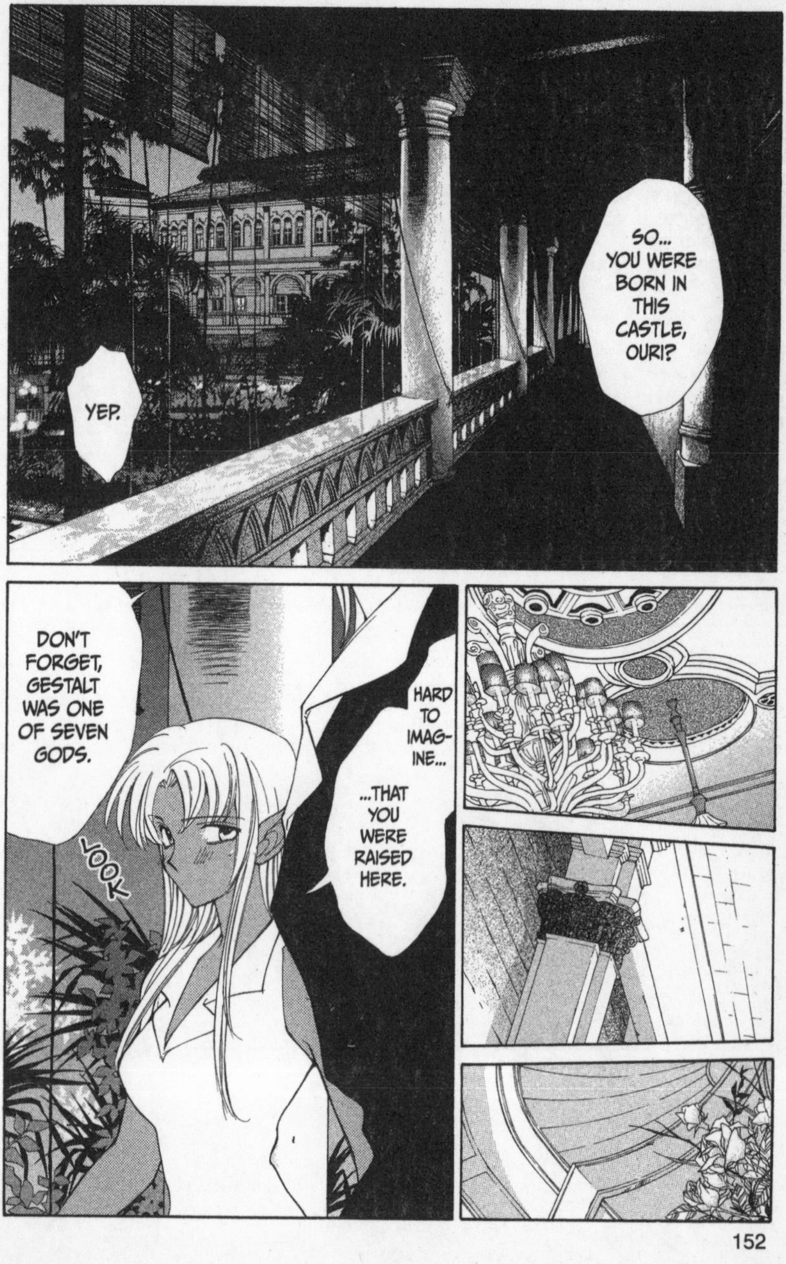
SO... YOU WERE BORN IN THIS CASTLE, OURI?
YEP.
HARD TO IMAG-INE...
...THAT YOU WERE RAISED HERE.
DON'T FORGET, GESTALT WAS ONE OF SEVEN GODS.
YOOK

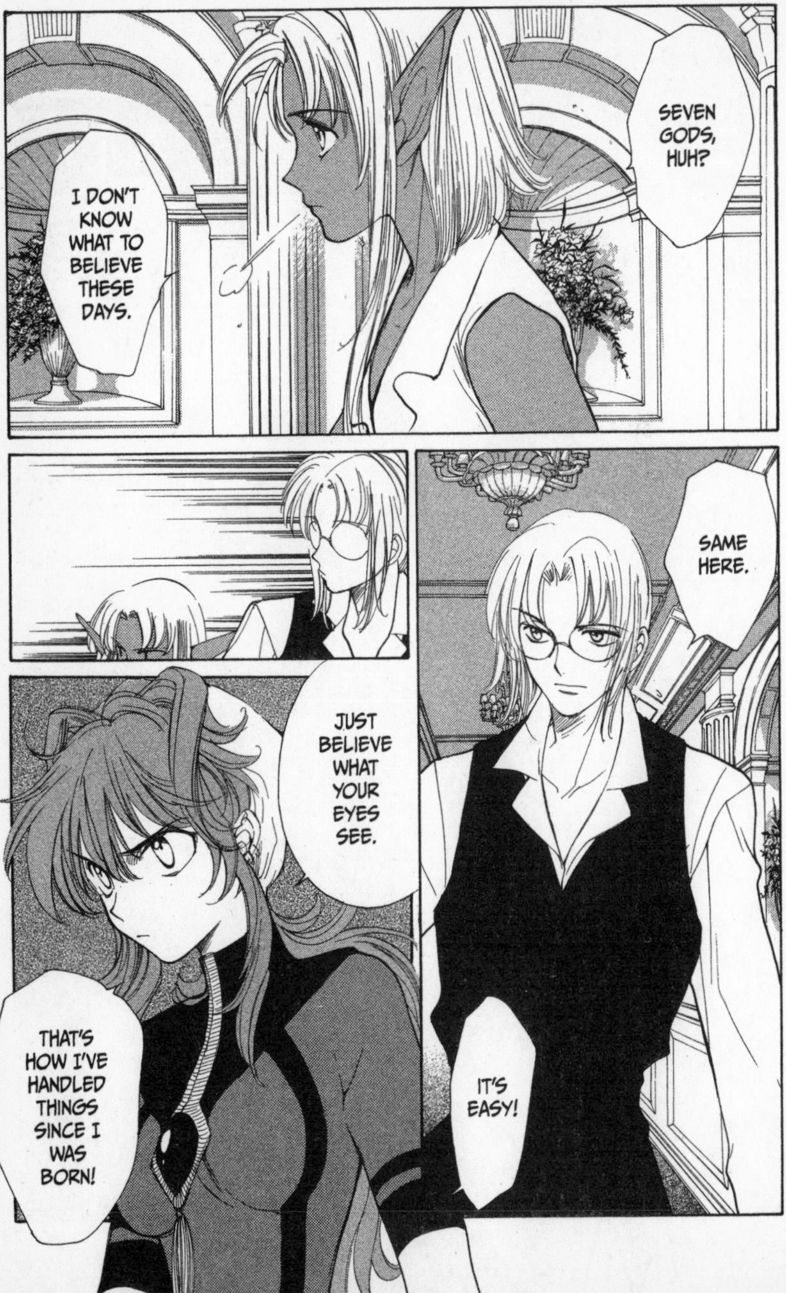
SEVEN GODS, HUH?
I DON'T KNOW WHAT TO BELIEVE THESE DAYS.
SAME HERE.
IT'S EASY!
JUST BELIEVE WHAT YOUR EYES SEE.
THAT'S HOW I'VE HANDLED THINGS SINCE I WAS BORN!

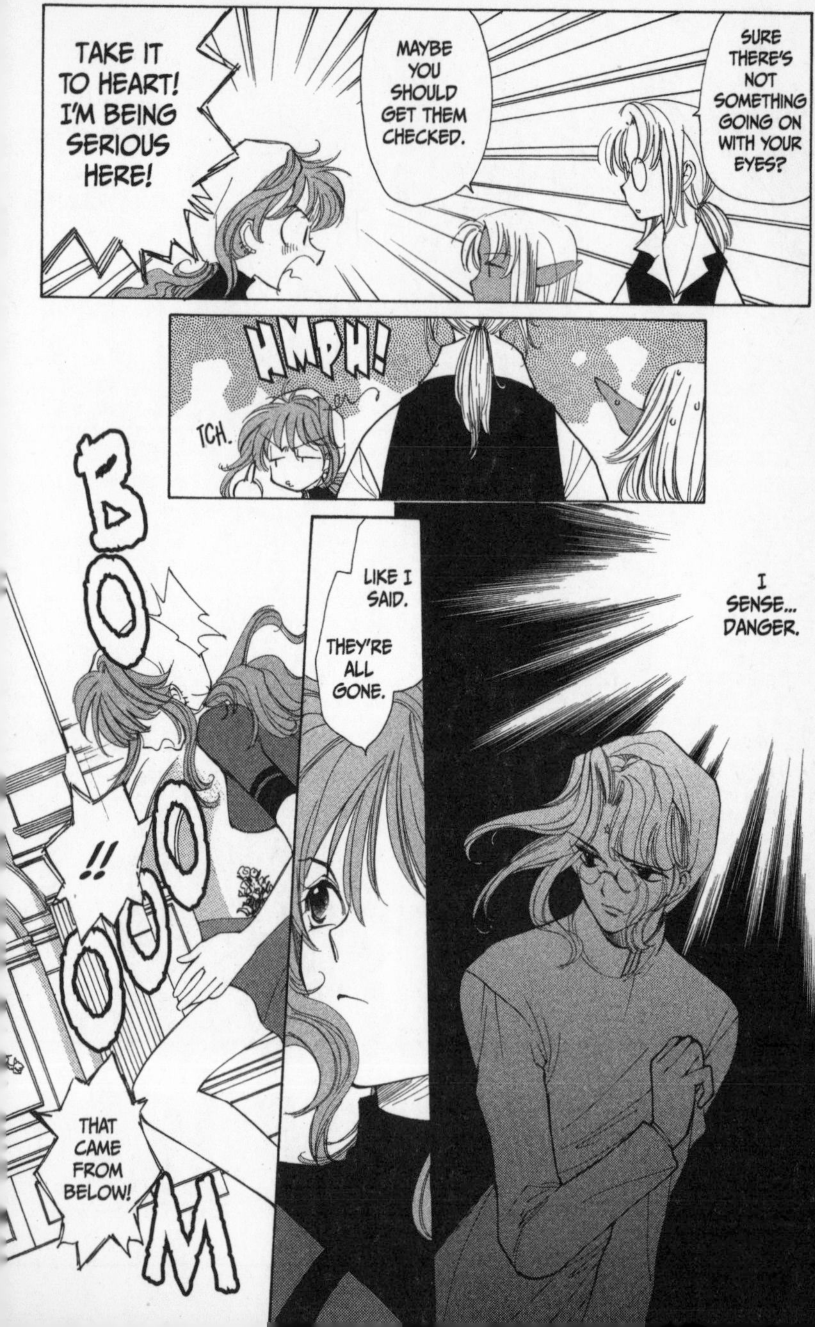
SURE THERE'S NOT SOMETHING GOING ON WITH YOUR EYES?
MAYBE YOU SHOULD GET THEM CHECKED.
TAKE IT TO HEART! I'M BEING SERIOUS HERE!
HMPH!
TCH.
I SENSE... DANGER.
LIKE I SAID.
THEY'RE ALL GONE.
BOOOOOM
!!
THAT CAME FROM BELOW!

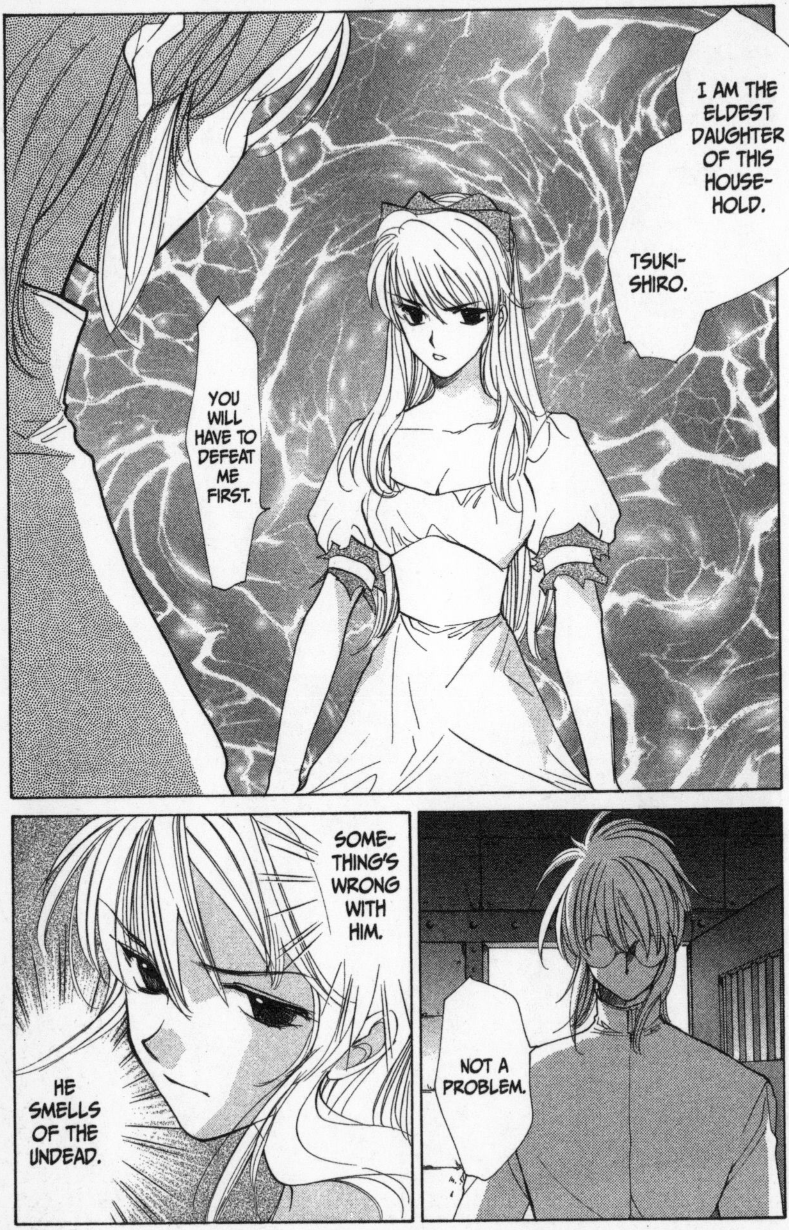
I AM THE ELDEST DAUGHTER OF THIS HOUSE-HOLD.
TSUKI-SHIRO.
YOU WILL HAVE TO DEFEAT ME FIRST.
NOT A PROBLEM.
SOME-THING'S WRONG WITH HIM.
HE SMELLS OF THE UNDEAD.

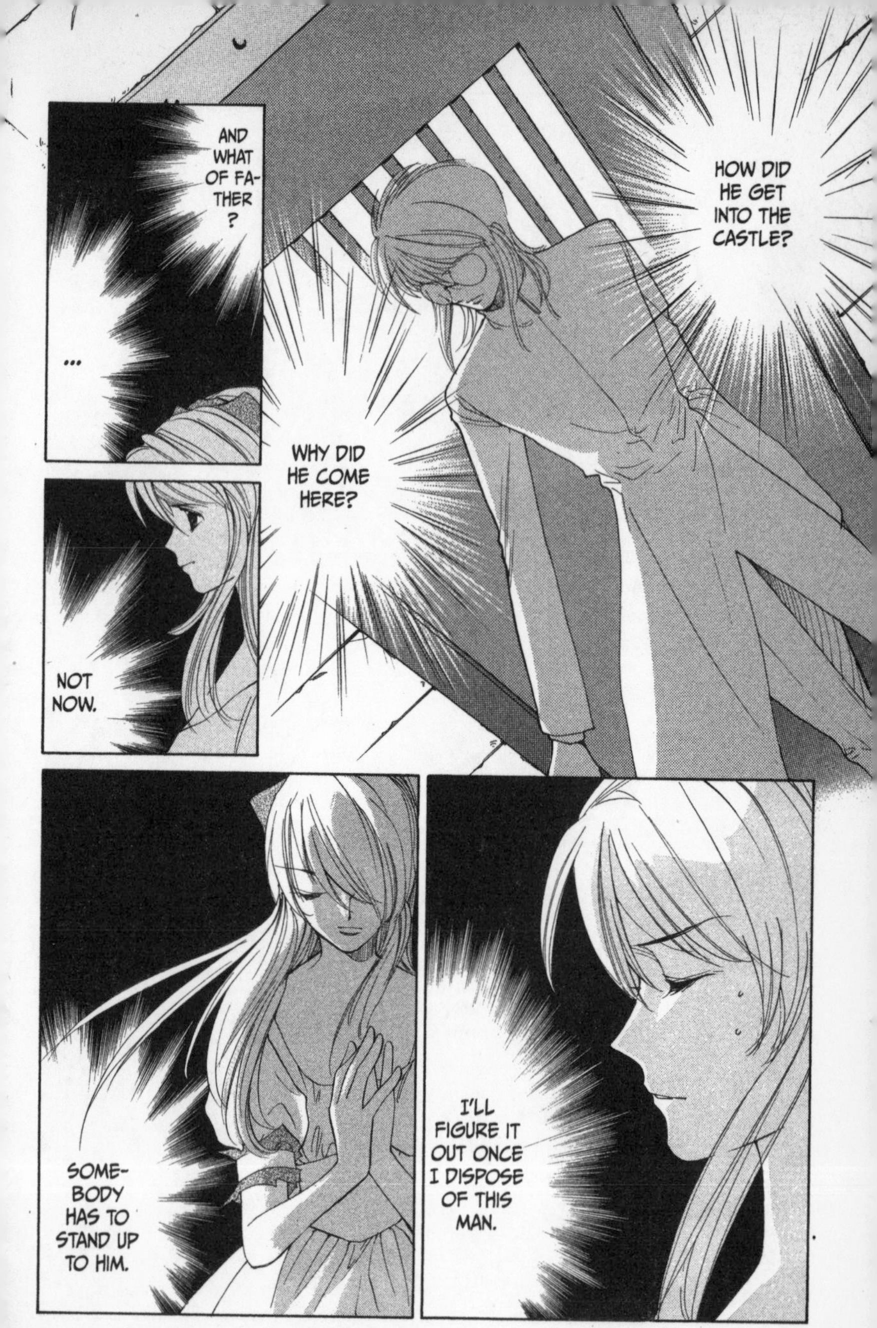
HOW DID HE GET INTO THE CASTLE?
WHY DID HE COME HERE?
AND WHAT OF FA-THER?
...
NOT NOW.
I'LL FIGURE IT OUT ONCE I DISPOSE OF THIS MAN.
SOME-BODY HAS TO STAND UP TO HIM.

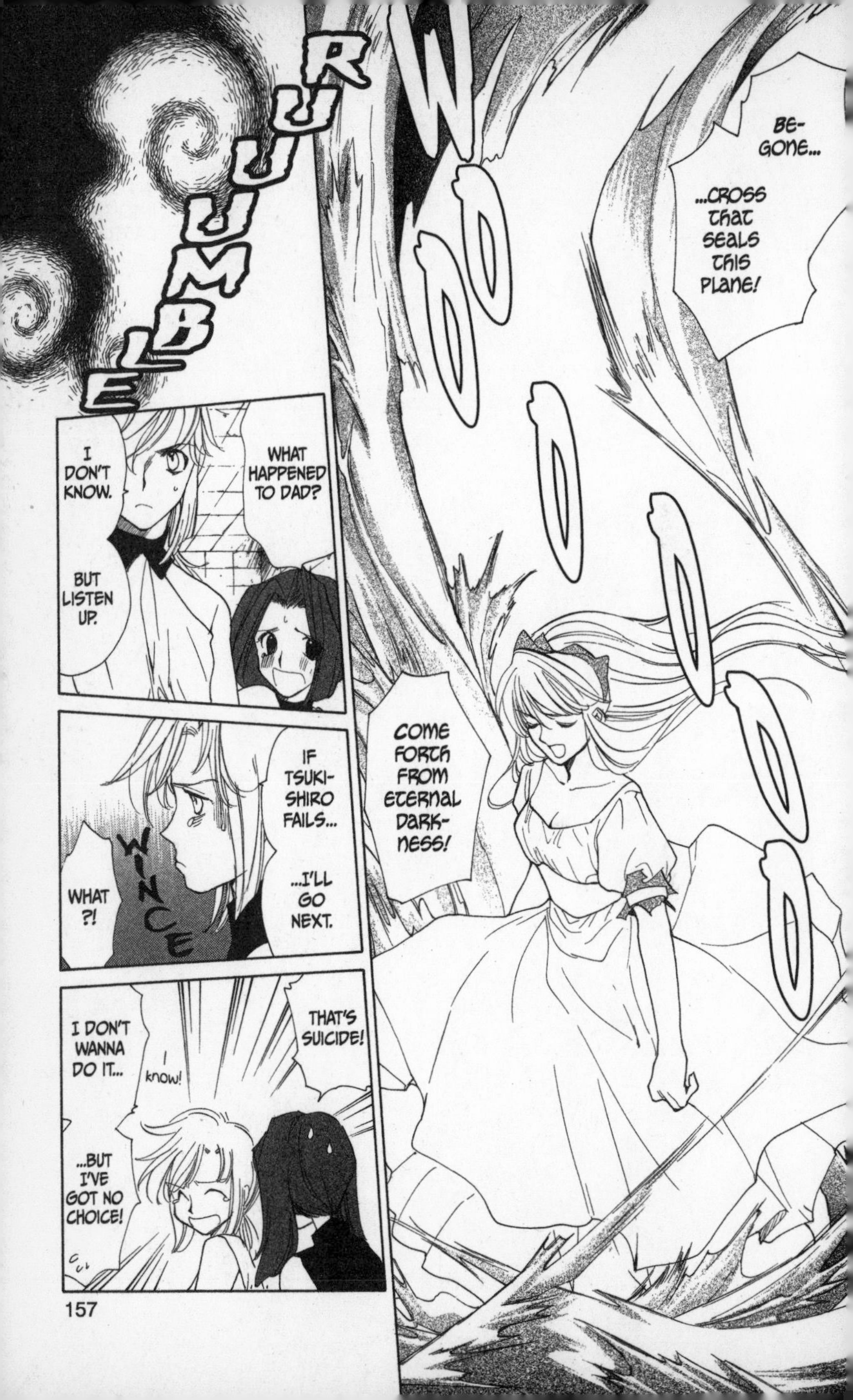
BE-GONE...
...CROSS THAT SEALS THIS PLANE!
WOOOOOOOO
COME FORTH FROM ETERNAL DARKNESS!
RUUUMBLE
WHAT HAPPENED TO DAD?
I DON'T KNOW.
BUT LISTEN UP.
IF TSUKI-SHIRO FAILS...
...I'LL GO NEXT.
WINCE
WHAT?!
THAT'S SUICIDE!
I know!
I DON'T WANNA DO IT...
...BUT I'VE GOT NO CHOICE!

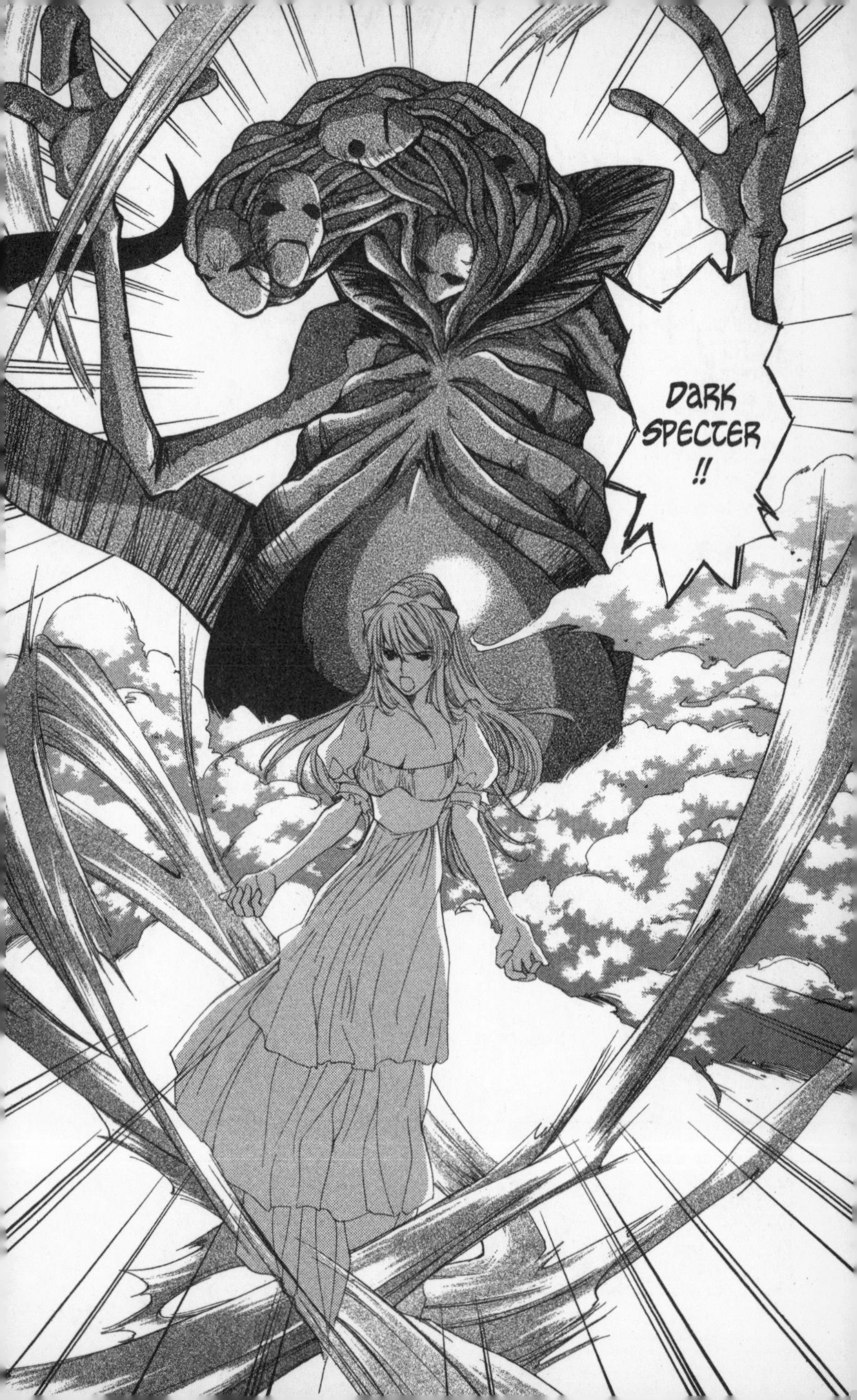
DARK SPECTER !!

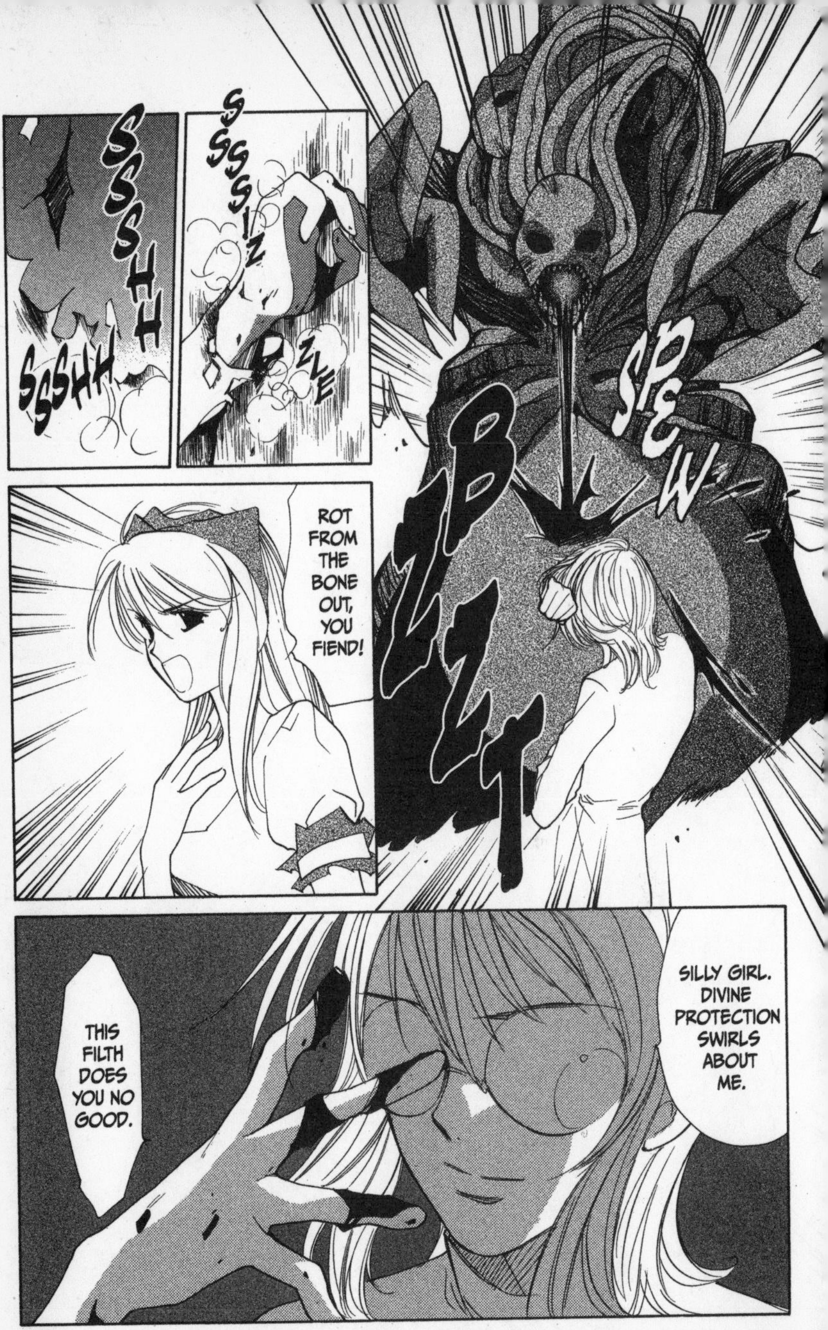
SPEW
BZZZT
SSSSIZZLE
SSSHHH
SSSHH
ROT FROM THE BONE OUT, YOU FIEND!
SILLY GIRL. DIVINE PROTECTION SWIRLS ABOUT ME.
THIS FILTH DOES YOU NO GOOD.

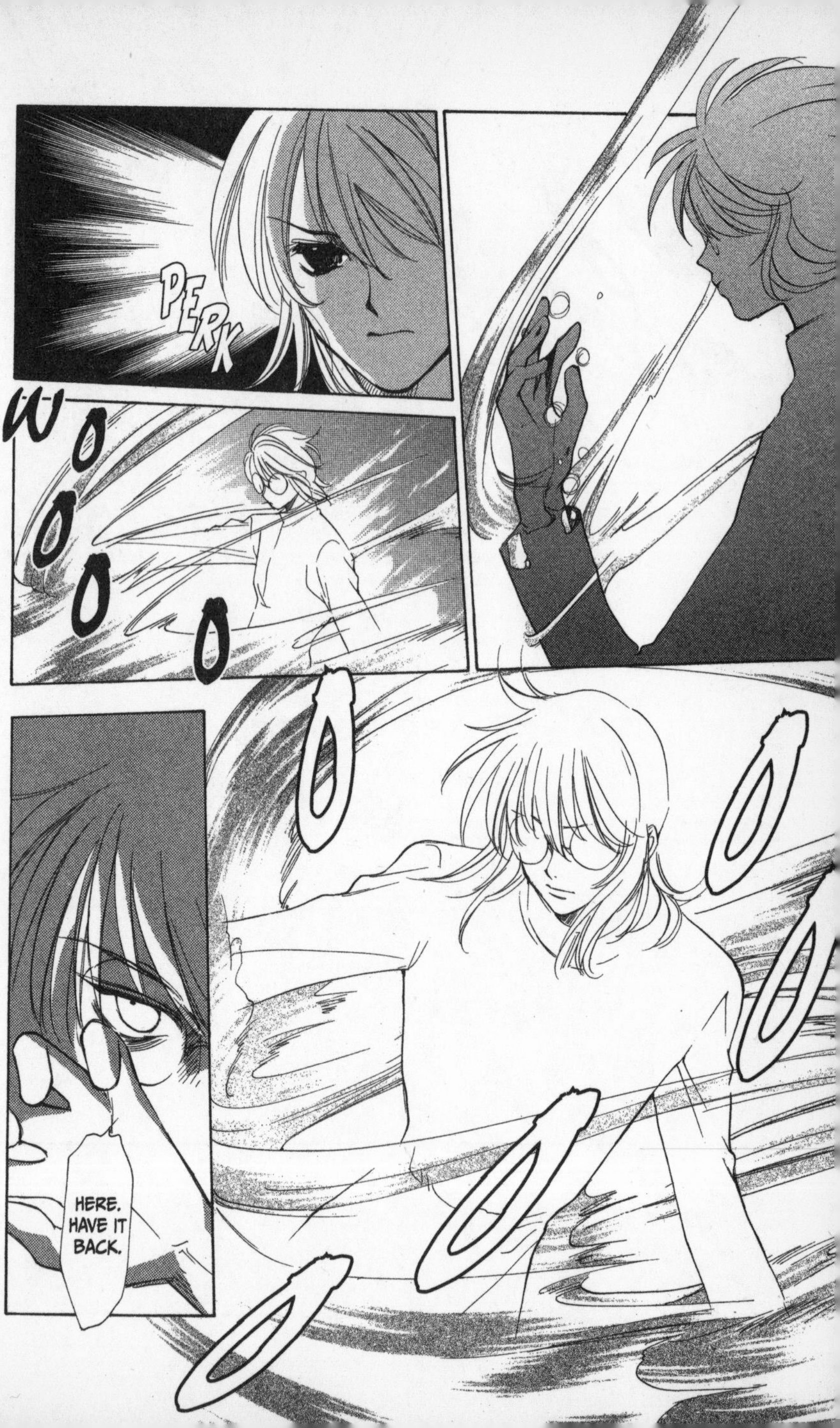
PERK
WOOOOO
HERE. HAVE IT BACK.

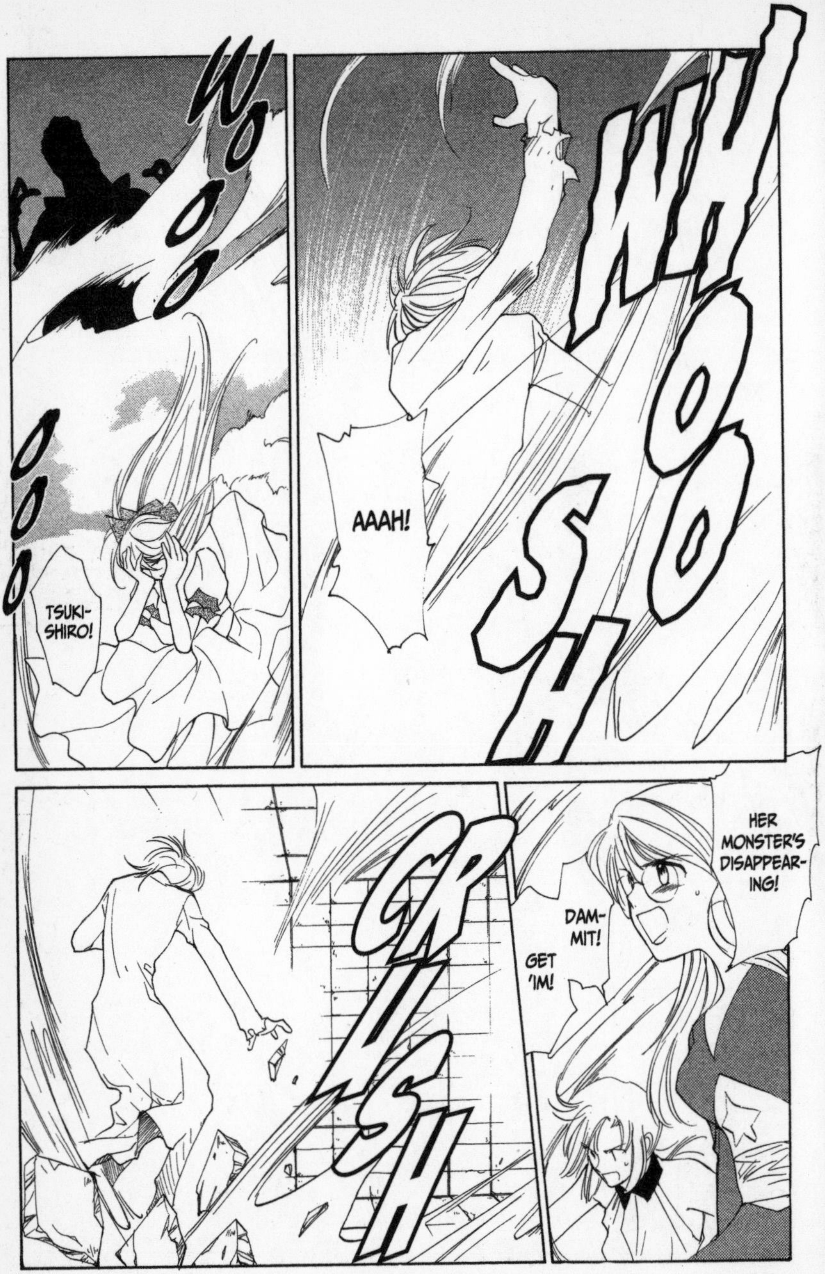
WHOOOSH
AAAH!
WOOOO
OOOOO
TSUKI-SHIRO!
HER MONSTER'S DISAPPEAR-ING!
DAM-MIT!
GET 'IM!
CRUSH

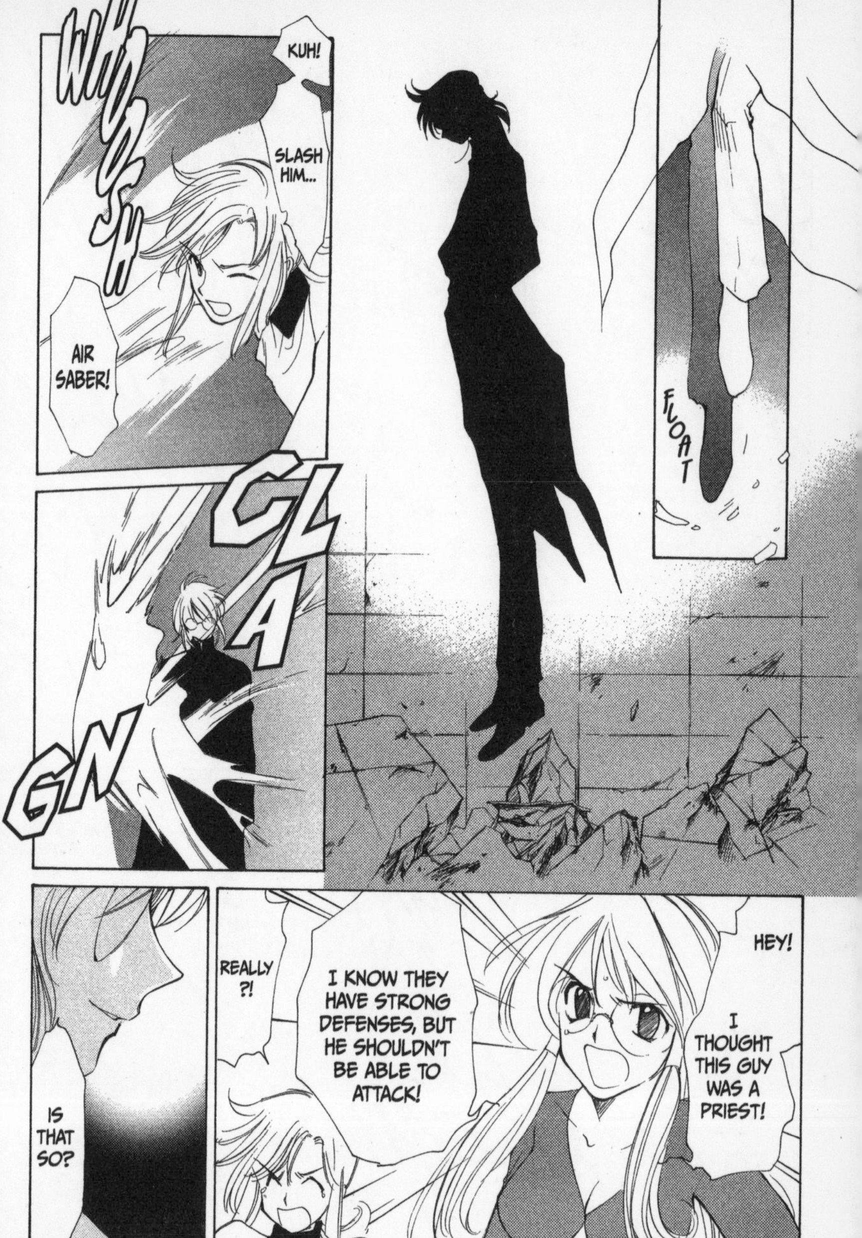
FLOAT
KUH!
SLASH HIM...
AIR SABER!
WHOOSH
CLANG
HEY!
I THOUGHT THIS GUY WAS A PRIEST!
I KNOW THEY HAVE STRONG DEFENSES, BUT HE SHOULDN'T BE ABLE TO ATTACK!
REALLY?!
IS THAT SO?

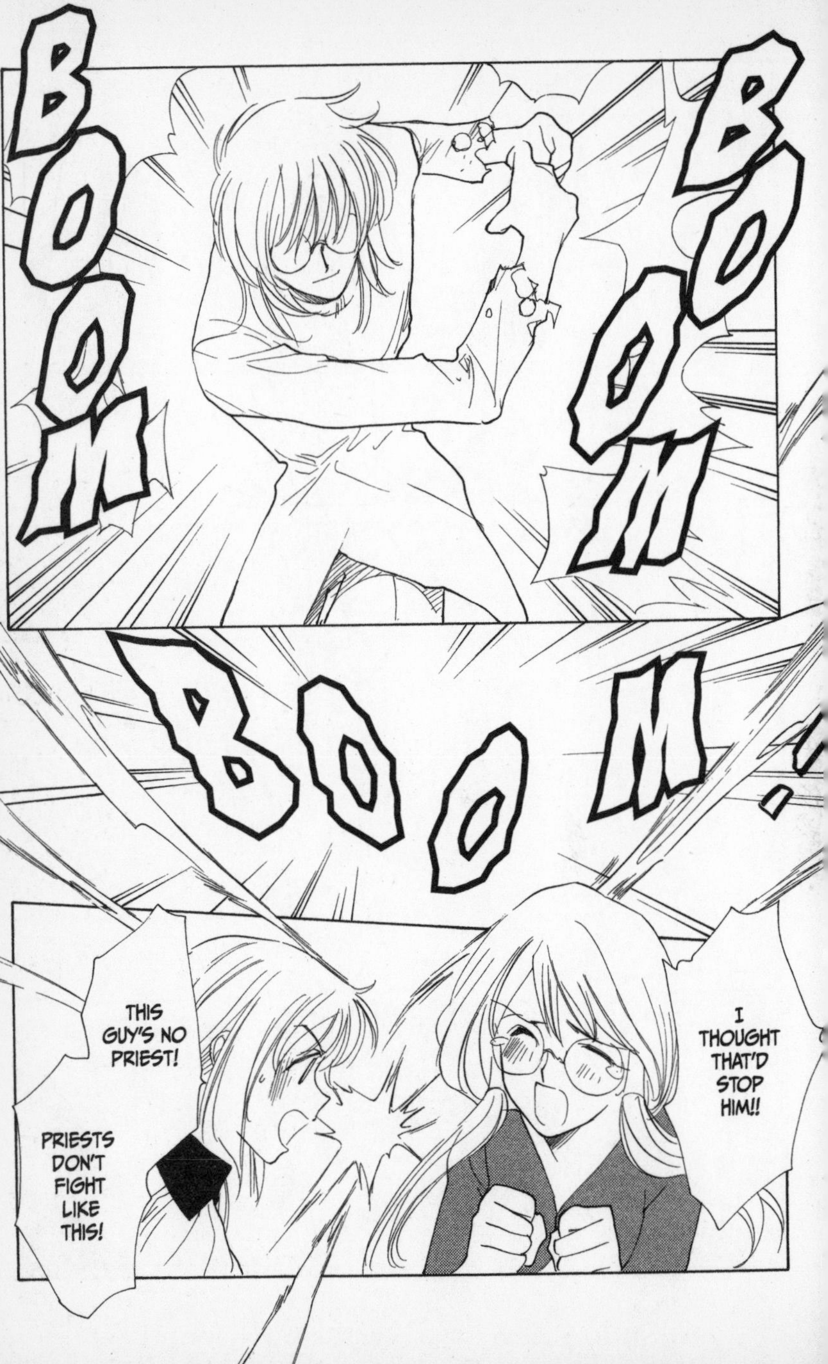
BOOM
BOOM
BOOOM!
I THOUGHT THAT'D STOP HIM!!
THIS GUY'S NO PRIEST!
PRIESTS DON'T FIGHT LIKE THIS!

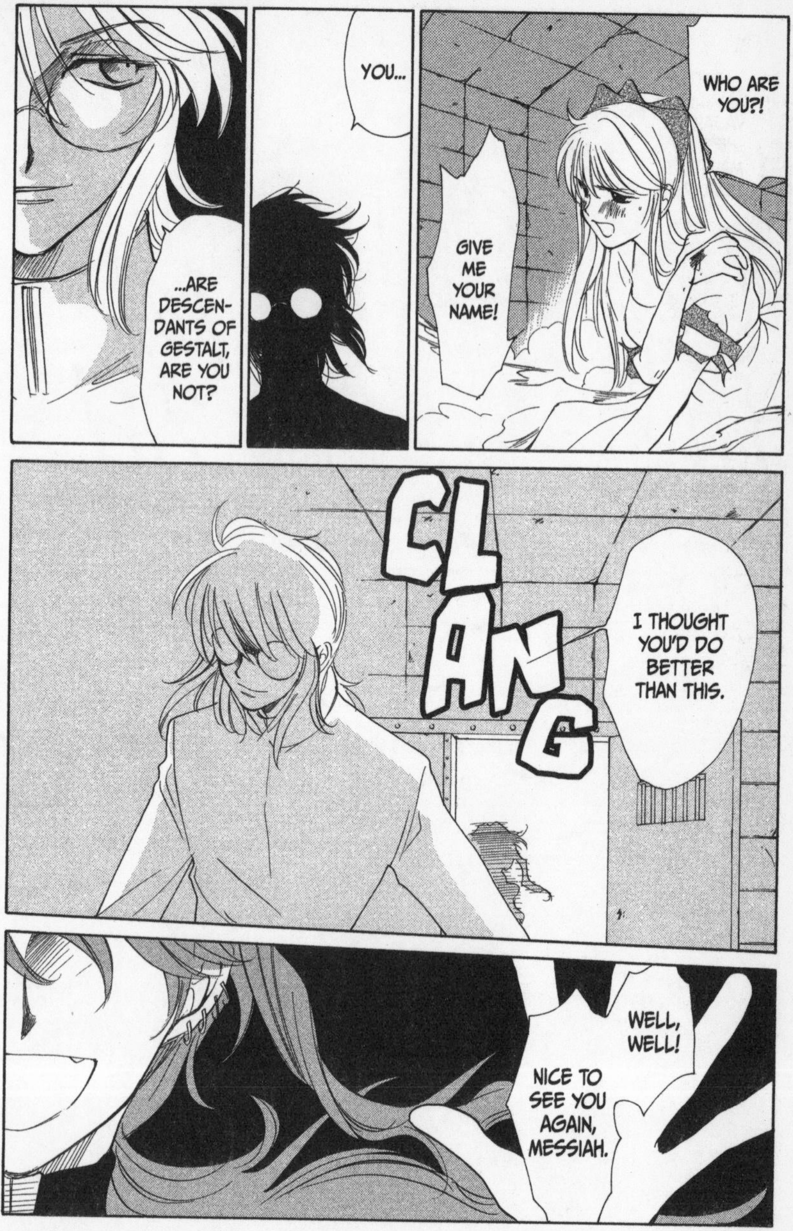
WHO ARE YOU?!
GIVE ME YOUR NAME!
YOU...
...ARE DESCEN-DANTS OF GESTALT, ARE YOU NOT?
CLANG
I THOUGHT YOU'D DO BETTER THAN THIS.
WELL, WELL!
NICE TO SEE YOU AGAIN, MESSIAH.

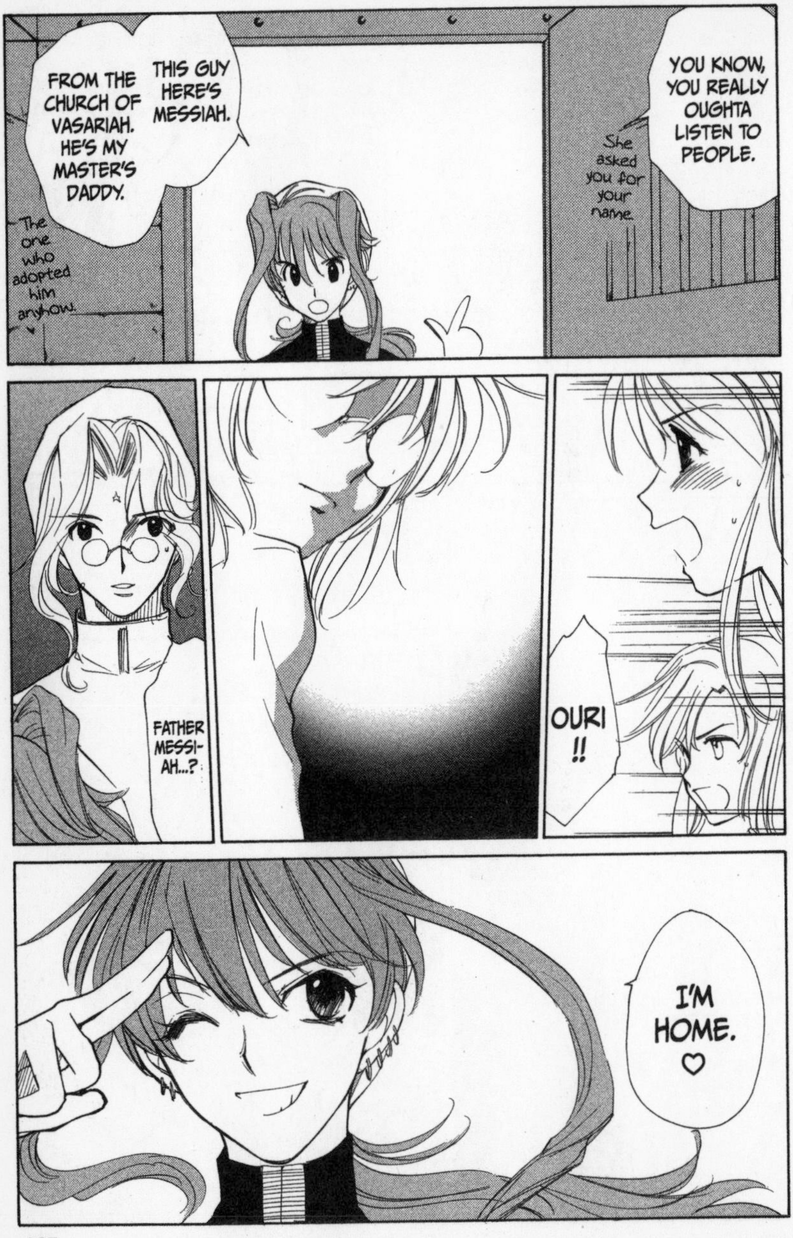
YOU KNOW, YOU REALLY OUGHTA LISTEN TO PEOPLE.
She asked you for your name.
THIS GUY HERE'S MESSIAH.
FROM THE CHURCH OF VASARIAH. HE'S MY MASTER'S DADDY.
The one who adopted him anyhow.
OURI !!
FATHER MESSIAH...?
I'M HOME. ♡

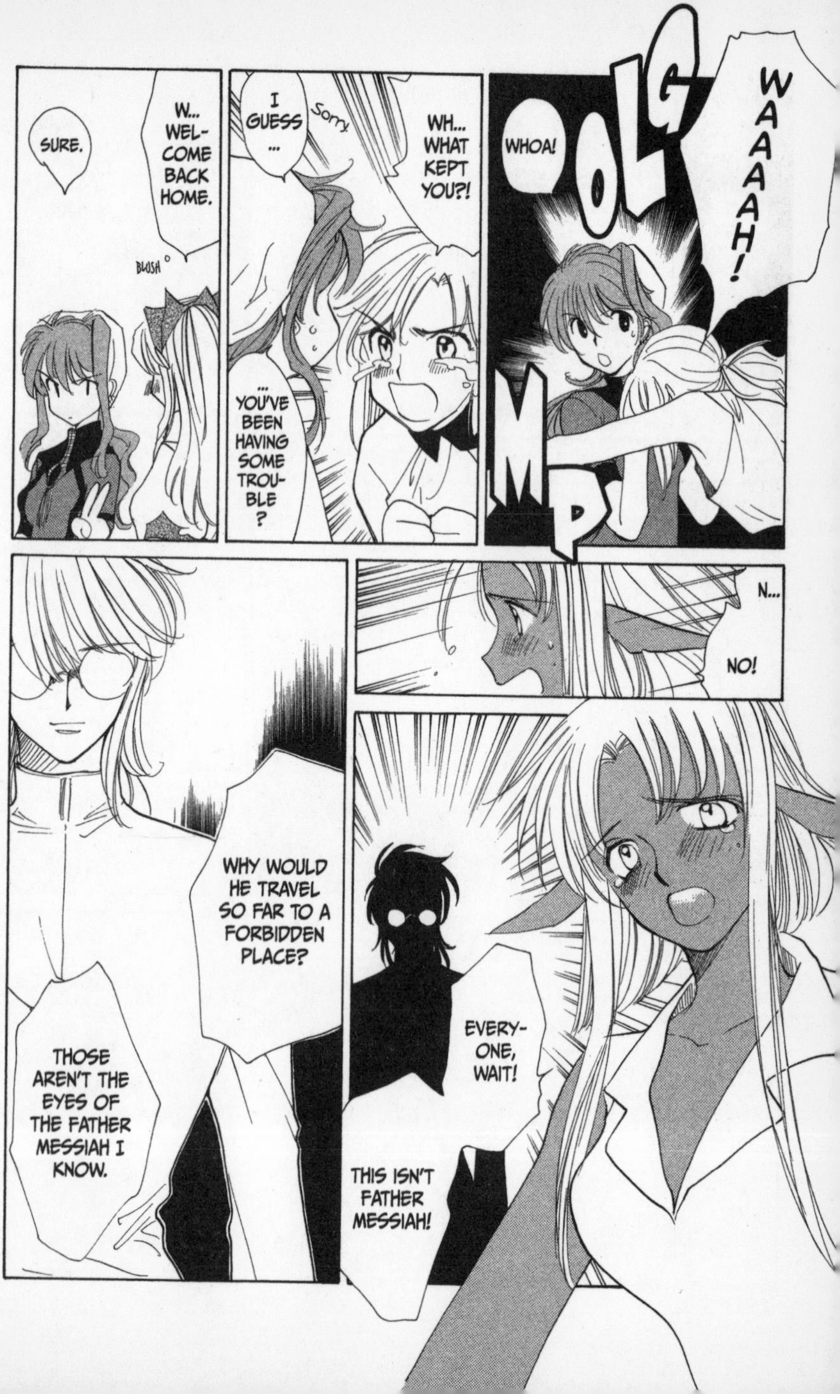
WAAAAAH!
WHOA!
GLOMP
WH... WHAT KEPT YOU?!
Sorry
I GUESS...
...YOU'VE BEEN HAVING SOME TROU-BLE?
W... WEL-COME BACK HOME.
BLUSH
SURE.
N...
NO!
EVERY-ONE, WAIT!
THIS ISN'T FATHER MESSIAH!
WHY WOULD HE TRAVEL SO FAR TO A FORBIDDEN PLACE?
THOSE AREN'T THE EYES OF THE FATHER MESSIAH I KNOW.

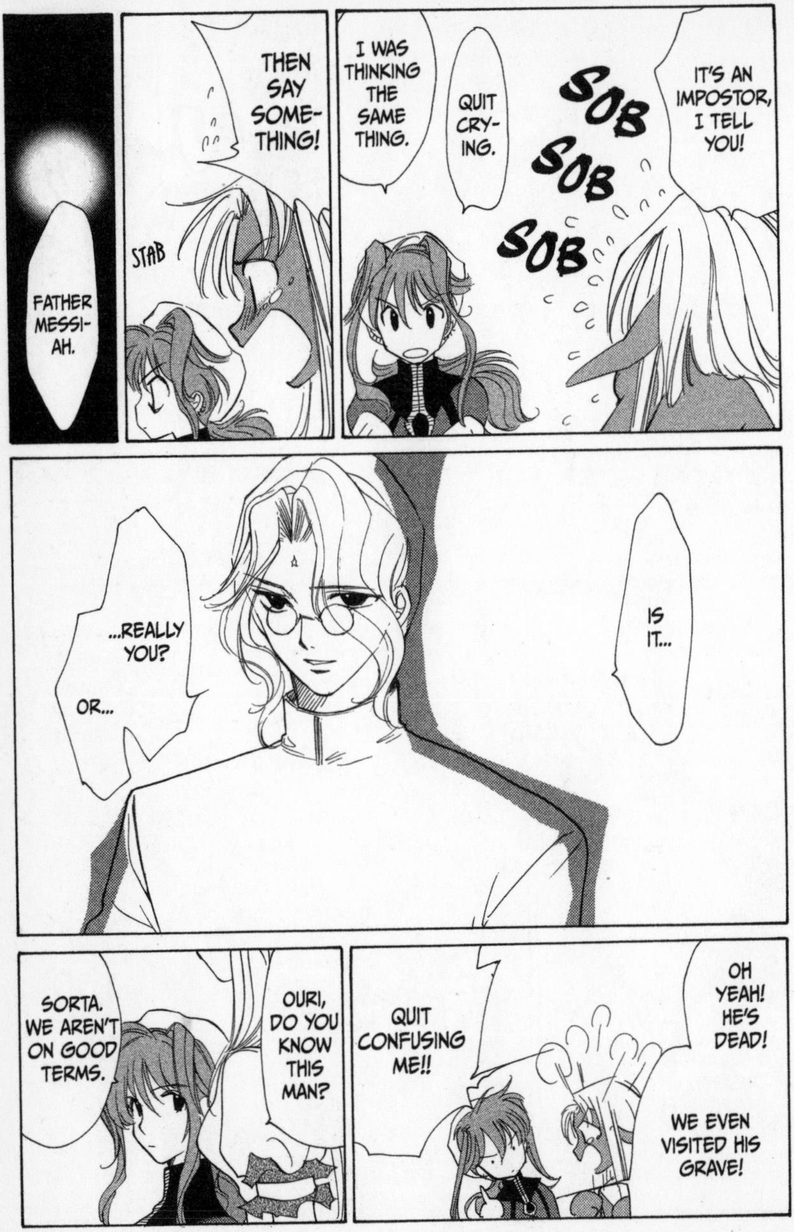
IT'S AN IMPOSTOR, I TELL YOU!
SOB SOB SOB
QUIT CRYING.
I WAS THINKING THE SAME THING.
THEN SAY SOMETHING!
STAB
FATHER MESSIAH.
IS IT...
...REALLY YOU?
OR...
OH YEAH! HE'S DEAD!
WE EVEN VISITED HIS GRAVE!
QUIT CONFUSING ME!!
OURI, DO YOU KNOW THIS MAN?
SORTA. WE AREN'T ON GOOD TERMS.

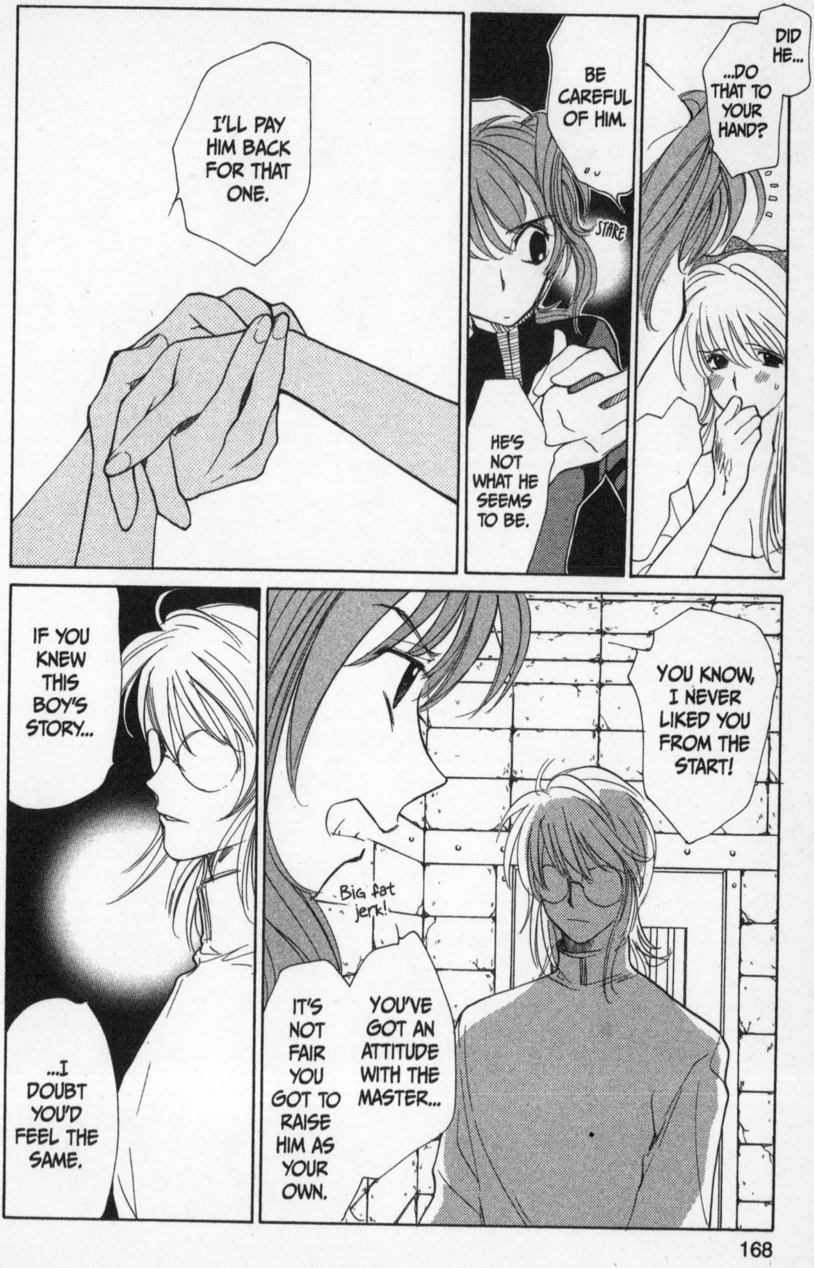
DID HE...
...DO THAT TO YOUR HAND?
BE CAREFUL OF HIM.
STARE
HE'S NOT WHAT HE SEEMS TO BE.
I'LL PAY HIM BACK FOR THAT ONE.
YOU KNOW, I NEVER LIKED YOU FROM THE START!
Big fat jerk!
YOU'VE GOT AN ATTITUDE WITH THE MASTER...
IT'S NOT FAIR YOU GOT TO RAISE HIM AS YOUR OWN.
IF YOU KNEW THIS BOY'S STORY...
...I DOUBT YOU'D FEEL THE SAME.

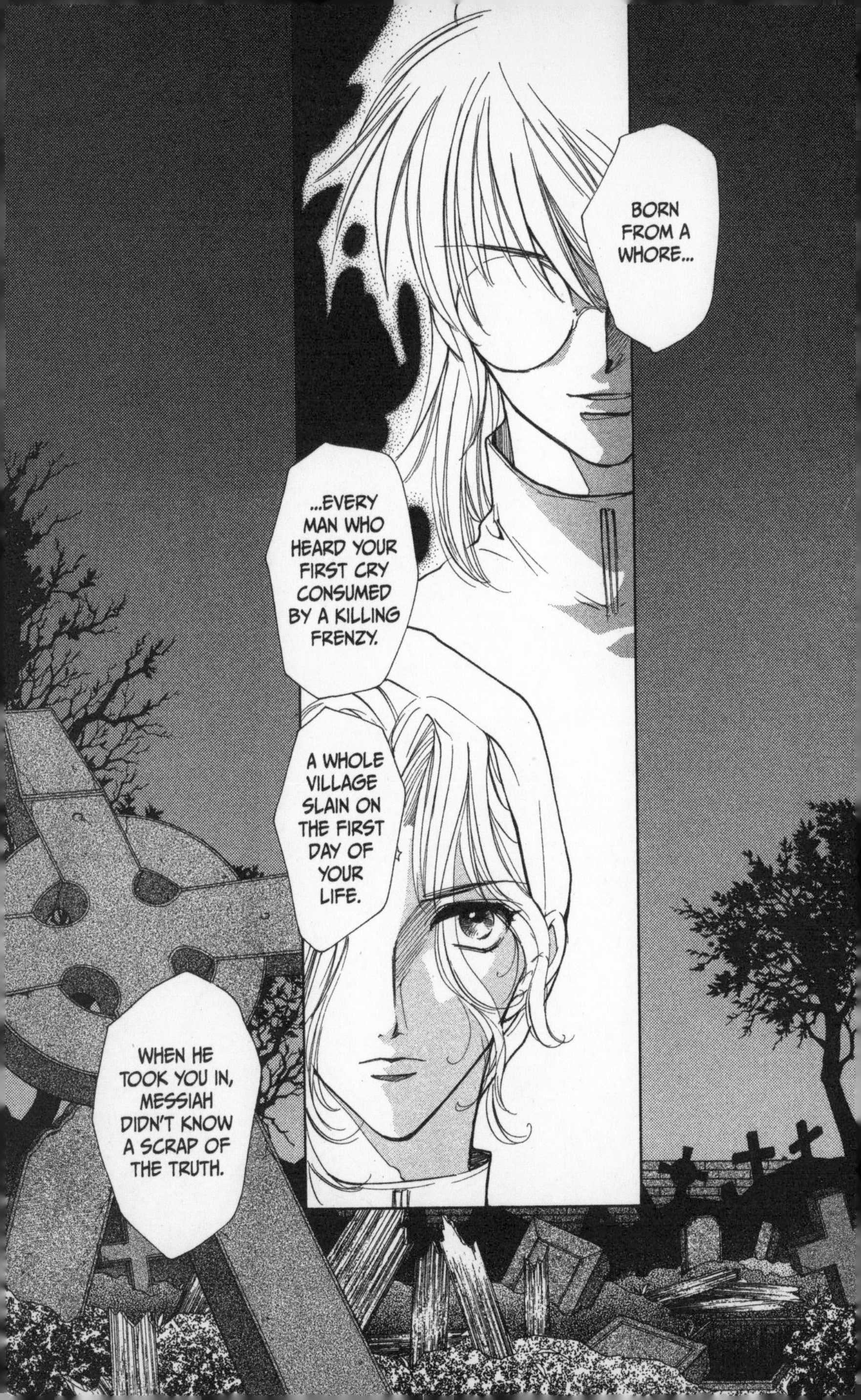
BORN FROM A WHORE...
...EVERY MAN WHO HEARD YOUR FIRST CRY CONSUMED BY A KILLING FRENZY.
A WHOLE VILLAGE SLAIN ON THE FIRST DAY OF YOUR LIFE.
WHEN HE TOOK YOU IN, MESSIAH DIDN'T KNOW A SCRAP OF THE TRUTH.

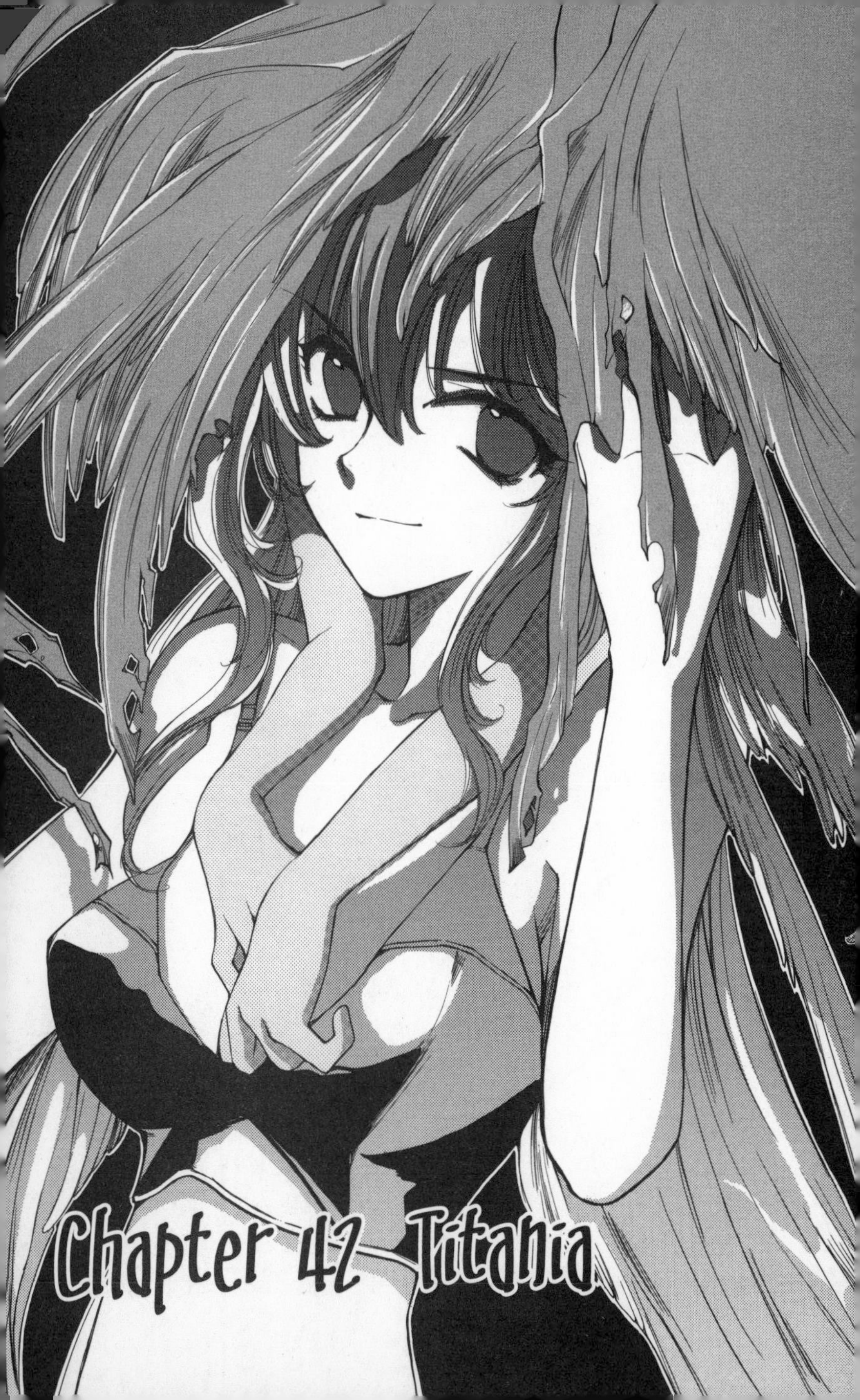

Chapter 42 Titania

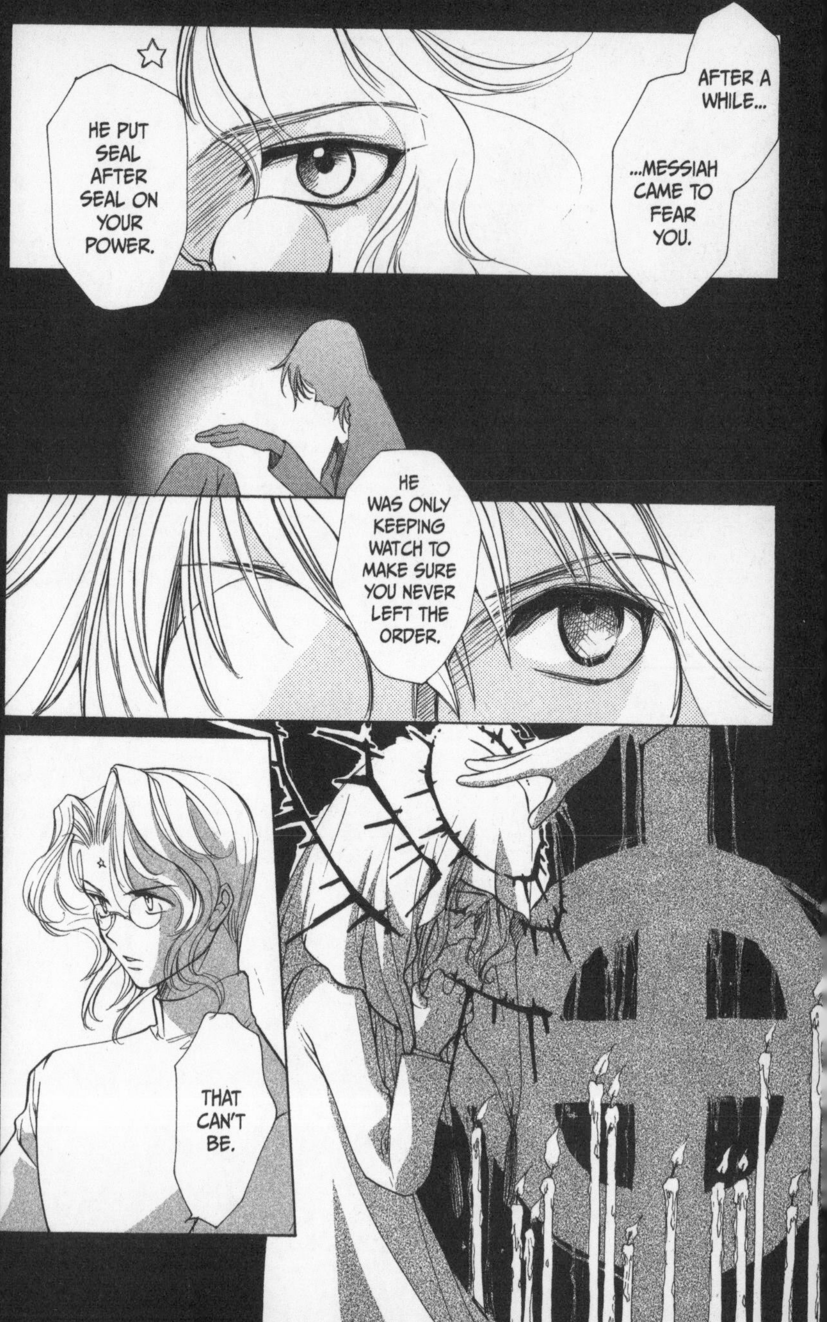
AFTER A WHILE...
...MESSIAH CAME TO FEAR YOU.
HE PUT SEAL AFTER SEAL ON YOUR POWER.
HE WAS ONLY KEEPING WATCH TO MAKE SURE YOU NEVER LEFT THE ORDER.
THAT CAN'T BE.

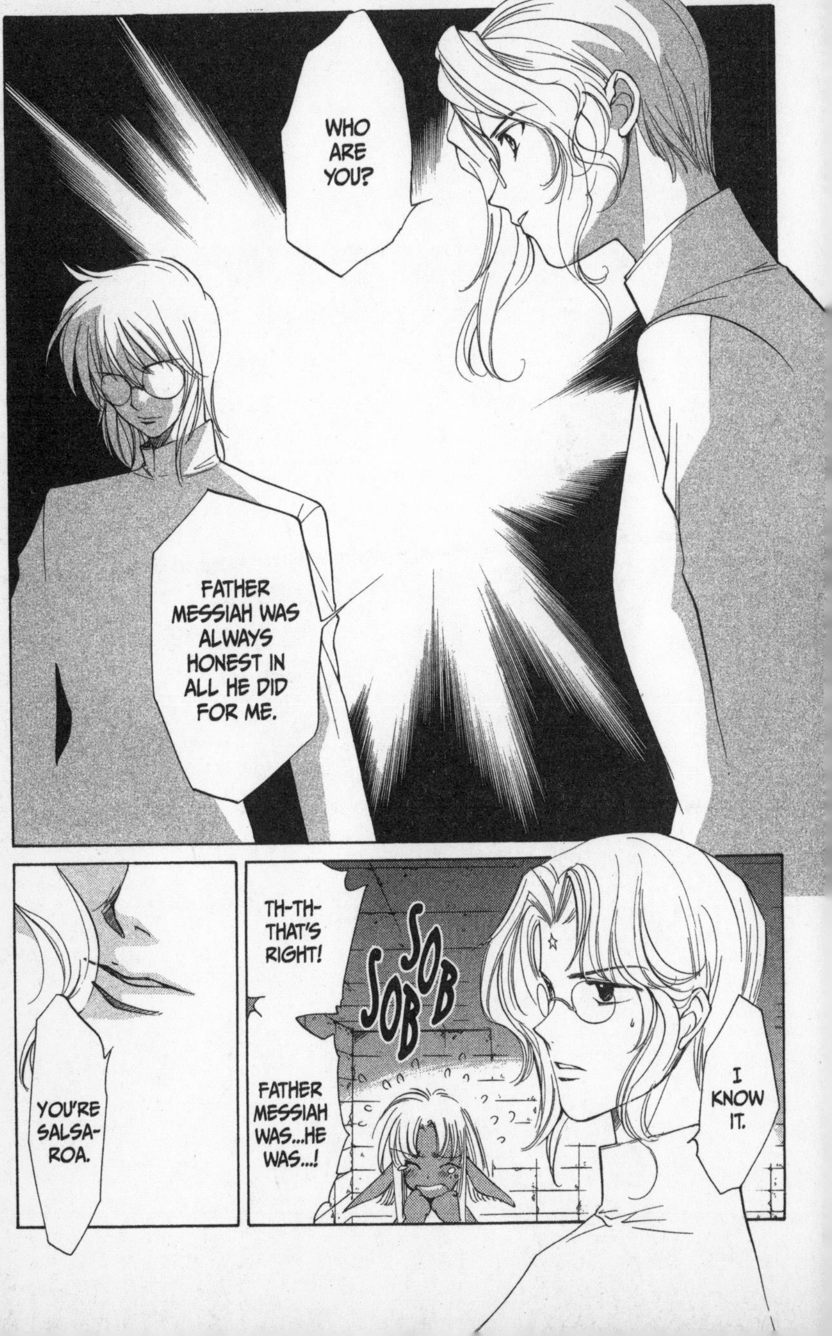
WHO ARE YOU?
FATHER MESSIAH WAS ALWAYS HONEST IN ALL HE DID FOR ME.
I KNOW IT.
TH-TH-THAT'S RIGHT!
SOB SOB
FATHER MESSIAH WAS...HE WAS...!
YOU'RE SALSA-ROA.

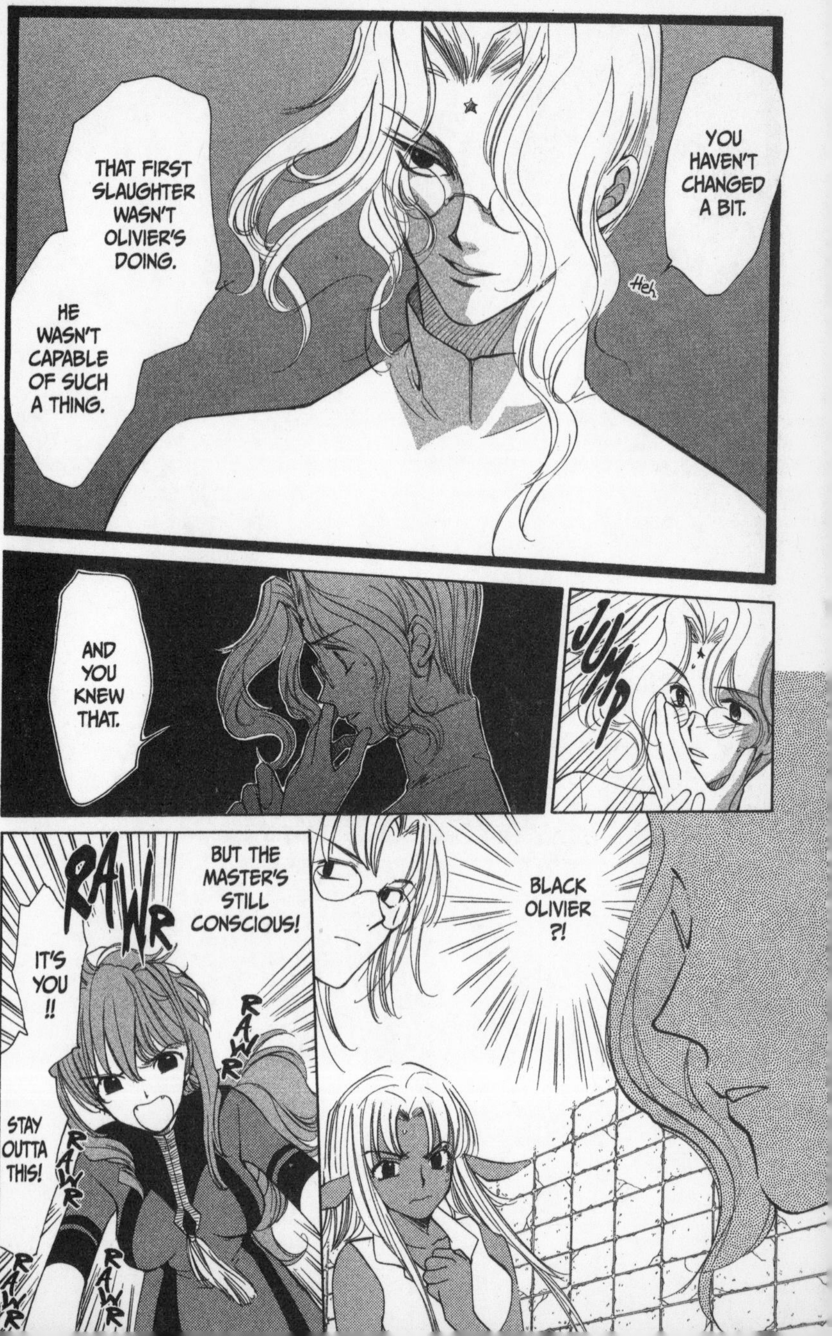
YOU HAVEN'T CHANGED A BIT.
Heh
THAT FIRST SLAUGHTER WASN'T OLIVIER'S DOING.
HE WASN'T CAPABLE OF SUCH A THING.
JUMP
AND YOU KNEW THAT.
BLACK OLIVIER ?!
BUT THE MASTER'S STILL CONSCIOUS!
RAWR
IT'S YOU !!
RAWR
STAY OUTTA THIS!
RAWR
RAWR
RAWR

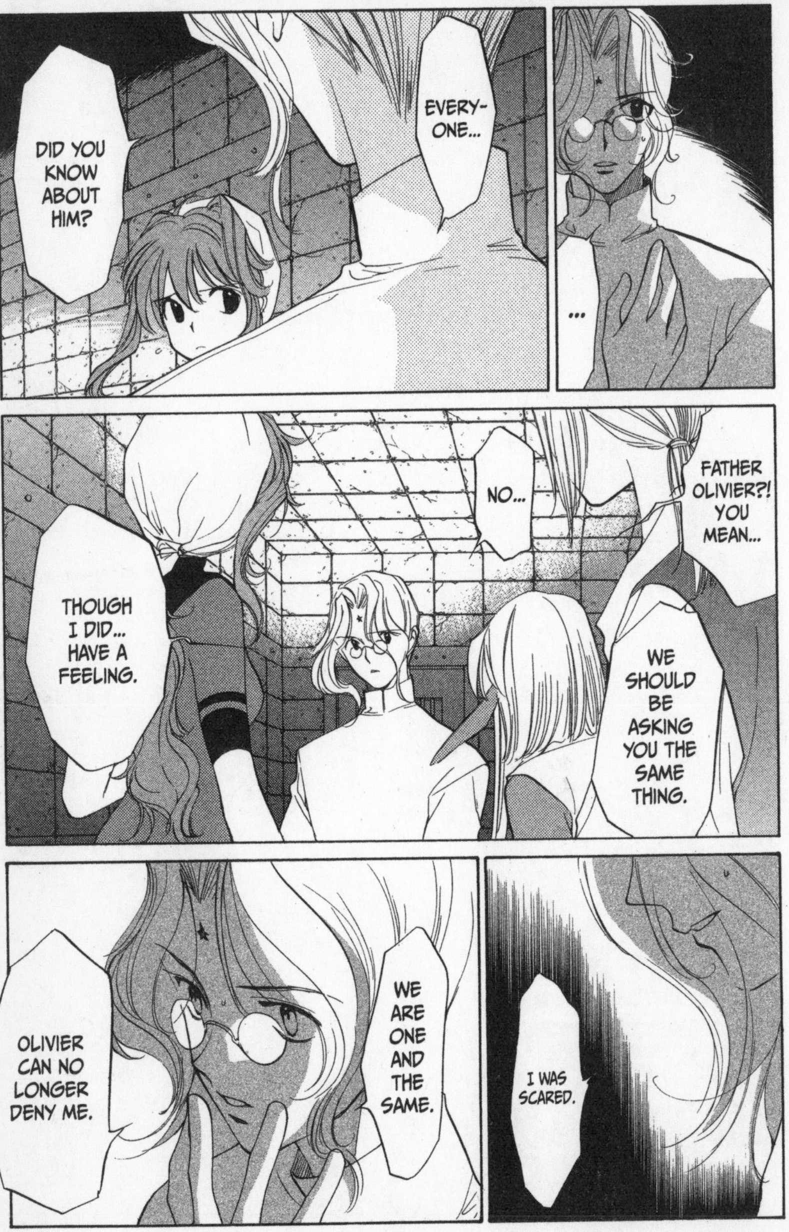
...
EVERY-ONE...
DID YOU KNOW ABOUT HIM?
FATHER OLIVIER?! YOU MEAN...
NO...
WE SHOULD BE ASKING YOU THE SAME THING.
THOUGH I DID... HAVE A FEELING.
I WAS SCARED.
WE ARE ONE AND THE SAME.
OLIVIER CAN NO LONGER DENY ME.

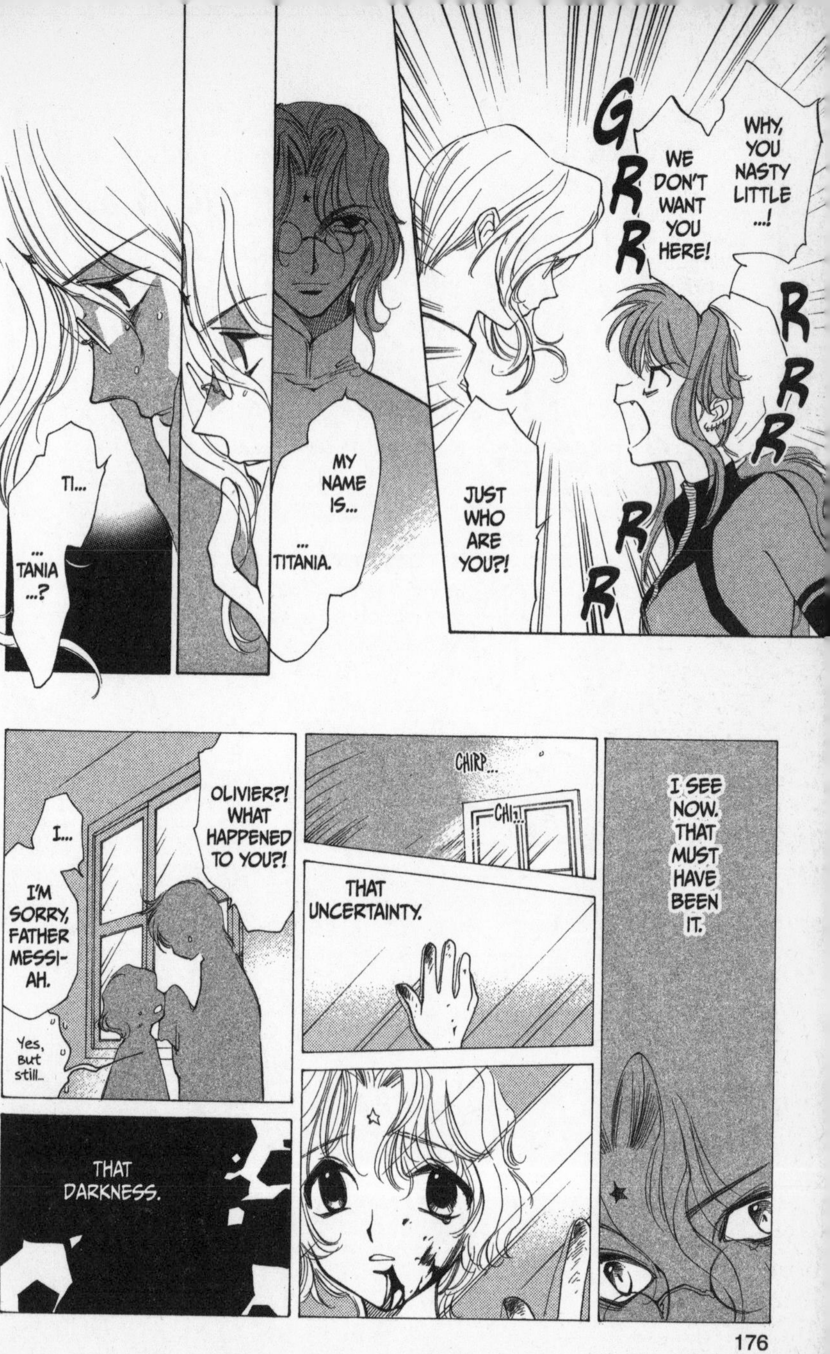

WHY, YOU NASTY LITTLE ...!
GRRRRRRR
WE DON'T WANT YOU HERE!
JUST WHO ARE YOU?!
MY NAME IS...
... TITANIA.
TI...
... TANIA ...?
I SEE NOW. THAT MUST HAVE BEEN IT.
CHIRP...
CHI...
THAT UNCERTAINTY.
OLIVIER?! WHAT HAPPENED TO YOU?!
I...
I'M SORRY, FATHER MESSIAH.
Yes, but still...
THAT DARKNESS.

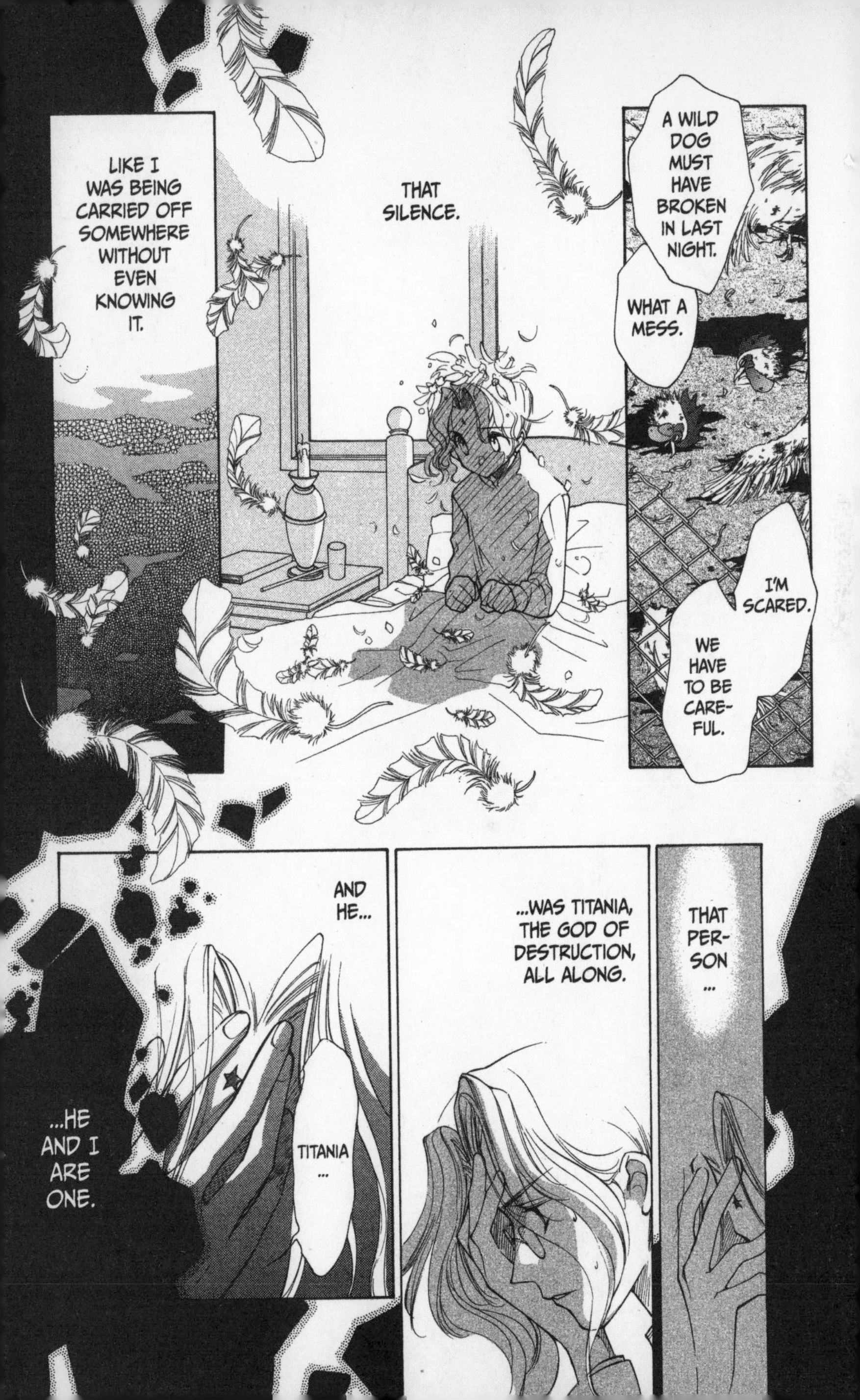
A WILD DOG MUST HAVE BROKEN IN LAST NIGHT.
WHAT A MESS.
I'M SCARED.
WE HAVE TO BE CARE-FUL.
THAT SILENCE.
LIKE I WAS BEING CARRIED OFF SOMEWHERE WITHOUT EVEN KNOWING IT.
THAT PER-SON ...
...WAS TITANIA, THE GOD OF DESTRUCTION, ALL ALONG.
AND HE...
TITANIA ...
...HE AND I ARE ONE.

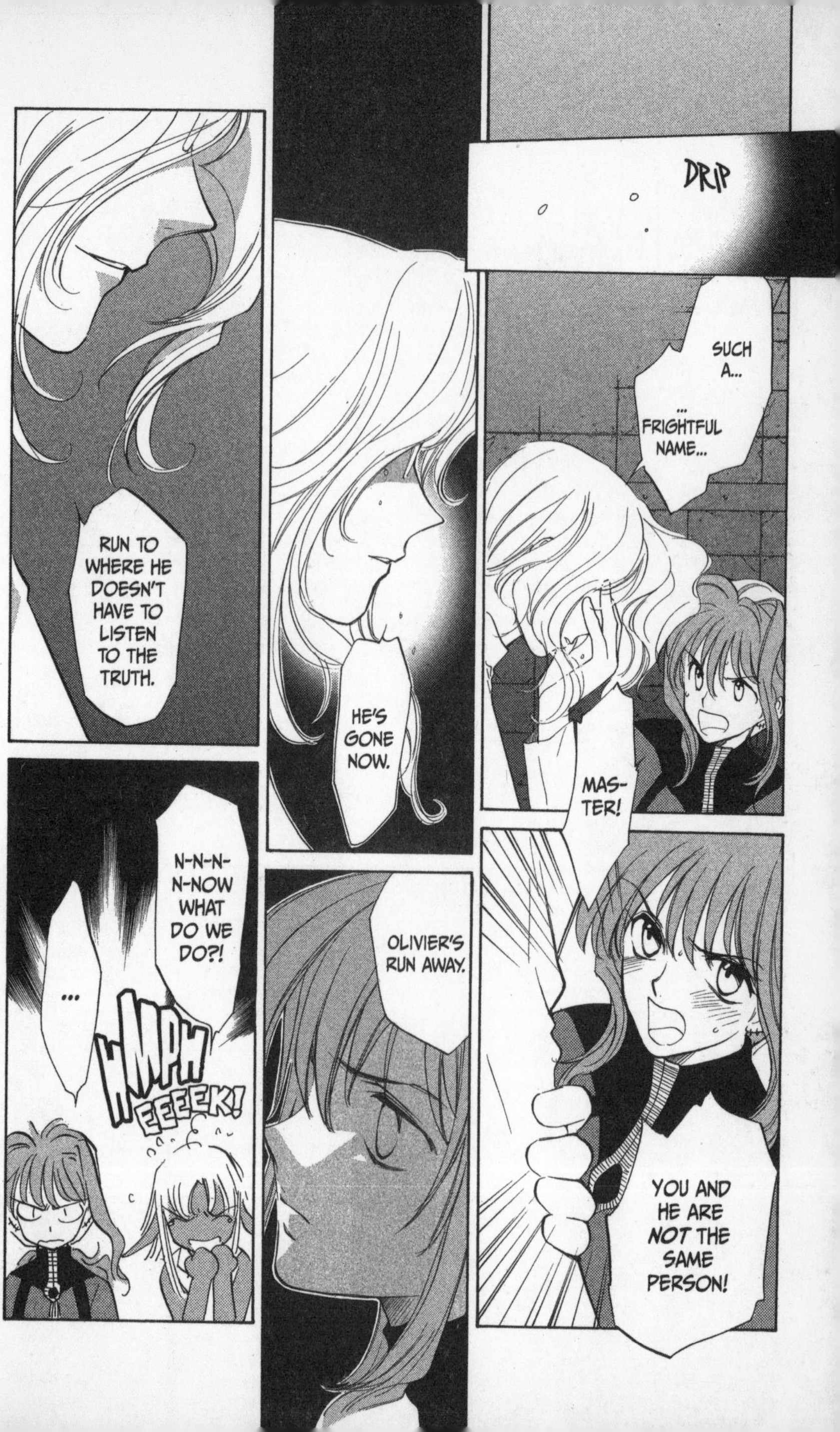
DRIP
SUCH A...
...FRIGHTFUL NAME...
HE'S GONE NOW.
RUN TO WHERE HE DOESN'T HAVE TO LISTEN TO THE TRUTH.
MAS-TER!
YOU AND HE ARE *NOT* THE SAME PERSON!
OLIVIER'S RUN AWAY.
N-N-N-N-NOW WHAT DO WE DO?!
...
HMPH
EEEEK!

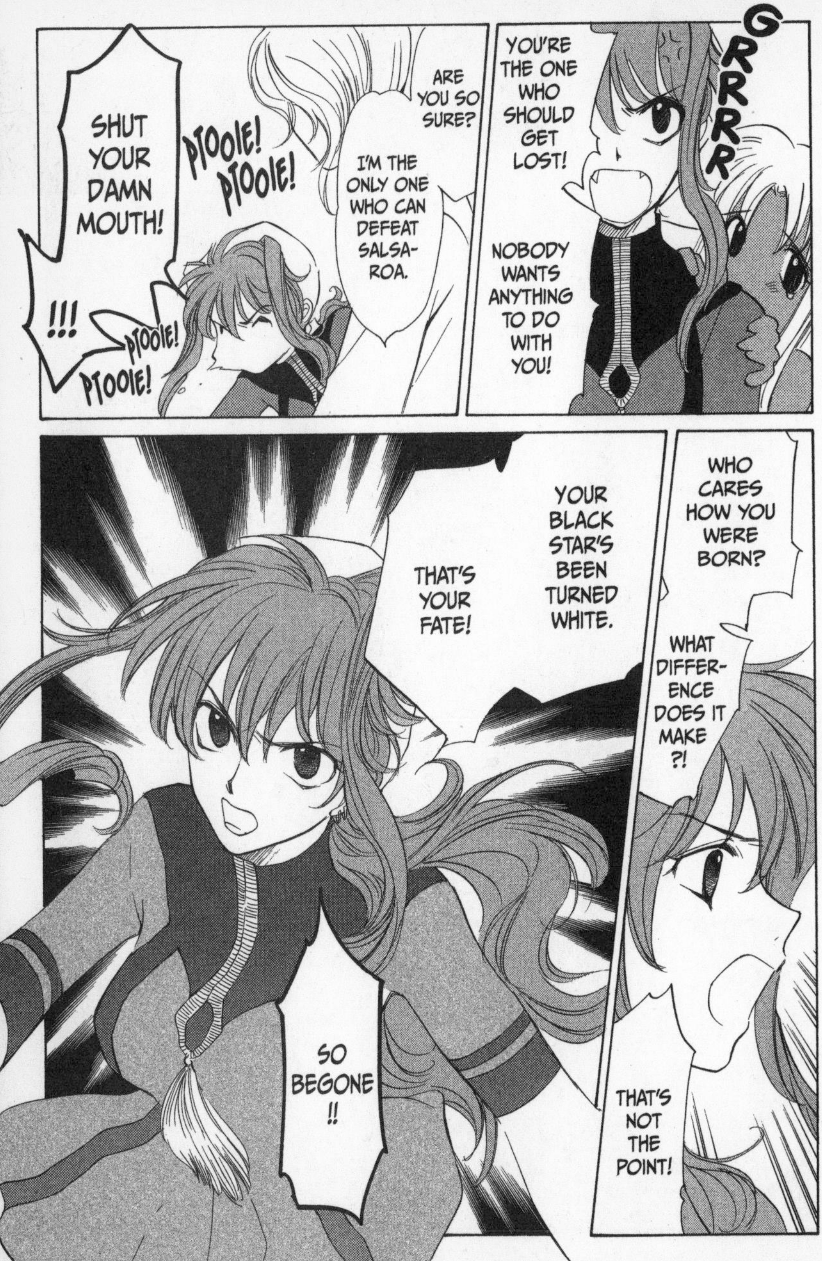
GRRRR
YOU'RE THE ONE WHO SHOULD GET LOST!
NOBODY WANTS ANYTHING TO DO WITH YOU!
ARE YOU SO SURE?
I'M THE ONLY ONE WHO CAN DEFEAT SALSA-ROA.
PTOOIE! PTOOIE!
SHUT YOUR DAMN MOUTH!
!!!
PTOOIE! PTOOIE!
WHO CARES HOW YOU WERE BORN?
WHAT DIFFER-ENCE DOES IT MAKE ?!
THAT'S NOT THE POINT!
YOUR BLACK STAR'S BEEN TURNED WHITE.
THAT'S YOUR FATE!
SO BEGONE !!

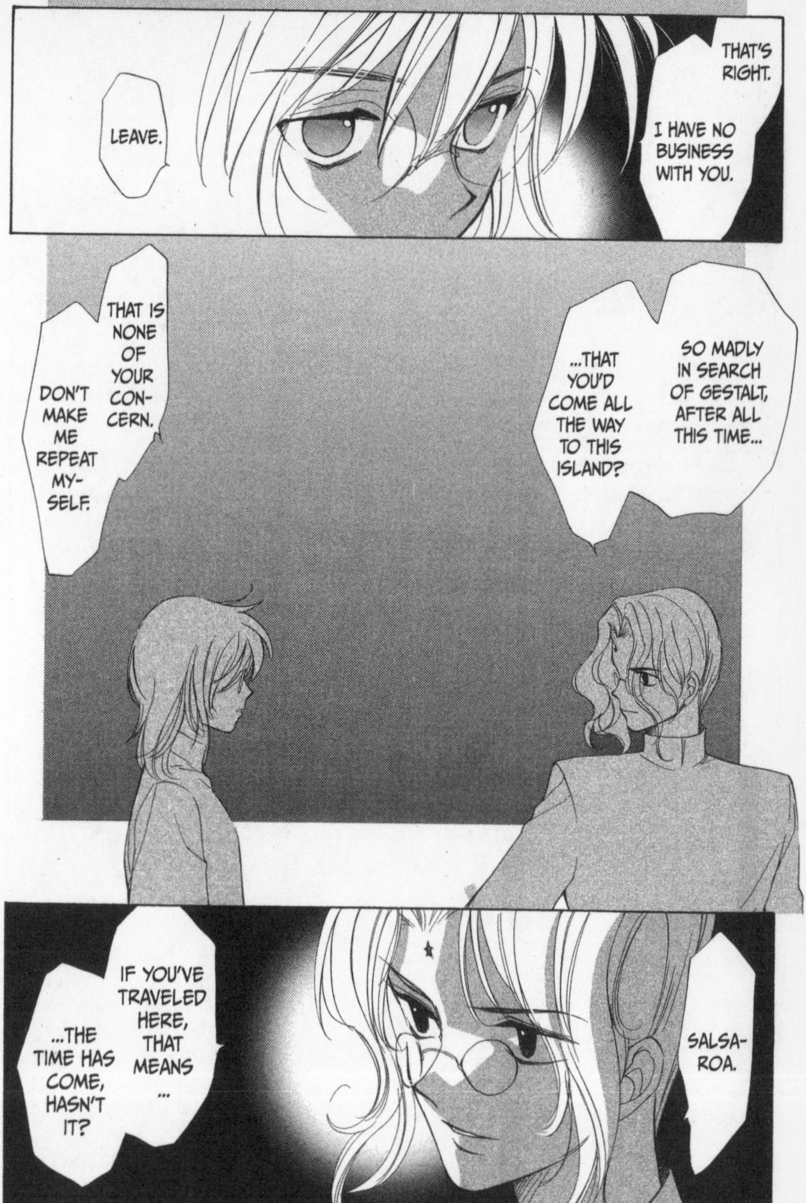
THAT'S RIGHT. I HAVE NO BUSINESS WITH YOU.
LEAVE.
SO MADLY IN SEARCH OF GESTALT, AFTER ALL THIS TIME... ...THAT YOU'D COME ALL THE WAY TO THIS ISLAND?
THAT IS NONE OF YOUR CON-CERN. DON'T MAKE ME REPEAT MY-SELF.
SALSA-ROA.
IF YOU'VE TRAVELED HERE, THAT MEANS...
...THE TIME HAS COME, HASN'T IT?

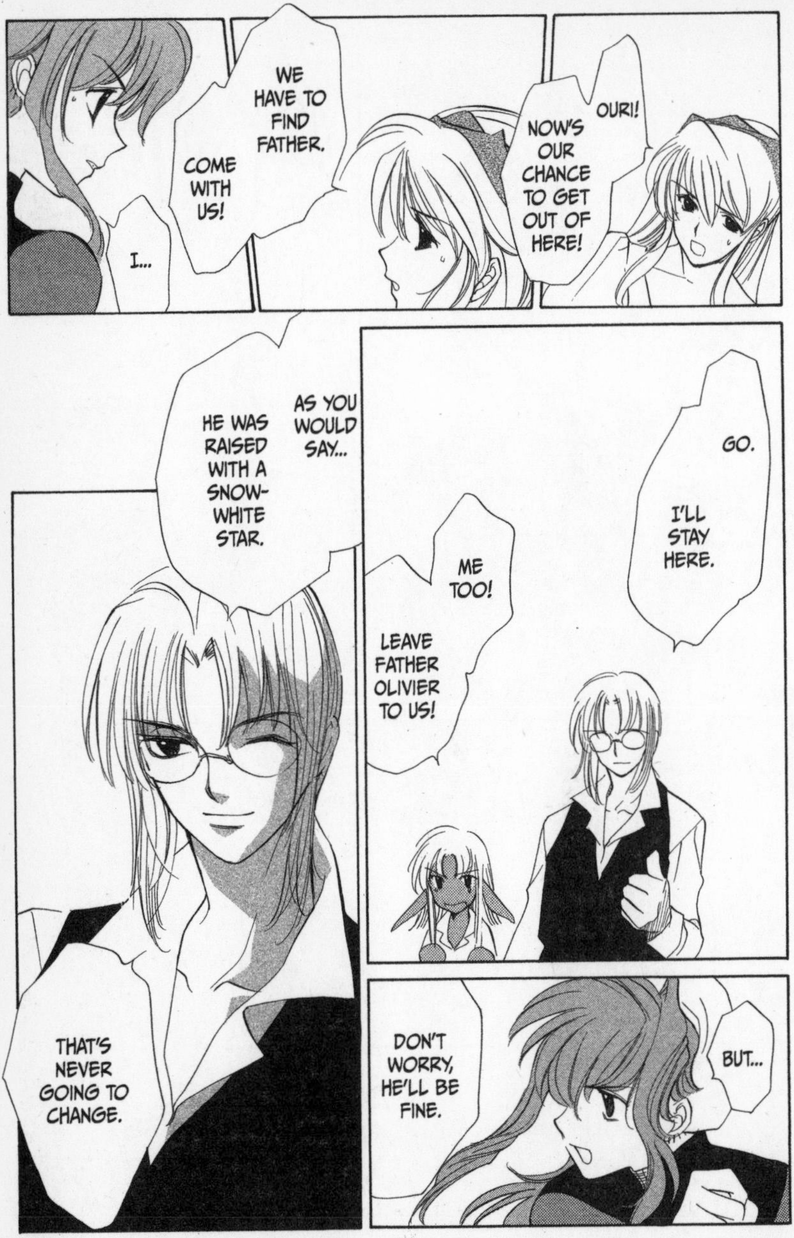
OURI!
NOW'S OUR CHANCE TO GET OUT OF HERE!
WE HAVE TO FIND FATHER.
COME WITH US!
I...
GO.
I'LL STAY HERE.
ME TOO!
LEAVE FATHER OLIVIER TO US!
BUT...
DON'T WORRY, HE'LL BE FINE.
AS YOU WOULD SAY...
HE WAS RAISED WITH A SNOW-WHITE STAR.
THAT'S NEVER GOING TO CHANGE.

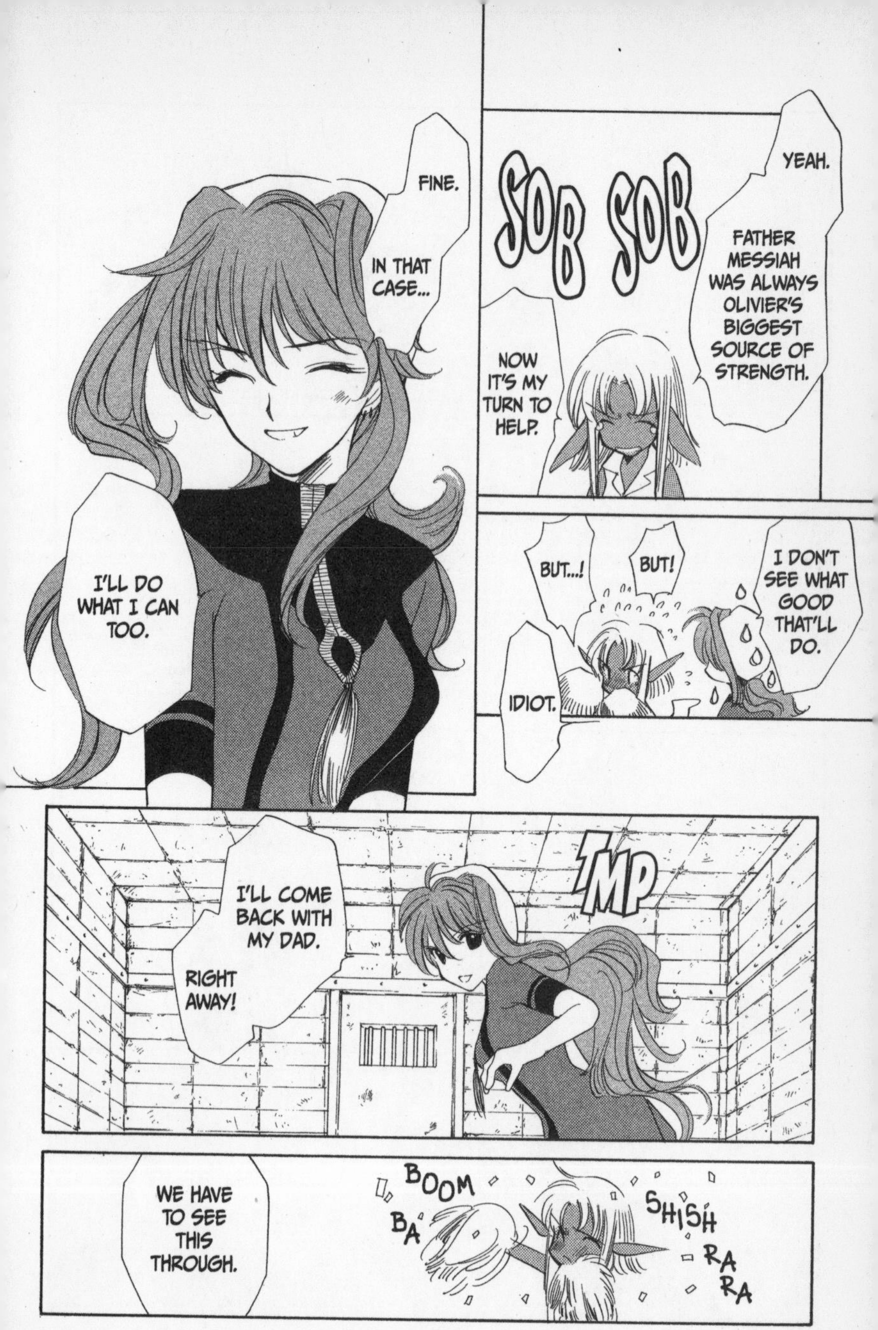
YEAH.
FATHER MESSIAH WAS ALWAYS OLIVIER'S BIGGEST SOURCE OF STRENGTH.
SOB SOB
NOW IT'S MY TURN TO HELP.
I DON'T SEE WHAT GOOD THAT'LL DO.
BUT!
BUT...!
IDIOT.
FINE.
IN THAT CASE...
I'LL DO WHAT I CAN TOO.
TMP
I'LL COME BACK WITH MY DAD.
RIGHT AWAY!
SHISH
RA RA
BOOM
BA
WE HAVE TO SEE THIS THROUGH.

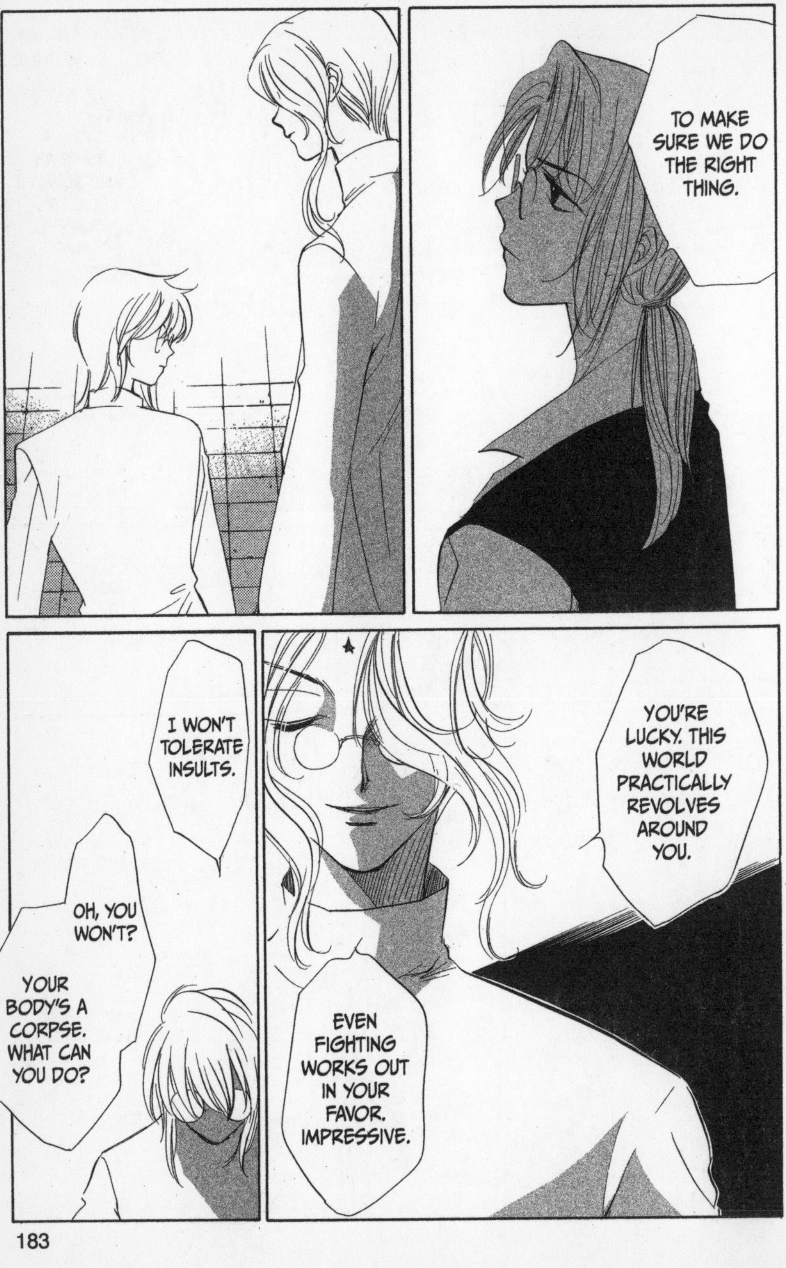
TO MAKE SURE WE DO THE RIGHT THING.
YOU'RE LUCKY. THIS WORLD PRACTICALLY REVOLVES AROUND YOU.
EVEN FIGHTING WORKS OUT IN YOUR FAVOR. IMPRESSIVE.
I WON'T TOLERATE INSULTS.
OH, YOU WON'T?
YOUR BODY'S A CORPSE. WHAT CAN YOU DO?

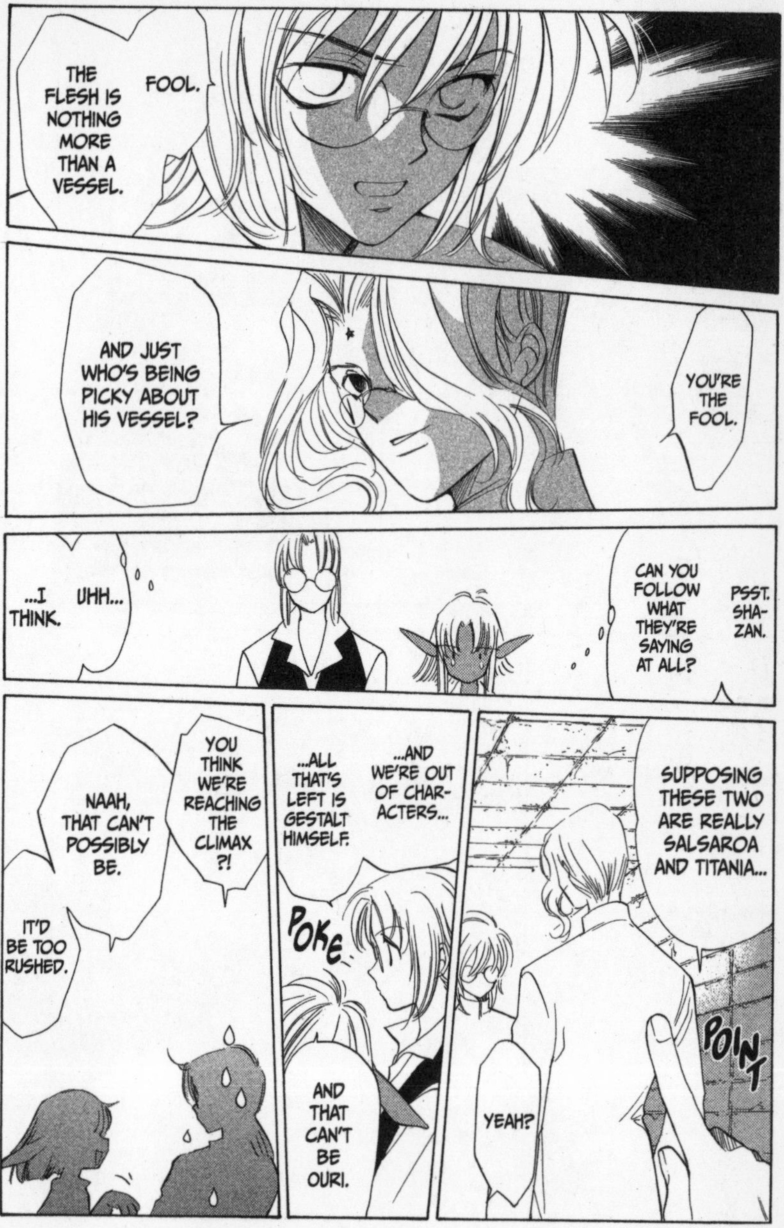
FOOL.
THE FLESH IS NOTHING MORE THAN A VESSEL.
YOU'RE THE FOOL.
AND JUST WHO'S BEING PICKY ABOUT HIS VESSEL?
PSST. SHAZAN.
CAN YOU FOLLOW WHAT THEY'RE SAYING AT ALL?
UHH...
...I THINK.
SUPPOSING THESE TWO ARE REALLY SALSAROA AND TITANIA...
POINT
YEAH?
...AND WE'RE OUT OF CHARACTERS...
...ALL THAT'S LEFT IS GESTALT HIMSELF.
POKE
AND THAT CAN'T BE OURI.
YOU THINK WE'RE REACHING THE CLIMAX?!
NAAH, THAT CAN'T POSSIBLY BE.
IT'D BE TOO RUSHED.

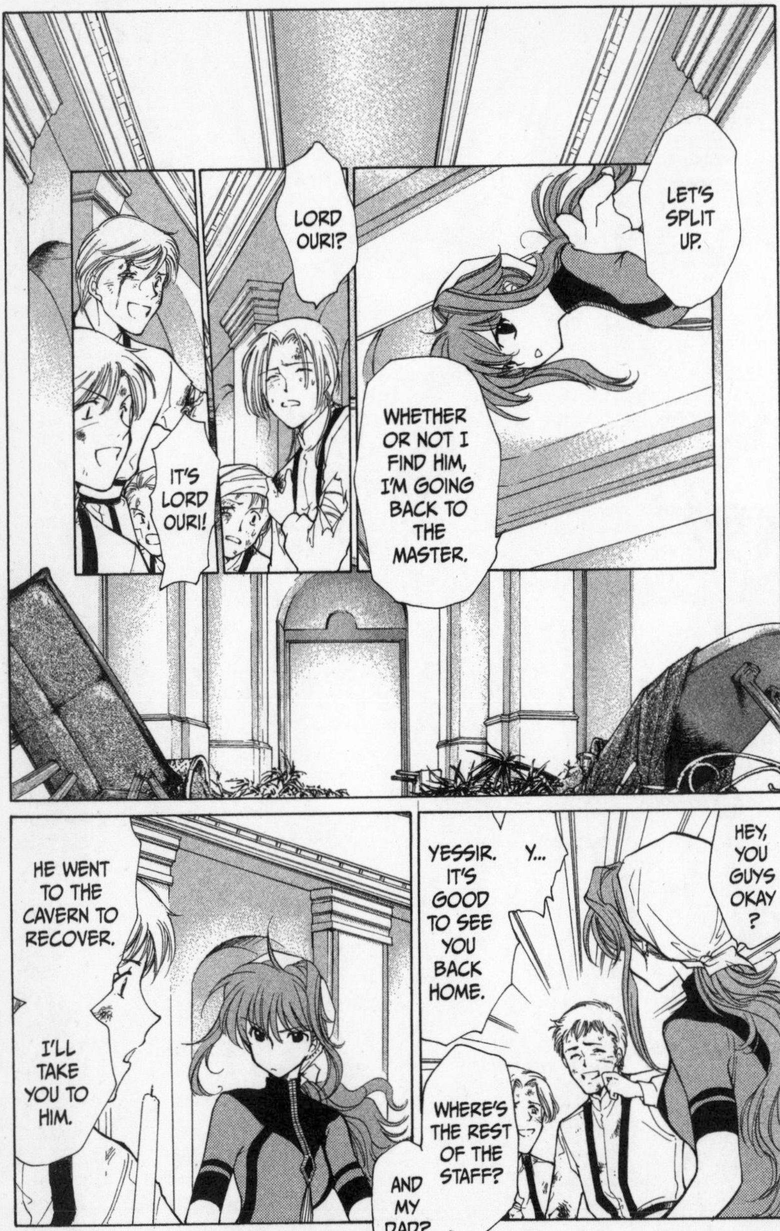
LET'S SPLIT UP.
WHETHER OR NOT I FIND HIM, I'M GOING BACK TO THE MASTER.
LORD OURI?
IT'S LORD OURI!
HEY, YOU GUYS OKAY?
Y...
YESSIR. IT'S GOOD TO SEE YOU BACK HOME.
WHERE'S THE REST OF THE STAFF?
AND MY DAD?
HE WENT TO THE CAVERN TO RECOVER.
I'LL TAKE YOU TO HIM.

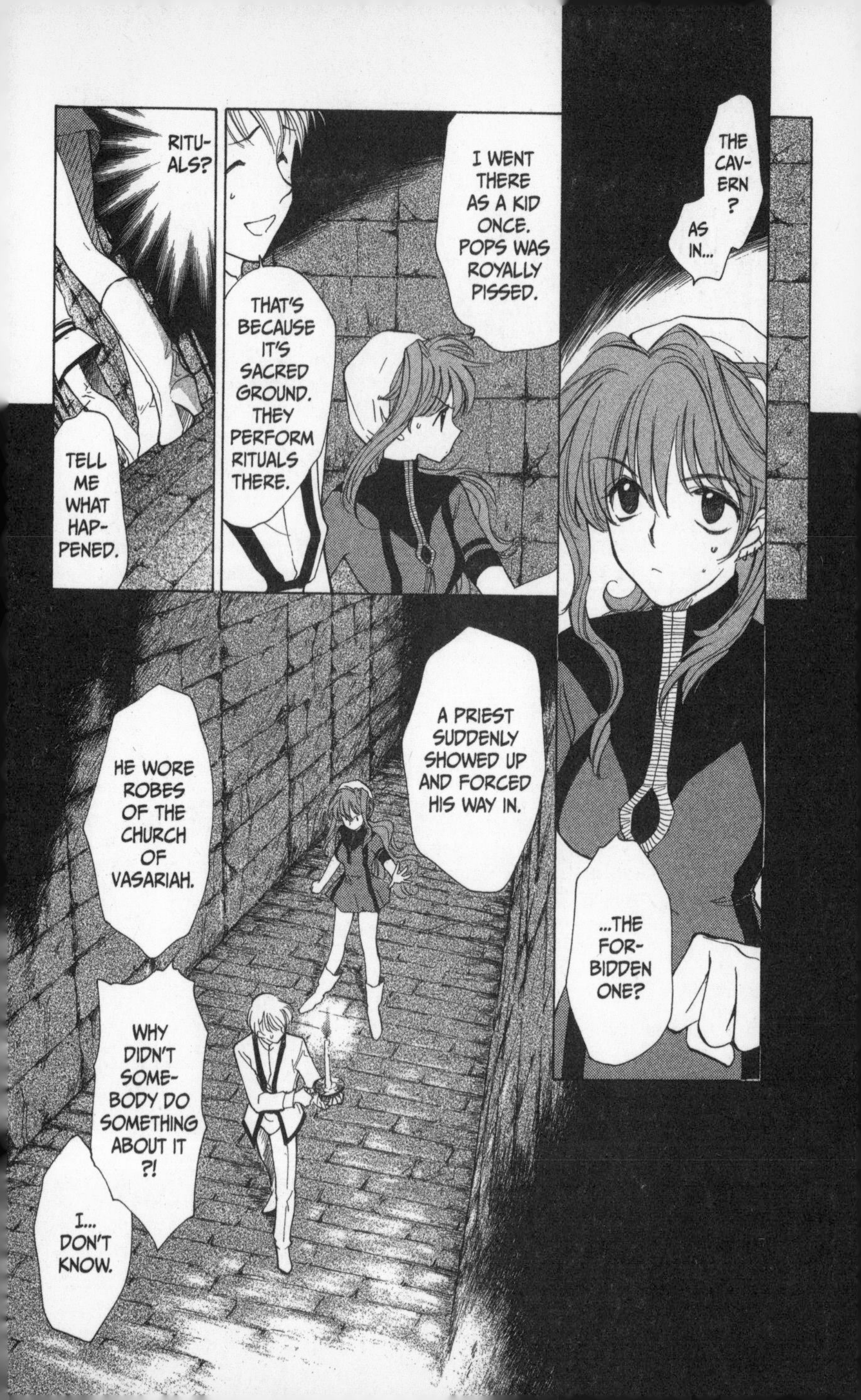
THE CAVERN? AS IN...
...THE FORBIDDEN ONE?
I WENT THERE AS A KID ONCE. POPS WAS ROYALLY PISSED.
THAT'S BECAUSE IT'S SACRED GROUND. THEY PERFORM RITUALS THERE.
RITUALS?
TELL ME WHAT HAPPENED.
A PRIEST SUDDENLY SHOWED UP AND FORCED HIS WAY IN.
HE WORE ROBES OF THE CHURCH OF VASARIAH.
WHY DIDN'T SOMEBODY DO SOMETHING ABOUT IT?!
I... DON'T KNOW.

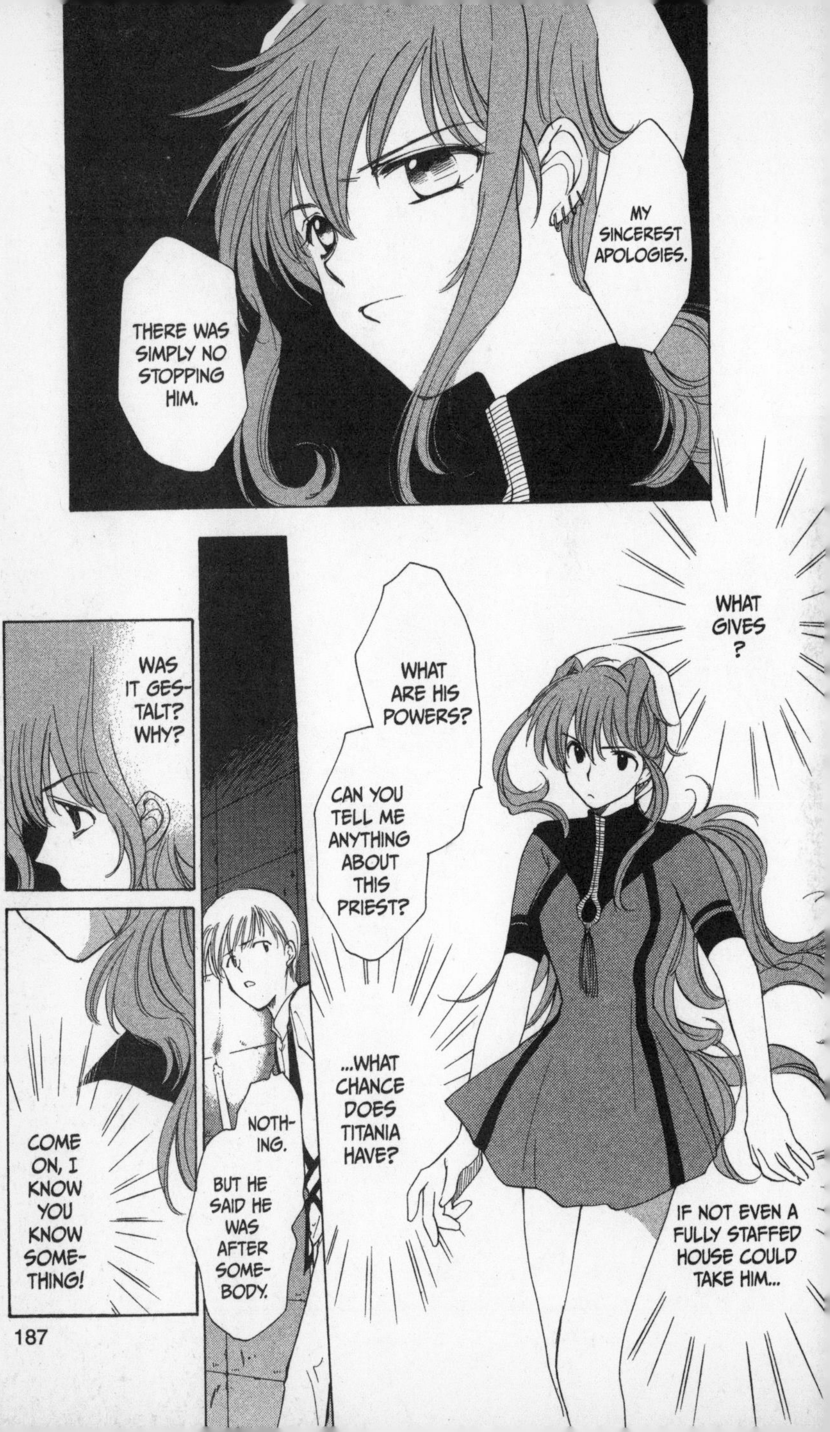
MY SINCEREST APOLOGIES.
THERE WAS SIMPLY NO STOPPING HIM.
WHAT GIVES?
WHAT ARE HIS POWERS?
CAN YOU TELL ME ANYTHING ABOUT THIS PRIEST?
NOTHING.
BUT HE SAID HE WAS AFTER SOMEBODY.
...WHAT CHANCE DOES TITANIA HAVE?
IF NOT EVEN A FULLY STAFFED HOUSE COULD TAKE HIM...
WAS IT GESTALT? WHY?
COME ON, I KNOW YOU KNOW SOMETHING!

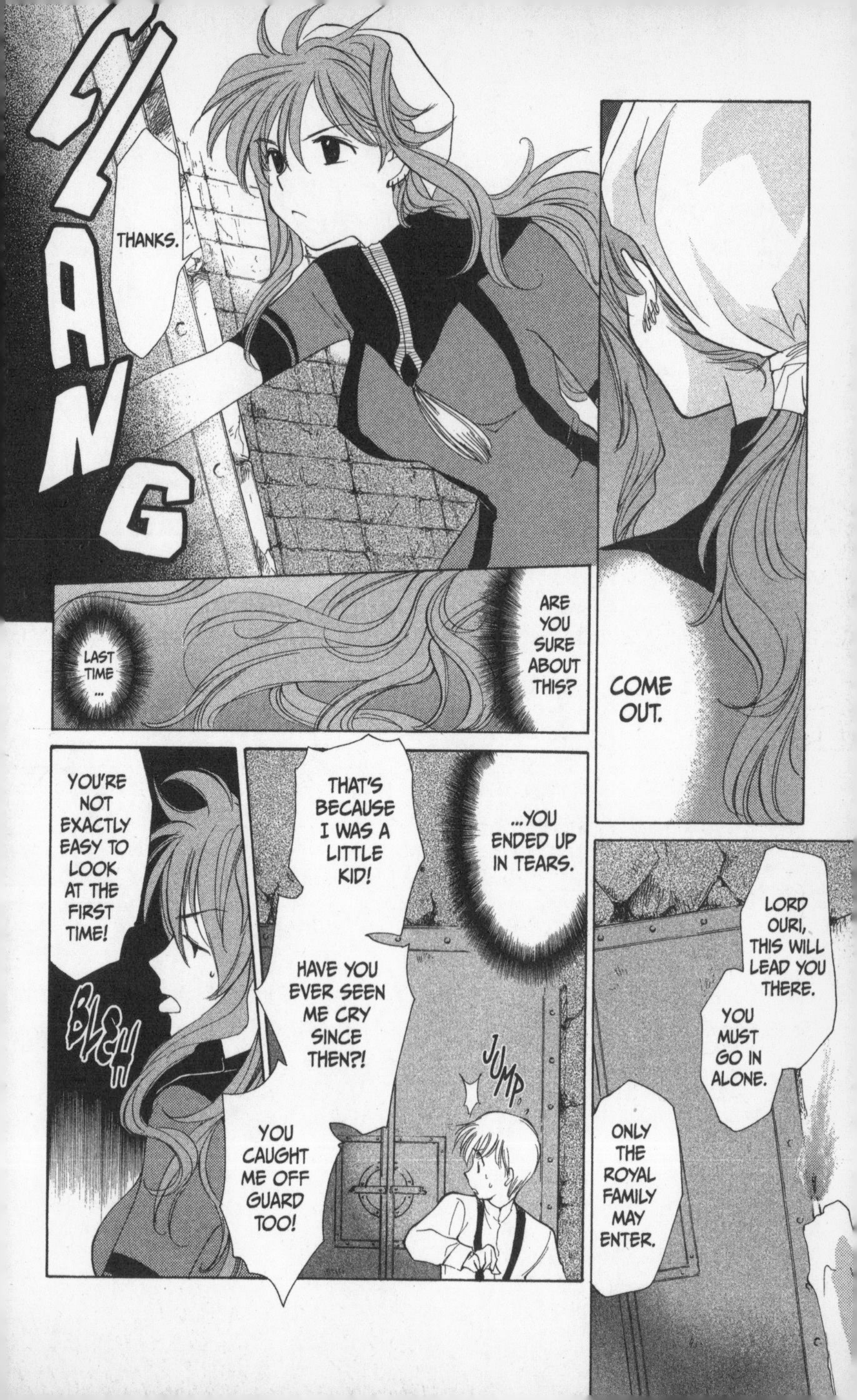
COME OUT.
CLANG
THANKS.
ARE YOU SURE ABOUT THIS?
LAST TIME ...
LORD OURI, THIS WILL LEAD YOU THERE.
YOU MUST GO IN ALONE.
ONLY THE ROYAL FAMILY MAY ENTER.
...YOU ENDED UP IN TEARS.
THAT'S BECAUSE I WAS A LITTLE KID!
HAVE YOU EVER SEEN ME CRY SINCE THEN?!
JUMP
YOU CAUGHT ME OFF GUARD TOO!
YOU'RE NOT EXACTLY EASY TO LOOK AT THE FIRST TIME!
BLEH

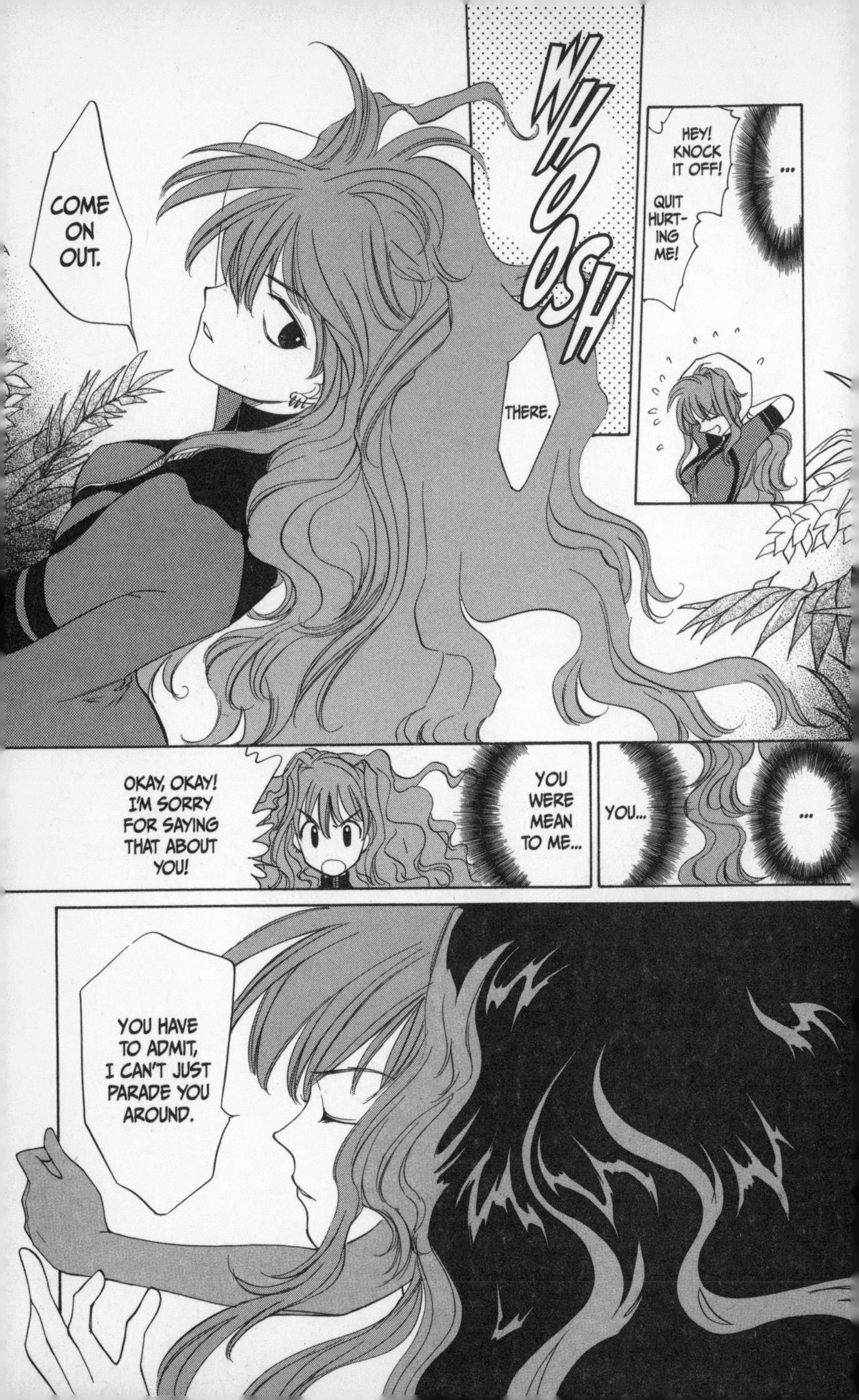
...
HEY! KNOCK IT OFF!
QUIT HURTING ME!
WHOOSH
THERE.
COME ON OUT.
...
YOU...
YOU WERE MEAN TO ME...
OKAY, OKAY! I'M SORRY FOR SAYING THAT ABOUT YOU!
YOU HAVE TO ADMIT, I CAN'T JUST PARADE YOU AROUND.

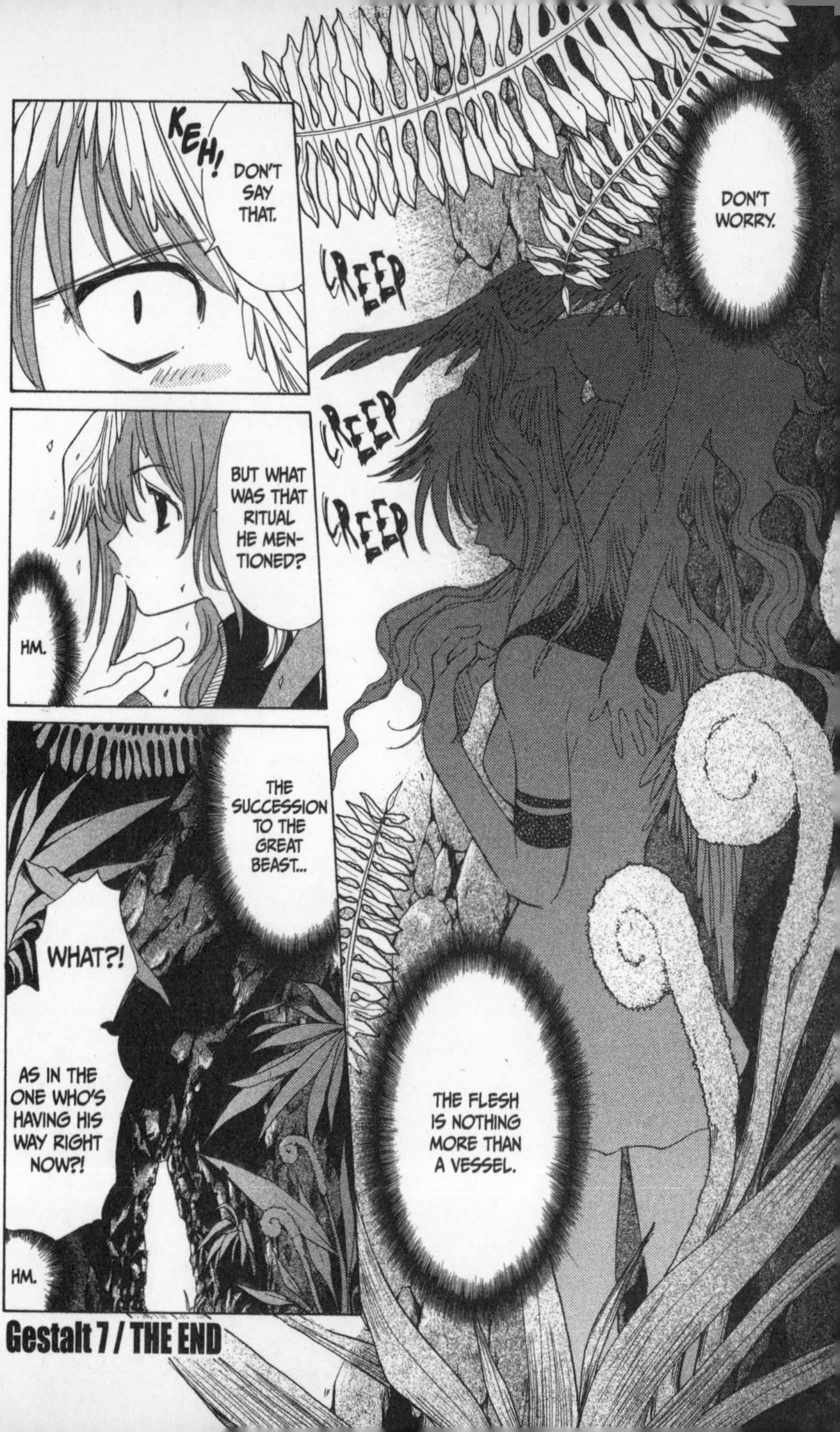
DON'T WORRY.
CREEP
CREEP
CREEP
THE FLESH IS NOTHING MORE THAN A VESSEL.
KEH!
DON'T SAY THAT.
BUT WHAT WAS THAT RITUAL HE MEN-TIONED?
HM.
THE SUCCESSION TO THE GREAT BEAST...
WHAT?!
AS IN THE ONE WHO'S HAVING HIS WAY RIGHT NOW?!
HM.

Gestalt 7 / THE END

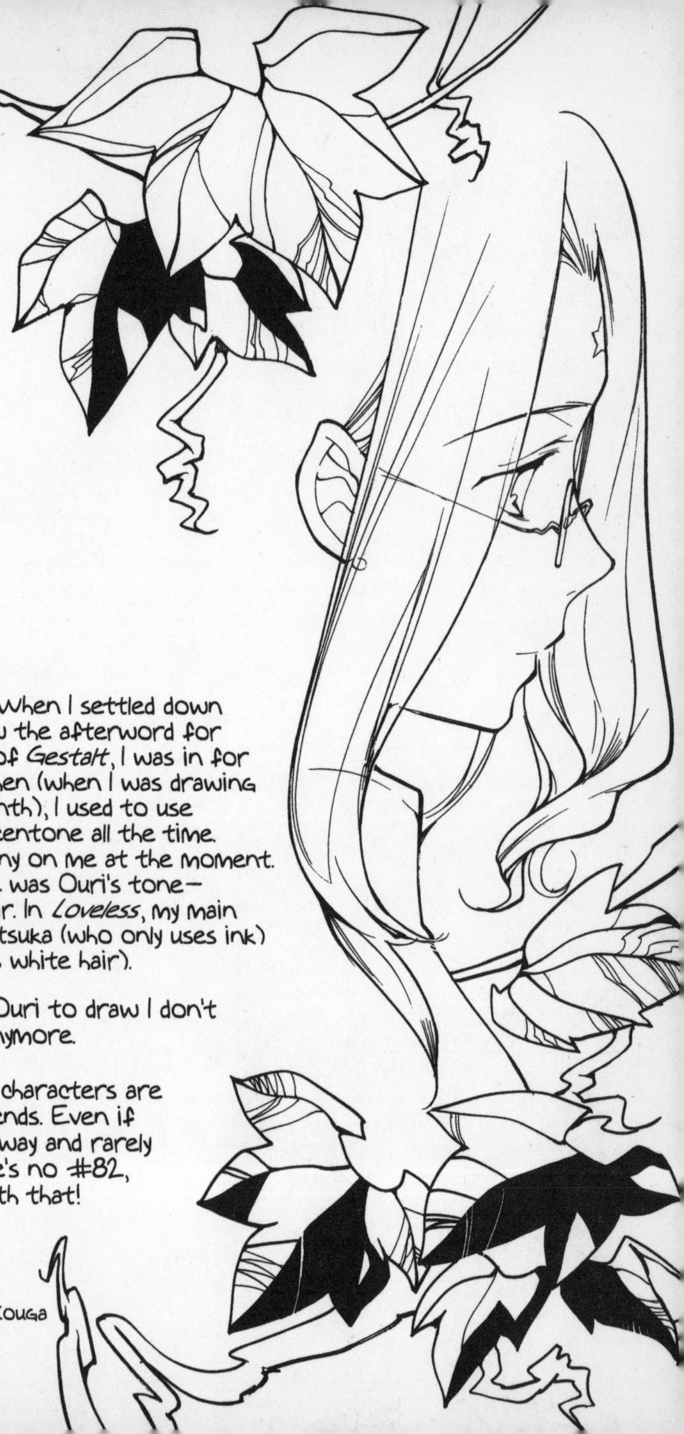

Hi, this is Kouga. When I settled down to write and draw the afterword for this new edition of *Gestalt*, I was in for a surprise. Back then (when I was drawing *Gestalt* every month), I used to use LETRA #82 screentone all the time. But I didn't have any on me at the moment. In my studio, #82 was Ouri's tone—mostly for her hair. In *Loveless*, my main characters are Ritsuka (who only uses ink) and Sobi (who has white hair).

So without Ouri to draw I don't carry #82 anymore.

Either way, my characters are all like best friends. Even if they're all far away and rarely meet and there's no #82, they're okay with that!

Summer 2006 Kouga

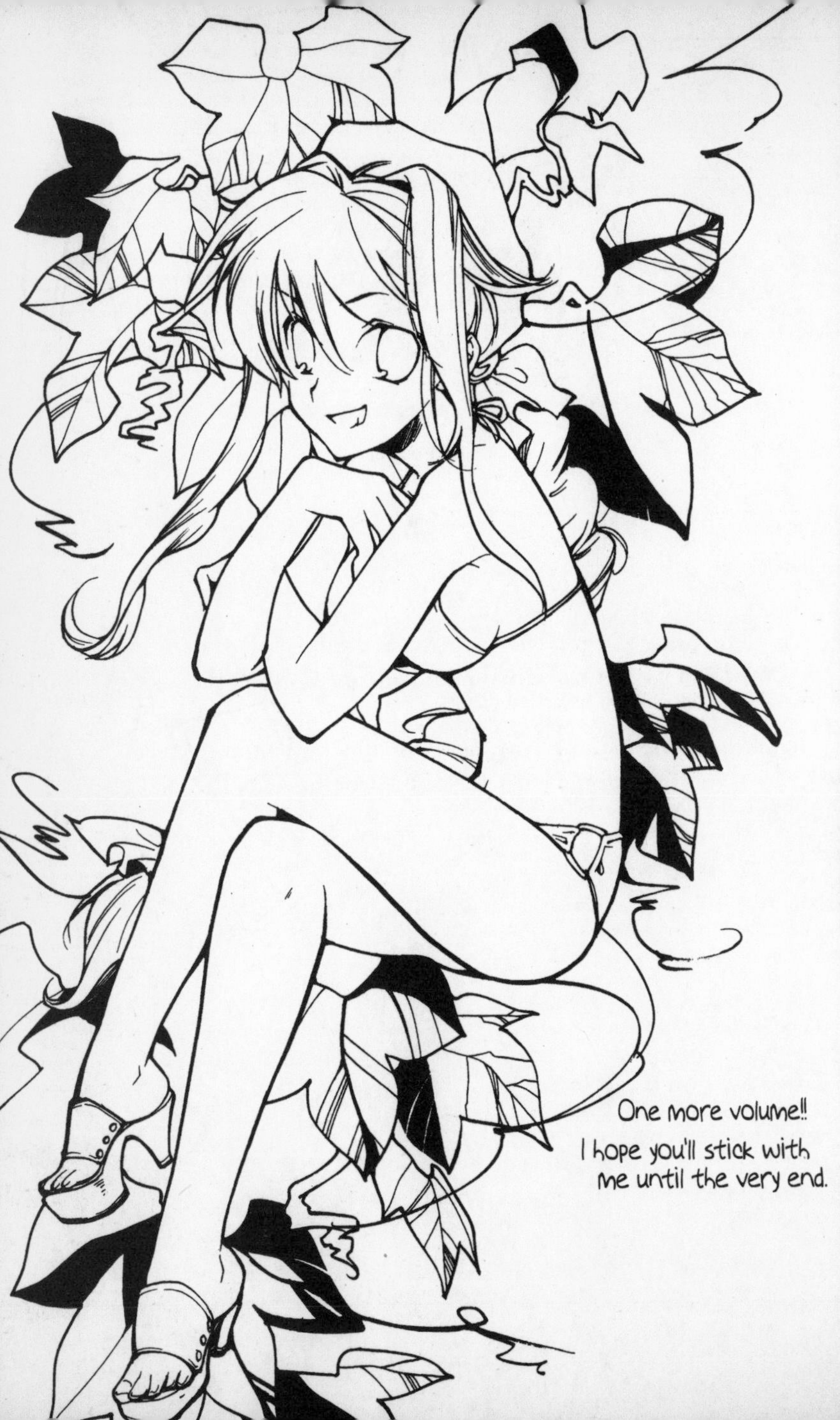
One more volume!!
I hope you'll stick with me until the very end.

JUMPING ROPE
I'M REALLY GETTING INTO IT. SUCH A GOOD WORKOUT!
WHOOSH
WHOOSH

While I was drawing this manga, I went through all kinds of emotions. After all, I worked on it long enough! There were times when I had a lot of fun and times when I felt worn down... times when I felt really pumped and times when I felt really bored...

Still, throughout it all, my love for Ouri never faltered. Whenever I felt too worn down or too wound up, Ouri was always there to make me laugh! Of course, I love all the other characters too.

Yun Kouga began her career as a doujinshi and debuted in 1986 with the original manga *Metal Heart*, serialized in *Comic VAL*. She is the creator of the popular series *Loveless* and *Earthian*, along with many manga and anime projects, including character design for *Gundam 00*.

Gestalt
Vol. 7
VIZ Media Edition

Story and Art by Yun Kouga

Translation & English Adaptation/Christine Schilling
Touch-up Art & Lettering/Mark McMurray
Design/Sean Lee
Editor/Chris Mackenzie

VP, Production/Alvin Lu
VP, Sales & Product Marketing/Gonzalo Ferreyra
VP, Creative/Linda Espinosa
Publisher/Hyoe Narita

CHOUJUU DENSETSU GESTALT
© Yun Kouga/ICHIJINSHA

Printed in Canada

Published by VIZ Media, LLC
P.O. Box 77010
San Francisco, CA 94107

10 9 8 7 6 5 4 3 2 1
First printing, June 2010

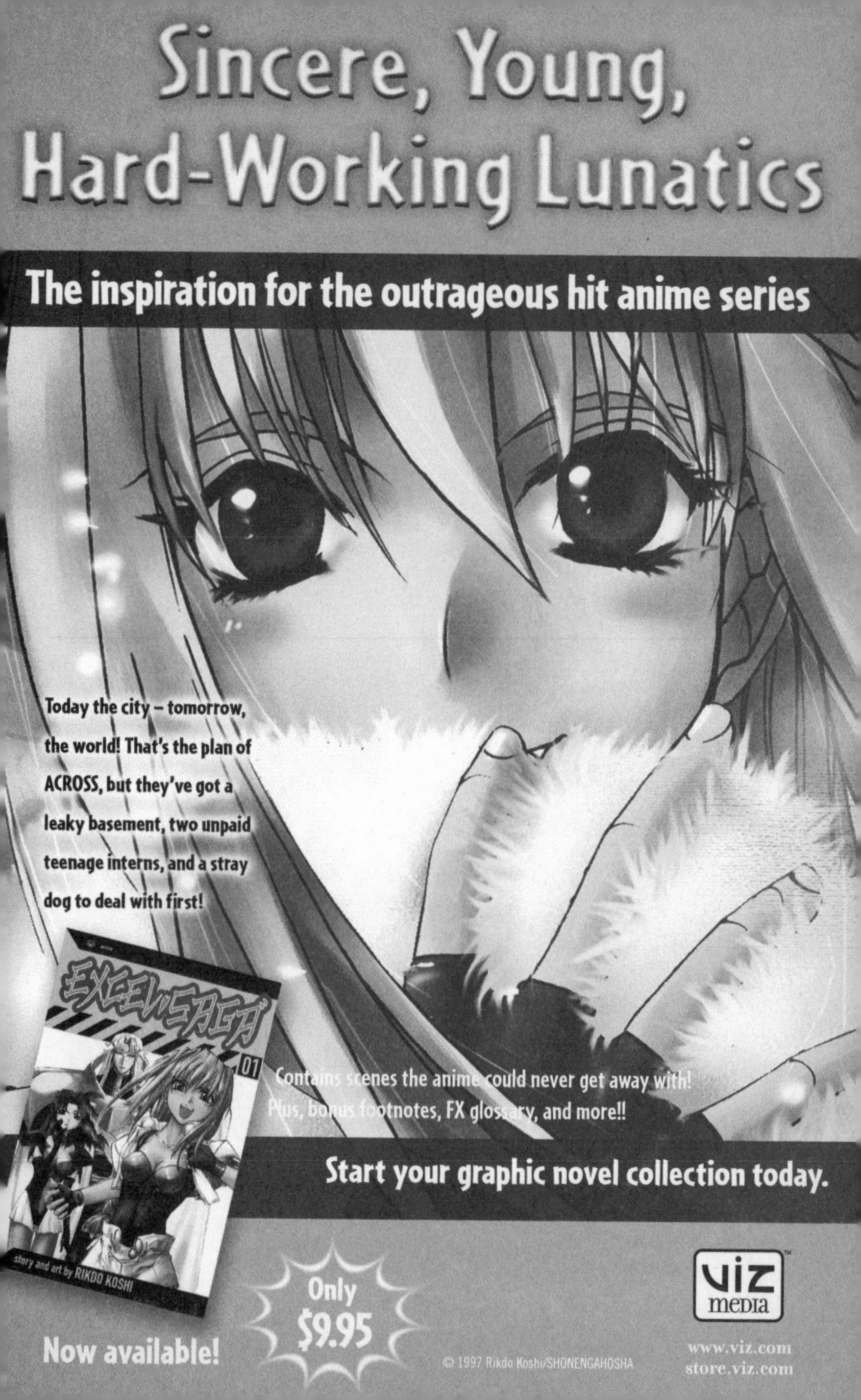
Sincere, Young, Hard-Working Lunatics
The inspiration for the outrageous hit anime series
Today the city – tomorrow, the world! That's the plan of ACROSS, but they've got a leaky basement, two unpaid teenage interns, and a stray dog to deal with first!
EXCEL SAGA
01
story and art by RIKDO KOSHI
Contains scenes the anime could never get away with!
Plus, bonus footnotes, FX glossary, and more!!
Start your graphic novel collection today.
Only $9.95
Now available!
viz media
www.viz.com
store.viz.com
© 1997 Rikdo Koshi/SHONENGAHOSHA